WHEN DAY AND NIGHT CEASE

A prophetic study of world events and how prophecy concerning Israel affects the nations, the Church and you.

RAMON BENNETT

ARM of SALVATION

P.O. Box 32381, Jerusalem 91322, ISRAEL

"This is what the LORD says, he who appoints the sun to shine by day, who decrees the moon and stars to shine by night, who stirs up the sea so that its waves roar — the LORD Almighty is His name: 'Only if these decrees vanish from my sight,' declares the LORD, 'will the descendants of Israel ever cease to be a nation before me'"

(Jer 31:35&36 NIV).

DEDICATION

I dedicate this work to the Jew, who has given so much to the world in the fields of Science, Medicine and the Arts. Through the Jew came the Bible which taught a pagan world about his God, the God of Abraham, Isaac and Jacob—the Holy One of Israel. And through the Jew came the Messiah, the Hope of Israel, and the Hope of every true Christian.

ACKNOWLEDGEMENTS

I am deeply indebted to many great men of God such as Oswald Chambers, A.W. Tozer, Charles Finney, Andrew Murray, G. Campbell Morgan and others who, *"though dead, still speak"* (Heb 11:4) and continue to challenge and encourage me in my daily walk with Christ.

I am also indebted to Marilyn Bryant who contributed so much to this work—her editing, advice and encouragement was invaluable. A very big thank-you goes to Kathy Kist who gave both of herself and her expertise so generously. And to Frank Gill who graciously made time available in his busy schedule to proof this second edition. The contribution of these talented people has been so valuable that I consider the work as much theirs as mine.

Grateful thanks are extended to Steve Barker who, with his artistic talent, produced the artwork for the cover.

I wish to acknowledge all the wonderful people who gave up the privacy of their homes that I might work undisturbed between ministry engagements in the United States. Especially remembered are Charlotte and Teddy in New York and Ella and Joe in Tennessee. Always unforgettable will be our "hillbilly" friends in Tennessee, Roy and Ella-Jane, whose hearts are so big that they enter and exit through doorways with difficulty. Ella-Jane also proved to be the greatest cook I have met in all my years and travels.

Most of all, I thank my dear companion, friend, wife and lover, Zipporah, who, for months, patiently endured so little communication with me while I devoted myself to this work.

CONTENTS

PART I

LAYING FOUNDATIONS

PART II

FROM ANCIENT TIMES

PART III

SPOKEN BY PROPHETS

PART IV

PEACE! PEACE!

PART V

AN UNFRUITFUL CHURCH

PART VI

THE ETERNAL PURPOSE

PREFACE

If people could see into the spirit realm, we would be seen walking about wearing spiritual "blinders." In the natural realm these two leather flaps are attached to a horse's bridle to curtail side vision. In the spiritual they curtail our view of any movement of God that is not directly in line with our narrow field of vision. These "blinders" are worn for a variety of reasons. Cultural, racial, doctrinal or credal biases, are but a few examples. For whatever reason, we are all wearing them to a greater or lesser degree. In the gospel of Mark we see an example of "blinders" worn by religious people:

"Then some Sadducees, who say there is no resurrection, came to Him; and they asked Him, saying: 'Teacher, Moses wrote to us that if a man's brother dies, and leaves his wife behind, and leaves no children, his brother should take his wife and raise up offspring for his brother. Now there were seven brothers. The first took a wife; and dying, he left no offspring. So the seven had her and left no offspring. Last of all the woman died also. Therefore, in the resurrection, when they rise, whose wife will she be? For all seven had her as wife.' Jesus answered and said to them, 'Are you not therefore mistaken, because you do not know the Scriptures nor the power of God? For when they rise from the dead, they neither marry nor are given in marriage, but are like angels in heaven. But concerning the dead, that they rise, have you not read in the book of Moses, in the burning bush passage, how God spoke to him, saying, 'I am the God of Abraham, the God of Isaac, and the God of Jacob?' 'He is not the God of the dead, but the God of the living. You are therefore greatly mistaken'" (Mark 12:18-27).

The Sadducees did not believe in a resurrection. They taught as truth a doctrine that had no basis in truth. The fact that they believed and taught a lie did not in any way alter the truth concerning the resurrection. The Sadducees wore "blinders" that curtailed spiritual perception and, as has happened down through the ages, concocted hypothetical situations aimed at proving the validity of their particular heresy. Jesus circumvented their trap, designed for the unwary or uninitiated, and pointed out that:

a) They were in error.
b) They were in error because they did not know the Scriptures.
c) They were in error because they did not know the power of God.

After travelling and teaching the Bible in a number of countries, I am aware of a sizeable amount of error in Christian doctrine. We have that error, for the same reason that the Sadducees had error in their day, because we know neither the Scriptures nor the power of God.

I remember leading a Bible Study group in Christchurch, New Zealand, years ago when suddenly the class erupted into a furor over something being discussed. Members were almost shouting at each other over an issue, each forcibly expressing his own particular point of view. I sensed the Lord speaking into my mind, "Ask how many of them have read the whole Bible." When I finally gained their attention, I put the question to them. To my utter amazement, not a single person in the entire class had read all of the Bible, yet they were arguing with ferocity on a question they only partially understood.

The amount of error in Christian doctrine concerning Israel and the Jewish people is vast. I submit this book with the strong hope that some of that error might be corrected. My desire and prayer is that eyes may be opened to the current move of God among His covenant people, which may safely be called the greatest move of God among Jews in world history.

*"The secret things belong to the LORD our God, **but those things which are revealed belong to us** and to our children forever"*
(Deut 29:29).

If we do not choose to take hold of the revealed truth that does not, in any way, stop it from being true—it only causes us to remain ignorant.

Ramon Bennett
Jerusalem
March 1993

"I know that whatever God does, It shall be forever. Nothing can be added to it, and nothing taken from it. God does it, that men should fear before Him. That which is has already been, and what is to be has already been; and God requires an account of what is past"

(Eccl. 3:14 &15).

INTRODUCTION

There have been hundreds, or perhaps even thousands, of books written about Israel. I have read only a few. The content of some I cannot recall; that of others was questionable, and most were factual and historical but ignored the spiritual. My interest remains in the Bible, which I consider to be the definitive work on Israel. I have read this fascinating and spiritually illuminating Book of books many times since I first yielded my life to Christ.

My desire, therefore, in this particular book is to present a thesis different from any that I have heard or read. The work that I offer is a progression of revelation facts from the first page unto the last. To omit reading even the Preface could mean remaining ignorant of something that might help set a person free from doctrinal bondage and release him into the glorious freedom to which he has been called.

Each chapter stands on its own. Each contains its own message and progressively leans toward the following chapter until we reach our destination—the glorious Church, reaping the harvest fields of the world. In the early chapters I provide some basic foundational truths apart from which we would have nothing to build a secure structure.

Neither Hebrew nor Greek text has been introduced to complicate reading. Those having an understanding of the original languages of the Bible will easily follow the few transliterations included.

The question has been asked of me in regard to these pages: "What books are you using for reference?" My answer has been, "Very few!" This is because I desire to introduce revelation, not a rehashed pottage from previously published works. This work is certainly not confined to the study of books listed in the Select Bibliography but is, rather, the result of nearly thirty years of Bible study, meditation, prayer and the reading of, perhaps, thousands of books, newspapers, magazines and assorted articles. I have relied heavily on the greatest and most accurate source of all, the Bible, and used numerous clippings from the world's news media to give credence to what I have written. Some of the books that I have taken quotations from are long out of print. An appreciable amount of additional information that I was unable to access for the first printing has now been included. This in no way alters either the facts or the message of the previous edition but distinctly corroborates the facts and strengthens the message. This second edition is, therefore, an expansion of all that is contained in the first edition, and we have attempted to correct inadvertent errors contained in the previous one.

Although I have written much concerning Israel here, the central point of my life is Jesus Christ, not Israel. Just as Jesus is the focal point of my life so He is also the focal point of everything pertaining to Israel. The centrality of Christ is readily perceived everywhere we care to look in the history of the nation of Israel. During the Passover, for example, the blood put upon the doorposts of the houses of the children of Israel pointed forward to the blood of Jesus that is put upon the doorposts of our hearts so that we, also, may be passed over in the day of God's judgement. Today we look back to the time of the Passover in order to understand the work that was wrought on the cross at Calvary. The blood spilled in Egypt points to Jesus, and we look back to Him, to the central place, in order to understand. God has given Jesus the central, pivotal position and intends *"to sum up all things in Christ"* (Eph 1:10 ASV). ***"For of Him and through Him and to Him are all things, to whom be glory forever. Amen"*** (Rom 11:36).

The Bible places tremendous importance upon Israel and the Jewish people. The Israel of the Old Testament affected the inhabited world known at that time. It caused the rise and fall of nations and empires according to how they viewed or treated these people of God's choice. Today, as promised in the Bible, there is a re-created state of Israel. This little country, of very small population, is once more stirring up the ire of many nations. This tiny speck on world maps will not and cannot be ignored. Israel demands our attention. Her insistence becomes louder each day. Whether we like it or not, Israel very much affects you and me, our parents, our children and our children's children. The Bible teaches that modern Israel will affect every nation, great and small. Whether it will be for good or for bad depends upon each one's attitudes towards her, together with the relationship that each may or may not have with the God of Israel and with His Son Jesus Christ. Israel affects the entire world and determines the course of its history.

I write from a prophetic perspective, not from a spiritualising one. My purpose is to look at Biblical prophecy concerning Israel to see where she is now in light of that prophecy and how that affects you and me.

The Bible is a love story. It is not just a simple love story but a classic one. It is not based on fact; it is fact. The characters were, and are, real. Every act and every scene is truth, and no names have been changed to protect individuals or nations.

Much of the Bible is taken up with an unhappy marriage between a hurting husband, the LORD, and His unfaithful wife, the nation of Israel. This sordid story is written for the eyes of all to see. Neither the affairs of the wife nor the anger of the deeply offended, jealous husband is hidden from the reader. It is all there—all the adulterous scenes and all the pain and pathos of wounded love.

The story has a happy ending, but most Christians do not grasp it the way that it is written. Some will not grasp it because they do not want to—prejudice is always more powerful than fact. Others cannot grasp it due to their particular doctrinal views which, honestly, have never been seriously questioned, only naively accepted. There is a passage of Scripture recorded in the Book of Acts which describes the arrival of Paul and Silas in Berea from Thessalonica. They first went to the local Synagogue and there preached the gospel to the assembled Jews. This passage tells us:

*"These were **more fair-minded** than those in Thessalonica, in that they received the word with all readiness, and **searched the Scriptures daily** to find out whether these things were so"* (Acts 17:11).

A great man of God, G. Campbell Morgan, said, "The whole truth lies not in 'It is written,' but in, 'Again it is written.'" Only the whole truth is the truth. Any part of the truth can become an error. Let us never accept without question what is handed to us on a plate. Let us be "fair-minded," and let us, also, imitate the Berean and "search the Scriptures daily."

Ancient Israel mistook the election to God's purposes to be an election of favouritism:

> **"She did not consider her destiny;** *therefore her collapse was awesome"* (Lam 1:9).

She did not then, and does not now, consider her destiny. Spiritually, she is blind still. Her destiny still awaits her. In every generation there has arisen one to destroy her: a Joseph Stalin, an Adolf Hitler or a Saddam Hussein. The reason for the unique survival of the Jews is that the purposes of God have yet to be fulfilled through them. Israel, therefore, will be opposed, and Satan will fight harder and bring greater controversy to bear on her. Any important, vital, theological or doctrinal truth will suffer in the same way.

For many years my burden has been for spiritual revival within the Church. Israel and the Jewish people are a key to that revival. In this work we explore the purposes of God for Israel and also for the Church. Israel has a distinct and definite role to play in the plan of world evangelism, as does the Church. Neither can fulfill its purpose apart from the other—their destinies are intertwined. At present there is a wide gulf between them; but, as shall be seen in these pages, the day is coming when they shall walk together as God's *"One New Man"* (Eph 2:15). Clear signs of the dawning of this new day are already perceived by those watching for the Day Star. Bonded together by the love of Jesus, Israel and the Church will move as one, reaping the greatest spiritual harvest imaginable. It shall no longer be "them," but "She"—the radiant, beautiful and spotless Bride of Christ. My prayer here is that the Lord of Glory might use this book to hasten that day.

"God elected a certain nation to be His bondslave, and through that nation a knowledge of His salvation is to come to all the world. The history of that nation is a record of awful idolatry and backsliding, they remained neither true to God's prophets nor to God Himself; but in spite of everything the fulfilment of God's purpose for the nation of His choice is certain. The election of the nation by God was not for the salvation of individuals; the elect nation was to be the instrument of salvation to the whole world. The story of their distress is due entirely to their deliberate determination to use themselves for a purpose other than God's."

Oswald Chambers, *So I Send You* (Pennsylvania: Christian Literature Crusade, 1930).

PART I

LAYING FOUNDATIONS

"According to the grace of God which was given to me, as a wise master builder I have laid the foundation, and another builds on it. But let each one take heed how he builds on it"

(1 Cor 3:10).

1

WHO KILLED JESUS CHRIST?

Anti-Semitism defiles. It defiles those who are the object of discrimination, and it defiles those who discriminate. "The Jews killed Jesus—they deserve all they get!" This statement, however incredible it may appear to some readers, can be heard from individuals throughout the entire spectrum of the Church and verbalises an attitude held by a great number of professing Christians. Anti-Semitism has been with us for thousands of years and shows no sign of abating. The probability today is that the majority of Gentiles have a deep-seated resentment toward Jews. This resentment, much like a dormant volcano, has a habit of erupting violently and unexpectedly bringing death and destruction to those living in its shadow. For almost two millennia the Jew has suffered verbal and physical abuse from the "Christian world" for being a "Christ-Killer."

If it were only unregenerate men involved in this arena of hate it would be a little more understandable. Unregenerate Cain killed his brother Abel because of jealousy, and unregenerate twentieth-century man will kill his brother for even less reason. But it is a far greater shame when the redeemed, the born-again members of the Church who carry the name of Christ, have hate and prejudice in their hearts. What shame has come upon the Church and upon the very name of Jesus, who is the personification of love and mercy! This shame and disgrace has come by way of those who profess His Name and Nature, yet have hate and prejudice toward those through whom came their Bible and their Lord. Can a person really love the King of the Jews while hating His very family according to the flesh? The Bible says that he cannot.

It was sin, not the Jew, that ended the earthly life of Jesus. It was our sin—yours and mine. The Son of God came to rid our hearts of deceit and hatred, as well as the resentment and envy that we harbour toward others. He came to take away the inherent sin that has been in all of us from the very moment of conception in our mother's womb. The sin that has caused our governments to become corrupt and our cities to become immoral and full of theft and violence, so that the women and children in them are no longer safe to be left alone. Jesus came because of the sin that causes even professing born-again Christians to pilfer from employers or to cheat on income tax assessments. When rebuked for breaking speed laws on Californian highways a local pastor replied, "Who hears a tree fall in a forest?" God does! That is why He sent His Son—to die for you and for me. Jesus was not backed into a corner, and no one took away His life; He gave it to the world as a love offering:

> *"Therefore My Father loves Me, because I lay down My life that I may take it again. **No one takes it from Me, but I lay it down of Myself. I have power to lay it down, and I have power to take it again.** This command I have received from My Father"*
>
> (Jn 10:17,18).

No honest, sane and reasonably-educated person would deny the involvement of the Jew in the crucifixion of the Christ. Admittedly, for fear of repercussions from the Gentiles, the average Jew refuses to publicly acknowledge his people's part in the crucifixion and loudly declares their innocence. He counters the charge by saying that the Gentiles committed the deed themselves. We have heard the charges of both the Gentiles and the Jews, but what does God have to say—at whose feet does He lay the blame?

> *"Why did the nations rage, and the people plot vain things? The **kings of the earth** took their stand, and the **rulers** were gathered together against the Lord and against His Christ. For truly against Your holy Servant Jesus, whom You anointed, both **Herod** and **Pontius Pilate**, with the **Gentiles** and the **people of Israel**, were gathered together to do whatever Your hand and Your purpose **determined before** to be done"*   (Acts 4:25-28).

He charges the inhabitants of all nations, the kings of the earth and the rulers of the people. It was all of mankind that was against the LORD and against His Son. He reinforces this statement by bringing our attention to focus on the joint act and stating plainly and bluntly that both Herod (the Jewish King) and Pilate (the Gentile governing ruler), together with the Gentiles and the Jews, carried out the crucifixion. This was His pre-determined purpose even before the foundation of the earth (see Rev.13:8, 1 Pet.1:20, Eph.1:4, 2 Tim.1:9 and Tit.1:2).

According to the evidence, every one of us stands guilty before the LORD for the crucifixion of His Son, but there is good news:

"And when they had come to the place called Calvary, there they crucified Him, and the criminals, one on the right hand and the other on the left. Then Jesus said, 'Father, forgive them, for they do not know what they do.' And they divided His garments and cast lots" (Luke 23:33,34).

Jesus cried to His Father for our forgiveness, and that cry was heard:

*"As He also says in another place: 'You are a priest forever according to the order of Melchizedek'; who, in the days of His flesh, when He had offered up prayers and supplications, with vehement cries and tears to Him who was able to save Him from death, **and was heard** because of His godly fear"* (Heb 5:6,7).

Jesus is our eternal High Priest. The function of a priest is to stand between holy God and sinful man and intercede on man's behalf. The Scripture tells us that Jesus was heard because of His piety, and, because He was heard, we now stand without condemnation in the sight of God on the charge of crucifying His Son. And God not only forgave Gentiles—He forgave the Jew, too. Surely the Jew stands in need of a pardon from the Gentiles.

All of mankind is forgiven the offence of nailing Jesus to a rough wooden cross with iron nails, but there is better news yet:

*"Christ died for our sins according to the Scriptures, and that He was buried, and that **He rose again the third day** according to the Scriptures, and that He was seen by Cephas, then by the twelve. After that He was seen by over five hundred brethren at once, of whom the greater part remain to the present, but some have fallen asleep"* (1 Cor 15:3-6).

*"This Jesus **God has raised up**, of which we are all witnesses"*
                                                    (Acts 2:32).

Jesus is alive! Let this fact sink into the depths of our souls. Jesus is not dead, He is alive! There were witnesses, many witnesses. Witnesses who were not given to vivid and fanciful imaginings, and, furthermore, He was seen by hundreds of people at the same time. We serve a risen, vivified Lord. The cross is bare, the tomb is empty, and He is alive. He lives to change bad men into good men and sinful men into holy men—Gentile and Jew alike. Because He is alive and because He lives all those who receive Him live eternally. The crucifixion was not a murder that a people committed; it was a sacrifice freely offered. The cross was the altar, and the condemned man was the lamb.

Dear LORD,
Grant me grace that I may in my heart grant mercy to the Jewish people. Help me to see that it was my own personal sin that put Jesus on the cross. Reveal to me the depth of the atonement that was made at Calvary. Let me taste the sweet love of the One who bore my guilt in order to bring about my reconciliation with You. Amen.

2

HOW BIG
IS GOD?

The awesomeness of God is lost to us by our shallow concept of both Him and His power. Our concept of God will always determine the quality of our Christianity. Gone from the Church is the dependency upon Him for our sustenance which includes our very life's breath:

> *"If He should set His heart on it, if He should gather to Himself His Spirit and His breath, all flesh would perish together, and man would return to dust"* (Job 34:14&15).

The average Christian unconsciously restricts his God to the confines of a box, the dimensions of which will vary according to his particular doctrinal view and his level of faith. Not only is our concept of Him cabined within the limits of our human minds, but we actually expect Him to perform when we speak a command. We have reduced the capability and sovereignty of our Creator to a form of servitude to His own creation. Forgotten, it seems, are the words of the prophets who uttered the heartbeat of the Almighty throughout the millennia. Forgotten is God's declared sovereignty over all creation and history:

> *"I am God, and there is no other; I am God, and there is none like Me, declaring the end from the beginning, and from ancient times things that are not yet done, saying, 'My counsel shall stand, and I will do all My pleasure,' Calling a bird of prey from the east, the man who executes My counsel, from a far country. Indeed I have*

spoken it; I will also bring it to pass. I have purposed it; I will also do it"   (Isa 46:9-11).

Forgotten is God's sovereignty over eternity which He inhabits:

"Indeed before the day was, I am He; and there is no one who can deliver out of My hand; I work, and who will reverse it?"
(Isa 43:13).

Forgotten is God's sovereignty over peoples and nations:

"The LORD brings the counsel of the nations to nothing; He makes the plans of the peoples of no effect"   (Psa 33:10).

Forgotten is the fact that God's sovereignty is absolute:

"But He is unique, and who can make Him change? And whatever His soul desires, that He does"   (Job 23:13).

The fear of the LORD needs to fall upon mankind again. This fear needs to penetrate the hearts of millions of Christians who profess trust in Him—Catholics, Protestants, Traditionals, Evangelicals, Charismatics and Pentecostals alike:

"On this one will I look: on him who is poor and of a contrite spirit, and who trembles at My word"   (Isa 66:2).

We need to tremble not only at His word but tremble also at every remembrance of this awesome being:

"...who gives life to the dead and calls those things which do not exist as though they did"   (Rom 4:17).

Who among us can give life to the dead? Who among us can call into existence that which does not exist?

With all our twentieth-century, sophisticated equipment and high technology, the best we can attain to is to shine a light into a dark area. But God simply **spoke** into the darkness:

"'Let there be light'; and there was light"   (Gen 1:3).

Not only did light appear at the spoken word of the LORD, but it also shone **out** of the darkness:

*"God ... **commanded** light to shine out of darkness"*   (2 Cor 4:6).

On the first day of creation God called forth light out of darkness. There never had been light until that time. Not until the fourth day did He create the sun and moon to rule day and night, which He had created by separating light from darkness.

Creating light was a small thing compared with some of His other accomplishments. The late A.W. Tozer said something to this effect:

"God can do anything as easily as He does anything. It is as simple for Him to cure a common cold as it is to create an entire universe. We find things harder or easier to do because we have limits, but God does not have limits and neither does He strain:"

*"**By the word of the LORD** the heavens were made, and all the host of them **by the breath of His mouth**"*   (Psa 33:6).

Venture out beyond the city limits on a clear night and contemplate the stars and planets that can be seen with the naked eye: Mars, Saturn, Jupiter and Venus. Consider also:

*"By God's word the heavens existed and the earth was formed **out of water** and by water"*   (2 Pet 3:5 NIV).

Consider the mass and density of this planet, Earth, and then consider that it was formed out of **water!** Modern science now believes that matter was created out of gas. Many Christians mistakenly believe that the Bible bears out Science but this is not true. Scientists are constantly changing or reforming their theories while the Bible is forever the same. Science may, eventually, bear out the Bible but never vice versa.

Have you ever really considered the heavens and the earth? King David, the *"sweet psalmist of Israel"* (2 Sam 23:1), did. And he was *"a man after God's own heart"* (Acts 13:22):

*"I consider your heavens, **the work of your fingers**, the moon and the stars, which you have set in place"*   (Psa 8:3 NIV).

The heavens are the work of God's fingers. He set the moon and the stars in place. This awesome God plays with planets as a boy would play with marbles! The heavens proclaim the glory of God. They make known to us His great majesty, knowledge and wisdom. Let us examine His handiwork.

THE SOLAR SYSTEM

Our planet Earth is a body of matter with a diameter of nearly 13,000 km. (8,100 mi.). This body of matter rotates on its axis at a speed of 1,700 km. (1,100 mi.) per hour while revolving around the sun at a speed in excess of 100,000 km. (62,000 mi.) per hour. Wherever we are and whatever we are doing, we are spinning like a top on a gigantic merry-go-round. When did we last feel dizzy from the spin of the earth, or when did we last fear to release our grips on sturdy trees lest we spin off into space? A little closer to the sun and the earth would burn up; a fraction further away and it would become ice. The knowledge and wisdom of the Designer took it all into account.

Earth is one of nine planets revolving around the sun and is third in distance from the sun. The closest planet is Mercury, followed by Venus. The order, after Earth, is Mars, Jupiter, Saturn, Uranus, Neptune and, finally, Pluto. Earth has its own satellite planet called Moon. Only Mercury and Venus are without satellite planets. Pluto has one satellite, Mars has two, Neptune eight, Uranus fifteen, Jupiter sixteen and Saturn seventeen. All of these satellites are turning on their axes while revolving around their mother planet, which is also spinning on its axis and revolving around the sun.

Scientists are fascinated with the movement of atoms seen through a microscope. When we look to the heavens, we observe in our own solar system a similar pattern on a huge scale—planets up to 300 times the mass of earth, twirling and whirling through space at immense speeds. Consider the intelligence and power required to create such majesty on high:

"The LORD by wisdom founded the earth; by understanding He established the heavens" (Prov 3:19).

*"He stretches out the north over **empty space**; He hangs the earth on **nothing**"* (Job 26:7).

Richard Wurmbrand, a dear Christian brother who spent fourteen years in a Communist prison because of his love for God's Son, had much time to contemplate the heavens. He acknowledges the wisdom of the LORD when he says:

"Our earth, this huge ball with its five billion inhabitants, was hung by God upon nothing. If he had hung it on a thick cable of steel, the cable would long since have broken. But 'nothing' is a resistant material."[1]

THE HEAVENS[2]

The known area of space is so vast that distances are calculated in light years, a light year being the distance that light, travelling at 299,792 km. (186,282 mi.) per second, travels in one full year. Therefore, a light year is a distance of (and I will try to make it easier for the reader) 9 trillion, 460 billion, 716 million, 19 thousand, 200 km.[3] (5 trillion, 878 billion, 612 million, 843 thousand, 200 mi.)![4]

The sun has a diameter of nearly 1 million 400 thousand km.[5] (870 thousand mi.)[6] which is 109 times the diameter of Earth and has a surface area 12,000 times greater than the earth. The sun is just an average size star. Giant stars have diameters up to 30 million km. (18 million 650 thousand mi.)! Supergiants have diameters of 1 billion 500 million km. (933 million mi.)! That is approximately 1,000 times that of the sun. Betelgeuse, the largest star in the constellation of Orion, is so huge that Earth and Jupiter together could orbit within its dimensions! An average temperature reading of the sun is approximately 18 million degrees Celsius[7] (32 million 400 thousand degrees Fahrenheit)! Compare this with the boiling point of water at 100 degrees Celsius (212 degrees Fahrenheit) and molten lava spewing from a volcano at 2,000 degrees Celsius (3,600 Fahrenheit).

The sun is part of the Milky Way galaxy which contains approximately 200 billion other stars. Each star rotates in its own orbit and the **entire galaxy** also orbits! All the stars that can be seen from earth with the naked eye (about 6,000) belong to this one galaxy and most are brighter than the sun. The sun is 30,000 light years from the centre of the galaxy—a mere 283,821 trillion, 480 billion, 576 million km. (176,358 trillion, 385 billion, 296 million mi.)! Yet it is only little more than thirteen light minutes, or 150 million km. (93 million mi.), from Earth.

No one knows exactly how many stars there are. They number about 200 billion billion in the **known** universe. Every living person on earth would have to count 50 billion stars each before one star would be counted twice. Understandably, our scientists have names for only a few stars, but the LORD created the stars, set them in place and:

"He counts the number of the stars; he calls them all by name" (Psa 147:4).

Stars can be found in groups of thousands and hundreds of thousands. Our nearest neighbouring star is 4.3 light years away or just 40 trillion, 681 billion, 78 million, 882 thousand, 560 km. (25 trillion, 278 billion, 35 million, 225 thousand, 760 mi.), while our most distant neighbour inhabits a galaxy billions of light years away.

The nearest galaxy to the Milky Way is approximately 200,000 light years away which is a distance of (wait for it!) 1,892,143 trillion, 203 billion, 840 million km. (1,175,722 trillion, 568 billion, 640 million mi.)! And there are approximately 100 billion galaxies, each containing at least 100 billion stars. Does your head spin with these numbers? Can your mind comprehend such figures? Is not our God an awesome God?

SPACE TRAVEL

Having looked at the gigantically enormous area of space, let us look briefly at efforts to explore it. The United States has recorded some remarkable successes in this area.

The planets in our solar system come into line every 176 years and one such event took place during the 1980s. The United States, taking advantage of the line-up, launched the spacecraft Voyager 2 from Cape Canaveral in August, 1977, on a data-gathering trek through space. Voyager 2 cruised at 60,000 km. (37,000 mi.) per hour, accelerating to 98,000 km. (61,000 mi.) per hour when pulled by the gravitational force of the planets. It reached Jupiter in 1979, Saturn in 1981, Uranus in 1986 and Neptune in 1989, after travelling some four billion kilometres (two and one half billion miles). By using the gravitational pull of each planet during the line-up reduced the length of the trip by eighteen years.[8]

Another report informs us that in early October 1990 the space shuttle, Discovery, dispatched Europe's Ulysses probe on a five-year journey to the sun.[9]

Consider:

Voyager 2 cruised at speeds up to 98,000 km. (61,000 mi.) per hour. This was a very fine achievement on behalf of the American people, and I do not want to detract from that achievement. But the journey took twelve years and was helped by the planets lining up on their 176 year cycle. Without that help, a similar journey would take thirty years. The distance that Voyager 2 travelled in those twelve years was equal to passing across the face of just two big stars. The spacecraft will continue travelling into interstellar space, remaining inside Neptune's orbit until 1999.[10] Adding the necessary five years of travel from Earth to sun, together with the years required to reach Pluto in its erratic orbit, means that just travelling the length of our own solar system from the sun to Pluto, other than during a planetary line-up, would take longer than half a century!

No one knows for certain if other solar systems exist. Planets, at least in comparison to stars, are small and dark, and optical telescopes used by twentieth century astronomers lack the power to detect them in orbit. It is believed that there might be other solar systems similar to ours existing somewhere, possibly on the far side of the galaxy and beyond. Assuming this were true, Voyager 2, travelling consistently at 60,000 km. (37,000 mi.) per hour would require **545 million years** to reach even the centre of our galaxy on a quest to find them!

There is not a calculator available to man that is capable of holding sufficient actual digits to determine the dimensions of the heavens in kilometres or miles. Known space extends into decillions of decillions (a decillion is: 1, followed by thirty-three zeros)[12] of kilometres or miles. And, in the first week of September 1989, scientists made a startling announcement:

"Evidence had been found of a cosmic version of gestation: a galaxy preparing for birth. The new galaxy of stars is 'ten times as large as the Milky Way.' Scientists have been convinced for years that a cataclysmic explosion took place fifteen billions of years ago that spawned the universe. Last week this new galaxy 'shook the conviction of that theory.'"[13]

Many billions of cubic miles of new space appear between the galaxies every day[14] and new galaxies are being born into this vacuum. Man believed the heavens to have been completed billions of years ago; but it was God who did the creating, and, in the words of His Son:

"My Father is always at his work to this very day"   (Jn 5:17 NIV).

God's ability to shatter our pet theories concerning His creation can be most aptly summed up thus:

"If the works of God were such as they might be easily comprehended by human reason they could not be justly called marvellous or unspeakable."[15]

HOW BIG IS GOD?

Having considered the magnitude of God's creation, let us now consider the immensity of God Himself:

*"Is not God in **the height of heaven**? And see the highest stars, how lofty they are!"*   (Job 22:12).

*"But who is able to build Him a temple, **since heaven and the heaven of heaven cannot contain Him**?"*   (2 Chr 2:6).

Our human minds cannot adequately perceive the immense distances in space. A trillion trillion kilometres or miles in any direction will only get us into the backyard of some of our nearer neighbours. Yet even dimensions of such magnitude are insufficient for the creator God—*"it cannot contain Him, He fills the heavens and the earth"!*

"'Do I not fill heaven and earth?' says the LORD"   (Jer 23:24).

What man's body is to his spirit, so all of creation is to God! Consider this also:

*"God is **Spirit**"*   (Jn 4:24)

*"For **in Him** we live and move and have our being"*   (Acts 17:28).

God is nearer to us than we are to ourselves. He is not far away as some think; He is distant only insofar as we have alienated ourselves from Him:

*"Your **iniquities have separated you** from your God; and your sins have hidden His face from you"*   (Isa 59:2).

Our sin separates us from God. Separation creates an ignorance of God, and ignorance of God widens the gap further.

God, as revealed in the Bible, is big enough to believe in. But, seriously, how big is your God? Your God is as big as your mind will allow him to be. He is as potent or as impotent as your faith in Him, and He is as real to you as your need of Him.

A charge Jesus made against the Sadducees, in Mark 12:24, was that they did not know the power of God (see the Preface). Not knowing the power of God blinded them to the truth of the Scriptures. Too many Christians are in the same category. We need to repent and take off our blinders.

Dear LORD,
Open my eyes to Your awesomeness so that I may behold Your majesty, glory and power. Allow me to see my own smallness alongside Your greatness so that I might prostrate myself before You in holy fear and loving adoration. Amen.

3

BIBLICAL PROPHECY

A popular phrase used in Christian circles and Christian publications is "It depends on how you interpret prophecy." With this I disagree.

Bible teaching does not stand or fall upon "interpretation" of prophetic Scripture. Prophecies are not, and should not be, interpreted. The question is not one of "interpretation;" the question, when it comes to prophecy, is "Has there been fulfillment?"

The Church ought not to have been trying to predict or determine future events. The consistency in which she has been wrong has undermined, even further, her credibility with an unbelieving world. I, personally, am not aware of even a single instance where a prophecy of Scripture has been fulfilled as someone has predicted it would be. Predictions are made concerning future events based on "interpretations" of prophetic Scriptures. Multitudes of books have been written concerning "End Times" and how prophecy will be fulfilled. Bible prophecy, however, is not recognised until after the fulfillment has taken place, or during the actual fulfilling itself, leading to the statement:

"This is what was spoken by the prophet ..."　　　　(Acts 2:16).

To illustrate the above, let us look at examples from both the Old and New Testaments:

*"So **Solomon removed Abiathar from the priesthood** of the LORD, **fulfilling the word the LORD had spoken** at Shiloh about the house of Eli"*   (1 Kg 2:27 NIV).

The historical writer records the fulfillment of a prophecy. King Solomon did not remove Abiathar to consciously fulfill the word of the Lord; he removed him for treachery. In so doing, prophecy is seen being fulfilled.

*"When Herod realized that he had been outwitted by the Magi, he was furious, and he gave orders to kill all the boys in Bethlehem and its vicinity who were two years old and under, in accordance with the time he had learned from the Magi. **Then what was said through the prophet Jeremiah was fulfilled**: 'A voice is heard in Ramah, weeping and great mourning, Rachel weeping for her children and refusing to be comforted, because they are no more'"*
(Matt 2:16-18 NIV).

The writer of this gospel records for us the actual fulfillment of a Scripture. The same writer records twelve more fulfilments as they happen: Matthew 2:15, 2:17, 3:3, 4:14, 8:17, 12:17, 13:14, 13:35, 21:4, 26:54, 26:56 & 27:9. He merely continues a pattern that runs throughout the Bible from Genesis to Revelation.

Another aspect of Biblical prophecy that can throw its students off course is double fulfillments. A number of prophecies have two fulfillments: a literal and a second, or double, fulfillment. The literal fulfillment is the exact fulfillment. The double fulfillment looks like the literal fulfillment but does not quite fill all details. The double fulfillment sometimes takes place first, followed by the literal. An example of this phenomenon will be seen in a later chapter.

Here is an example of two fulfillments of the same prophecy:

*"When Israel was a child, I loved him, and **out of Egypt I called My son**"*   (Hos 11:1).

*"He took the young Child and His mother by night and departed for Egypt, and was there until the death of Herod, that it might be fulfilled which was spoken by the Lord through the prophet, saying, '**Out of Egypt I called My Son**'"*   (Matt 2:14,15).

The literal fulfillment is a distinct and definite reference to Israel and the exodus from Egypt. Moses was sent by God to Pharaoh with specific words:

> *"Then you shall say to Pharaoh, "Thus says the LORD: 'Israel is My son, My firstborn. So I say to you, let My son go that he may serve Me. But if you refuse to let him go, indeed I will kill your son, your firstborn'"* (Ex 4:22,23).

Through the prophet Hosea, the LORD Himself is speaking of Israel being His son and of actually calling him out of Egypt. Matthew, a Jew writing to fellow Jews, gives us a classic example of Jewish exegesis. Applying the prophecy to the return of Mary and Joseph from Egypt where they had fled from Herod with the infant Jesus, he draws our attention to the double fulfillment.

SPIRITUALISING SCRIPTURE

If we are to understand Bible prophecy we must learn at least one rule of exegesis. The basic rule of exegesis is what Rabbinical scholars call *"Mi l'mi?"* meaning "from whom, to whom?" Exegesis is the critical explanation or analysis of a text. Taking a Scripture directed to a particular person, nation or event and applying it elsewhere is not exegesis—it is "spiritualising." Spiritualising a Scriptural promise often strengthens an individual's faith and draws him closer to God. This is not only acceptable but is also to be encouraged. We can often take a promise that is specifically directed to a particular nation, person or situation, "spiritualise" it and apply it to our own country, to ourselves or to our own situation and find that God honours the application. But no matter how wonderful the benefits or how wonderful the spirituality, that is not exegesis!

THE JEWISHNESS OF THE BIBLE

Eighty percent of the entire Bible is made up of the Old Testament and quotations from the Old Testament. Ten percent of all that is recorded as spoken by Jesus is from the Old Testament.

To whom did Jesus address His actual words?

*"I was sent **only** to the lost sheep of Israel"*   (Mt 15:24 NIV).

To whom did Jesus send His disciples after commissioning them?

*"These twelve Jesus sent out with the following instructions: '**Do not go among the Gentiles or enter any town of the Samaritans.** Go rather to the lost sheep of Israel'"*   (Matt 10:5,6 NIV).

Obviously Jesus was directing His ministry and the ministry of the disciples to the Jewish people at that time. It was not until after His resurrection, during the forty days prior to His ascension, that we find:

*"**Go into all the world** and preach the gospel to every creature"*
(Mk 16:15).

The Bible is a Jewish book. I did not say that the Bible was only for Jews; I said that it is a Jewish book. Scholars agree that every writer of the sixty-six books of the Bible is known to be Jewish with the exception of Luke. He wrote the gospel that bears his name and also the book of Acts. Sixty-four books written by Jews out of a total of sixty-six makes the Bible a Jewish book.

Consider also, if you will, the following excerpts from "Introductions to New Testament books," in the New King James "Slimline" Bible printed by Thomas Nelson, Inc., Bible Publishers.

From the introduction to the Gospel of Matthew:

"Matthew is the gospel written by a Jew to Jews about a Jew."

From the introduction to the Epistle to the Hebrews:

"Many Jewish believers, having stepped out of Judaism into Christianity, want to reverse their course in order to escape persecution by their countrymen. The writer of Hebrews exhorts them to 'go on to perfection ...'"

From the introduction to the Epistle of James, beginning in the sixth sentence:

"Throughout his epistle to Jewish believers, James integrates true faith and everyday practical experience by stressing that true faith must manifest itself in works of faith."

From the introduction to the First Epistle of Peter, beginning in the third sentence:

"In writing to Jewish believers struggling in the midst of persecution, Peter encourages them to conduct themselves courageously for the person and program of Christ."

In summarising, we find that:

a)   Eighty percent of the entire Bible is made up of the Old Testament and quotations from the Old Testament.

b)   Ten percent of all of the recorded words of Jesus are taken from the Old Testament.

c)   The three-year ministry of Jesus was directed only to Jews.

d)   The ministry of the disciples was initially directed only to Jews.

e)   The writers of at least sixty-four of the sixty-six books of the Bible were Jews.

f)   Much of the New Testament was written directly to Jews.

We must now conclude that over ninety percent of both Old and New Testaments was written directly to, or concerning, the Jews.

Please understand what I am about to say, because it is very important. I am not saying that the Bible is for Jews only nor am I even hinting at such a thing. The Bible, of course, is for all mankind equally. What I am saying is that we must understand that, with such a huge predominance of Jewish involvement and content in the Bible, the Jews are the central people in the drama. They are the actors on centre stage, and all others play only supporting roles.

Having established that ninety percent of the Bible is centred on Israel and the Jewish people, we also establish that ninety percent of the prophetic content concerns them, too. Remember, the first rule of exegesis is *"Mi l'mi?"*—from whom to whom? We cannot hope to find literal fulfillment of prophecy in any other place than to whom or where it is directed; spiritual fulfillment can be found, but literal fulfillment cannot be found. And literal fulfillment can only be found after, or during, the actual event. In light of the above, we see that we neither have the licence nor the liberty to "interpret prophecy" for the purpose of foretelling the future.

Dear LORD,
Open my spirit to the wonders of Your word. Stop me from seeking something in it that would bolster a particular theory. And help me not to be so preoccupied with future events that I forget to live the 'todays.' Amen.

4

MEASURED HEAVENS

In the Preface attention was given to doctrinal error fostered by the Sadducees of Jesus' day. Jesus said that they were "greatly mistaken." During His discourse He chided the Sadducees and said to them, "Have you not read?" He reproached them because they prided themselves on their knowledge of the Scriptures yet, with all their knowledge, they were still greatly mistaken and in grave error. How Jesus would chide us today for the same reason!

Perhaps the greater portion of the Western Church has error in its doctrine concerning Israel. The most commonly held misbelief is that Israel was rejected by the LORD and that the promises made to the Jewish people were then given over to the Church. This doctrine is known as "Replacement Theology." There are variations of this doctrine, each with greater or lesser degrees of error. It is true that the Church is "spiritual Israel," but this truth needs to be balanced with Scripture; we must be *"rightly dividing the word of truth"* (2 Tim 2:15).

A big percentage of the Church, consciously, or unconsciously, refuses to acknowledge the actual existence of the State of Israel. If mention has to be made of that country, instead of Israel, they use the name Palestine.

Often Christians criticise the Jewish people for their blindness concerning spiritual matters, and that is not without reason for the Jews are blind to the truth about their Messiah. I remember being in a synagogue in New Zealand with a Christian group, many years ago, when a member of the group asked the Rabbi a question concerning the

New Testament. The Rabbi replied, "To me, that book does not exist; therefore, it is an irrelevant question." His blindness is, in part, caused by his stubbornness which refuses to recognise the existence of something that affects a major portion of the world. But, in reality, is the Christian any more open than the Jew? The stubborn resistance by a large portion of Christendom (due to its own erroneous doctrinal view) to acknowledge the State of Israel is no more acceptable than the stance of the Rabbi.

Due to its belief that the Roman Catholic Church, herself, is the true Israel, the Vatican attempted to gain control of Palestine at the end of World War I. The Vatican failed in its move, and, instead, the Mandate to control Palestine was given to the British. But as a consequence of its belief, the Vatican, for more than forty years, refused to recognise the State of Israel. Of late the Vatican has begun the process necessary to establish diplomatic relations with Israel, not because it now recognises Israel as such, but because it now recognises that it has no chance of ever controlling "Palestine" and desperately wants to take part in the current Middle East "peace" process. Within the framework of this "peace" process the Vatican will be assured of a hearing when "her" city, Jerusalem, is placed on the agenda for discussion.

When Prince Andrew of the British Royal Family married Sarah Ferguson in August 1986 it was requested that no mention of Israel, Jacob, Jerusalem or Zion be made during the wedding ceremony in Westminster Abbey. Queen Elizabeth is the head of the Anglican Church of England and also of the British Commonwealth. The royals, having set the precedent, were soon followed by the New Zealand Anglican Church which removed the words Israel, Jacob, Jerusalem and Zion from the order of service and prayer books. No doubt the New Zealand government's extreme pro-Arab/anti-Israel stance contributed to this, but the name Israel occurs in the Bible 2,564 times, Jacob 358 times, Jerusalem 812 times and Zion 160 times; a total of 3,894 occurrences. That is a lot of Scripture to lay aside in order to enforce doctrinal error.

The "New Israel" doctrine stems from the early centuries of Church history and carries with it a latent but dangerous anti-Semitism (this subject is addressed in a later chapter). It is not just the Catholic and traditional sections of the Church that has such radical belief in Replacement Theology. Some major mainline denominations hold to this doctrine and also large numbers of "independent," nondenominational churches. The doctrine is fostered from the pulpit and through various Christian publications, Bible commentaries and even Bibles, including a popular chain-reference Bible.[1] These Bibles encourage the doctrine by the wording employed in their chapter headings, especially those in the books of the major prophets. For example, this chain-reference Bible in the heading to Isaiah 41 says, "God speaks of his merciful providence in regard to his church." This refers to: *"But thou, Israel, art my servant, Jacob whom I have chosen, the seed of Abraham my friend ..."* etc. Natural Israel, in the view of the composer of this particular study Bible, has been totally rejected by God and replaced by a "New Israel," namely, the Church, and therefore every encouraging passage is applied to the Church while every calamity or projected destruction is applied, no longer to Israel but to "the Jews." For example, the heading of Isaiah chapter 50: "... the Jews dereliction." Millions of its readers are therefore constantly indoctrinated with Replacement Theology as they read headings such as that of Isaiah 59: "The Jews sins ... ." And then, of the next chapter, Isaiah 60: "Glory of the church ... ."

There are, of course, exceptions to almost every rule and many individuals in every stream of the Church deny the doctrine of Replacement Theology, but they become voices crying in a vast wilderness.

We find that in Mark chapter twelve Jesus lays the blame for the doctrinal error of the Sadducees on three points:

a) Not knowing the Scriptures.
b) Not knowing the power of God.
c) Not reading the Scriptures correctly.

Today, as in the days of Jesus, the same spiritual condition prevails for the same reasons:

a) The average Christian today is woefully ignorant of the Bible. He has never read the whole Bible, preferring to leave out much of the Old Testament and anything else that is of little interest to him. He is apparently unaware that it is simply not possible to comprehend the New Testament until the Old Testament is first understood, since the New is concealed in the Old, and the Old is revealed in the New.

*"**All** Scripture is given by inspiration of God, and is profitable for doctrine, for reproof, for correction, for instruction in righteousness"*   (2 Tim 3:16).

b) Our low image of God is not conducive to knowing His power. The average Christian (be he Catholic, Protestant, Traditional, Evangelical, Charismatic or Pentecostal) has more faith in his own ability, his insurance policy or his doctor than he does in his God. Thus we forget:

*"What is **the exceeding greatness of His power toward us who believe**, according to the working of His mighty power"* (Eph 1:19).

c) Few, indeed, are they who approach their Bibles with an open heart and an open mind to hear a living word from a living God. Daily freshness is lost to so many of us because our minds are closed. We come to the Bible to bolster our particular doctrinal beliefs. We are not believing what we are reading but reading that which we are already believing. The large portions of our Bibles that are not underlined are the areas that we need to work on:

*"That the God of our Lord Jesus Christ, the Father of glory, may give to you the spirit of wisdom and revelation in **the knowledge of Him, the eyes of your understanding being enlightened; that you may know ...**"*   (Eph 1:17,18).

The basis of Replacement Theology is a supposition that God had cast off Israel because of her sins and unfaithfulness, and then replaced her with the Church, the new Israel. That God put Israel aside due to her sins and unfaithfulness is completely true; however, it was a temporal measure. He "suspended" the relationship, not "severed" it, and He determined her punishment very carefully so that it would neither exceed her powers of endurance, nor threaten her existence as a nation. I do not want to discuss this issue further at this point because it will be dealt with later on. I want to focus our attention now on specific Scripture that reveals the heart of the God of Israel:

*"Thus says the LORD, who gives **the sun** for a light by day, the ordinances of **the moon and the stars** for a light by night, who disturbs the sea, and its waves roar (The LORD of hosts is His name): '**If those ordinances depart** from before Me, says the LORD, then the seed of **Israel shall also cease from being a**"*

nation before Me forever'. Thus says the LORD: 'If heaven above can be measured, and the foundations of the earth searched out beneath, I will also cast off all the seed of Israel for all that they have done', says the LORD"   (Jer 31:35-37).

The LORD makes it perfectly clear, that when day and night cease Israel will cease to be a nation. Israel in the natural realm may well be a scattered people, but, in the eyes of God, they are a nation merely waiting to be gathered together into a whole.

The LORD says that if the heavens can be measured and the intricacies of Earth in orbit can be fathomed then He will cast off all the seed of Israel for all that they have done. Day and night continue with us. And the heavens? They are so vast in magnitude that they defy man and his equipment and technology. The heavens issue a challenge to determine their origin, content and dimension. Man has taken up the challenge, but the answers elude him. Israel remains a nation before God and the continuance of Israel as the chosen people of God is as continual as the laws of nature.

The LORD is fully aware of the Church's response to Israel:

"Have you not considered what these people have spoken, saying, 'The two families which the LORD has chosen, He has also cast them off'? Thus they have despised My people, as if they should no more be a nation before them. Thus says the LORD: 'If My covenant is not with day and night, and if I have not appointed the ordinances of heaven and earth, then I will cast away the descendants of Jacob ... For I will cause their captives to return, and will have mercy on them'"   (Jer 33:24-26).

The two families that the LORD mentions are the northern kingdom of Israel and the southern kingdom of Judah. Simply saying that God has cast off natural Israel is to despise His chosen people, and, as we shall see in Chapter Eight, this is dangerous ground indeed. In the above passage the LORD again mentions the fixed order of day and night in connection with the casting away of the Jewish people.

Even before the LORD brought the Israelites into the land of Canaan He foresaw their being taken away as captives to other lands because of their apostasy. But great are His promises to them:

*"The land also shall be left empty by them, and will enjoy its sabbaths while it lies desolate without them; they will accept their guilt, because they despised My judgments and because their soul abhorred My statutes. **Yet for all that**, when they are in the land of their enemies, **I will not cast them away, nor shall I abhor them**, to utterly destroy them and **break My covenant with them**; for I am the LORD their God. But for their sake **I will remember the covenant of their ancestors**, whom I brought out of the land of Egypt in the sight of the nations, that I might be their God: I am the LORD"*   (Lev 26:43-45).

We have seen that the LORD has made specific promises to Israel concerning her destiny despite the gravity of her offences against Him:

a) Only when day and night cease will she cease to be a nation.
b) Only when the heavens are measured will He cast her off because of her sins.
c) Even while she is in captivity, He will not cast her off nor abhor or detest her; neither will He totally destroy her nor break His covenant with her.
d) He will bring her exiled people back to their own land.

It is argued by some that, due to the grave abominations that they committed against Him, the LORD changed His mind concerning the election of Israel. Can we in all conscience charge the LORD with being fickle? Let Scripture both argue the case and answer the charge:

*"**God is not a man, that He should lie**, nor a son of man, that He should repent. Has He said, and will He not do? Or has He spoken, and will He not make it good?"*   (Num 23:19).

*"God, who **cannot lie**"* (Tit 1:2).

*"It is **impossible** for God to lie"* (Heb 6:18).

*"Indeed, **let God be true** but every man a liar. As it is written: 'That You may be **justified in Your words**, and may overcome when You are judged'"*   (Rom 3:4).

It is easy to bring charges against the LORD and attempt to blacken His name, because He does not defend Himself. The four Scriptures quoted above, however, do defend Him. Let all those that truly love Him agree with the apostle Paul who said, *"Let God be true but every man a liar."* It is not merely a matter of the LORD not lying; He simply cannot lie, because it is not His nature—His nature is truth.

Concerning the validity of God's word, there is an interesting little play on words that the LORD engages in with the prophet Jeremiah. The LORD wants to catch Jeremiah's attention and focus it on an important point:

> *"The word of the LORD came to me: 'What do you see, Jeremiah?' 'I see the branch of an **almond** tree,' I replied. The LORD said to me, 'You have seen correctly, for **I am watching** to see that my word is fulfilled'"*   (Jer 1:11,12 NIV).

Since the above only makes sense to those that read and understand Hebrew, I will explain the interchange. The Hebrew language is made up of consonants only; there are no vowels, as such. The Hebrew word for "almond" has only three letters *Shin, Kof* and *Dalet* and is pronounced *shaked*. The Hebrew word for "watching" also has the same three letters, *Shin, Kof* and *Dalet*, but is pronounced *shoked*. The LORD, wanting to enforce His point into Jeremiah's mind, first shows him an almond branch and then brings him to the issue at hand, namely, that He is watching to ensure that His word is fulfilled.

Just as the LORD needed to remind Jeremiah that the words spoken by Him would come to pass and that He was watching over those words to ensure this, so He would remind us again today that He is watching to see that all His words will come to pass:

> *"For I am the LORD. **I speak, and the word which I speak will come to pass**"*   (Eze 12:25).

To say that the LORD has rejected the Jewish people and that the promises made to them have passed to the Church is more than Scripturally wrong, it is blasphemous.

Dear LORD,
Give me a right understanding of Your word concerning Your people Israel. Help me to realise that I am fighting You personally when I withstand Your divine purposes. Give me a teachable spirit and grant me the grace to change what needs to be changed in my thinking. Amen.

PART II

FROM ANCIENT TIMES

"I am God, and there is no other; I am God, and there is none like Me, declaring the end from the beginning, and from ancient times things that are not yet done, saying, 'My counsel shall stand, and I will do all My pleasure'"

(Isa 46:9&10).

5

THE END
FROM
THE BEGINNING

The LORD is as sovereign over Israel as He is over every other created thing or entity. In fact, concerning Israel, He says:

> *"As the clay is in the potter's hand, so are you in My hand, O house of Israel"* (Jer 18:6).

And the reality of this is to be seen in the actual outworking of His dealings with Israel. Despite many and varied catastrophes brought about by prolonged periods of idolatrous and unrighteous behaviour, Israel still needed to be reminded as to Who held the reigns of power. It is from one of these reminders that we locate the starting point for our particular study of that nation:

> *"Listen to Me, O house of Jacob, and all the remnant of the house of Israel ... I am God, and there is no other; I am God, and there is none like Me, **declaring the end from the beginning**, and from ancient times things that are not yet done, saying, '**My counsel shall stand, and I will do all My pleasure**,' Calling a **bird** of prey from the east, the **man** who executes My counsel, from a far country. Indeed **I have spoken it; I will also bring it to pass. I have purposed it; I will also do it**"* (Isa 46:3, 9-11).

The LORD declares His sovereignty over Israel and His sovereignty over both man and beast also. He establishes His authority over creation by informing us that He commands at will man, bird or beast to carry out His pleasure or to expedite His judgements. And at the same time, He alerts us as to where to find His declared counsel and pleasure concerning *the house of Jacob and the remnant of the house of Israel.*

God said that He had declared *the end from the beginning* and gives us assurance of the absolute certainty that what He has *spoken will come to pass.*

Obviously, we must look for words spoken by the LORD at the beginning of the history of the nation of Israel that would foretell the most distant future. But where does the nation of Israel really begin? Does it begin with Abraham? Does it begin with the change of name: Jacob into Israel? Does it begin with Joseph in Egypt who was later joined by Jacob and the entire patriarchal family? No, the nation of Israel begins in Egypt with the acknowledgement by the LORD that those descended from the loins of Abraham, through Isaac, are His people.

> *"Now it happened in the process of time that ... the children of Israel groaned because of the bondage, and they cried out; and their cry came up to God because of the bondage. So God heard their groaning, and God remembered His covenant with Abraham, with Isaac, and with Jacob. And God looked upon the children of Israel, and **God acknowledged them**"*   (Ex 2:23-25).

It is here, in Egypt, that the **nation** of Israel begins and consequently, the history of that nation also. Because Scripture says that *"God remembered His covenant"* it does not mean that the LORD has a memory that fails with age like that of man. It means that He now gives full attention to that covenant. The LORD gives recognition to the children of Israel that they are indeed His people and puts into motion certain events in order to bring them up out of the land of Egypt that they may enter His own land. (We shall discuss the LORD'S land later).

The LORD then proceeds to capture the attention of the man, Moses, whom He plans to send into the court of Pharaoh and whom He had already prepared for this task by having him raised in the protocol of Egypt. Moses was currently looking after his father-in-law's sheep in a desert, and the LORD causes a bush in that desert to ignite and burst into flame but not be consumed by the flames. A burning bush that is not consumed arouses the curiosity of Moses, and he approaches for a closer look at the phenomenon. Having gained his attention, the LORD spoke to him from out of the bush:

*"Come now ... I will send you to Pharaoh that you may bring **My people**, the children of Israel, out of Egypt"*   (Ex 3:10).

This is the first instance, among many, of the children of Israel being termed *My people* which follows hard on the heels of God's acknowledgement of the descendants of His friend Abraham.

Most everyone knows how Moses went before Pharaoh demanding the release of the children of Israel and how, at Pharaoh's obstinacy, the LORD brought ten calamities upon the land and people of Egypt. Those ten plagues brought the required response from Pharaoh, and Egypt released the children of Israel and allowed them to depart the ravaged country.

After the exit from Egypt, the LORD opened up the Red Sea by holding back the waters, allowing His people to travel through on dry ground into the *Wilderness of Shur* (Ex 15:22). They went from there into the *Wilderness of Sin* (Ex 16:1) and then:

*"**In the third month** after the children of Israel had gone out of the land of Egypt, on the same day, they came to the Wilderness of Sinai"*   (Ex 19:1).

For nearly three months the children of Israel had been laboriously travelling toward the Wilderness of Sinai. Shortly after their entering it, the LORD began to give His commands, judgements and statutes to the fledgeling nation of Israel. They received the Ten Commandments and the *Torah* (Law) and were informed of what would befall them in the future.

The book of Deuteronomy records the second reading of those laws and ordinances to the children of Israel and provides some details not available to us in Exodus, Leviticus or Numbers. It is here, in the book of Deuteronomy, written *from ancient times*, that we find the future of Israel—the things that have not yet happened. Here, recorded from antiquity—three months out of Egypt, at the very beginning of Israel's long trek—are the basic things that would take place in the millennia to come:

*"Now it shall come to pass, when **all these things come upon you**, the blessing and the curse which I have set before you, and you call them to mind among all the nations where the LORD your God drives you, and you return to the LORD your God and obey His*

voice, according to all that I command you today, you and your
children, with all your heart and with all your soul, that the LORD
*your God **will bring you back from captivity**, and have*
*compassion on you, and **gather you again** from all the nations*
where the LORD your God has scattered you. If any of you are
*driven out to the **farthest parts under heaven**, from there the*
LORD your God will gather you, and from there He will bring you.
*Then the LORD your God will **bring you to the land which your***
***fathers possessed, and you shall possess it**. He will prosper you*
and multiply you more than your fathers. And the LORD your God
*will **circumcise your heart** and the heart of your descendants, to*
love the LORD your God with all your heart and with all your
*soul, that you may live. Also the LORD your God will put **all these***
***curses on your enemies** and on those who hate you, who perse-*
cuted you. And you will again obey the voice of the LORD and do
all His commandments which I command you today"

(Deut 30:1-8).

In the above passage are recorded several major events that will take
place in their appointed times. Most of these events directly concern
Israel, but one relates to Gentile nations. I summarise these events as:

a)   The blessing.
b)   The curse.
c)   The exile.
d)   The re-gathering.
e)   The land.
f)   The revival.
g)   The economic and physical collapse of Gentile nations.

In a capsulated form we have the declared history of Israel from beginning to end. And we have the sure failure of the economies of
nations coupled together with wars, famines and diseases within those
nations. We shall be looking into all these events separately, but for our
purposes here, we simply need to clarify the list of events.

THE BLESSING:
The blessing of the Jewish people is found in the twenty-eighth
chapter of Deuteronomy. The first thirteen verses of the chapter contain
twelve verses of blessing. For the sake of a better understanding, I

encourage you to read the passage from your own Bible. The reader who has some knowledge of the remarkable talent, high intelligence and abundant wealth of the Jewish people can appreciate the blessings promised to them.

THE CURSE:

The curse that would befall the Jewish people as a result of careless and wilful neglect of their spiritual responsibilities is spelled out in fifty-four verses of that same chapter of Deuteronomy. Again, I encourage you to read this from your Bible; only then do we gain an appreciation of the anguish that the Jewish people were to endure throughout the millennia.

As we consider the history of the Jews we clearly see the truth of the terrors promised. They have been cursed in city and countryside; scattered into almost, if not every, country in the world; and made the scapegoat for all the ill-winds of misfortune that befell those countries. The Jews have been oppressed and plundered continuously; hounded from country to country; their little ones torn from their arms and killed or, as in thousands of cases after the birth of the Church, forcibly baptised and reared in Gentile homes.

The Jew has, indeed, been driven nearly mad because of what they have had to watch and endure. Nearly fifty years have passed since the Holocaust, yet my wife's aunt still cannot sleep soundly due to reoccurring nightmares that haunt her from terrible years spent in German death camps. She has a number that the Nazis tattooed on her forearm that, during the daylight hours, keep her mindful of the horrors she witnessed. Her own immediate family and her husband's extended family (seven brothers and their wives and children) do not suffer from terrible dreams—they were all exterminated by poison gas and incinerated in the great gas-fired ovens of those German camps. There was no rest for their souls and no assurance of life. They longed for the night, and when it came they longed for the day. They offered themselves as slaves, but no one wanted them. Scripture harrowingly describes the suffering of the Jewish people:

"You have fed them with the bread of tears, and given them tears to drink in great measure"   (Psa 80:5).

Their food and drink, which were found in abundance, were their own salty tears of despair. And after the death of the millions of Jews who died before World War II and the six million that were murdered by the Nazi regime during the war, the Jewish people, as the LORD foretold, were left few in number.

The blessing and the curse is part of the foretold future of Israel. When the Scripture says, *"when **all** these things come upon you,"* it plainly indicates that a long period of time is involved. It was not something that happened during the course of a generation or two. The blessing came as Israel walked in the ways of her God, and the curse came as she spurned Him. Reading the Biblical account of Israel, we see them vacillate back and forth over millennia of time with blessing following repentance and cursing following disobedience. The pattern commenced within a few short years after the death of Joshua, who led the children of Israel into the promised land, and it continues until the present day.

THE EXILE:

The Deuteronomy account that foretells the future for Israel was communicated to the children of Israel only a matter of months after the Exodus from Egypt. This was forty years prior to the crossing of the river Jordan into the promised land. Yet, before the children of Israel had set foot in the land, or had even set their eyes upon the land, they were told that they would leave it. They were told that they were going to go into captivity in many nations and that some of them were going to go *"to the farthest parts under heaven."* From this we know that Israel's history must incorporate exile from the land and great dispersion of the Jewish people into many nations, even to the extent of being scattered to the most distant lands on earth.

THE REGATHERING:

Just as we see reference to dispersion of the children of Israel from the land, so, too, we see reference to regathering from the nations back into that very same land. By the construction of the passage, *"gather you **again** from all the nations,"* we have cause to see not one, but two, exiles. This tells us that there must be two regatherings also because at the time of Deuteronomy, the LORD had not gathered the children of

Israel from the nations but had simply *"brought the children of Israel up out of the land of Egypt."*

THE LAND:

Throughout Genesis, Exodus, Leviticus and Deuteronomy, constant referral is made to the land that would be given to the children of Israel as their inheritance. In the passage concerning the history of Israel, the LORD says that He would bring them *"to the land which your fathers possessed, and you shall possess it."* The history of Israel obviously involves possession of a particular land, a land that had been previously possessed by earlier generations of the children of Israel.

THE REVIVAL:

In the sixth verse of the Deuteronomy passage we have another interesting event that must take place during Israel's history: the total conversion of Israel.

The LORD spoke to the children of Israel: *"the LORD your God will circumcise your heart and the heart of your descendants."* He addresses them as one man, as one entity. The promise is made to every member of the congregation of Israel and to all their descendants.

Circumcision of the heart means to cut away the excess, callused flesh in order to expose the tender portion to God. We see an example of this type of usage in the words of the LORD when speaking to Josiah, King of Israel:

*"Because **your heart was tender, and you humbled yourself** before God"*   (2 Chr 34:27).

Those that understand Hebraic terms understand that circumcision of the heart means a turning to God. When a person turns to God there is a voluntary humbling that accompanies the action. We will be having an in-depth look at this subject later on, and the circumcision mentioned here will clearly be seen as the reception of Jesus as Messiah and Lord.

THE COLLAPSE OF GENTILE NATIONS:

In the seventh verse of our passage, we are told that the LORD will put all of the curses upon the *enemies* of Israel, *"and on those who hate you, who persecuted you."* These curses will not necessarily come as the culmination of events at the end of Israel's long trek. If we take an historical glance over our shoulders to the past we see that quite the opposite has happened. Several nations and a few empires butchered and oppressed or persecuted the children of Israel. Some of these nations, such as Edom, not only collapsed, but no trace of them remain today—not even enough for a tombstone to remind the present generation that here lies a dead civilisation.

The great majority of the enemies of Israel during the past 1,900 years, those that both hated and persecuted them, were "Christian" nations. We shall be looking at Anti-Semitism in a separate chapter, and most readers will be horrified at the actual history of the Christian Church. While we can look back over the past and see fulfillment of the LORD'S words regarding the cursing of the enemies of Israel, we obviously cannot document that which has not yet come to pass. We can, however, expect grave economic and physical chaos to happen in the near future to some of the longer established sections of Christendom and also to other cultures and religions that treat Israel with contempt. We expect this because it is simply impossible for this last promise to be unfulfilled if all the other promises are to have fulfillments.

We have looked very briefly at the prophetically recorded history of Israel before it happens. We shall, as time and space permit, deal with each of these events. But suffice to say, this history, given to us some 3,500 years ago, is an accurate forecast and is, indeed, the declaration of the end from the beginning.

Dear LORD,
Terrible curses came upon the Jewish people because of their stubborn refusal to walk in Your ways. You also plan to put these curses upon other nations. I humbly ask that my nation be brought to repentance. As Nineveh of old repented before You in sackcloth and ashes, so I ask You to turn the heart of my people to repentance that they too may be spared the awful judgement decreed against them. Amen.

6

TIMES
AND
SEASONS

Again I want to stress the sovereignty of God at the commencement of this new chapter. If we do not grasp the fact of the absolute sovereignty of the LORD in the affairs of man, we are left with a very large group of somewhat irrational beings with highly divergent opinions and personalities who are in charge of their own personal destiny and also that of the world in which they live. We human beings are fickle and find little contentment for any length of time because we tire of things quickly. If we were left entirely to ourselves we would self-destruct because our moods are in a state of constant change. What pleased us yesterday will not please us tomorrow because we are dissatisfied within a brief space of time. For example, when the weather gets hot we desire it to be cooler; and when it becomes cooler we would like it warmer. Then when the weather is dry we want rain, and when the rains come we quickly tire of grey skies. Imagine the chaos if individuals had control of the weather. Just one average family could have the day take on the appearance of a discotheque! How fortunate we are that the LORD has absolute sovereignty over all the elements:

*"He makes His **sun** rise on the evil and on the good, and sends **rain** on the just and on the unjust"* (Matt 5:45).

*"Have you entered the treasury of **snow**, or have you seen the treasury of **hail**, Which I have reserved for the time of trouble, for the day of battle and war?"*   (Job 38:22&23).

*"He makes **lightning** for the rain; he brings the **wind** out of His treasuries"*   (Psa 135:7).

When man began to think he could control the weather elements by seeding the clouds, etc., the LORD simply opened a hole in the ozone layer which brought about a global warming that has thrown much of our world into chaos. Even though man had no great success over the natural elements he marches proudly and defiantly on proclaiming that he, the master of this planet, controls his destiny and steers the direction and ideologies of the nations. Simply declaring himself to be in control did not put control in or even near his grasp. The fact of the matter is that he is no more in control of the nations than he is of the weather. The constant round of political or military coups and the many surprise election results bear witness to this. Just as there is evidence concerning the LORD'S sovereignty over the weather so there is concerning nations and kingdoms:

*"O LORD God of our fathers, are You not God in heaven, and do You not rule over **all the kingdoms** of the nations?"*   (2 Chr 20:6).

*"**He makes nations great, and destroys them**; he enlarges nations, and guides them"*   (Job 12:23).

*"**God reigns over the nations**; God sits on His holy throne"*
                                                          (Psa 47:8).

*"He changes the times and the seasons; **He removes kings and raises up kings**"*   (Dan 2:21).

People often wonder why even the most intelligent person elected to government office makes so many seemingly unintelligent decisions. In many instances better decisions appear to be made by children than by mature statesmen. It is essential that we see the hand of the LORD in the affairs of men and realise that:

*"He **deprives of intelligence** the chiefs of the earth's people, and makes them wander in a pathless waste"*   (Job 12:24 NASB).

"The LORD foils the plans of the nations; he thwarts the purposes of the peoples"   (Psa 33:10 NIV).

"He brings the princes to nothing; he makes the judges of the earth useless"   (Isa 40:23).

"I will destroy the wisdom of the wise, and bring to nothing the understanding of the prudent"   (1 Cor 1:19).

Do we deduce then that God is in control of the natural elements and the destiny of nations but has no control over the individual? The argument that, as individuals having a free choice, we are in control of our personal destiny does not find support in the Bible:

"A man's heart plans his way, but the LORD directs his steps"   (Prov 16:9).

"The lot is cast into the lap, but its every decision is from the LORD"   (Prov 16:33).

"All the days ordained for me were written in your book before one of them came to be"   (Psa 139:16 NIV).

Some people balk at the idea of God being in control of them:

"But indeed, O man, who are you to reply against God? Will the thing formed say to him who formed it, 'Why have you made me like this?' Does not the potter have power over the clay, from the same lump to make one vessel for honor and another for dishonor?"   (Rom 9:20&21).

Obviously, we have little control over anything at all. Even our apparent free-choices turn out to be God's foreordained decrees. This may sound logically absurd but is, nevertheless, true. We are not discussing fate or kismet. We are talking about the tremendous power and intelligence of our God. He created the heavens by the word of His mouth, but it will take us a trillion lifetimes to explore those heavens—which He fills with His presence. He declares from antiquity what will happen in eternity, because He knows the thought and intention of the heart of man. He acts and plans hundreds, thousands and millions of years ahead, according to His own sure foreknowledge

of the thoughts and intentions of men, in order to accomplish His divine
purpose and will. The LORD is not some insignificant god, competing
against other petty gods. The LORD our God is the creator, possessor
and absolute, sovereign ruler of everything existing and is in complete
control of the work of His hands:

> *"He is **unique**, and who can make Him change? And whatever His*
> *soul desires, that He does"*   (Job 23:13).

The LORD is unique—Hebrew, *echad,* the prime #1. This means that
He has no equal or equivalent. He is incomparable, matchless and
unrivalled—the only One of a kind. This is the meaning in the great
Jewish *Shema:*

> *"Hear, O Israel: The LORD our God, the LORD is **one**!"*
>   (Deut 6:4).

The same Hebrew word is used here. The meaning of this passage is
not that there is only one God of Israel. That is very true, but it is not
what the passage is telling us. The passage is saying: *"Hear, O Israel:*
*The LORD our God, the LORD is **unique**!"*

All of the above, thus far, is merely to get us to the place where we
see the sovereignty and centrality of the LORD in the affairs of what we
call nature, the world and man. Now we can see more clearly His
involvement with Israel.

A TIME FOR EVERYTHING

As we saw briefly in the last chapter, there are certain events that
must happen during the history of Israel. That which we looked at was
the backbone of the history. Flesh and blood will be added to this
skeleton as we proceed further into our study of the nation.

We saw also that there had to be a beginning, a time when the people
came to be a nation in actuality. The beginning of their history as a
nation came in the land of Egypt where the children of Israel were
oppressed as slaves. The LORD had spoken to Abram, who became
Abraham, who became the father of Isaac, who in time was the father of
Jacob, later named Israel. The LORD spoke to Abram shortly after he
had come out of Haran, and then made a covenant with him that he

would possess the land of Canaan. Immediately after making the covenant, Abram fell into a deep and dreadful sleep, and the LORD spoke to him:

> *"**Know** certainly that your descendants will be strangers in a land that is not theirs, and will serve them, and they will afflict them **four hundred years**"*   (Gen 15:13).

Why did the descendants of Abram need to be strangers in a foreign land for 400 years? Actually, for a number of reasons, and one was that the LORD might show His mighty sovereign power in Egypt. To Pharaoh, King of Egypt, the LORD said:

> *"For this purpose I have raised you up, **that I may show My power** in you, and that My name may be declared in all the earth"*
> (Ex 9:16).

Another reason why they were to be strangers for 400 years becomes obvious:

> *"In the fourth generation they shall return here, for **the iniquity of the Amorites is not yet complete**"*   (Gen 15:16).

The period in Egypt was a stopgap measure that the LORD used to great advantage. At the time when the covenant was made it was not opportune for the LORD to supplant the Amorites with Abram and his offspring. The Amorites were an iniquitous people, but their sin was not yet at the level where He would sanction destruction of an entire nation. This would take a further 400 years. The oppression of the Israelites during their sojourn in Egypt was also necessary to prevent them from becoming too comfortable to leave.

These verses from Genesis tell us that the LORD knows the details of what will happen in the centuries to come and that there are definite pre-determined times for definite pre-determined events. This is borne out by King Solomon, who, aside from the Lord Jesus, was the wisest man that ever lived:

> *"**To everything there is a season, a time for every purpose** under heaven"*   (Eccl 3:1).

We add to the words of that wise man those of Jesus Himself, in whom dwelt the fullness of the Father:

*"It is not for you to know **times** or **seasons** which **the Father has put in His own authority"***   (Acts 1:7).

We find that the wise king and the Son of God both said the same thing. Jesus adds that God also has sovereignty over the times and the seasons.

For some strange reason much of Christianity feels that the LORD'S plans were totally upset by the fall of man in the garden of Eden. They feel that He then needed to find a solution to the problem and, eventually, after careful consideration, decided to send His Son in the likeness of sinful flesh to restore man back to Himself. Again, none of this finds any support in the Scriptures. Speaking of Jesus, we are assured that He is:

*"The Lamb slain **from the foundation** of the world"*   (Rev 13:8).

We are plainly told that Jesus, the Lamb of God, was sacrificed from the foundation of the world, which was eons before Adam and Eve existed. The Bible goes further:

*"He indeed was **foreordained before the foundation** of the world, but was **manifest in these last times** for you"*   (1 Pet 1:20).

Now we are told that Jesus was foreordained or predestined before the foundation of the world. And we see the "times and seasons" aspect come to the fore, but nowhere clearer than in the following:

*"**When the fullness of the time had come**, God sent forth His Son"*   (Gal 4:4).

The shedding of the blood of our Lord Jesus for the life of the world was an integral part of the planning of the LORD when He made the heavens and the earth. To use a figure of speech, Jesus "was as good as dead" in the mind of the Father when the foundations of our world were laid. But it was not until many long ages had passed in time that the appointed season became actual and the appointed time arrived. We then have the words of Jesus recorded for us approximately 1,000 years before He came to carry out His Father's will:

"Behold, I have come—in the volume of the book it is written of Me—to do Your will, O God" (Heb 10:7, Psa 40:7&8).

Eternal life was part of the great plan of God too:

*"In hope of eternal life which God, who cannot lie, **promised before time began"*** (Tit 1:2).

It was promised before time began to all who would receive Jesus as Lord by exercising their apparent free-choice:

"He chose us in Him before the foundation of the world"
(Eph 1:4).

Free choice? Positively yes! Sovereignty of God? Absolutely! Contradictory? Never! Do we yet understand that the LORD'S intelligence is so far superior to ours that we do not even possess the intelligence to comprehend His? Before the earth was formed, before the sun, moon and stars were created, Jesus, the Son of the Father's love, was ready to be sacrificed for our sin. Jesus was and is *"the Lamb of God who takes away the sin of the world"* (Jn 1:29). The sin of the world is yet to be taken away. At present, the vast majority of the world's population remains unsaved and still in its sin: this will not always be so. The Bible says otherwise: the LORD has a plan. The central point of the LORD'S plan for the salvation of the world is very much Jesus. And, as we shall see, He is to be revealed to the world through Israel in conjunction with a pure and holy church which is His body.

MODERN ISRAEL

We dare not divorce modern Israel from the Israel of the Bible. Modern Israel is the fulfillment of the prophecies concerning Biblical Israel.

In the natural realm, modern Israel is chaotic, and I would define chaos as the absence of God. At the beginning of creation we see an interesting fact:

"In the beginning God created the heavens and the earth. The earth was without form, and void; and darkness was on the face of

*the deep. And the Spirit of God was hovering over the face of the
waters. Then **God said, 'Let there be light'; and there was** light"*
(Gen 1:1-3).

Most English Bible translations give the same rendering, *"without
form, and void."* This is not the best translation of the Hebrew *tohu ve
vohu* which really means "empty and chaotic." Of course the earth had
form. The hills, mountains and valleys were formed and in position, but
it was empty of life and there was no order. Then the LORD
commences to speak into the chaos *"Let there be ..."* and order
proceeds to come. When we put God into modern Israel, order begins to
come into the chaos that is seen with the natural eye. Israel will never
make any sense all the while we look at her with the natural eye.
Consider the words of Jesus that He spoke to the Samaritan woman at
the well:

*"You worship what you do not know; we know what we worship,
for **salvation is of the Jews**"*   (Jn 4:22).

That is a remarkable statement: *"Salvation is of the Jews."* The
Greek word *ek* rendered here as "of" means "the point where action
proceeds from," and it is often used in connection with "completion."
Let us paraphrase what Jesus said. "Salvation proceeds from, and is
completed in, the Jewish people." Perhaps now we can understand the
following Scripture a little better:

*"For if their **rejection is the reconciliation** of the world, what will
their acceptance be but **life from the dead**?"*   (Rom 11:15 NIV).

Through the rejection, or putting to one side, of Israel, salvation came
to the Gentile nations. The culmination of the plan of salvation, the
resurrection, comes **after** the Jews are grafted back into their own Olive
tree—which is nothing short of "life from the dead." The gospel, or
good news, of Jesus Christ is so intertwined with the Jewish people and
with Israel that the two cannot be separated. And the gospel is not
directed to reason, it is directed to faith. Looking at modern Israel with
eyes of faith means that a degree of order will easily be seen that could
never be perceived otherwise.

*"So then **faith** comes by hearing, and hearing by **the word of
God**"*   (Rom 10:17).

Faith, we are told, comes from the word of God. In our study of Israel we shall be looking at much of the word of God, and we shall see the actuality of times and seasons, events *"which will be fulfilled in their own time"* (Lk 1:20). Faith will rise in the heart of the reader because God will be seen speaking into the chaos, not only into the chaos of modern Israel, but also into the world of chaos in which we live.

Dear LORD,
Help me to realise that You are in complete control of every situation and that nothing escapes Your all-seeing eye. Grant me the ability to relax in the knowledge of You, knowing that You have a plan and purpose for our chaotic world, and that You will, at the right time, execute this plan to the glory of Your great name. Amen.

7

THE
PURPOSE

Although it is the common belief of many that Israel is to be a light to the Gentiles, this is only true insofar as it concerns the *"redeemed"* nation after the *New Covenant* comes into effect, and thus we read: *"Gentiles shall come to your light, and kings to the brightness of your rising"* (Isa 60:3). Scripture is adamant that it is not Israel that is to be the light to the Gentiles but Jesus, the Jewish Messiah:

> *"I, the LORD, have called You in righteousness, and will hold Your hand; I will keep You and **give You as a covenant** to the people, as a light to the Gentiles, **to open blind eyes, to bring out prisoners from the prison,** those who sit in darkness from the prison house"* (Isa 42:6&7).

> *"It is too small a thing that You should be **My Servant** to raise up the tribes of Jacob, and to restore the preserved ones of Israel; **I will also give You as a light to the Gentiles,** that You should be **My salvation** to the ends of the earth"* (Isa 49:6).

It was Jesus, not Israel, that was given as a *"covenant"* to the people. It was Jesus that became the *"Mediator"* (Heb 8:6, 9:15, 12:24) of the *"new covenant"* (Jer 31:31, Eze 16:60). It was also Jesus on whom the *"Spirit of the Lord"* rested *"to proclaim liberty to the captives and recovery of sight to the blind"* (Lk 4:18). It is Jesus whom God describes as *"My Righteous Servant"* (Isa 53:11). And it is Jesus (Heb. *Yeshua*) who is the Salvation (Heb. *Yeshuah*) of God *"to the ends of the earth."*

On completion of the prescribed forty days of cleansing after the birth of a male child, Mary and Joseph brought the little, circumcised baby to Jerusalem to be presented to the LORD in accordance with the law of Moses that required every first-born male opening the womb to be set apart to the LORD. At that time, Simeon, a devout and righteous man with the Holy Spirit upon him, took Jesus in his arms and said:

"A light to bring revelation to the Gentiles, and the glory of Your people Israel"   (Lk 2:32).

But He is not just to be a light to the Gentiles, He is to be a light to the Jewish nation also:

"Christ ... light to the Jewish people and to the Gentiles"
                                                                      (Acts 26:23).

With the above in mind we should now ask ourselves that if the nation of Israel was not given to be a light to the Gentiles, as generally believed, then what is her purpose? The Jews as a nation, themselves, were also wrong in their perception of why the LORD chose them. They thought that their election to the purposes of God was an election of favouritism, and this has led them through a long, long valley of tears. The reason for the unique survival of the Jews is that the purposes of God have yet to be fulfilled through them. The appointed purpose, the destiny, of the Jewish nation still awaits them. But, as the pendulum of time continues to swing relentlessly on, we are seeing the very powers of hell rising up in rage against her in a futile effort to stop the fulfillment of her destiny.

THE PURPOSE OF ISRAEL

To find the purpose of Israel we must search it out, and to do that we need to return once more to the beginning of the nationhood of Israel. Remember, the LORD heard the groaning of the children of Israel in Egypt and acknowledged them as His own people. He appointed and anointed Moses to lead His people out of Egypt, and, having accomplished that, He then said to the whole nation of Israel:

*"I am the LORD **your** God, who brought you out of the land of Egypt, out of the house of bondage. You shall have **no other gods**

*before Me. You shall not make for yourself a carved image, or any likeness of anything that is in heaven above, or that is in the earth beneath, or that is in the water under the earth; you shall not bow down to them nor serve them. For I, the LORD **your** God, am a jealous God"*   (Ex 20:2-5).

The LORD does not say to Israel "I am the LORD God." He says two times *"I am the LORD your God."* Significant? Very much so. He was to be their **personal** God. *"You shall have no other gods."* For Israel, there were to be no other gods besides Him—there was to be no confusing His power with some demonic force. They were to be a holy people, that is, a people **set apart** from all other nations:

*"For **you are a holy people to the LORD your God;** the LORD **your** God has chosen you to be a people for Himself, a special treasure above all the peoples on the face of the earth"* (Deut 7:6).

In contrast to the last two Scriptures, consider the following:

*"And when you look up to the sky and see the sun, the moon and the stars—all the heavenly array—do not be enticed into bowing down to them and worshiping things the LORD your God has **apportioned to all the nations** under heaven"*   (Deut 4:19 NIV).

An interesting passage. The LORD became the personal God of Israel, but He apportioned (NKJ), allotted (RSV & NASB), and divided (KJV) the sun, moon, stars and all the heavenly host among the nations to be their gods. These gods would be rather useless in the area of answering petitions, whereas the LORD would be seen to be the most benevolent of Gods. Obviously He wanted the other nations to notice this fact. We shall develop this train of thought by using the account of King David, but before we do so let us look at David's authority. We read of David in the Old Testament:

*"Thus says David the son of Jesse; thus says the man raised up on high, the anointed of the God of Jacob, and the sweet psalmist of Israel: **'The Spirit of the LORD spoke by me, and His word was on my tongue. The God of Israel said, the Rock of Israel spoke to me ...'"***   (2 Sam 23:1-3).

Not only did the LORD speak **to** David, He also spoke **through** David. And we are also told six times in the New Testament that David spoke by the power of the Holy Spirit. Even Jesus Himself is recorded as having said it on, at least, one occasion:

*"For **David himself said by the Holy Spirit**: "The Lord said to my Lord, 'Sit at My right hand, till I make Your enemies Your footstool'"*   (Mk 12:36).

David was not only a man that prophesied by the Holy Spirit, but he was also in touch with the LORD, and had His very thoughts:

*"Then David gave his son Solomon the plans for the vestibule, its houses, its treasuries, its upper chambers, its inner chambers, and the place of the mercy seat and the plans for **all that he had by the Spirit,** of the courts of the house of the LORD, of all the chambers all around, of the treasuries of the house of God, and of the treasuries for the dedicated things"*   (1 Chr 28:11&12).

*"The LORD made me understand **in writing, by His hand upon me,** all the works of these plans"*   (1 Chr 28:19).

King David was so much in harmony with the LORD that the LORD could communicate explicit detail through him by His Holy Spirit. Knowing this helps us to refrain from reading into his words that which is not there:

*"And who is like Your people, **like Israel,** the one nation on the earth whom God went to redeem for Himself as a people, **to make for Himself a name**—and to do **for Yourself** great and awesome deeds **for Your land**—before Your people whom You redeemed **for Yourself** from Egypt, the nations, and their gods?"*   (2 Sam 7:23).

This is the purpose of Israel! They were the smallest of all nations (Deut 7:7) and the one which the LORD took for Himself to confound the great nations and *"to make for Himself a name."* The deeds that He would do were not for Israel, they were for Himself and His land. Some English Bible translations drop the Hebrew word *aretz* "land" from the text and this, unfortunately, leads the reader to an erroneous concept of what the text is actually saying.

The purpose of Israel is not to make Israel look good among the nations but to make the LORD look good among the nations. The purpose of Israel is to make a name for the LORD so that the nations might turn to Him and desire Him. Everything that the LORD does is for Himself, not for Israel. He will use Israel to make a name for Himself in our world. The deeds that He does are done for Himself, to enhance His name. Much of what will take place will take place on His land (we will discuss this in a later chapter)—the land that He covenanted to give to Israel. Militarily we can expect to see great conflicts in that land as military might always brings about a certain awe and reverence:

*"To make for Yourself a name ... **by driving out nations** from before Your people"*   (1 Chr 17:21).

Miraculous signs also have this effect:

*"**You showed signs and wonders** ... You made a name for Yourself, as it is this day"*   (Neh 9:10).

The concept of the LORD making a name for Himself through Israel in order to bring the nations to Himself is not isolated by any means. It runs throughout the Bible:

*"Thus says the Lord GOD: 'I do not do this for your sake, O house of Israel, but **for My holy name's sake** ... **and the nations shall know** that I am the LORD'"*   (Eze 36:22&23).

During the future war with Gog, of the land of Magog, He will use Israel to bring her enemies to their knees in holy reverence:

*"You will come up **against My people Israel** like a cloud, to cover the land. It will be in the latter days that I **will bring you against My land, so that the nations may know Me,** when I am hallowed in you, O Gog, before their eyes"*   (Eze 38:16).

The purpose of Israel is to be a vehicle by which the LORD will make for Himself such a great name that every nation will voluntarily seek after Him and worship Him for who He is.

*"For the LORD your God is **God of gods and Lord of lords, the
great God, mighty and awesome"*** (Deut 10:17).

The LORD has every intention of being seen for who He is; Israel is
a chosen medium through whom He will bring it about. Sometime in
the future, all the awesome power that created the universe will be
unleashed in military conflict through Israel and:

*"The one who is feeble among them in that day shall be **like David,
and the house of David shall be like God, like the Angel of the
LORD** before them"* (Zech 12:8).

The world will stand aghast at the display of His might and:

*"In those days ten men from every language of the nations shall
grasp the sleeve of a Jewish man, saying, 'Let us go with you, for
we have heard that God is with you'"* (Zech 8:23).

Dear LORD,
I want to be on the winning side with You. Help me, and help my nation,
to see at an early hour what You are staging for the future. Grant us the
humility to comprehend our extreme weakness, and grant that we might
surrender to You before meeting You in battle. Amen.

8

THE
BLESSING
AND
THE CURSE

There is a Scripture in the twelfth chapter of Genesis of which one particular piece is often quoted by Christians. Although it is quoted mostly in reference to the Christian community, literally the Scripture is directed toward Abraham and his descendants. There is great misunderstanding concerning this passage, and that misunderstanding will remain with us as long as translators of major, English-Bible versions follow "traditional" renderings rather than stepping out of the Christian comfort zone. Most, but certainly not all, English versions render the passage the same as does the New King James version given below. The portion in question is highlighted and quoted in context with its two preceding verses.

> *"Now the LORD had said to Abram: 'Get out of your country, from your family and from your father's house, to a land that I will show you. I will make you a great nation; I will bless you and make your name great; and you shall be a blessing. **I will bless those who bless you, and I will curse him who curses you;** and in you all the families of the earth shall be blessed'"* (Gen 12:1-3).

The LORD is telling Abram, the grandfather of Jacob who became Israel, that he would become a *"great nation."* That nation, obviously, is Israel. The LORD continues by saying that He would make the name of Israel *"great; and **you shall be a blessing** ... in you **all the families of the earth shall be blessed."***

We need not spend a great deal of time on the aspect of the greatness of the Jewish people nor on the aspect of the blessing that they have been to all the nations of the earth. They are a unique and wonderful people—creative and talented, with a passion for life and culture. The contribution the Jews have made to the world is enormous. They comprise less than one quarter of one percent of the world's population, yet they have produced more than ten percent of the world's Nobel Prize winners.[1] The genius of the Jews in the fields of Science, Medicine and the Arts is legendary. And through the Jewish people came the Bible and Jesus, the Lamb of God who takes away the sin of the world. Of course we know that Jesus was and is the Son of God, but Jesus came into this world of men as a Jew, and we have this sure word of Scripture:

*"Jesus Christ is the **same yesterday, today, and forever"***
(Heb 13:8).

Jesus was and is a Jew! Focusing upon Jesus, at this time, and laying aside, momentarily, everything else that the Jewish people have contributed, we are told that Gentiles were:

*" ... strangers from the covenants of promise, **having no hope** and without God in the world"*   (Eph 2:12).

Without the Jew there would still be no Jesus, and without Jesus there would still be no hope and no God for the Gentiles; a huge debt is owed to the Jewish people.

Returning back to our first passage of Scripture, we isolate the portion where the misunderstanding lies:

"I will bless those who bless you, and I will curse him who curses you"   (Gen 12:3).

The blessing and cursing is dependent upon man's attitude toward Abraham and his descendants. What is done to them is as doing it to the LORD, and, thus, we find written concerning the Jewish people: *"He who harms you sticks his finger in Jehovah's eye!"* (Zech 2:8 TLB). To "bless" means "to honour or to bestow favour upon" and God promises to do this to those who honour and favour Israel. However, the next segment, *"I will curse him who curses you,"* misleads us by being wrongly translated. At first glance (at least in the popular English versions), it would seem to be a divine tit-for-tat statement. But in Hebrew it is not at all moderate. First, the two words rendered here as curse are quite different in Hebrew. Secondly, they are not only different but actually poles apart in meaning and do not even come from the same root. The first Hebrew word is *arar,* and the second is *kilel.* Even without a knowledge of Hebrew the reader can see that these words are greatly dissimilar. There are only two instances in the entire Bible where these two words come together in a single verse, namely, the one that we are giving attention to and the following:

> *"You shall not **revile** God, nor curse a ruler of your people"*
> (Ex 22:28).

Here, the word *kilel* is translated as "revile." It is exactly the same Hebrew word used in our verse in Genesis but translated quite differently. Now let us proceed and analyse what this means to us in real terms.

We must remember that in this passage it is the LORD who is speaking, and it is the LORD who will "bless," and it is the LORD who will "curse." God's powerful blessing causes us to rejoice:

> *"The blessing of the LORD makes one rich, and He adds no sorrow with it"*   (Prov 10:22).

> *"I will ... open for you the windows of heaven and pour out for you such blessing that there will not be room enough to receive it"*   (Mal 3:10).

The LORD'S judgement and power are found in His curses:

> *"So the LORD God said to the serpent: 'Because you have done this, you are **cursed** more than all cattle, and more than every beast of the field; **on your belly you shall go**, and you shall eat dust all the days of your life'"*   (Gen 3:14).

That serpent, or snake, once walked upon this earth like other four-legged animals. Most people are not aware that snakes have atrophied legs tucked up inside their bodies—a perpetual, living reminder to the dreadful power of God's curse.

> *"Then to Adam He said, 'Because you have heeded the voice of your wife, and have eaten from the tree of which I commanded you, saying, You shall not eat of it:* **Cursed** *is the ground for your sake;* **in toil you shall eat of it all the days of your life.** *Both* **thorns and thistles it shall bring forth** *for you, and you shall eat the herb of the field"* (Gen 3:17&18).

Adam originally ate food that was self-perpetuated from the soil. After the LORD cursed, mankind sweated, and still sweats, to extract food from the earth. The several hundred varieties of thistles that wage war against farmers and gardeners substantiate the curse upon the earth, as do the thousands of awful thorn bushes that tear our skin and clothing.

We see the tragic results of the curse of the LORD concerning Jericho (uttered from the lips of Joshua but, nevertheless, the word of the LORD):

> *"***Cursed*** be the man before the LORD who rises up and builds this city Jericho; he shall lay* **its foundation with his firstborn,** *and* **with his youngest he shall set up its gates"** (Josh 6:26).

And later we read:

> *"In his days Hiel of Bethel built Jericho. He laid its foundation* **with Abiram his firstborn,** *and* **with his youngest son Segub he set up its gates,** *according to the word of the LORD, which He had spoken through Joshua the son of Nun"* (1 Kg 16:34).

Hiel thought to rebuild Jericho and his first-born son died as he laid the foundations. When he hung the gates to the city his youngest son died also.

In all three of the passages given above (there are a number of others) the word rendered "curse" is, in the original Hebrew, the word *arar*. The word means: "to execrate," or "to denounce evil against" – "something that brings great harm or trouble." In contrast to this terrible word, we look at our second Hebrew word *kilel*. I have highlighted the word in its context and have used several versions of the Bible so that we may clearly see its meaning:

"When she saw that she had conceived, her mistress became **despised** *in her eyes"*   (Gen 16:4 NKJ).

"You shall not **revile** *God, nor curse a ruler of your people"*
(Ex 22:28 NKJ).

"Do not **blaspheme** *God or curse the ruler of your people"*
(Ex 22:28 NIV).

"Forty blows he may give him and no more, lest he should exceed this and beat him with many blows above these, and your brother be **humiliated** *in your sight"*   (Deut 25:3 NKJ).

"They went into the temple of their god, ate and drank, and **ridiculed** *Abimelech"*   (Jdg 9:28 NRSV).

"I am **unworthy**—*how can I reply to you?"*   (Job 40:4 NIV).

"The LORD of hosts has purposed ... to bring into **contempt** *all the honorable of the earth"*   (Isa 23:9 NKJ).

We have six passages with seven different renderings of the same word from three major English versions of the Bible published in the United States. The following definitions are taken from the foremost English Dictionary published in the United States:[2]

Despise: "to look down upon, to have a low opinion of."
Revile: "to be reproachful or abusive in speech."
Blaspheme: "to revile or speak reproachfully."
Humiliate: "to lower the pride or dignity of; to humble."
Ridicule: "words or actions intended to express contempt and excite laughter."
Unworthy: "without merit or value."
Contempt: "the feeling or actions of a person toward something he considers low, worthless, or beneath notice."

With these definitions before us, we now have a much clearer understanding of what is really being said in Genesis 3:12. The LORD has promised to curse; to bring great trouble and harm to those who have a low opinion of the Jewish people. The LORD promises to curse and bring great trouble upon those who cause the dignity or the personal pride of the Jewish people to suffer. The LORD promises to curse and bring great trouble upon those who subject the Jewish people to ridicule. The LORD promises to curse and bring great trouble upon those who reproach the Jewish people or subject them to abusive language. The LORD promises to curse and bring great trouble upon those who think that the Jew is lacking in worth or that an individual Jew, or the Jewish people as a whole, are inferior or beneath notice. The LORD promises to curse and bring great trouble upon those that speak reproachfully of His holy people, Israel. Just as the LORD, through Joshua, issued a warning concerning Jericho, so He also issues a warning to the world regarding the Jews.

At the very beginning, when Abram, the father of the Jewish people, stood alone and without offspring, the LORD identifies the cause of Abram with His own. He declares him to be essentially connected with the prosperity and the misfortune of all who come in contact with him. The LORD promises to bless those that bless Abram and his offspring and, conversely, promises to curse those who hold them lightly in esteem. He issued the promises more than 4,000 years ago and the passing of the eons of time has not devoured the blessing nor worn down the severity of the curse. He who has ears to hear, let him hear. What the LORD said to Abram still stands today and many of us are skating on extremely thin ice with regard to the curse. In addition to the world's unregenerate population, there are countless thousands of professing Christians who have testimonies of troubled lives, saying, "Everything I touch turns to dust." It behooves us to heed the warning of the LORD concerning Israel, and in blessing, we shall surely be blessed.

Dear LORD,
Forgive me for my unwitting, wrong understanding of Your word. Forgive me, too, for the times that I have either consciously or unconsciously spoken against Your chosen people. Forgive me for the Jewish jokes I laughed at and for holding the Jews lightly in esteem. I repent, LORD, and ask that You put my sin under the blood of Jesus, the King of the Jews. Grant me now the grace to bless Your people in deed and in speech, and help me to put right the wrong committed. Amen.

PART III

SPOKEN BY PROPHETS

"The LORD has sent to you all His servants the prophets, rising early and sending them, but you have not listened nor inclined your ear to hear"

(Jer 25:4).

9

TIMES
OF
REFRESHING

In Chapter Five we looked briefly at that which I termed the "backbone," or "skeleton," of the history of the Jewish people. I later said that "flesh and blood" would be added to the skeleton. The entire third section of this book leads us to a vantage point where a panoramic vista of Israel—past, present and future—opens before us. Having such a view before us allows us to see not only the flesh clinging to the historical bones but also the blood flowing from the throbbing heart of modern Israel into ancient veins made new again.

In the book of Acts, after the healing of the man who was born lame, Peter preaches in the portion of the temple known as Solomon's porch where Jesus had often taught. We know from verse twelve of the same chapter that he is addressing Jews, and he hands us a key that unlocks a gate obstructing our view of Israel. This enables us to see order where previously we had seen only disorder.

> *"Repent, then, and turn to God, so that your sins may be wiped out, that times of refreshing may come from the Lord, and that he may send the Christ, who has been appointed for you—even **Jesus.** **He must remain in heaven until the time comes for God to restore everything, as he promised long ago through his holy prophets"***
> (Acts 3:19-21 NIV).

To fairly explain this passage would take the space of two volumes; therefore, we shall confine ourselves to three points only: a statement, a time period and a promise.

THE STATEMENT

Jesus must remain in heaven until:

Scripture declares that Jesus will not return until certain events take place. He must remain in heaven *"until the time comes ... ."* Remember the chapter about "Times and Seasons"? Here is a perfect example. No matter what our theological, eschatological or apocalyptical opinions might be, Jesus will not—indeed, cannot come—until some particular happenings happen. Why can He not come? Because God's word says that He cannot! We can beg, plead, cajole, offer bribes, tear our clothes, pluck out our hair, put dust upon our heads, beat our breasts and fast and pray until there is no breath or strength left to us, but Jesus shall not come. It can be argued that the LORD can do anything that He desires, and with that I concur whole-heartedly. At the same time there are some things that the LORD will not do, and one of those things is that He will never contradict His word. Just accept the LORD'S word that Jesus cannot come back until particular conditions are met.

THE TIME PERIOD

His holy prophets:

We know from the previous paragraph that Jesus cannot come again until certain pre-determined events shall have been fulfilled. These foreordained events are spoken of by the prophets of the LORD. The first great prophet was Abraham, the father of the Jewish people. Speaking of Abraham the LORD says:

*"**He is a prophet**, and he will pray for you ..."*   (Gen 20:7).

The last of the great prophets was the Lord Jesus:

*"Jesus of Nazareth, who was **a Prophet mighty in deed and word**"*   (Lk 24:19).

I am not saying that there are no prophets today. I believe that there are true, modern-day prophets but not nearly as many as are unashamedly laying claim to the title. I am saying that the first of the **great** prophets was Abraham and the last of the **great** prophets was the Lord Jesus Christ. Within the period of time that includes the life-spans of Abraham and Jesus, we shall find everything that must be restored and which will precede and usher in the greatest of all events—the return, or second coming, of Jesus, the Messiah.

THE PROMISE

To restore everything:

If we should read this passage as the average Christian reads it we would nod our heads as if in agreement with what it says, then pass on by without much idea of what we perfunctorily agreed with. Let me explain what I have just said. We read the passage and see that the LORD has promised to *restore everything*. Without questioning, pondering or researching the statement, we continue reading the page and by doing so we have agreed that what we have read is correct and true. But what is the "everything" that God has promised to restore?

Taking the word "restore" at its face value, we understand that it means "to make restitution"; "to bring back into existence"; "to give back" etc. At the time when Peter was speaking Israel was under Roman occupation. Thus, we could assume that the nation could have their sovereignty returned. Israel as a whole was in a spiritually backslidden state, and we could assume, also, that they would be restored to a vital relationship with the LORD. Our assumptions and suppositions nevertheless remain conjecture because we took the word "restore" at its face value.

There are several words in the Greek text of the New Testament that are translated "restore." We shall be looking at two of those words both now and in a later chapter of this section. The word that is translated "restore" in this passage is the Greek word *apokatastasis*. This word is not used anywhere else in the New Testament and it is not used at all in the *Septuagint* (the 2,000 year old, Greek version of the Old Testament). It has a distinct meaning that is not apprehended by casual referral to a Greek lexicon. The profound meaning of this word is of inestimable value to the understanding of the passage.

The word *apokatastasis* was the subject of several theological debates from the third century onwards. The Church at that time was becoming increasingly anti-Semitic, and in her desire to purge herself of everything Jewish she not only cut off the Judaic roots to her faith but also denied herself the Judaic mind that was so essential to explaining the faith. Consequently, when trying to understand this passage, great theologians such as Origen went looking in the wrong direction and no universally accepted definition of the word was ever laid down. The *Theological Dictionary of the New Testament*, edited by Kittel and Friedrich, regarded as the foremost critical Greek Theological Dictionary available, rightly notes that the word is not used in the LXX (*Septuagint*) and that it was rarely used even in Judaism, and this was an important clue the Fathers missed when trying to arrive at the meaning of *apokatastasis*. Josephus, the Jewish historian who wrote in Greek during the first century A.D., used it in the context of the Jews returning from exile. And Philo of Alexandria, the great Jewish philosopher and historian who was born at the end of the last century B.C. and whose writings in Greek are also extant, uses it in the context of the redemption of the Jewish people from Egypt.

The word is rarely used due to the fact that the need for its use is rare. It means "to re-enact historical events." Therefore, let us paraphrase what Peter said almost two millennia ago. **"Jesus must stay in heaven until the times and seasons come to pass when Israel's historical events are re-enacted."**

Knowing what to look for is always helpful in a search. We now know that we should focus attention on significant events that affected the nation of Israel from its inception until the time of Peter's sermon in the temple porch.

ISRAEL'S MAJOR EVENTS

Listed below in the order that they occurred in the Bible are the most important events of Israel's history that had the greatest effect upon that nation. Everything in this list was spoken of by the prophets, beginning with Abraham and ending with the Lord Jesus.

Giving of the land of Canaan

Special relationship with the LORD

Exodus from Egypt

Wandering in the desert

Entering the promised land

Capture of Jerusalem

Establishment of the state of Israel

Kingdom of King David

Jerusalem made capital of Israel

All these great events came and went during the course of ancient Israel's long history. These are the events that we are told must be re-enacted before Jesus can return for His bride. In the succeeding nine chapters we take each event individually, as it occurred in the Biblical account, and look towards modern Israel for its counterpart. As we look to modern Israel and find re-enactments spoken of by Peter, we remember the thesis concerning prophecy in Chapter Three, that it is not a question of "interpretation" but of "fulfillment." We shall now see the truth of that thesis.

Dear LORD,
Open my spiritual eyes to behold wonderful things, and open my heart that I may have understanding. Allow me to see Your faithfulness in the keeping of Your promises to Israel, and allow me to see that the same faithfulness extends also to me. Amen.

10

THE
COVENANT

When the term "Abraham's covenant" is mentioned, usually the "covenant of circumcision" comes to mind. But there is a greater covenant than that of circumcision, a covenant made with Abraham some twenty years earlier. This covenant concerns the land of Canaan, and the making of that covenant is described in Genesis chapter fifteen. We have in that passage the sole recorded instance in the Bible of the actual making, or "cutting," of a covenant.

The essentials, and the implications, of this covenant provide several pieces of the puzzle that bewilders experts, upsets Muslims, frustrates the White House and vexes many leaders of other nations. Let us start at the beginning when Abraham was still Abram, living in the land of his birth, at the time when the LORD first spoke to him:

"Now the LORD had said to Abram: **'Get out of your country,** *from your family and from your father's house,* **to a land that I will show you'"** (Gen 12:1).

Abram, the Bible informs us (Gen 12:4), was seventy-five years of age when he departed the land of his fathers. He left because the LORD commanded him to leave. And he left for a particular land that was to be shown him by the LORD. He came, we are told, to the land of Canaan, and shortly thereafter the LORD actually appeared to Abram and spoke to him for the second time:

"Then the LORD **appeared** *to Abram and said,* **'To your descendants I will give this land'"** (Gen 12:7).

The LORD promised to give the land of Canaan to Abram's descendants and, symbolically, Abram would possess the land through them. We know from the account in Genesis that Abram wandered around in Canaan and, because of a severe famine in the land, went down into Egypt for a while. He got himself into trouble with Pharaoh and the entire royal household and was escorted to the border and deported (Gen 12:20). Abram went up into the land of Canaan, again, where he continued his nomadic life. Here the LORD spoke to him for the third time:

> *"And the LORD said to Abram ...'Lift your eyes now and look from the place where you are—northward, southward, eastward, and westward; for **all the land which you see I give to you and your descendants forever** ... Arise, walk in the land through its length and its width, for **I give it to you**'"*   (Gen 13:14,15&17).

This is the second time that the LORD promised to give the land of Canaan to Abram and his descendants. Then the LORD spoke to him personally for the fifth time which was the fourth recorded occasion regarding the land. This time the LORD spoke more earnestly:

> *"He said to him, 'I am the LORD, who **brought you out** of Ur of the Chaldeans, **to give you this land** to inherit it'"*   (Gen 15:7).

When the LORD commanded Abram to leave the land of his birth, it was for one purpose only: to give him the land of Canaan as an inheritance. We now have three separate instances where the LORD promised to give this land to Abram and his offspring. On this occasion Abram asked for a confirmation, a sealing of the repeated promise:

> *"And he said, 'Lord GOD, **how shall I know** that I will inherit it?'"*   (Gen 15:8).

To which the LORD replied: *"Bring Me ... ."*

These two words begin a passage that we will look at in a moment. They actually tell us a great deal. Abram, not staggering at the magnitude of the promise, desires to follow the custom of that time and seal the promise. The LORD graciously consents to this and told Abram what was required:

"'Bring Me a three-year-old heifer, a three-year-old female goat, a three-year-old ram, a turtledove, and a young pigeon.' Then he brought all these to Him and cut them in two, down the middle, and placed each piece opposite the other; but he did not cut the birds in two ... And it came to pass, when the sun went down and it was dark, that behold, there appeared **a smoking oven and a burning torch that passed between those pieces.** *On the same day* **the LORD made a covenant with Abram,** *saying:* **'To your descendants I have given this land, from the river of Egypt to the great river, the River Euphrates—the Kenites, the Kenezzites, and the Kadmonites, the Hittites, the Perizzites, and the Rephaim, the Amorites, the Canaanites, the Girgashites, and the Jebusites'"** (Gen 15:9,10,17-21).

In consenting to Abram's request for a confirmation of the promise, the LORD told him to bring certain animals and birds. Abram brought them and, as he was familiar with the custom, cut the animals in two and laid the pieces opposite each other. The LORD manifested Himself in the form of smoke and fire, much like He did at the burning bush (Ex 3:2) and in the pillars of cloud and fire (Ex 13:21). The LORD then passed between the pieces of the cut animals and sealed the promise made to Abram. The carcasses were not consumed because it was not a sacrifice offered but a covenant made. This type of covenant was common in Abram's day and was still in vogue at least 1,500 years later:

"The words of **the covenant** *which they made before Me, when* **they cut the calf in two and passed between the parts of it—***the princes of Judah, the princes of Jerusalem, the eunuchs, the priests, and all the people of the land who passed between the parts of the calf ... "* (Jer 34:18&19).

The two parts of the animals represented the two parties to the covenant. The parties would walk down the aisle flanked by the pieces of the slaughtered animals which signified an oath:

"May it be so done to me if I do not keep my oath and pledge."[1]

The LORD promised on oath to give the land of Canaan to Abram and his descendants. He later confirmed the promise to Isaac and his descendants:

"Dwell in this land, and I will be with you and bless you; for to
you and your descendants I give all these lands, and I will
perform the oath which I swore to Abraham *your father"*
(Gen 26:3).

The LORD also reaffirmed the promise to Jacob and his descendants:

"I am the LORD God of Abraham your father and the God of
Isaac; ***the land on which you lie I will give to you and your***
descendants"   (Gen 28:13).

Not only did the LORD promise the land individually to Abraham,
Isaac and Jacob, but He had personally ratified the covenant with an
oath. We see too, that the LORD defined the boundaries of the covenanted land:

"From the river of Egypt to the great river, the River Euph-
rates"   (Gen 15:18).

Although the land is normally termed the land of "Canaan," it en-
compassed far more than the land of the Canaanites. It included all the
land of the following ten nations:

"The Kenites, the Kenezzites, and the Kadmonites, the Hittites, the
Perizzites, and the Rephaim the Amorites, the Canaanites, the
Girgashites, and the Jebusites"   (Gen 15:19-21).

Thus there is a fully confirmed covenant with fully confirmed boundaries. Now the term of the covenant needs to be ascertained:

*"I give to you and your descendants **forever**"*   (Gen 13:15).

The usage here of *"forever"* is ambiguous and we are not to understand
from this that the covenant has no end, because, in fact, it does have a
definite length of duration. The length of the covenant is recorded two
times in Scripture. One of these is found in Psalms:

*"He remembers His **covenant** forever, the word which He com-*
*manded, for a **thousand generations**, The covenant which **He***
made with Abraham**, and **His oath to Isaac**, And **confirmed it to
***Jacob** for a statute, **to Israel** as an **everlasting** covenant, saying,*

'To you I will give the land of Canaan as the allotment of your inheritance'" (Psa 105:8-11).

The duration of the covenant is described as *"a thousand generations"* and *"everlasting."* It appears to be a contradiction but it is not. The use of the word *"everlasting,"* is, like *"forever,"* ambiguous, and describes *"a thousand generations."* The length of one of these *"generations"* is defined by the LORD moments before He ratified the covenant with Abram:

*"Know certainly that your descendants will be strangers in a land that is not theirs, and will serve them, and they will afflict them **four hundred years** ... but in the **fourth generation** they shall return here"* (Gen 15:13&16).

On the day the covenant was made, the LORD Himself defined a generation as "one hundred years." In the entry for "generation" in perhaps the world's most authoritative dictionary of the English language,[2] we find written *inter alia*: "In reckoning historically by 'generations,' the word is taken to mean the interval of time between the birth of the parents and that of their children ... ." And thus Scripture declares:

*"Abraham was **one hundred years** old when his son Isaac was born to him"* (Gen 21:5).

The duration of the covenant is, therefore, 1,000 generations multiplied by 100 years which is 100,000 years. Now, what does this mean to you and me?

Abraham was born in the year 2111 B.C. He was seventy-five years of age when he left the land of his birth and travelled to the land of Canaan where the LORD made the covenant with him. Thus we calculate:

$$2,111 - 75 = 2,036 + 1993 = 4,029$$

$$100,000 - 4,029 = 95,971$$

With nearly 96,000 years left of the duration of the covenant, who has the sole right of possession today? Obviously, the descendants of Abraham through the line of Isaac and Jacob.

Please realise that the above has absolutely nothing to do with the second coming of Jesus. It simply tells us that the literal, physical seed of Abraham, through Isaac and Jacob, namely Israel, has absolute right of possession of the land of Canaan for that length of time. The earth will be dissolved many thousands of years before the covenant runs its course, but perhaps the reader can now understand why the covenant is described as *"forever"* and *"everlasting."*

The LORD established a covenant of defined duration for a defined land with defined borders and defined the people who were to possess it. We always need to remember that the Jewish people are the possessors, not the owners of the land. The actual title belongs to the LORD himself, which He makes clear to the children of Israel before they crossed the Jordan to possess their inheritance:

> *"The land shall not be sold permanently, for **the land is Mine**; for you are **strangers and sojourners** with Me"*   (Lev 25:23).

The ownership of the land still belongs to the LORD today. When referring to the war between Israel and Gog, of the land of Magog, which is yet to come, the LORD reiterates His ownership:

> *"It will be in the latter days that I will bring you against **My land...**"*   (Eze 38:16).

Other references where the LORD describes the land as being personally His are: 2 Chr 7:20, Isa 14:25, Jer 2:7, 16:8, Eze 36:5, Joel 1:6 & 3:2. The importance of knowing that ultimate ownership rests with the LORD will be seen shortly.

EXILE FROM THE LAND

The children of Israel crossed the Jordan into Canaan around 1410 B.C. under the leadership of Joshua, defeating most of the nations militarily, and dispossessing others. In time, under Samuel, Israel rejected the LORD as their King and called for the establishment of a physical monarchy that would make them like the nations around them. According to the personal tastes of the succeeding kings, disobedience to the LORD and adulterous worship of other gods waxed and waned throughout the centuries. But, few, indeed, were the kings who had a heart to follow the LORD. Angry with their behaviour toward Him the LORD first brought Shalmaneser, king of Assyria, against Israel's northern kingdom. Samaria fell to Shalmaneser in 722 B.C. and he took the captives back to Assyria. The southern kingdom of Judah failed to heed the warning, and the LORD brought Nebuchadnezzar, king of Babylon, down to Jerusalem. In 597 B.C. the city was destroyed, and he carried most of the surviving population back to Babylon as captives. Their years of captivity were set at seventy years:

*"For thus says the LORD: **After seventy years** are completed at Babylon, I will visit you and perform My good word toward you, and cause you to return to this place"* (Jer 29:10).

The books of Ezra and Nehemiah record for us the accounts of how, after the seventy years were completed, the captives came back to the land, rebuilt the cities and the temple, and life returned to the way it had been before the exile. Life, for the Israelites, became so much in the same vein as previously that the LORD brought the might of the Roman army against Israel in 63 B.C., and this war took a recorded 2,504,490[3] Jewish lives. The war culminated in A.D. 70 with the city of Jerusalem and the temple being razed to the ground once more. During the siege of Jerusalem alone 1,100,000[4] Jews died either by starvation or by the sword, and 97,000[5] were carried away captive. A large Jewish presence was left in the land, however, but when Rome renamed Jerusalem *Ælia Capitolina* and built a temple to Jupiter on the site of the Jewish temple, the Jews revolted under the leadership of Simon Bar-Kochba. The Romans took three and a half years to quell the revolt with great loss of life for the Jews. At the end of the revolt, in the year 135 A.D., there were few Jews left in the land which the Romans now renamed *"Syria Palaestina,"* in an effort to eradicate the Jewish connection. Desolation was heaped upon desolation in this degraded land that, in time, was Anglicised into Palestine. Succeeding armies of "Christian" Byzantines, Arab-Muslims, "Christian" Crusaders, Mongols, and finally Turkish-Muslims conquered, built and destroyed until the Promised Land was but a dusty, rocky and treeless waste. The famous American author, Mark Twain, a visitor to the land in 1867 wrote:

"A desolate country whose soil is rich enough, but is given wholly to weeds—a silent mournful expanse. We never saw a human being on the whole route ... ."[6]

It was a land that could barely produce enough to sustain a sparse population, a far cry from the *"land of milk and honey"* that the children of Israel had inherited.

ISRAEL REBORN

During World War I, Britain ran out of acetone, a chemical imported from Germany and from which cordite, an essential component of gunpowder, was made. Britain, unable to manufacture high explosives, was in dire straits. Defeat by her enemies was almost inevitable if synthetic cordite were not produced. A brilliant Jewish chemist, Chaim Weizemann, was summoned to the British War Office by the First Lord of the Admiralty, Winston Churchill, and asked to produce thirty thousand tons[7] of synthetic cordite. Weizemann, with every available government facility at his disposal, manufactured a synthetic cordite that actually produced a higher explosive than cordite from acetone.

At the time Weizemann was producing cordite, British forces, led by General Edmund Allenby, were fighting the Turks for control of Palestine. After Weizemann had produced the requested amount of cordite he was asked what he wanted as recompense. His reply was:

"If Britain wins the battle for Palestine, I ask for a national home for my people in their ancient land."

To this Britain agreed. Shortly afterward, on November 2, 1917, the British Foreign Minister Arthur James Balfour, on behalf of the government, issued the following statement which had been submitted to, and approved by, the Cabinet:

"His Majesty's Government view with favour the establishment in Palestine of a national home for the Jewish people, and will use their best endeavours to facilitate the achievement of this object ... ."[8]

Just as the LORD promised the land of Canaan to the children of Israel while other nations occupied it so, also, Britain promised the same land to the descendants of the children of Israel while others occupied it.

In December of the same year General Allenby was in sight of the Old City of Jerusalem. He ordered planes to fly over the city and ascertain the number of troops and armaments facing his forces. He also ordered leaflets to be dropped from the planes calling for the Turks to surrender. These leaflets were signed with the signature of Allenby.

Following orders, the pilots of the planes flew several sorties over the Old City during the daylight hours, dropping leaflets and gathering information. That night the Turkish troops retreated from the rear of the city. The dropped leaflets, signed with the name of "Allenby," were taken by the Turkish Muslims to be a directive from *"Allah"* for them to leave the city. No shots were fired in the capture of the Old City of Jerusalem. General Allenby, a devout Christian, would not ride his horse into the city. He dismounted and, cap in hand, led his horse and his troops into the City of the Great King. Now consider the following:

*"Like **birds flying about**, so will the LORD of hosts defend Jerusalem. Defending, He will also **deliver it; passing over, He will preserve it**"*   (Isa 31:5).

A remarkable passage indeed. With planes, *like birds flying about,* the LORD *"delivered"* the city from the Turks and *"preserved"* it from destruction.

At the end of the War, with victory in the hands of the Allied forces, Britain was voted a mandate to administer Palestine and to oversee the establishment of a Jewish national home there. Soon after, however, they found that they had a "hot potato" in their hands. There was heavy resistance by Muslims to a larger Jewish presence in Palestine and due, no doubt, to the growing oil deposits being found in the region, Britain reneged on the Balfour Declaration. She issued the infamous "White Paper" which called for the establishment of an Arab state in Palestine within ten years. Britain then proceeded to restrict the immigration of Jews into Palestine.

On September 3, 1939, German armies invaded Poland, catapulting the world into World War II. Soon thereafter began Adolf Hitler's "Final Solution" to the Jewish problem—the calculated and systematic murder of the world's Jewish population.

After five terrible years of warfare, Hitler's military machine was finally defeated, leaving in its wake the world's highest number of war dead. And six million Jewish civilians (men, women, children and babes-in-arms) were murdered in special extermination camps constructed throughout Europe for that purpose. The Jews had been stripped of their possessions and their clothing and herded into rooms which were then pumped full of poison gas. Their bodies were burnt in giant gas cremation ovens. One third of all world Jewry had perished:

*"Alas! For that day is great, so that none is like it; and **it is the time of Jacob's trouble,** but he shall be **saved out of it"** (Jer 30:7).*

It was the day of Jacob's trouble indeed. Had Hitler not been stopped every living Jew would have eventually perished at his command. Jacob not only was saved by the defeat of the German armies, but, because of what he had endured at their hands, his dream, which had lain in his bosom for centuries, was about to become a reality.

Jewish refugees had been stopped from entering Palestine at the time of their greatest need. Britain patrolled the seas and intercepted refugee ships, escorting them to detention camps in Cyprus. One ship, the "Exodus," carrying more than 4,500 Jewish refugees from Europe, was intercepted with such a display of military force that several of the Jews were killed. That ship was actually sent back to **Germany** of all places!

Owing to the lot that had befallen the Jewish people during the war, the League of Nations (forerunner of the United Nations) met on November 29, 1947, to vote on the issue of partitioning Palestine in order to establish a Jewish state. The vote was taken, and the result was thirty-three in favour and thirteen against. Jacob was saved. He was in possession of his beloved Promised Land for the third and final time. The vote had taken less than half an hour:

*"**Who has ever heard of such a thing? Who has ever seen such things?** Can a country be born in a day or a nation be brought forth in a moment?"*   (Isa 66:8 NIV).

No one had ever heard of such a thing! No one had ever seen such a thing! There was no precedent in all of world history where a people had come back to their own land after a lapse of almost 2,000 years!

Can a country be born in a day? It was born in the length of time that it took to cast the vote! Can a nation be brought forth in a moment? The nation was brought forth the very moment that the first Prime Minister of the fledgeling state, David Ben-Gurion, declared on May 14, 1948, that this tiny piece of land was, indeed, the new "State of Israel."

A tiny piece of land it was too. Palestine was divided this way: seventy-seven percent to the Arabs and twenty-three percent to the Jews. A land mass of approximately 8,000 square kilometres (3,000 square miles) fell to the Jews. Remember, the LORD made a covenant with Abram. The boundaries were to extend: *"from the river of Egypt to the great river, the River Euphrates"* (Gen 15:18).

The day after Israel was declared a "State" seven Arab armies attacked Israel with the sole intention of liquidating it. Israel won that war. Not only did she win the war, but she also extended her territory from 8,000 to 21,000 square kilometres (3,000 to 8,000 square miles).

In 1967, Arab nations began massing troops and war machinery on Israel's borders in another attempt to destroy the Jewish presence. Vastly outnumbered in men and equipment, the Israeli cabinet decided to strike first to ensure survival. On June 5, they launched the now famous pre-emptive strike. Having the advantage of surprise, the Israeli forces routed the forces of five nations in just six days. Another war was won. Her 21,000 square kilometres (8,000 square miles) had expanded to 67,000 square kilometres (26,000 square miles).

Again in 1973, the powerful, Soviet-equipped Arab armies were intending to deal a death-blow to the cursed Jewish state. This time the Arabs had the element of surprise on their side. On Yom Kippur (the Day of Atonement), the holiest day of the Jewish calendar, when the Jews were in their synagogues, the Arab forces poured over the Suez Canal, over the Golan Heights and across the Jordan River. Israel was caught off guard. The tiny army mobilised, fought back and pulverised the enemy, driving them far from her borders in only ten days. It was yet another war fought and won by a people weary of fighting. After the war, her 67,000 square kilometres (26,000 square miles) had now become 88,000 square kilometres (34,000 square miles).

At the time this chapter was written the borders of Israel extend from the River of Egypt up into Lebanon. Only Syria stands in the way of Israel's presence at the Euphrates. Syria spends heavily on armaments. Her regular standing army is more than four times that of Israel's; her tanks divisions exceed that of Israel and so, too, her number of fighter-planes. Syria is watching for an opportune moment, waiting to pounce like a cat upon a mouse. She says:

"War is inevitable."[9]

"War with Israel will go on as long as time is."[10]

Sometime in the future, perhaps soon, Israeli forces will arrive at the Great River, the Euphrates.

The LORD made a covenant with Abraham and his descendants, and we have seen that He has re-established that covenant in our time. By acts of aggression waged against His people, the land is being returned to them, and in a later chapter we shall look at the ramifications of this.

Many nations, however, are displeased with the status quo and some seek to influence it by pouring massive amounts of arms into the region:

"Five nations, namely (in the order of highest contributor), the Soviet Union, the United States, France, China and Britain, have themselves poured 163 billion dollars in arms into the Middle East between the years 1976 and 1990."[11]

Of this vast amount Israel received fifteen and one half percent,[12] the remaining eighty-four and one half percent went to her enemies. Only the United States supplied any arms to Israel, but she also supplied the Arab nations who are in a state of war with Israel. The United States says that she wants to keep a military balance between nations. What type of balance has a ratio of eighty-four to fifteen? Israel is merely a pawn in a game played between powerful nations, and the United States is playing both sides of the board. The objective of the game is to control the flow of oil that lies beneath the desert sands belonging to the Arabs. With the recent economic and physical collapse of the Soviet Union, the United States no longer considers its former enemy to be a threat or even a serious player in the game. Therefore, the Bush administration, with vested interests in Middle East oil, turned aggressively against Israel, its only real ally in the region, in favour of its newly acquired Arab "friends". This turn against Israel was very noticeable as a U.S. news editorial remarked:

"Washington appears to have gone out of its way to accommodate the Arabs at the expense of the Israelis. The United States ... should not lose all sense of fairness towards the Israelis."[13]

Influenced by anti-Israel rhetoric, many Americans now think less of Israel than they do of Arab countries.[14] Israel is expendable—a sacrificial lamb to a New World Order.

An international "Peace Conference" has been forced upon Israel, the terms and conditions dictated by the same nations made fat from the profits of death and destruction. But there will be no lasting peace, and can be no lasting peace, either for Israel or for the nations, until Jesus, the Prince of Peace comes, the One in whom peace is found.

Earlier we brought to the reader's attention that the ownership of the land belongs to the LORD, that the title deed is vested in Him. Only the owner of something has the right to give it away. We cannot give what does not belong to us.

There are among the leaders of the world's most powerful nations those that profess to be Christians and readers of the Bible—the inerrant word of God. Apparently, they do not see that the land that Israel now holds belongs to the God of Israel, the same God in whom they themselves profess trust. The "New World Order," which was created in 1990 to deal with Saddam Hussein in Kuwait, has already stated that Israel must make land a concession for peace. What it does not seem to understand is that Israel was not given authority to barter with the LORD'S land, selling it for peace. What Israel might negotiate with any Arab party will quickly be found to be non-binding upon the Owner. The Jews, as tenants of a Landlord who makes no provision for sale, subleasing or gifting of His property, will find that their agreements are null and void. And it is this stubborn refusal on the part of the LORD to negotiate with His neighbours and their brokers that has much of the world currently gnashing their teeth at Israel. And, any nation forcing Israel's hand on the question of land will, ultimately, find itself in a confrontation with the Owner. This would be like stepping into a bear trap wired to a high voltage power line. Somebody should inform the world's leaders that it is far more advantageous to be the friend of Israel than the enemy of her God.

Dear LORD,
Thank You that Your word is sure, that all of Your promises will come to pass as surely as Day follows Night. LORD, Your ways are not my ways; as the heavens are higher than the earth, so are Your ways higher than my ways. Help me, not so much to understand You, as to know You. Help me to know the Prince of Peace and be ready to meet Him when my journey here is over. Amen.

11

THE
RELATIONSHIP

The intimate relationship that the nation of Israel has enjoyed with the LORD has never been duplicated. Of Israel, the LORD says:

*"**You only have I known** of all the families of the earth"*
(Amos 3:2).

And again He says:

*"When Israel was a child, **I loved him**, and out of Egypt I called* ***My son*** *"*
(Hos 11:1).

This special bond between the LORD and Israel was that of the imagery of father and son. More than that, it was as a father and first-born son:

*"Israel is My son, **My firstborn** ..."*
(Ex 4:22).

As the first-born son, Israel, even in the midst of apostasy and fornication with other gods, inherits the double portion:

*"If a man has two wives, one loved and the other unloved, and they have borne him children, both the loved and the unloved, and if the firstborn son is of her who is unloved, then it shall be, on the day he bequeaths his possessions to his sons, that he **must not bestow firstborn status on the son of the loved wife in preference to the son of the unloved, the true firstborn.** But he shall acknowledge the son of the unloved wife as the firstborn by giving him **a double***

portion of all that he has, for he is the beginning of his strength; the right of the firstborn is his" (Deut 21:15-17).

Although the LORD is speaking to the fathers of the families of the children of Israel, He is not a hypocrite. What holds true for the families holds true for the nation. Israel **must** inherit the double portion from the Father as it is written:

*"Instead of their shame **My people will receive a double portion**, and instead of disgrace they will rejoice in their inheritance; and so **they will inherit a double portion** in their land, and everlasting joy will be theirs"* (Isa 61:7 NIV).

Even being the first-born son with all the accompanying advantages and blessings did not complete the relationship. It went much further than that. Speaking to Israel, the LORD says:

*"I looked at you and saw that you were old enough for love, **I spread the corner of my garment over you** and covered your nakedness. **I gave you my solemn oath and entered into a covenant with you**, declares the Sovereign LORD, **and you became mine"*** (Eze 16:8 NIV).

The LORD now moves into new imagery. Spreading His garment over Israel, making a solemn oath and entering into a covenant with her means that He first redeemed the nation and then took her to be His wife. We have an exact example of such redemption and marriage with Boaz and Ruth:

*"In the middle of the night something startled the man, and he turned and discovered a woman lying at his feet. 'Who are you?' he asked. 'I am your servant Ruth,' she said. '**Spread the corner of your garment over me, since you are a kinsman-redeemer"*** (Ruth 3:8&9 NIV).

*"So **Boaz took Ruth and she became his wife**"* (Ruth 4:13).

That the LORD took Israel as His wife is manifestly clear:

"I am married to you ..." (Jer 3:14).

This, then, was the unique and intimate relationship that Israel enjoyed with the LORD. Indeed, they were a special people with a special relationship:

*"For you are a holy people to the LORD your God; the LORD your God has chosen you to be a people for Himself, **a special treasure above all the peoples** on the face of the earth"* (Deut 7:6).

Israel was a holy (set-apart) people, a people for God alone. Their segregation was by the will of the LORD. They were a *"special treasure"* for God. Most parents understand God's heart. Lots of little ones, babies and small children, live in our neighbourhoods, but there is none like one's own. They may not be prettier or healthier, but they are a treasure above all treasures: a *"special treasure"* that one would not part with for all the world.

BROKEN RELATIONSHIP

The most common term used by the LORD to describe Israel in the above relationship is *"My people."* This first appears in the book of Exodus shortly after God acknowledges the children of Israel:

*"And the LORD said: 'I have surely seen the oppression of **My people** who are in Egypt'"*   (Ex 3:7).

This term is recorded for us sixty-seven times in Scripture up until the sixth chapter of Isaiah. Here, in Isaiah, the LORD, distressed beyond measure at Israel's record of conduct, institutes punitive measures. The prophet Isaiah sees the LORD exalted in His temple:

*"Also I heard the voice of the Lord, saying: 'Whom shall I send, and who will go for Us?' Then I said, 'Here am I! Send me.' And He said, 'Go, and tell **this people** ...'"*   (Isa 6:8&9a).

The prophet responds to the LORD'S call and is commissioned to *"Go, and tell this people ... ."* It is now no longer *"My people,"* but *"this people."* The honeymoon is over, and Israel is put aside for a season of discipline.

Isaiah received a message for *"this people"*: a message of despair that held only one spark of hope:

*"Tell **this people:** 'Keep on hearing, but **do not understand;** keep on seeing, but **do not perceive.** 'Make the heart of this people dull, and their ears heavy, and shut their eyes; lest they see with their eyes, and hear with their ears, and understand with their heart, and return and be healed'"*   (Isa 6:9&10).

The Israelites were now, largely, shut up for discipline. They would not be able to turn back in repentance and be healed of their afflictions. The prophet is overwhelmed with the severity of the LORD'S decree:

"Then I said, 'Lord, how long?' And He answered: 'Until the cities are laid waste and without inhabitant, the houses are without a man, the land is utterly desolate'"   (Isa 6:11).

The only spark of hope in a message decreeing death and destruction was the word *"until."* Israel would not be able to hear spiritually, see spiritually nor respond spiritually, until … . That word, "until," is always a point in time. It is the moment when a situation changes. Israel was, at this point, out of favour, but the situation would change at a given point in time.

The prophet Hosea was a contemporary of Isaiah. Hosea was told by the LORD to marry a prostitute and have children by her. She was to be a sign to Israel and signified the nation's unfaithfulness. Hosea married a harlot named Gomer, and she gave birth to three children. The children were also to be signs to the nation. Each child was named by the LORD. The first was a son:

*"Call his name **Jezreel** … I will break the bow of Israel in the Valley of Jezreel"*   (Hos 1:5).

Jezreel, or *yizreel,* in Hebrew, means, "God Scatters," and the valley of Jezreel had been the site of many great military battles. It was literally a graveyard of kingdoms. And it was in this valley that Shalmaneser, king of Assyria, inflicted a decisive defeat upon Israel before capturing Samaria and taking the Israelites to Assyria as captives. The next child was a daughter:

*"Call her name **Lo-Ruhamah,** for I will no longer have mercy on the house of Israel …"*   (Hos 1:6).

In Hebrew, *lo-ruhamah* means "No Comfort" or "No Compassion." Finally, Gomer gave birth to another son:

*"Call his name **Lo-Ammi**, for **you are not My people**, and I will not be your God"* (Hos 1:9).

In Hebrew, *lo-ammi* literally means "Not My People." In the first chapter of Hosea we have the same message as that contained in the sixth chapter of Isaiah! Death and destruction were to come upon Israel. There would be no comfort for her—no mercy extended to her. She was put aside by the LORD. The children of Israel, for the time being, were no longer "His people."

RELATIONSHIP RESTORED

In Isaiah's message there had been a glimmer of hope—the word "until." The discipline would end at a given point in time. Following on from our last Scripture, the Holy Spirit, through Hosea, indicates when this is to be:

*"The number of the children of Israel shall be as the sand of the sea, which **cannot be measured or numbered**. And it shall come to pass **in the place where it was said to them**, 'You are not My people,' **there it shall be said to them**, 'You are **sons of the living God'"*** (Hos 1:10).

This passage indicates that there was to be a lengthy period of time in which natural regeneration would take place. It also informs us that in the same place where the children of Israel were told they were no longer the people of the LORD, they would hear again that they were the people of the LORD.

Question: Where was it that they were told, *"You are not My people"*?
Answer: In the land of Israel.
Question: Where will they be told they are, *"Sons of the living God"*?
Answer: In the land of Israel.

From this we know that the massive spiritual restoration of Israel, or, to couch it in evangelical terminology, the great revival, will take place in the land of Israel.

It was pointed out in Chapter Five that the "circumcision of the heart" alluded to the reception of Jesus as Messiah and Lord. We are told that Israel shall be called *"Sons of the living God."* How does one become a child of the living God? By receiving Jesus as Messiah and Lord!

> *"As many as **received Him**, to them He gave the right to become **children of God**, to those who believe in His name"*   (Jn 1:12).

It is the reception of the Messiah and the indwelling of the Holy Spirit that is promised to Israel by the LORD through the prophet Ezekiel:

> *"I will give you a new heart and put a new spirit within you; I will take the heart of stone out of your flesh and give you a heart of flesh. **I will put My Spirit within you** ..."*   (Eze 36:26&27).

The LORD is looking ahead through the centuries of time to the moment when Israel as a nation acknowledges the Messiah-King and undergoes spiritual rebirth. It is then that God will fulfill His promise to *"put My Spirit within you."* There is no other way possible to receive the Spirit of the living God except by receiving Jesus as Messiah and Lord. And tens of thousands of Jews today testify that they received the Holy Spirit from the God of Abraham, Isaac and Jacob when they personally received *Yeshua* (Jesus) as Messiah, Lord and King.

CURRENT FULFILLMENT

It has been estimated by scholars that there were approximately 63,000 Jewish believers in *Yeshua* (Jesus) at the time of the destruction of the second temple. It is interesting to note that numbers given for Jews believing in *Yeshua* (Jesus) in the United States in 1988 were double that figure—approximately 120,000[1]—and that there were then around one hundred Messianic Synagogues[2], where *Yeshua* (Jesus) is worshipped regularly on the Sabbath.

Also, in 1987, a young Jew from the then Underground Church in Russia said categorically, "Between twenty and twenty-five percent of the total Underground Church is Jewish"! After the Russian Jews began to enter by hundreds and thousands into Israel, during 1990, an entire congregation of Russian believers in Jesus was formed. Another four Russian congregations have been formed since that time and some twenty-nine groups have sprung up that are as yet too small to be classed as congregations.

The Israeli government began a clandestine operation in 1979 to bring *Beta Israel*, the Ethiopian *Falasha* Jews, home to Israel. Thousands were smuggled out through the Sudan and Kenya. These, together with the nearly 7,000 airlifted to Israel in "Operation Moses" in 1984-85, brought half the entire Ethiopian Jewish community to Israel. Due to the publicity given to "Operation Moses" the Ethiopian government stopped the airlift, causing many hundreds of family members to be separated from each other for years. It was soon found, however, that many of these black Jews who were brought to Israel believed in Jesus. There were so many, in fact, that the religious authorities in Israel wanted to "reconvert" the entire community back to Judaism! The Ethiopians demonstrated their opposition by camping in the open, opposite the main synagogue in Jerusalem for two weeks. Eventually a compromise was worked out, and the demonstrators dispersed. In May 1991 after payment to the Ethiopian government of approximately US$2,000 per head, another airlift, "Operation Solomon," brought the other half of the Ethiopian Jewish community home and reunited the splintered families. There are now several congregations in Israel solely made up of Ethiopians, who worship Jesus as the holy Lamb of God.

Groups of Jews believing in Jesus are to be found in many countries of the world. Some groups are large, others are small. But wherever Jews are to be found in reasonable numbers there will be found those who worship Jesus.

Although Jews are coming to the knowledge of their Messiah all around the world, it is in Israel that both excitement and tension mount. There is excitement because of what the LORD is doing and tension due to the opposing of His work by the religious, who wield great power in the government and also in society. In the late 1970's and early 1980's there were only about 300 Jewish believers in Messiah Jesus throughout the entire country. As a slow trickle of Jews came to know their Messiah a constant cry ascended to heaven pleading for an "increase in the momentum."

The Lord communicated to us that He could not do this because "we had no vehicle to carry a revival." On pondering this we realised the absolute truth of the statement. We were a motley bunch. Some groups were so small that they could not be termed "congregations" without vivid imagination! Over the years, however, congregations have sprung up in every city and in most towns throughout Israel. Most believers are strong in the Lord; many have suffered a great deal of harassment and persecution for their faith.

In contrast to the 300 Jewish believers in 1980 there are now thousands, spread as a network over the entire country. These numbers came from children born to married couples, by evangelism and by dreams and visions revealing Jesus as Messiah. They did not come from immigration. That is a very recent event.

Looking at the thousands of believers coming to know Messiah Jesus during the past decade, we now see well over 2,000% increase in numbers. Number-wise it is small compared with such countries as China. Percentage wise it is definitely one of the greatest, if not the greatest, move of our time.

One evening in 1978, two years before I was invited to Israel, I was in a Charismatic Christian meeting in Christchurch, New Zealand. During that meeting a prophetic word came forth:

"The torch has been lit and is on its way to Jerusalem."

This word pierced my spirit even though I was then at a loss to understand it. I shelved it in the archives of my mind. Some months later I witnessed the lighting of the torch that was to be carried to the country where the next Olympic Games were to be held. The prophetic word was instantly recalled and the significance of it revealed. Christchurch, New Zealand, is, as many people know, the farthest city in the world from Jerusalem. And the Scriptures tell us that:

*"You shall be **witnesses** ... **to the end of the earth**"*   (Acts 1:8).

The gospel had gone out to Christchurch, to the literal end of the earth, and was now returning back to Jerusalem!

This excited me. In 1986, just prior to *Yom Kippur* (Day of Atonement), a small group of us were preparing to go out onto the streets of Jerusalem with 1,000 tracts, in Hebrew, showing Jesus to be the *kapparah* (Atonement). Mass tract distribution had not been attempted in Jerusalem, previously, due to the very real dangers involved. Both religious and non-religious Jews are capable of inflicting serious injuries upon the persons or property of "missionaries," as all the believers in Jesus are called. We formed a strategy that we hoped might prevent a religious conflict that evening. Staying in our home at the time was a black Nigerian Christian friend, Chinyere. Chiny, as she preferred to be called, was shy and went to her room while we finished our preparations for going out. We were praying and laying hands on the tracts, asking for the Lord's protection on them, as well as on ourselves, and requesting that none of the tracts might be wasted.

While we were praying, Chiny had a vision. She shared the vision with my wife, Zipporah, and Zipporah suggested that she share it with the group. The vision was this. As we laid hands on the tracts, Chiny saw a "stick" with flames coming out of the end of it. "A 'torch' I suppose you would call it," she said, "and it went right down the middle of your main street!"

Immediately I remembered the prophecy given many years ago concerning the Olympic torch. It had been on its way to Jerusalem all that time. It had arrived on the very day a major move was first undertaken to bring the knowledge of Messiah Jesus to Jerusalem!

MERCY!

The LORD is again showing great mercy to the house of Israel. He has planted her back in His land and is building a vehicle there to carry the great revival that is to come. The children of Israel have but a short time to wait for the *"until"* of Isaiah six. For many that moment has arrived—they are again *"My people."* And the following is in process of fulfillment:

> *"I will sow her for Myself in the land, and I will have mercy on her who had not obtained mercy; then I will say to those who were not My people, 'You are My people!' And they shall say, 'You are my God!'"* (Hos 2:23).

The apostle Paul states that: *"All Israel will be saved"* (Rom 11:26).

Some believe and teach that the *"all Israel"* referred to is the Church but the context does not support such a conclusion. Some see it rightly in its relationship to the Jews, yet believe and teach that *"all Israel"* is made up of those who call upon the Name of the Lord out of the *"remnant"* of the Jewish people referred to in that chapter. Personally, I have never believed that "all" equates to "some." The *"all Israel"* must literally be all of Israel. No matter how difficult we find this fact to accept, we should bow to Scripture which is both adamant and repetitious on the subject. For example:

> *"'Behold, the days are coming,' says the LORD, 'when I will make a **new covenant** with the **house of Israel** and with the **house of Judah**—not according to the covenant that I made with their fathers in the day that I took them by the hand to lead them out of the land of Egypt, My covenant which they broke, though I was a husband to them,' says the LORD. 'But this is the covenant that I will make with the house of Israel after those days,' says the LORD: 'I will put My law in their minds, and write it on their hearts; and I will be their God, and they shall be My people. No more shall every man teach his neighbor, and every man his brother, saying, "Know the LORD,' for **they all shall know Me, from the least of them to the greatest of them**, says the LORD. For I will forgive their iniquity, and their sin I will remember no more'"*   (Jer 31:31-34).

> *"**All the house of Israel, all of them** in the land, shall serve Me"*   (Eze 20:40).

A **"new"** covenant will be made with Israel. It will not be like the old covenant, laid before them to accept or reject, but it will be written on their hearts by the Holy Spirit. It will be placed within their very being becoming a life principle, and thus they shall truly be "God's people." Every Jew alive will be part of this covenant when it is made in full, from the most important to the least important of them. That is the promise made to them by the Holy One of Israel. And He never has made, nor ever will make, an idle promise.

Dear LORD,
Thank You for what You are doing among the Jewish people. Thank You for promises made and kept. Help me to see Your workings in my day, and give me the grace to help pray it to fulfillment, so that Jesus might return and take His Bride to Himself. Amen.

12

THE
EXODUS

Our word "exodus" comes from the Greek word *"exodos,"* which means "a going out, a release." The Alexandrian Jews, when they translated the Hebrew Scriptures into the Greek *Septuagint* during the third century B.C., applied it to the Israelites coming out of their bondage in Egypt and named the second book of the Greek Scriptures *Exodos,* and this carried over into the English versions.

The date of the Exodus has been estimated to be around the year 1450 B.C. and, without doubt, has been the subject of much discussion over the centuries by both the world's religious and non-religious communities. A secular neighbour of mine in Jerusalem made me laugh one day when he jokingly said, "We Jews haven't worked since we came out of Egypt." But whether the Exodus is referred to in terms of awe or in a joking manner, the fact remains that it is still talked about some 3,500 years after the event. And that was exactly the reason that the LORD brought the children of Israel out of Egypt in the manner that He did. The LORD said to Pharaoh:

> *"I have raised you up, that I may show My power* in you, and that *My name may be declared in all the earth"* (Ex 9:16).

Remember the thesis of Chapter Seven, namely, that the LORD does everything ultimately for Himself, to make a name for Himself in the world. The excellence of His strategies are borne out by time! Also remember the content of Chapter Eight regarding blessings and curses, that is, that the LORD would *"bless those who bless"* the Jewish people, and, conversely, would *"curse him who holds you lightly in esteem."* In Chapter Ten, when speaking to Abram concerning his descendants being oppressed, the LORD looks ahead and declares punishment upon Egypt 430 years before it took place:

"I will punish the nation they serve ..."   (Gen 15:14 NIV).

The Exodus is a documented event in history. It was foretold centuries before the advent and discussed millennia after the event.

THE SECOND EXODUS

Even though the Israelite Exodus from Egypt is a fact of history and still a topic of conversation today, there is to be another Exodus of even greater magnitude:

*" 'Behold, the **days are coming,**' says the LORD, "that **it shall no more be said**, 'The LORD lives who brought up the children of Israel from the land of Egypt,' "but, 'The LORD lives who **brought up the children of Israel from the land of the north** and from all the lands where He had driven them.' For **I will bring them back into their land which I gave to their fathers"**   (Jer 16:14&15).*

First, we are told that *"it will no more be said ... but ..."* which means that something of greater importance will replace that particular topic of conversation. Second, it tells us what will replace it. *"The children of Israel [coming out] from the land of the north and from all the lands ... ."* We are informed that the children of Israel, the Jews, coming out of the land of the north and from other lands, will overshadow the event of the children of Israel coming out of Egypt. The emphasis is on the land of the north and by the construction of the passage we see an analogy to two Pharaohs. The first Exodus involved a ruler that refused to release the children of Israel. The country was ravaged by sequential disasters until the Israelites were allowed to leave. The second event, the passage tells us, will eclipse the first. Therefore, the Israelites of the second advent are also held against their will in a northern land, and sequential disasters will also come upon that country until the Israelites are free to leave.

Directly north of the land of Israel lies the Commonwealth of Independent States, better known until the latter half of 1991 as the Soviet Union. The Soviet Union had the third largest Jewish population in the world. Only Israel and the United States had greater Jewish populations.

Whereas the children of Israel were slaves in Egypt, doing the most menial work, those in the Soviet Union are mainly scientists, doctors, lawyers and other highly intelligent professional people, making up a large part of the working elite. Just as Moses was sent by the LORD to Pharaoh in Egypt requesting the release of the Israelites, so leaders of nations and God-fearing men and women of renown went to the Kremlin in Moscow for years requesting the same right for the Jews in Soviet Russia, that they be allowed to emigrate. These people received the same answer as Moses received from Pharaoh—No!

Ten disasters from the hand of the LORD came upon Egypt, and the country was ruined. Has the reader considered the plight of the Soviet Union of late? Newspapers and magazines from around the world tell us of the awful conditions prevailing inside Russia and other member states of the C.I.S. The Chernobyl nuclear disaster in April, 1986, officially classified as, "The worst peacetime nuclear disaster in world history,"[1] has now been estimated to have killed not just the 3,000 souls officially reported by the Soviet press, but nearer to 300,000 persons with the area affected by radiation still spreading.[2] Financial collapse has come to the point where the once "superpower" is given "Third World" status, and Russian leaders ask the nations for "emergency credit" of billions of dollars to buy grain for the hungry masses to avoid starvation.[3] The ruble, as a currency, is now worthless.[4] Vodka buys more than the ruble and dulls the pain of the situation. Vegetables, especially potatoes, are disease ridden and rot in the ground causing grave shortages and near-famine conditions for the Russians. Most food is in such short supply that people stand in line for over four hours just to get a loaf of bread! Many times there is no bread left at the end of the rainbow when the shopper finally reaches it. Fist-fights and shoving-matches occur daily in food lines that stretch for blocks.[5] In October-November, 1990, food prices in privately owned stores rose 1,000% in just three weeks![6] A thirty centimetre (twelve inch) long sausage costs nearly half an average monthly salary.[7] Gasoline prices have sky-rocketed and it now costs the average Russian a week's salary to fill the gas tank of his car.[8]

"'I have been faithful to my country all my life,' says a seventy-nine year old widow as she waits for lunch at a soup kitchen, 'and this is what I get in return? I have no money and no hope.'"[9]

And shops are empty of goods—there is nothing to buy:

"'My daughter is seven. She wants a Barbie doll,' says Marina with her voice breaking in emotion. 'I am willing to pay more than a week's salary for a Barbie, but it is impossible to buy it.'"[10]

The final humiliation for the Soviet leaders was blazoned in banner headlines around the world in September, 1991:

"THE SOVIET UNION IS FINISHED"[11]

And a prominent Russian physicist surveyed the wreckage of the society around him and summed up the situation:

"Our economy is in absolute disarray, our Army is in retreat, our union is crumbled. We've had everything except a military defeat in the classical sense."[12]

Just as the collapse of Egypt under Pharaoh brought the children of Israel out of that oppression, the collapse of the Soviet Union has brought the Jews, with some bureaucratic passport hold-ups, freedom to leave their oppression, too. Emotional headlines around the world proclaimed the release of the Soviet Jews. A major New York newspaper devoted a full page to the event. It published a half page photo of Soviet Jews arriving in Israel, weeping on each others shoulders. The huge headline declared:

"THIS IS HOW IT FEELS TO COME HOME AFTER 2,000 YEARS"[13]

Even a Buddhist country announced the Jewish emigration as a front page feature under the headline:

"Thousands of Soviet Jews flood into Israel."[14]

The story tells us that:

"Immigrants are flooding in at a rate of three thousand a day."[15]

Hundreds of thousands of Soviet Jews have arrived in Israel. They tax the meagre resources of a tiny nation. They occupy all available housing, fill every spare hotel room and live in trailer-caravan villages throughout the land. There are, in Russia, another 1,200,000 Soviet Jews said to be:

"Sitting on their suitcases awaiting the opportune moment to migrate."[16]

Hundreds of thousands more await exit visas. Transportation to Israel is a problem because normal air-trafic was not designed for such-large scale operations. Ships are now being used to bring the people home, but even they are inadequate given the huge numbers to be moved.

Scandinavian Christians, awakened by the Holy Spirit to the reality of the coming Russian Exodus, have spent years in prayer and preparation. They have shelter and food ready for the masses. Fleets of buses and private cars wait patiently for their passengers.[17] They await the final phase of Exodus II, the moving out, overland and on foot, of the Russian-speaking Israelites.

Getting the Russian-born children of Israel to the Promised Land has, thus far, proven more difficult than getting the Egyptian-born children of Israel to the Promised Land. Even now, the event is far from completion. Undoubtedly, the LORD will have arranged that the latter portion of the operation should outshine the former. One thing we do know, the Russian Exodus is underway. The crossing of seas or skies will prove no greater obstacle to the Ruler of the universe than the parting of either the Red Sea or the River Jordan. He is the Architect of creativity. *Nyet,* we will not have long to wait.

Dear LORD,
We stand in awe of You. We stand in awe of Your power and might. You crush the world's most militarily powerful nation and bring it to its knees. You crush nations, hold back the waters of seas and rivers and cause a city's wall to come tumbling down, all for the sake of Your people. Oh, God, bring Your people home. Bring them home that nations might speak of Your works and glorify Your Name for all eternity. Amen.

13

THE WANDERING

The children of Israel, after the Exodus from Egypt, spent forty years wandering around in circles in a desert. This sojourn in a dry and thirsty land came upon them because of their unbelief. But it was here, in a harsh environment, at Mount Sinai, that the LORD made a covenant with the house of Israel and gave them the *Torah*, the Law of Moses.

Israel was never able to keep the Law. Either through wilful disobedience or sheer human frailty they repeatedly broke the covenant they had entered into with the LORD at Sinai. Indeed, it was impossible for them to keep God's laws; they were:

> *"**Held prisoners** by the law, **locked up** until faith should be revealed. So the law was put in charge to lead them to Christ ..."*
> (Gal 3:23&24 NIV).

The inability on the part of the Israelites to keep the Law held them prisoners to that Law. If they kept all but one commandment it was as if they had failed every commandment; they had broken the Law. The constant failure to keep the Law only made them more aware of their wretched state:

> *"**Cursed is everyone** who does not continue in **all things which are written in the book of the law**, to do them'"* (Gal 3:10).

The Law was designed to bring the children of Israel face to face with the insurmountable barrier of trusting in their own goodness to bring salvation. It was designed to embed into the heart of the Israelite his need of a Saviour. And it is with the Saviour in mind that the LORD promises to make a new covenant with the house of Israel:

> *"Behold, **the days are coming**, says the LORD, when **I will make a new covenant** with the house of **Israel and with the house of Judah**—not according to the covenant **that I made with their fathers** in the day that I took them by the hand to lead them out of the land of Egypt, My covenant which they broke, though I was a husband to them, says the LORD. But this is the covenant that I will make with the house of Israel after those days, says the LORD: **I will put My law in their minds, and write it on their hearts**; and I will be their God, and they shall be My people"*   (Jer 31:31-33).

The new covenant that the LORD will make will be a spiritual covenant, one that is written on the hearts and minds (see final paragraph on page 116) of the children of Israel through the Messiah of God, Jesus. The new covenant will be made with a unified Israel. The northern kingdom of Israel and the southern kingdom of Judah will again be united, and both will be party to the new covenant. That it will be made with the entire house of Israel is plain from the above Scripture and also from other passages, of which the following is but an example:

> *"Thus says the Lord GOD: 'Surely I will take the stick of Joseph, which is in the hand of Ephraim, and **the tribes of Israel**, his companions; and **I will join them** with it, with the stick of **Judah, and make them one** stick, and they will be one in My hand'"*
>   (Eze 37:19).

The wilderness that the children of Israel dwelt in for forty years after leaving Egypt was a physical wilderness. The covenant that they received at Sinai by the hand of Moses was a physical covenant, written on physical tablets of stone.

Since the declaration of the State of Israel in May 1948 the children of Israel have wandered in a "spiritual" wilderness in the literal sense of the word. There has been one ambition during that time—to survive! After thousands of years of persecution, the survival instinct is strong within the Jewish people. There is little thought given to God or to His reality by the average Israeli. Most Israelis are secular, that is to say, disinterested in things pertaining to religion. Of those that are religious, it is said of them by one of their own people:

"The Jewish community is the most agnostic in the world."[1]

Even among those ritually performing the requirements of Judaism, there are many who subscribe to doubts concerning proof of the existence of God. And what does the Scripture say concerning this?

*"God hath **concluded them all in unbelief,** that he might have mercy upon all"*   (Rom 11:32 KJV).

The word translated here as "concluded" is the Greek word *sugkleio*, which means "shut up together." We may therefore freely translate the passage thus: *"God has shut them all up in unbelief, that He might show mercy to them all."* Remember, the message in Isaiah chapter six was to *"Make the heart of this people dull, and their ears heavy, and shut their eyes; lest they see with their eyes, and hear with their ears, and understand with their heart, and return and be healed."*
During the past few years, reports have been published and circulated concerning those involved in religious sects and the occult. Figures for Jewish involvement have ranged between fifty and seventy per cent! I cannot verify the accuracy of these statistics, but I can truthfully say that of the large number of Jewish believers in Messiah Jesus that I know personally, each one, as part of their unconscious search for the Truth, became involved in the occult. The Jewish people are wandering in circles in a spiritual desert, blindly groping, hoping to fill the great vacuum in their souls with the Reality for which they were created to serve.

Just as the soul of the average Jew wanders in a "spiritual" wilderness so, too, does the Jewish State. There was much support for the establishment of a Jewish national home back in yester-year. But with increased Arab-blackmail pressure upon nations to boycott Israel or lose their supply of oil imports, support for Israel dwindled and continues to dwindle. All the member states of the Arab League uphold the boycott that not only forbids trade between the "Zionist entity" and themselves but also blacklists Western businesses with links to Israel and, sometimes, even "companies that do business with companies that do business with Israel."[2] Hundreds of European companies regularly honour requests to forswear Israeli links.[3] It is almost unbelievable to what extent European companies will debase themselves in their slavish attempts to placate the Arabs. Hundreds of companies regularly certify that they have no Jewish employees![4] It is not only Europe that complies to Arab blackmail. Japanese companies also have histories of capitulating to the Arab boycott.[5] Even *Time* and *Newsweek,* the magazine giants, appease the Arabs by including Israel in their European editions rather than their Middle East editions![6] They then print special European ex-Israeli editions (editions that carry no Israeli advertising and are not circulated within Israel).[7] These editions:

"Cater to companies that wish to avoid the taint of having even pictures of their wares seen by Israeli eyes. And, though it is impossible to put an exact figure on it, the boycott has cost the Israeli economy billions of dollars in lost trade and foreign investment."[8]

Coupled with the commercial isolation of Israel is the bad press that this nation receives at the hand of the world's news media. To say that the press is generally "slanted" against Israel is a great understatement. Israel has suffered compounded insults to her integrity from the foreign media. The question could be asked, "Does the media deliberately mislead the public?" And the answer would be an unequivocal, "Yes!" The media, especially American television networks, are both aware and proud of their immense power to influence the decisions and policy making of their nation's government. Big budgets, massive salaries (senior American television reporters receive salaries equivalent to that of film stars[9]) and equally hefty egos are involved. Both the politicians and the masses are manipulated by carefully chosen subliminal and background pictures, lighting and sound effects shown at hours when people are hungry or tired and only partially attentive (for a full exposé of these techniques read veteran American journalist Jim Lederman's book, *Battle Lines: The American Media and the Intifada.* New York: Henry Holt, 1992). There are no factual errors or lies as such in the individual clips. The media is, therefore, almost beyond judicial proceedings. But when individual clips (sometimes separated by the space of several years) are spliced together and viewed as a whole, the viewer can be manipulated perceptually to react emotionally at the whim of those responsible for the program.

For example, the reporting by Dean Reynolds, chief correspondent for ABC-TV, one of America's major networks, on the "Temple Mount" episode in October 1990, helped cause negative repercussions to fall upon Israel, from both the White House and the UN, by the deliberate joining together of two separately filmed events to make them appear as one. With a false visual view of events and, in this case, an equally false audio story to match the visual, the viewers reacted negatively to Israel, which was a prime intention. Reynold's reporting was vehemently criticised by the Israeli press as —

"Unadorned, blatant fabrications ... lies ... ."[10]

Splicing film to control the viewer's perception of events is an old trick. The Nazis made full use of it in many of their 1,400 anti-Semitic propaganda films produced between 1939 and 1945 to maintain support for "The Final Solution"—the extermination of the Jewish people.

Mike Wallace, star of CBS-TV *60 Minutes* (CBS is another of America's major networks, and *60 Minutes* has been one of the most popular shows for years), reporting on the same incident, also used the same technique to further discredit Israel in the eyes of the American people. He deliberately used a segment of an old press conference with Binyamin Netanyahu, former Deputy Foreign Minister, purporting it to have been made at the time, and also spliced portions of an interview with Teddy Kollek, Jerusalem's mayor, out of both context and sequence. Kollek had been led to believe that he was being interviewed for something entirely different, which is a breach of television's rules. Kollek protested to CBS and stated *inter alia*:

"... Mike Wallace deliberately used me ... ."[11]

Wallace's main production consultant was a well-known, PLO terrorist propagandist,[12] and, between the two of them, they gave a grossly distorted and untruthful version of events which not only influenced the White House and American television audiences but also further inflamed Muslim hatred against Israel. Concerning this screening of events, a noted Israeli newspaper editor condemned both Wallace and CBS in a series of three articles. The third article had a *postscript* which ended with:

"Innocent Jewish victims of Islamic knifers have paid with their lives for this lie. But we can hardly expect Wallace and his colleagues to think about such matters when making a sensational television show."[13]

Just as big television networks are not beyond deliberately misleading their viewers, neither are the big magazine publishers beyond misleading their readers. Both *Time* and *Newsweek* have been exposed in their faking of pictures used to illustrate the Israeli "oppression" of the Palestinian Arabs.[14] Like the television networks they well know the power of the visual image that, "one picture is worth a thousand words."

Not all foreign newsmen or news editors are unethical or anti-Israel. One honest journalist[15] spoke out against what he called "unfair" and "biased" reporting on Israel. His article concluded with a correct evaluation of the media's reason for its anti-Israel presentations:

"So what causes this bias ... Esteem for Jewish ethics or for Arab oil?"[16]

It is a known fact that those who own the media determine when and what the media will broadcast or publish. In 1988, while ministering in New Zealand, we were informed, via the person in charge of incoming news for the government-owned New Zealand Broadcasting Corporation, that the government only allowed items to be broadcast on its single channel television network that showed Israel in a poor light. But the American media is by far the world's most powerful media and has been the most damaging to Israel. And so we may ask, "Who owns the American media?" Consider the following:

"Ten financial and business corporations control three of the four major television and radio networks, 59 magazines, including *Time* and *Newsweek*, 58 newspapers, including the *New York Times*, the *Washington Post* and the *Los Angeles Times*. Three-quarters of the major stockholders of ABC, CBS and NBC are banks like Chase Manhattan, Morgan Guarantee Trust, Citibank and Bank of America ... some corporate owners intervene directly to control the news and public information."[17]

And what happens when the oil industry has a large influence in the governing of the news media? This is not just an academic question:

"Oil representatives sit on the boards of the most powerful news media."[18]

Each of these directors is legally obligated to act in the best interest of each corporation on whose board he sits, thus —

"In the Arab-Israeli conflict, where hundreds of billions of petrodollars are involved, it requires little imagination to guess where the interests of the oil-banking-investment directors lie."[19]

Many journalists are forced to compromise their personal and moral ethics in order to provide for themselves and their families:

"In the normal hiring and firing of reporters, editors, writers and producers, the owning corporations quietly eliminate those who do not conform to corporate wishes ... Anyone who believes that writers have complete freedom also believe in the tooth fairy."[20]

Faked, fraudulent and biased reporting against Israel emanates from the same black ooze that brings economic and political bias against Israel. And the acquisition by a Saudi Arab of *United Press International* (UPI) in June 1992 can only fuel anti-Israel sentiments throughout the world. *United Press International* is one of the major wire services of the world, and most local newspapers in the West get their Middle East news from wire services. In the few short weeks since Walid Ibrahim, owner of the London-registered *Middle East Broadcasting Center,* bought the bankrupt UPI for $4 million, Israel has already felt the sting of its new ownership. Because of an anti-Israel dispatch from Jerusalem published in *The Toronto Sun*, David Bar-Illan, Executive Editor of *The Jerusalem Post*, took UPI to task and publicly charged them with publishing —

"... an unmitigated, vicious lie ... ."[21]

For the sake of oil, nations line-up against Israel. For profits, companies move speedily to sever their ties with this nation. And for the same reasons much of the news media is willing to foul the minds of the world's masses with anti-Israel fodder.

And what about the "impartial" United Nations in its mediating role? Here, also, Israel has no illusions. Israel doubts that it is coincidental that the UN headquarters are located on the site known as the "Hill of Evil Counsel" (where Ahithophel advised Absalom on how to wrest the kingdom from David (2 Sam 16:21-17:2). Boutros Boutros-Ghali, the present secretary general, is an Arab and the Security Council, itself, includes a permanent PLO representative and two Arab members! The bias of the United Nations against Israel is very apparent:

"The UN Security Council ... has managed to devote some 30% of all its meetings, and a full one-third of its resolutions to Israel."[22]

And not until Saddam Hussein invaded Kuwait was there ever a resolution made against an Arab country, not even in 1982 when Hafez Assad of Syria personally ordered the slaughter of 20,000 people in the city of Hama, who were from a rival sect, and had the city bulldozed under a mound of dirt.[23] In 1982 Israel located UN facilities in Lebanon that were routinely used as PLO training bases![24]

With regard to the United Nations' "investigating" team's going to Jerusalem over the episode on the Temple Mount in 1990, overseas articles about the Israeli government's refusal to allow the team into Israel give these reports:

"What credit can one give to this as an authentic information-seeking mission when the Security Council ... has already declared the guilty party? Whatever the facts, a majority against the Jewish State is axiomatic."[25]

"Given the United Nations' history of anti-Israeli and anti-Jewish rhetoric, it is not surprising that the Israeli government declined to cooperate."[26]

And thus the UN's outburst was summed up by the unbiased section of the foreign press as:

"This latest manifestation of the UN's anti-Israel reflex."[27]

Political, commercial and religious bigotry against a tiny country in an effort to isolate and destroy her very existence manifests itself in different ways. Governments, for example, "leak" false information to the media with the intention of creating adverse public reaction to Israel. The United States has led the field, of late, with several malicious "leaks." One of the most recent involved the Patriot missile, the "hero" of the 1991 Gulf war, which Israel was reported as having sold to China. An indignant American newsman asks:

"Whatever happened to the big Patriot missile 'leak' story? Was it allowed to fade away because it did not damage Israel's image, as planned? It did prove, however, that the Bush administration had moved the art of leakage to unprecedented heights, or depths, depending on which side of the leak you find yourself ... when it was proved the that the Patriot allegations were a deliberate lie."[28]

On October 6, 1973, Israel was observing her most holy, solemn day of the year—*Yom Kippur*, the Day of Atonement. The population was fasting, as commanded by the Law, and attending synagogue. On that fateful day, armies of Arab nations, led by Egypt and Syria, invaded Israel with massive numbers of troops and armaments. Most of the Israeli regular army was home for the high holy-day. The few remaining troops left at their posts on the Golan Heights and at the Bar-Lev Line in the Sinai desert were literally annihilated by the attacking armies. Coming out of the synagogues after a five hour service, the country found itself at war—again. Mobilising as fast as they could, the Israelis struck back, but not before they had sustained heavy loss of life among the country's prime young men. Israel was in very real danger of losing that war and being exterminated as a Jewish nation. The wives and mothers wept, the IDF (Israel Defence Forces) fought and the enemy was overcome, driven out of Israel and far back into their own lands. After the war, as Israel counted her dead, **sixty-one nations broke off diplomatic relations**! Black gold had again "convinced" the governments of the nations that the aggressors were really the innocent party and Israel the usurper of Arab lands.

The modern state of Israel is in a wilderness surrounded by hostile nations, just as the children of Israel were when they marched through the desert at the command of their God. The children of the Exodus experienced neither mercy nor help from those who surrounded her. And neither mercy nor help is given to the children of today's miraculously reborn state of Israel.

Tempted by reward, the corrupt prophet Balaam was willing to curse the Jewish people. Many today, for the same reason, are willing to curse those whom the LORD has blessed.

Israel, barred from competing in much of the world's market place and burdened with unjust condemnation, gropes wildly about in a hostile environment, and is isolated, but not by choice. Because she is spiritually blind, she does not see where her isolation leads her:

"I will allure her, I will bring her into the wilderness and speak comfort to her"   (Hos 2:14).

Israel is being enticed into the wilderness. It is there that the LORD will speak tenderly to her. It was in the wilderness of Sinai that the children of Israel received the Law and entered into a covenant with the LORD: the covenant that they could not keep and that was designed to bring them into the knowledge of the Messiah. It is in her empty and broken state, with increasing isolation from the nations of the world, that Israel is entering into the promised covenant of Jeremiah chapter thirty-one. Over 2,000% increase in the body of Christ in Israel during the past few years bears witness to the new covenant being made in the wilderness today.

Dear LORD,
Justice is found only in You. Thank You for the comfort of knowing that even in the world's injustice, Your purposes are fulfilled. Speak tenderly to the house of Israel, LORD. Open their eyes and open their ears. Remove the veil of blindness that lies over their hearts. Remove it, that they may now turn and be healed. Remove that veil in Christ, Father, for the honour of Your name. Amen.

14

THE
PROMISED
LAND

It has often been suggested, and even plainly stated on occasions, that taking the land of Canaan away from those that lived there and giving it to strangers was an unjust act on the part of the LORD. But what do we gain by charging God with what we consider to be a mistake? Unquestionably, *"Shall not the Judge of all the earth do right?"* (Gen 18:25). Only the owner of something has the right to give it away. The LORD, therefore, has the absolute right to dispose of His land to whomever He will:

> *"**I have made the earth**, the man and the beast that are on the ground, by My great power and by My outstretched arm, **and have given it to whom it seemed proper to Me**"* (Jer 27:5).

Large sums of money have been paid to governments, local bodies, companies and individuals for land, but, nevertheless, most people today probably live on land with tenuous rights. Scripture records only three occasions when the Divine right to dispose of land was exercised:

1. To Israel

> *"The LORD made a covenant with **Abram**, saying: 'To your descendants **I have given this land**, from the river of Egypt to the great river, the River Euphrates'"* (Gen 15:18).

2. To Moab

*"Do not harass **Moab**, nor contend with them in battle, for I will not give you any of their land as a possession, because **I have given Ar to the descendants of Lot** as a possession"*   (Deut 2:9).

3. To Ammon

*"And when you come near the people of **Ammon**, do not harass them or meddle with them, for I will not give you any of the land of the people of Ammon as a possession, because **I have given it to the descendants of Lot** as a possession"*   (Deut 2:19).

The ten nations occupying "Canaan" had no right to be there. They were squatters. They also indulged in unspeakable practices with their gods on the LORD'S private land. Even after He had deeded the land to the children of Israel, the Israelites had to wait more than 400 years to take possession of their inheritance because of God's mercy extended toward the Amorites.

Around 1410 B.C., performing the oath which He swore to Abraham, the LORD brought Israel, under the command of Joshua, over the Jordan into the land of their inheritance. From that time Scripture specifically refers to the land thirty-one times as *"the land of Israel."*

Because of their continued infidelity toward the LORD, Israel was conquered and the people were taken away captive. Unlike other nations who were conquered, taken captive and assimilated so effectively that they ceased to exist as nations, Israel resisted assimilation as all other peoples were "unclean" to them (Acts 10:28). They were a people who were to dwell alone and never to be reckoned with the nations (Num 23:9). They also had incumbency of their land from the Holy One of Israel, who swore His oaths with an arm raised to heaven (Deut 32:40). Therefore, even though they were to be punished for their unfaithfulness, He would not entertain the thought of reneging on His promise. In their captivity, the land that is such an integral part of the relationship between Israel and the LORD was ever before Him:

*"**I will remember My covenant with Jacob, and My covenant with Isaac and My covenant with Abraham I will remember; I will remember the land.** The land also shall be left empty by them, and will enjoy its sabbaths while it lies desolate without them; they*

will accept their guilt, because they despised My judgments and
because their soul abhorred My statutes. Yet for all that, when they
are in the land of their enemies, I will not cast them away, nor
shall I abhor them, to utterly destroy them and break My covenant
*with them; for I am the LORD their God. But for their sake **I will***
***remember the covenant of their ancestors**, whom I brought out of*
the land of Egypt in the sight of the nations, that I might be their
God: I am the LORD"   (Lev 26:42-45).

The LORD banished Israel from the land for a decreed period of
seventy years. After those seventy years had been completed:

"I, Daniel, understood by the books the number of the years
specified by the word of the LORD through Jeremiah the prophet,
*that **He would accomplish seventy years in the desolations of***
***Jerusalem**. Then I set my face toward the Lord God to make*
request by prayer and supplications, with fasting, sackcloth, and
ashes"   (Dan 9:2&3).

We may never know why the LORD requires intercession or prayer
from His people before He acts to implement that which He has
declared in Scripture. But, for whatever reason, Daniel discovered the
truth of it. The example should spur us to lift the promises of God to His
throne for His attention just as Daniel did. The LORD responded
quickly to the *"fervent prayer"* of this *"righteous man:"*

***"At the beginning of your supplications** the command went*
out..."   (Dan 9:23).

The command in the heavenlies went forth and the Israelites were released from their captivity and returned to the land to rebuild the temple
and the ruined cities. The books of Ezra and Nehemiah chronicle the
events at the end of the Babylonian exile.

Unfortunately, the children of Israel did not learn from the harsh
lessons of their history. Given time, they abandoned the LORD for a
corrupt human-religious-system, and each man did what was good in
his own eyes. In 70 A.D. the Romans destroyed Jerusalem and the
temple once more. A protracted revolt against Roman rule was finally
put down in 135 A.D. with great loss of Jewish life. Jews were then
banished from Jerusalem, which the Romans renamed, and Jewish

presence dwindled from the land. That, as far as most of the Church is concerned, was that. The Jews were "out," and the Church was "in." Nothing could be farther from the truth. The Jews were out of the land, certainly, but out of the covenant? Never!

"For the gifts and the calling of God are irrevocable"
                                                        (Rom 11:29).

RETURN FROM EXILE

In Chapter Five, under the heading "The Regathering," we saw that there would not be one but two exiles. Many proponents of the "New Israel" doctrine, and others who teach on the subject of Israel, say that the passages of Scripture dealing with the regathering of Israel only refer to the return from the Babylonian exile. The following Scriptures entirely negate such erroneous doctrine:

*"It shall come to pass in that day that the LORD shall set His hand **again the second time** to recover **the remnant of His people who are left**, from Assyria and Egypt, from Pathros and Cush, from Elam and Shinar, from Hamath and the islands of the sea. He will set up a banner for the nations, and will assemble the outcasts of **Israel**, and gather together the dispersed of **Judah** from the **four corners of the earth"**   (Isa 11:11&12).*

The passage clearly tells that the LORD will set His hand *"again the second time"* to recover the *"remnant of His people who are left."* There is to be **a second gathering of a remnant from the tribes of both Israel and Judah**. First, it was not a *"remnant"* that came out of Egypt, it was an entire nation. Second, those that returned from Babylon came only from Judah. Third, the exiles who returned from Babylon were few in number (42,360—Ezra 2:64, Neh 7:66) and came from the area of Babylon. Our passage tells us that the second gathering will come from many nations and from islands in the sea—from the four corners, or four quarters, of the earth! It is *"in that day"* that the gathering will take place, but when is *"that day"* that the passage speaks of? Putting the passage back into its context and beginning at the commencement of the chapter, we find *"that day"* is defined:

*"There shall come forth **a Rod from the stem of Jesse**, and a **Branch** shall grow out of his roots. **The Spirit of the LORD shall rest upon Him**, the Spirit of wisdom and understanding, the Spirit of counsel and might, the Spirit of knowledge and of the fear of the LORD. **His delight is in the fear of the LORD**, and He shall not judge by the sight of His eyes, nor decide by the hearing of His ears; but with righteousness He shall judge the poor, and decide with equity for the meek of the earth ... **a Root of Jesse**, who shall stand as a banner to the people; for **the Gentiles shall seek Him, and His resting place shall be glorious"*   (Isa 11:1-4&10).

The *"Rod from the stem of Jesse,"* the *"Branch,"* and the *"Root of Jesse,"* refer to Jesus, the Jewish Messiah. It is upon *"Him,"* that *"the Spirit of the LORD shall rest,"* and His *"resting place"* is the Church. It is clearly **after** the advent of Jesus, during the dispensation of the Church, that the second gathering will take place which precludes any thought of the Babylonian exile. The second gathering is to be very much greater in magnitude than the first gathering, so much so that it is described by the LORD as raising a *"banner,"* which, along with trumpet fanfares, heralds the approach of a Monarch. The second gathering began with a trickle of Jews into "Palestine" after the turn of the last century. The trickle became a stream after 1948 and a river during the 1950s and 1960s. The river is now in flood-stage and in danger of bursting its banks with the masses arriving from the last vestiges of the Soviet Union. Another Scripture passage, that also describes the outstanding feat of gathering the vast multitude, is the following:

*"Behold, I will bring them **from the north country**, and gather them **from the ends of the earth**, among them **the blind and the lame, the woman with child and the one who labors with child**, together; **a great throng** shall return there. They shall come **with weeping**, and **with supplications** I will lead them. I will cause them to walk by the rivers of waters, in a straight way in which they shall not stumble; for I am a Father to Israel, and Ephraim is My firstborn. **Hear the word of the LORD, O nations, and declare it** in the isles afar off, and say, '**He who scattered Israel will gather him**, and keep him as a shepherd does his flock'"*   (Jer 31:8-10).

The people who are to be gathered will come *"from the north country"* and from *"the ends of the earth."* Russia is the *"north country"* and, as mentioned in Chapter Eleven, New Zealand is the farthest country from Jerusalem. From New Zealand and its neighbour, Australia, the literal *"ends of the earth,"* come the greatest amount of Jewish immigrants per head of population![1] The children of Israel have, thus far, returned to the Promised Land from more than **140 nations**![2] There were, in the early 1980s, nearly one hundred languages spoken in Israel![3] The *"blind and the lame"* are received with open arms. Expectant mothers and those actually in labour come. "Operation Solomon" in May 1991 was history's greatest airlift of human cargo. In just thirty-three hours and twenty-seven minutes almost 1,500 Ethiopian Jews were brought to Israel, including many pregnant women. Three of those *"labouring with child"* gave birth during flight![4]

Newspapers around the world continue to declare other fulfillments of prophecy. Large photographs published of Soviet Jews weeping on each others necks after landing in Israel[5] fulfill *"with weeping ... they shall come."* And *"with supplications* (prayer) *they will come"* is fulfilled as the Ethiopians descended from the "steel doves":

"... grizzled Ethiopian men knelt in prayer and kissed the ground."[6]

"A great throng shall return" is being fulfilled. Millions have returned to Israel since 1948. The Jews continue to come, and articles continue to document the exodus from the nations. Perhaps we may better understand recent events in Europe from a newspaper article entitled "Albanian Jews land in Israel."[7] The article informs us:

"The last Jewish immigrants from Albania landed in Israel on Thursday, closing a clandestine saga that wrote one more footnote to the collapse of Europe's Communist dictatorships."[8]

Remember the Pharaohs of Exodus I and II? The Communist walls came down in order to let the Jews out! At the completion of the last article mentioned, we read the epitaph to a fallen regime:

"... the Jewish diaspora of Albania no longer exists."[9]

The nations of the world are enjoined to, *"Hear the word of the LORD"* concerning the gathering of His people. The nations are not just to *"Hear the word of the LORD,"* they are also to *"declare it in the isles afar off, and say, 'He who scattered Israel will gather him, and keep him as a shepherd does his flock'"* (Jer 31:10). All who see the truth of prophecy being fulfilled in regard to the regathering of the LORD'S people should be speaking about it continuously. It should be loudly declared what God is doing in our day. To do so will bring others into the kingdom of God. It was with this intent that the Apostle Paul magnified his ministry among the Gentiles:

"I magnify my ministry, if by any means I may provoke to jealousy those who are my flesh and save some of them"
(Rom 11:13b&14).

Precise Scripture passages concerning the second gathering continue to be fulfilled almost daily:

"I will say to the north, 'Give them up!' And to the south, 'Do not keep them back!' Bring My sons from afar, and My daughters from the ends of the earth"   (Isa 43:6).

The LORD says to the north, to Russia, *"Give them up!"* And the north spews out its captives. In the middle of a military conflict in the famine stricken Horn of Africa, south of Israel, He says to the armies fighting in Ethiopia, *"Do not keep them back!"* And twenty-nine planes make forty trips to finish bringing *"His sons and daughters home."*

The miracles of the second regathering are endless. Dramatic airlifts, like that which brought the Ethiopians, began with "Operation Ali Baba" in 1949, which brought 120,000 Iraqi Jews to Israel. Tales abound in Israel of how individual Yemenite Jews walked 3,000 km (1,850 mi.) across the deserts to reach the Promised Land! Then, in 1949-50, Israel airlifted nearly 50,000 Yemenite Jews into Israel in "Operation Magic Carpet." These adorable, olive-skinned people, having never seen an airplane other than high in the skies over Yemen, lined up to enter the great roaring birds without a second thought. The children of Israel had been carried on eagles wings out of Egypt:

"You have seen what I did to the Egyptians, and how I bore you on eagles' wings and brought you to Myself"   (Ex 19:4).

Now, the Yemenites turn had come to be carried by the big bird. They had waited for generations and the great eagle had come at last to carry them back to the land.

Another fulfillment of Scripture concerning the gathering of God's elect people is worthy of attention, due to its unusual nature:

*"Surely these shall come from afar; look! Those from the north and the west, **and these from the land of Sinim**"*   (Isa 49:12).

This passage seems to have been a headache for Bible translators. In Hebrew, *"the land of Sinim"* is the land of the Chinese. To the mind of some translators this could not be possible—who could believe such a thing—it must be a textual error! Therefore, of the popular translations, some have put "Syene" in the text with either a margin annotation or footnote indicating that the Hebrew text has *Sinim*, making their disbelief obvious. Some have followed the crowd and put "Syene" but without any gloss that the Hebrew text is different. One has left it out completely, and another is apparently undecided, having *Sinim* in earlier versions but changing to "Aswan" in recent years. But, happily, there are those that are well known for adhering more closely to the original texts and have translated it correctly.

The passage in question is constructed in such a way that we are meant to distinguish between *"those"* coming from the unnamed countries of the north and west, and *"these"* coming from afar—from *"Sinim"*—the "regular," as opposed to, the "irregular." The "expected," in contrast to, the "unexpected." The Hebrew text emphatically means China, and all of the most respected among the critical commentaries substantiate this fact. Franz Delitzsch, in his commentary on this passage, notes, "Concerning the Jews of China, in the *History of the Post-biblical Poetry of the Jews* (1836), it is not by accident that the 'land of the Sinese' is given as the 'farthest point to the east.'" With such emphasis made of gathering the dispersed Jews from *"the ends of the earth,"* we can understand the emphasis placed on *"these from the land of Sinim."*

Jews first arrived in China around 1,300 years ago but the West knew little of them until 1605, when the Jesuit missionary Matteo Ricci arrived. The Jewish community thrived and grew to 50,000 persons at its height.[10] In 1949, after the Communists had taken over, the community became almost extinct by dispersion as the Chinese Jews fled to escape Communism. Approximately 1,000 families from that community have thus far made their way back to Israel. Their presence in the land bears witness to the fulfilling of our prophecy.

Jews are returning to the Promised Land from all parts of the world. They come in all colours; white, olive, black, brown, yellow and every hue in between. They come from near, and they come from afar – from the north, the south, the east and the west, exactly as Scripture has foretold. And Isaiah, receiving revelation beyond his comprehension concerning airtravel, poses the prophetic question:

*"Who are these **who fly like a cloud**, and **like doves to their roosts?**"*   (Isa 60:8)

In just thirty months, from mid-December 1989 until mid-August 1992, over 785,000[11] returning Jews flew into the Promised Land. Jews are flying home from the exile, *"like a cloud, like doves"* with a homing instinct. Some religious Jews, some believing Jews, and many Gentile Christians, say that modern Israel is of the flesh. If modern Israel is of the flesh and not of God then God is either not God or there is no God at all! Modern Israel is fulfilling Scripture daily!

THE REMNANT

It took the death of six million Jews by the hands of Nazi Germany during World War II to establish the modern State of Israel. In this terrible event in both Jewish and world history, we have one of the double fulfillments of prophecy mentioned in Chapter Three. We also have the phenomenon mentioned there of the first fulfillment being the double fulfillment, with the second being the literal fulfillment.

Herod, if you remember the story in the Gospels, was paranoid that a King had been born. Fearing that he might lose his throne, he ordered all male children under the age of two years to be slaughtered in the Bethlehem area:

*"Herod ... sent forth and put to death all the male children who were **in Bethlehem and in all its districts**, from two years old and under, according to the time which he had determined from the wise men. **Then was fulfilled what was spoken by Jeremiah the prophet**, saying: 'A voice was heard in Ramah, lamentation, weeping, and great mourning, Rachel weeping for her children, refusing to be comforted, because they are no more'"*
                                                                (Matt 2:16-18).

Here we see a fulfillment of Scripture. But, let us return the Scripture to its context in Jeremiah and see the literal fulfillment in relation to the Holocaust:

> *"Thus says the LORD: 'A voice was heard in Ramah, lamentation and bitter weeping, Rachel weeping for her children, refusing to be comforted for her children, because they are no more.' Thus says the LORD: 'Refrain your voice from weeping, and your eyes from tears; for your work shall be rewarded, says the LORD, and **they shall come back from the land of the enemy**. There is hope in your future, says the LORD, that **your children shall come back to their own border"***   (Jer 31:15-17).

In Matthew's context of Herod murdering the children, we have the children being killed in their own land. In the original context of Jeremiah, the children were *"in the land of the enemy."* The LORD assures Israel that *"there is hope in your future,"* and that hope was, *"that your children shall come back to their own border."* They would return to the Promised Land, *"from the land of the enemy."* The literal fulfillment of this prophecy was the *"lamentation and bitter weeping"* of the Jews at the systematic murder of one third of their people by Nazi Germany. There is a museum to this Holocaust in Jerusalem, Israel. Inside the grounds of the museum there is a huge bronze sculpture of a woman with head covered and tears flowing down her face. The Hebrew inscription below the statue says, "Rachel, weeping for her children. She refuses to be comforted for her children, who are gone."

The hope that was held out to the Jews by the LORD is now actualising. The children are coming back to their own borders.

THE WHOLE HOUSE

We do not as yet see all the Jews returning to the Promised Land. Some, because of their wealth or life-style, chose to stay in the lands of their exile even though the doors opened for them to leave. Thousands of these Jews, most especially those in Iran or Arab lands, are now prisoners. They are held in ghettos against their will, and many suffer torture or even death, but the choice, ultimately, was theirs.

Most of the world's Jews do not wish to emigrate to Israel, preferring to live more affluent life-styles in other countries. This will not always be the case. The LORD has promised to gather the whole house of Israel back to the land:

*"But you, O mountains of Israel, you shall shoot forth your branches and yield your fruit to My people Israel, **for they are about to come**. For indeed I am for you, and I will turn to you, and you shall be tilled and sown. I will multiply men upon you, **all the house of Israel, all of it**; and the cities shall be inhabited and the ruins rebuilt"* (Eze 36:8-10).

It is obvious that the entire house of Israel was never gathered back to the land after the Babylonian exile; both the Bible and history bear out this fact. This promise is yet for a future date. It will be fulfilled in its own time—in its appointed season. And then, *"all the house of Israel—all of it,"* will be reunited after eons of separation. There are, of course, other Scriptures that support the gathering of every Jew to the land, for example:

*"The Gentiles shall know that the house of Israel went into captivity for their iniquity; because they were unfaithful to Me, therefore I hid My face from them. I gave them into the hand of their enemies, and they all fell by the sword. According to their uncleanness and according to their transgressions I have dealt with them, and hidden My face from them.' Therefore thus says the Lord GOD: 'Now **I will bring back the captives of Jacob**, and have mercy on **the whole house of Israel**; and I will be jealous for My holy name … .*

*When I have brought them back from the peoples and gathered them out of their enemies' lands, and I am hallowed in them in the sight of many nations, then they shall know that I am the LORD their God, who sent them into captivity among the nations, but also brought them back to their own land, **and left none of them captive** any longer. And I will not hide My face from them anymore; for I shall have poured out My Spirit on the house of Israel,' says the Lord GOD"* (Eze 39:23-25,27-29).

The passage also bears witness to what has previously been said elsewhere: that there will be a "great revival" among the Jewish people after they have been brought back to the land. But that is not the focus of our attention here. Here, the LORD promises to *"bring back the captives of Jacob."* Jacob in Scripture contexts such as this, is always a metaphor for the entire house of Israel. The LORD promises also to *"have mercy on the whole house of Israel."* It is upon the *"whole house"* that He will have mercy, not a "partial" house.

Any place outside of Israel is, for the Jew, either the *diaspora* (Greek), or the *galut* (Hebrew). These two words both mean "exile" and are commonly used among Jews to describe the Jewish exile from the land. Biblically, any Jew living outside of Israel is living in exile. Both *diaspora* and *galut* refer directly to the captivity of the Israelites. And what does the Scripture say? That He will leave *"none of them captive"!* At some point in history there will be no Jews left in the *galut.* There may, perhaps, be many dead bodies left there—the bodies of those that choose the way of wealth and temporal comfort over the way of the LORD—but there will be no live bodies left behind. It took the murder of six million Jewish souls to establish the modern state of Israel; what will it take to bring the unwilling Jew home?

THE AMERICAN JEW

There are approximately eight million Jews living in the United States. The vast majority have absolutely no desire or intention to move to Israel. Many salve their consciences by giving a few dollars to help the feeble Israeli economy and claim that if they moved there they would not be able to help financially. If the American Jews transferred their collective billions of dollars, together with their higher-than-average intelligence, to Israel, there would be no feeble Israeli economy needing to be propped up! According to a recent survey of nations by *Money magazine*:

"U.S. residents still enjoy the highest standard of living in the world ... the United States [is] ranked first among the world's 16 wealthiest nations."[12]

It is affluence that keeps the American Jew in his self imposed exile. Even a Jewish believer in Jesus patted his Cadillac and boasted to me a few years ago, "This is the second most expensive Cadillac made." And that sums up much of the average American-Jewish thinking.

The Jews in the U.S. are free to leave the *galut*, but they choose to stay. The Jews of the former Soviet Union were not free to leave, so the

LORD simply manoeuvred economic and physical events to cause the collapse of the Communist regime. Today, there is no Soviet Union. The superpower has been destroyed—it is now a disaster area begging for help from its former enemies, but the gates of exit opened for the Jews. Even though emigration became an option, few Jews actually desired to leave the land of their birth. It was not until anti-Semitism reared its ugly head in fresh waves of attacks upon Jews that lines began to form at the emigration offices. The upsurge of anti-Semitism continues to intensify and, according to the results of a survey released in September 1991:

"... more than half of the Soviets polled want all Jews to leave the country ... The results of the poll, conducted by the Institute of Sociology in Moscow, indicate that the country is becoming more rampantly anti-Semitic as it moves from Communism to democracy and the republics are flexing their increasingly ethnic muscles."[13]

So intense is the rise of anti-Semitism in the former Soviet Union that *Pamyat*, a Russian political party, even published in its periodical that, "... a world without Jews is closer than you think." The clear implication was that plans for exterminating the Jews were being made. Fear swept through the Jewish population and literally millions are going to the emigration offices for exit visas. At the time of the Gulf War in 1991 Russian immigrants in Israel were interviewed regarding the missiles raining upon Israel from Iraq. The consensus of opinion among those interviewed was that they feared Hussein's missiles less than anti-Semitism in Russia!

It will take no greater miracle to get the American Jew out of voluntary exile than it took to get the Soviet Jew out of forced exile. And the promise is sure: the whole house of Israel will return, none will be left. Only anti-Semitism seems to move the Jew, and it is steadily on the increase in many parts of the world. Reports are being published in the United States that anti-Semitism is at an "all-time-low," but the real authority on anti-Semitism there insists that in 1991 it was, in fact, at an "all-time-high:"

"Anti-Semitic incidents in the United States rose to record levels last year with attacks on people outnumbering attacks on Jewish-owned property."[14]

A later report from a difference source states:

"Anti-Semitic incidents in 1991 rose thirty-five percent world-wide and fully doubled in the United States."[15]

It has been repeatedly stated by authorities on anti-Semitism that every ingredient for another holocaust is present in America—only the affluence of the country prevents it. Edward H. Flannery, in his documentation of global anti-Semitism, is also of that opinion:

"Prolonged and gruelling poverty—breeder *par excellence* of the anti-Semitic growth—has never found a hospitable home in most parts of America. It is a sobering fact, however, that the relatively short-lived economic depression of the thirties was productive of a brand of anti-Semitism that in many ways resembled the European kind at its worst."[16]

Such a statement, from perhaps the world's leading authority on anti-Semitism, is indeed sobering. To even venture to equate the potential of anti-Semitism in America to that of Hitler, or the Cossacks, gives some indication of what could lie beneath the outer layers of the present opulence.

If the economy of the United States fails, and it could fail at anytime given its current huge debts and fiscal policies, the Jews will get the blame. The LORD has promised to bring the Jews home. He has several methods of accomplishing that task:

*"I will **whistle** for them and gather them"*   (Zech 10:8).

*" 'I will send for many **fishermen**,' says the LORD, 'and they shall **fish them**' "*   (Jer 16:16).

*"Afterward I will send for many **hunters**, and they shall **hunt them** from every mountain and every hill, and out of the holes of the rocks"*   (Jer 16:16).

When the LORD whistled in 1948, two million Jews began their journey home to Israel. He presently has fishermen casting their nets throughout the earth, bringing in hauls of "fish." Others are setting "baited hooks"—the word of God pertaining to the divine purposes for Israel, the Jews and the nations. But anti-Semitism, the great Jew hunter, is sharpening his weapons. The fishermen are still fishing, but the season is drawing to a close, and the hunters are coming.

The Soviet immigration will double Israel's population. It is stretching everything that can be stretched. Already, Russian has taken over as Israel's second language. The immigration of the North American Jews will again double Israel's population and strain its economy, but they are experienced in absorbing millions of people:

"The infrastructure exists in Israel to absorb 100,000 immigrants a month."[17]

Had the children of Israel not been afflicted and oppressed in Egypt, they would not have wanted to leave that land at all:

"We remember the fish which we ate freely in Egypt, the cucumbers, the melons, the leeks, the onions, and the garlic"
(Num 11:5).

So, too, with the modern Jew. The American Jew especially remembers the bagels, the lox and the cream cheese. What option does the LORD have but to bring affliction upon them to get them up out of their land of captivity? The LORD'S heart-desire is that His people might respond to His call, but, as history painfully points out, God's way frequently becomes the path of suffering—the way of the long, long trail.

Today, in the United States, God-fearing Christians are already preparing secret rooms and places of refuge for Jews. How will the American Jew return to Israel? In waves of voluntary immigration with their possessions or, as so often in the past, as refugees with just the clothes on their backs? Either way, Israel will welcome them home.

Dear LORD,
Thank You for daily working miracles in the affairs of men. Thank You for bringing Rachel's children back to their land. I remember Daniel's example. I lift before You the end of the years of exile from the land. Bring the children of Israel home, LORD, bring them home. Bring them all home, LORD; do not leave one of them out in the exile. And grant me the grace to raise a banner for the nations, telling of your mighty works. Amen.

15

JERUSALEM

Nestled among the Judean hills in Israel, nearly 1,000 metres (3,300 feet) above sea level, lies the city of Jerusalem. If those hoary hills could speak, what tales they would tell! No other city has ever seen such destruction, violence and horror from the hands of so great a succession of foreign armies. The blood of its inhabitants has flowed upon the cobbled streets since time immemorial. And, even today, the blood of many who live in the historic city, eking out a meagre living for themselves and their families, continues to trickle between the ancient stones or stain the twentieth-century bitumen. No other city has so repeatedly risen from the ashes of devastation, and no other city can lay claim to an eternal future.

Jerusalem today has a rare beauty; it is a jewel among cities. And it must have possessed a particular beauty in bygone days, too:

"It is beautiful in its loftiness, the joy of the whole earth ... Zion, **the city of the Great King"** (Ps 48:2 NIV).

"There is a river whose streams shall make glad **the city of God,** *the holy place of* **the tabernacle of the Most High"** (Psalms 46:4).

Jerusalem's status as *"the city of the Great King—the city of God"* is the very reason why terror, mayhem and murder prowl her streets, stalking their victims. The attributes and purposes of God, the Great King, are diametrically opposed to those of Satan and the hosts of hell. This conflict has raged for nearly 5,000 years. Originally, the Canaanites lived in this city. The Jebusites displaced the Canaanites and dwelt there until the first Israeli conquest. Under Joshua, the city was destroyed by the children of Israel:

"Now the children of Judah fought against Jerusalem and took it; they struck it with the edge of the sword and set the city on fire"   (Judg 1:8).

How fierce the battle must have been for the city in those days. The LORD, Himself, helped the Israelites, and, under the command of Joshua, Israel was an extremely efficient fighting machine, defeating and destroying nation after nation. Joshua, without doubt, was one of history's great military generals. But, even so, their expertise in warfare did not allow them to conquer the *"Stronghold of Zion,"* a small fortified village that stood near, but separate from the main city:

"As for the Jebusites, the inhabitants of Jerusalem, the children of Judah could not drive them out"   (Josh 15:63).

The Jebusites resisted all attempts at dislodging them for nearly 600 years and mocked Israel during that time:

"The Jebusites said ... 'You will not get in here; even the blind and the lame can ward you off'"   (2 Sam 5:6 NIV).

The battle for Jerusalem will continue until one side is totally vanquished, and the other emerges completely victorious. Only One inhabits eternity, and His name is graven into the substance of which the city is made. Indeed, He is the very essence of Jerusalem, which, ironically, means "City of Peace"!

"In Jerusalem, which I have chosen out of all the tribes of Israel, I will put My name forever"   (2 Kings 21:7).

CITY LOST

The children of Israel conquered Jerusalem around the year 1407 B.C. They took the main city and all the surrounding villages except the *"Stronghold of Zion."* The Jebusites remained firmly in possession of that until around 1000 B.C. when it was conquered by King David and became known as *"The City of David"* (2 Sam 5:7).

King Nebuchadnezzar of Babylon penetrated the Jerusalem defences, in 597 B.C., after a prolonged siege and the effects of famine had weakened the defenders. Beginning with Nebuchadnezzar, the sovereignty of the city passed to succeeding conquering armies. The

Babylonian empire itself fell to the Persians, who held Jerusalem until Alexander the Great added it to his kingdom in 333 B.C. Egypt took it in 323 B.C., and in 198 B.C. it became a tributary of Syria. The Jews, led by the Maccabees, rebelled and broke the yoke of Syrian rule in 165 B.C., rededicated the temple and clung to Jerusalem until Rome took the city away from them again in 63 B.C. After the abortive Bar-Kochba revolt against the Romans, the Jews were banished from the city. Banishing the Jews from the city did not quench the sword's thirst for blood. A new twist came into an old conflict—religion!

In the fourth century A.D. Christianity was made legal in Rome, and Jerusalem became a centre for Christian shrines. The city remained under Roman (later Byzantine) control until 638 A.D. when Muslim Arabs took it. Toleration of Christians gave way to persecution of Christians, which sparked the Crusades. The Christian Crusaders conquered the Muslims, and, later, Muslims reconquered the Christians. Finally the British, with the aid of both a Jewish Legion and Arab nationalists, in non-religious World War II, conquered it in 1917. They defeated the Muslim, Turkish-Ottoman empire, and Jerusalem became the capital of mandated "Palestine." How true were the words of Jesus when He said that Jerusalem would be *"trampled by Gentiles."* Referring to the coming Roman vanquishment of the Jews, He says:

*"And they will fall by the edge of the sword, and be led away captive into all nations. And **Jerusalem will be trampled by Gentiles until the times of the Gentiles are fulfilled"** (Lk 21:24).*

The city of Jerusalem has been well and truly *"trampled"* underfoot by the Gentiles since those words were spoken by Jesus. Both Christian Gentiles and Muslim Gentiles trampled His holy city and each in his turn caused it to revert again into a city of violent bloodshedding.

SOVEREIGNTY REGAINED

The hope that was held out by Jesus was that the times of the trampling were to have an end. Jerusalem was to be *"trampled—until."* There would come a time when the situation would change.

When Palestine was partitioned in 1947, 100,000 Jews lived in Jerusalem.[1] Full-scale war broke out between Jews and Arabs on May

15, 1948. And just as the children of Israel under Joshua could not take the *"Stronghold of Zion"* from the Jebusites neither could the Jews wrest the Old City of Jerusalem from the Arabs. They had to withdraw for lack of supplies, unable to bring the necessities of war up the tortuous winding hills to their positions. The convoys bringing supplies were mostly annihilated by the Arabs on the steeply inclined bends of the gorge that leads to the city. To save Jewish lives, the battle was discontinued, and the ancient city, that meant so much to them, was abandoned to the Jordanians. The Jews of modern Israel, like those of ancient Israel, had to be content with the city and surrounding areas that were outside the centuries-old walls of the Old City.

Millions of tourists visited Jerusalem between the wars of 1948 and 1967. Those wishing to explore the Old City had to first exit Israel and then enter Jordan in order to view the historic walled city. The Arab inhabitants on both sides of the River Jordan were then, and are today, Jordanian citizens.

By mid 1967 both Syria and Egypt had amassed enormous amounts of Soviet military hardware, along with Soviet-trained troops, close to their borders with Israel. Jordan also began to mobilise her army. Israel, seeing the apparent inevitability of another war and not wanting to fight an additional force on an additional front, appealed to Jordan and warned her not to attack. Israel declared that if Jordan did not fire a shot Israel would not fire a shot either. Israel promised not to touch Jerusalem nor the West Bank which were both held as Jordanian territories at that time. Jordan's response to Israel's appeal was given in a message to her citizens on the West Bank: "Get out of the way, we are going to drive the Jews into the sea."

The Jordanians on much of the West Bank left their homes on their own volition and went to "refugee" camps that the Arabs had built some twenty years earlier. They intended to return to their homes after the war was over and Israel was defeated. War broke out on June 6, 1967. In just six short days the bulk of the Arab's military equipment lay strewn across long miles of battlefield. Of the attacking armies, Jordan suffered the greatest loss. On the second day of the war, June 7, 1967, the Old City of Jerusalem was captured by Israeli troops, and by the end of the sixth day the entire West Bank had changed hands also. Most Jordanians that freely left their homes to make way for their army's "blitzkrieg" that would "drive the Jews into the sea" are still living in those same refugee camps. Thousands of these people today, wrongly called "refugees," in my estimation, are employed within Israel, mainly in the construction industry.

History has a habit of repeating itself, yet nations apparently never learn from it. When Israel, under King David, subdued her enemies, those that gave the enemy a helping hand paid dearly for their interference:

*"When the Syrians of Damascus came to help Hadadezer king of Zobah, **David killed twenty-two thousand** of the Syrians. Then David put **garrisons in Syria** of Damascus; and the Syrians became David's servants ..."* (1 Chr 18:5&6).

Jordan, like Syria of old, paid a heavy price for extending her hand to other enemies of Israel. Acting out of hatred, in an endeavour to help obliterate the Jewish state, Jordan had unwittingly ushered in the *"until"* of hope for the Jewish people. The sovereignty of the ancient city, the City of the Great King, had been returned to Israel. It will not leave the hands of the Jewish people again—*"the times of the Gentiles"* for the trampling down of Jerusalem *"are fulfilled."*

When General Allenby and the British forces entered Jerusalem on December 9, 1917, it not only ended 700 years of Muslim rule, but also started the countdown of fifty years until Jubilee:

*"That **fiftieth year** shall be a **Jubilee** to you ... **In the Year of Jubilee** the field **shall return** to him from whom it was bought, **to the one who owned the land as a possession"** (Lev 25:11&27:24).

On November 2, 1917 the British government had promised Jerusalem, along with the rest of Palestine, to the Jewish people as a national homeland (see "Israel Reborn" on page 100) but later reneged on their agreement. The LORD arranged that during 1967, the fiftieth year after the British captured Jerusalem, in the Biblical year of Jubilee, the city was returned to its rightful owners!

Jerusalem contains the holiest place for the Jewish people, the last vestiges of both the first and second temples. Part of the original lower three layers of huge stones that helped make up the western retaining wall for the temple area above still remain from the temple built by King Solomon. On top of those lower layers, King Herod built his retaining wall to support his renovations and additions to the second temple that also stood above on the same area. The importance of this site to the Jewish people cannot be expressed adequately. Perhaps an excerpt from an interview with the commanding officer who led the battle for that area in 1967 expresses some of the feeling:

"… said the tough commando leader who took the Wall: 'None of us alive has ever seen or done anything so great as he has done today.' And there by the Wall, he broke down and wept."[2]

That man stated, in a different way, the emotional words of an ancient Jewish psalmist:

"If I forget you, O Jerusalem, let my right hand forget its skill! If I do not remember you, let my tongue cling to the roof of my mouth—if I do not exalt Jerusalem above my chief joy"
(Ps 137:5&6).

The conflict over the city continues today and will continue for years to come. Peace can come to the City of Peace only when Jesus, the *Prince of Peace*, comes to rule and reign in her, and then:

"Out of Zion, the perfection of beauty, God will shine forth"
(Psalms 50:2).

The promise that God's *shekinah* glory will again illuminate Jerusalem is as sure as day follows night. The promise, however, is still in the future. And the conflict remains in the present.

Dear LORD,
Thank You that control of Your holy city has again come into the hands of Your chosen people. May they now be wiser in their ways than in the past. You have said in Isaiah 62:6&7 that I am to *"give You no rest, and take no rest, until You make Jerusalem the praise of the earth."* Oh, LORD, make that city the praise of all the earth to the glory of Your name. Bring back the *Prince of Peace* to rule the nations. Let the Eternal City enter her inheritance, the peace for which she was created. Amen.

16

MEDINAT YISRAEL

Shortly after crossing the river Jordan, around 1410 B.C., the Israelites began the conquest of Canaan. Day after day, month after month and year after year, they fought the many nations occupying the land, destroying or subjugating them. In the case of the Gibeonites, who tricked the Israelites into making a covenant of peace with them, the people were not put to the sword but were, instead, turned into a nation of slaves, *"woodcutters and water carriers"* (Josh 9:27). The Israelites, under the command of Joshua, who in turn was guided by the LORD Himself, gradually spread throughout the land establishing their right of possession by a superior military prowess—and more than a few miracles. Thus the first "state" of Israel evolved.

The destruction of the northern kingdom of Israel by Assyria and the southern kingdom of Judah by Babylon, together with the captivity of the Israelites from both kingdoms, did not put an end to the "state" of Israel. In each of the two kingdoms, but more especially in Judah, a large number of people remained in the land. The prosperous Jews and those of importance were taken away; the poor were left behind:

*"Nebuzaradan the captain of the guard **left in the land** of Judah the poor people, who had nothing, and gave them vineyards and fields at the same time"* (Jer 39:10).

*"Then he made Gedaliah the son of Ahikam, the son of Shaphan, **governor over the people who remained in the land** of Judah, whom Nebuchadnezzar king of Babylon had left"* (2 Kings 25:22).

A seemingly unending line of conquerors followed the Assyrians and Babylonians, but it was not until 135 A.D., during the Roman occupation, that the "state" of Israel ceased to exist. The Jews were banished from their holy city, and it was renamed *Ælia Capitolina* after the Roman Emperor Hadrian, whose name was *Ælius*. The land itself was renamed *Syria Palæstina*, putting a Syrian and Philistine (*Palæstina* is Latin for Philistia, the home of the Philistines) connection to the land. This was an obvious effort to uproot the Jewish connection. In time, *Palæstina* became Anglicised to the Palestine that we all know today.

The Jewish people were never banished from the land by the Romans, only from Jerusalem. Many had fled the Roman Army's wrath against a people who not only continually rebelled but also held the might of Rome at bay for years. Millions[1] had died during the revolt that ended with the destruction of Jerusalem and the temple. Another half million died by the hands of the Roman legions during the Bar-Kochba revolt, and a further 66,000 were taken in chains to Rome to be made sport of by gladiators in the great arenas.

The Jews, however, always maintained a presence in the land with constant natural growth adding to their numbers. A little trickle of Jews returning from other countries swelled the communities dotted throughout the land, and, from the time the Jews were allowed to enter the city once more, Jerusalem was ever the centre for the Jewish religion and religious studies.

A NEW STATE IS BORN

The "Balfour Declaration," that came forth from the British government in 1917, had given the Jews hope that a Jewish homeland might again be established. Their hopes were quashed when the British also promised Palestine to the Arabs.

After the Holocaust had taken such a terrible toll of the world's Jewish communities during World War II, the need for a homeland was greater than ever before. As the United Nations General Assembly gathered to vote on November 29, 1947, on the issue of partitioning Palestine, Jewish ears were glued to radios around the world. A two-thirds vote was needed to win final approval of the plan, and no one knew whether the UN would approve it. The actual process of casting the vote took only a matter of minutes. The vote was carried in favour of partitioning—thirty-three to thirteen. Arab members stormed out of the meeting in protest, but there was dancing in the streets and wild jubilation among the Jews:

"Who has ever heard of such a thing? Who has ever seen such things? Can a country be born in a day or a nation brought forth in a moment?"   (Isa 66:8 NIV).

Of course, no one had ever seen or heard of such a thing! A new country had been created that day—not an old country renamed, but a new birth that had had a quick delivery. The baby took only moments to arrive into a glaringly hostile world.

There was much violence in the land between Arabs and Jews. This had existed under British rule before the partitioning but greatly increased afterwards. The Arabs became bent on destroying any idea of a Jewish state. Threats of "all-out" war were made constantly against the Jews in the land. After months of deliberation, on Friday, May 14, 1948, at precisely 4 p.m.:

"David Ben-Gurion, first Prime Minister of the Jewish state, banged the table with his fist and began to read. As he reached the words proclaiming 'the establishment of the Jewish State in Palestine, to be called Israel,' the audience cheered and wept."[2]

The State of Israel, the Jewish homeland and place of refuge for world Jewry, was again in existence after nearly 2,000 years. For millions of Israelis *medinat yisrael*, Hebrew for "State of Israel," would be printed on their identity papers and engraved upon their hearts. Indeed, *"Who has ever heard of such a thing—a country born in a day and a nation brought forth in a moment?"*

No one had ever heard of a nation being re-established after two millennia—and on the original land too! There are no precedents, it was a sovereign work of the Holy One of Israel:

*"LORD, You have been favorable to **Your land; you have brought back the captivity of Jacob"***   (Ps 85:1).

The LORD'S eyes are ever upon His land and His people. He promised many, many times to bring back His people. Here are just three promises selected from just one book:

*"It shall be, after I have plucked them out, that I will return and have compassion on them and **bring them back, everyone to his heritage and everyone to his land"***   (Jer 12:15).

*"I will set My eyes on them for good, and **I will bring them back to this land**; I will build them and not pull them down, and I will plant them and not pluck them up"*   (Jer 24:6).

*"For behold, the days are coming,' says the LORD, "that I will bring back from captivity My people Israel and Judah,' says the LORD. And **I will cause them to return to the land that I gave to their fathers, and they shall possess it'"***   (Jer 30:3).

The God of Israel manipulates both individuals and nations to fulfill His pre-ordained purposes. His promises to Israel are as sure as they are pure:

*"**The words of the LORD are pure words**, like silver tried in a furnace of earth, **purified seven times"***   (Psalms 12:6).

The State of Israel has been reborn. As with the first state, the Israelites, day by day, month by month and year by year, must fight the inhabitants, the squatters who resent displacement. In the first conquest it was Israel that wanted no covenants of peace. Today they would make covenants with everyone, but those occupying the land and the friends of the occupiers desire to fight. One implacable enemy of the State of Israel speaks for all her enemies:

"The Zionist entity will be the only one of our enemies not to find a burial site. Because we are firmly resolved to transform this monstrous entity into dry leaves strewn on the ground, that will be noticed by no one."[3]

How else will Israel learn the art of war without such challengers for battle?

Dear LORD,
It is comforting to know that Your hand is upon every situation. Nothing escapes Your attention. I am as safe in Your arms as Israel is. And Your promises to me are as sure as those made to Israel. Fulfill Your every plan for Israel, LORD; let the world know how great You are. Oh, let the world bow down and worship before You. Amen.

17

DAVID'S KINGDOM

Two great yearnings have lain deeply buried within most Jewish souls throughout the ages. One is to be back in the Promised Land, and the other is to see again the days of the kingdom of King David. Not that Jews had cravings to conquer and subjugate; they merely desired to see Israel rise from her humiliations to a place of greatness once more. Under King David, and later under his son Solomon, Israel was at the apex of her power and influence. It was a golden era of prosperity, and under Solomon Israel experienced peace. The LORD established David as king over both the southern kingdom of Judah and the northern kingdom of Israel. Israel was united, and, with the help of the LORD, David established the borders of his Kingdom by military prowess:

*"The **fame of David** went out into all lands, and the LORD brought the **fear of him upon all nations**"* (1 Chr 14:17).

Solomon inherited the throne of his father David, and the LORD gave him riches, majesty and exceptional wisdom to rule a mighty nation in a time of peace and prosperity:

*"Judah and Israel were as numerous as the sand by the sea in multitude, eating and drinking and rejoicing. So **Solomon reigned over all kingdoms from the River to the land of the Philistines, as far as the border of Egypt. They brought tribute and served So-lomon** all the days of his life"* (1 Kings 4:20&21).

"Solomon surpassed all the kings of the earth in riches and wisdom" (1 Kings 10:23).

Solomon reigned from the river Euphrates to the border of Egypt, over all the land promised by the LORD to Abram, the father of the Jewish nation. But Solomon was unfaithful to the LORD; his heart was turned away by the hundreds of foreign women that he had lusted after during his lifetime:

*"He had **seven hundred wives, princesses, and three hundred concubines;** and his wives **turned away his heart"*** (1 Kings 11:3).

*"Solomon built a high place for **Chemosh the abomination of Moab**, on the hill that is east of Jerusalem, and for **Molech the abomination of the people of Ammon**. And he did likewise for all his foreign wives, who burned incense and sacrificed to their gods"* (1 Kings 11:7&8).

After the death of Solomon, Israel was again divided into two kingdoms due to his unfaithfulness to the LORD. One would think that past glories are relegated to history books, but, as we shall see, there is an exception to this rule also.

WILL YOU DO IT NOW, LORD?

The disciples of Jesus clung to Him with the expectation and hope of seeing the Kingdom of David re-established. That was the sum of the disappointment expressed to Jesus (whom they did not recognise) by the dejected disciples on the way to Emmaus after His resurrection:

"We were hoping that it was He who was going to redeem Israel" (Lk 24:21).

With the crucifixion of Jesus the hopes pinned upon Him to establish the kingdom again were dashed. During the forty days immediately following His resurrection Jesus appeared to His disciples on several occasions. Hopes, at least for some of them, obviously began to rise. At a time that seemed opportune, not knowing that within moments Jesus would ascend to the right hand of the Father, the disciples openly expressed their hope:

"They asked Him saying, 'Lord, will You at this time restore the kingdom to Israel?'"   (Acts 1:6).

The response of Jesus to that question is interesting:

"It is not for you to know times or seasons which the Father has put in His own authority"   (Acts 1:7).

Instead of responding in the negative to the rather blunt "Are You going to do it now?" He tells them that it is not for them to know when! For that is what underlies, *"It is not for you to know the times or the seasons which the Father has in His authority"* or power. The pre-supposition is that the kingdom will return but not at that particular moment. Jesus continues instructing the disciples:

"You shall receive power when the Holy Spirit has come upon you; and you shall be witnesses to Me in Jerusalem, and in all Judea and Samaria, and to the end of the earth"   (Acts 1:8).

He informs the disciples that they are going to be busy for some considerable time to come. The Good News had to first be taken to the end of the earth before the kingdom could be established again. Besides, had the disciples remembered the discourse concerning the coming destruction of Jerusalem, they might not have asked of Him what they had:

"When you see Jerusalem surrounded by armies, then know that its desolation is near. Then let those in Judea flee to the mountains, let those who are in the midst of her depart, and let not those who are in the country enter her. For these are the days of vengeance, that all things which are written may be fulfilled. But woe to those who are pregnant and to those who are nursing babies in those days! For there will be great distress in the land and wrath upon this people. And they will fall by the edge of the sword, and be led away captive into all nations. And Jerusalem will be trampled by Gentiles until the times of the Gentiles are fulfilled"
                                                         (Lk 21:20-24).

Foretelling the destruction of Jerusalem, the *"distress in the land and wrath upon this people"* should have been clear to them that any thought of a physical Messianic kingdom in the near future was simply out of the question. The disciples themselves were going to see the destruction and it would not be confined to Jerusalem; there would be *"great distress in the land."* It was to come upon *"this"* people, that is, those living at that time. There was to be great bloodshed because *"this people"* were to *"fall by the edge of the sword."* There was also to be another exile as *"this people"* were to *"be led away captive into all nations,"* and Jerusalem was to be under foreign occupation as signified by, *"And Jerusalem will be trampled by Gentiles until the times of the Gentiles are fulfilled."* All the length of time necessary for the above to be carried out fully, together with the task of taking the Good News to the end of the earth, precluded the establishment of David's Kingdom for a long, long time. However, the promise is sure—it will return!

David's kingdom was twofold. It was a kingdom of continual praise to the God of Israel, and it was a kingdom of great military power. We shall look at each part separately in the next two chapters.

Dear LORD,
Times and seasons, advents and events are in Your hand. Your word tells me in Psalms 31:15 that *"my times are in Your hand"* too. Thank You that they are not in my own hands. I feel so much safer with You in control. Amen.

18

THE KINGDOM OF PRAISE

King David exhibited qualities seldom found in man. These rare qualities brought him great grace and favour in the eyes of the LORD:

> *"He raised up for them David as king, to whom also He gave testimony and said, 'I have found **David the son of Jesse, a man after My own heart**, who will do all My will'"* (Acts 13:22).

Perhaps David's greatest quality was his ability to show his love for the LORD. David was totally uninhibited when it came to acknowledging the goodness and greatness of God. David was prolific in the writing of psalms, and the majority of those found in the Book of Psalms are attributed to him. The Book of Psalms was the song-book for temple worship. In the psalms David leads in examples of humility and repentance by public confession of sins. And in the psalms David leads the way in a constant declaration of unabashed love and adoration of his God. David left a legacy of poetic beauty to the world. Almost 3,000 years after his death, millions of people still find daily comfort and blessing in his love songs to the LORD. David wrote of his love for God, and God wrote an epitaph for David:

> *"Now these are the last words of David. Thus says David the son of Jesse; thus says **the man raised up on high, the anointed of the God of Jacob, and the sweet psalmist of Israel**"* (2 Sam 23:1).

In the Bible the LORD singled out just two men for special distinction. One was Abraham, the father of the Jewish nation, and the other was David. Of Abraham, the LORD said, *"Abraham My friend"* (Isa 41:8), and of David He said, *"A man after My own heart"* (Acts 13:22). Abraham and David had much in common, not the least of this was that they were both worshippers. This is a quality that the LORD earnestly seeks among men:

"The true worshipers will worship the Father in spirit and truth;
for the Father is seeking such to worship Him" (Jn 4:23).

Of those who have worshipped the LORD throughout history David excelled them all. His passion for God knew almost no bounds. He determined to have continuous praise sound day and night to the Holy One of Israel. David's extravagance for God has not been matched in 3,000 years:

"Four thousand praised the LORD with musical instruments,
'which I made,' said David, 'for giving praise'" (1 Chr 23:5).

David had thousands of musical instruments made and appointed 4,000 musicians to praise the LORD. This number was broken down into twenty-six divisions, so that 166 musicians performed for only one two-week period each year (A Jewish year is made up of forty-eight weeks, not fifty-two.). The divisions, therefore, practised for forty-six weeks before their turn came to minister to the LORD. This, obviously, meant technically perfect performance on the part of the musicians. Then there were the singers:

*"So the number of them, with their brethren who were instructed in the songs of the LORD, **all who were skillful, was two hundred and eighty-eight"*** (1 Chr 25:7).

There were 288 *"skilful"* singers. These were the "lead" singers and the soloists. Again, the number was broken down into twenty-six divisions of twelve singers. And finally we have the trumpeters:

"And the Levites who were the singers, all those of Asaph and Heman and Jeduthun, with their sons and their brethren, stood at the east end of the altar, clothed in white linen, having cymbals,

stringed instruments and harps, and with them **one hundred and twenty priests sounding with trumpets**" (2 Chr 5:12).

Can we really imagine what it must have been like? The temple itself was not very large. It was, in fact, no bigger than an average sized church. But the area was sufficient to accommodate 166 of the finest musicians in the land and some of the most talented singers imaginable (who often sang acappella), together with a unified group of 120 priests blowing golden trumpets in accompaniment. While it must have been a visual, and audio spectacular, it was only designed to bring pleasure to the LORD—and it obviously succeeded:

"It came to pass, when the trumpeters and singers were as one, to make one sound to be heard in praising and thanking the LORD, and when they lifted up their voice with the trumpets and cymbals and instruments of music, and praised the LORD, saying: 'For He is good, for His mercy endures forever,' that the house, **the house of the LORD, was filled with a cloud, so that the priests could not continue ministering because of the cloud; for the glory of the LORD filled the house of God**" (2 Chr 5:13).

How awesome it must have been! And it was not a show put on for special occasions either. The praise ascended to the LORD for the full twenty-four hours of every day:

"These are the singers, heads of the fathers' houses of the Levites, who lodged in the chambers, and were **free from other duties; for they were employed in that work day and night**" (1 Chr 9:33).

The "chambers" mentioned were the side rooms attached to Solomon's temple where those involved in the temple ministry lived during their division's term of ministry. But let us not think that this magnificence of praise and worship was restricted to the period of the temple:

"Now these are the men whom David appointed over the service of song in the house of the LORD, after the ark came to rest. **They were ministering with music before the dwelling place of the tabernacle of meeting, until Solomon had built the house of the LORD in Jerusalem,** *and they served in their office according to their order"* (1 Chr 6:31&32).

David set up a three-sided tent near his palace, and the ark of the LORD was there. David had a royal couch placed in the tent where he could spend hours sitting or reclining before the LORD. David's place of relaxation was in the presence of the LORD. Here in the tent dwelt the Source from Whom he drew his strength. David would often spend long lengths of time in the presence of his Beloved. David's tent was a place where religion did not interfere with worship, a place where God was accessible to man, and it was pleasing to the LORD:

"I will raise up the tabernacle of David, which has fallen down, and repair its damages; I will raise up its ruins, and rebuild it as in the days of old"   (Amos 9:11).

As much as David enjoyed being in the tent with the LORD, the LORD enjoyed being there with David. David was a true worshipper. Both he and his tent have passed away, but that fallen tabernacle of David is to be rebuilt. Praise and worship by individuals gifted in those arts will be restored. And the LORD will be accessible to His worshippers.

RESTORATION

Returning to a Scripture used in the last chapter, we look at our other Greek word that has been translated "restore" in English:

"When they had come together, they asked Him, saying, 'Lord, will You at this time restore the kingdom to Israel?' And He said to them, 'It is not for you to know times or seasons which the Father has put in His own authority'"   (Acts 1:6&7).

The Greek word translated here as "restore," is *apokathistemi*. This word, like the other Greek word in Chapter Nine, has its root in "restore." But, again, it is a particular type of restoration. The meaning of this word also goes beyond "bringing back into existence." It means to "reconstitute." Most of us would understand "reconstitute" best from our experience with items purchased from a grocery store. Some items need to have an ingredient added, usually water or milk, to bring the contents back to a required condition. The word *apokathistemi* is used six times in the New Testament, mostly in connection with healing:

*"And behold, there was a man who had **a withered hand** ... He said to the man, 'Stretch out your hand.' And he stretched it out, and **it was restored** as whole as the other"* (Matt 12:10&13).

In the beginning of the passage we are told that a man had a withered hand. The hand, obviously, was in existence but it was withered or shrivelled up. The Lord Jesus, by the Holy Spirit, healed the hand by supernaturally adding what was lacking—flesh, bone, sinew etc. Here we find a key to the restoration of David's Kingdom. Using the example of the withered hand, we can safely assume that the Kingdom actually exists but lacks a vital ingredient to bring it to its desired condition.

King David's great name and victories came by the supernatural power of the LORD. Solomon's great wisdom and wealth came by the supernatural power of the LORD. The Jewish people and the Jewish nation exist, but, like the man with the withered hand, they need an infusion of the Holy Spirit! The Jews today are endowed with much of the world's greatest musical talent. Each year the world mourns the loss of Jewish virtuosos. In 1991 we saw the passing of Leonard Bernstein whose conducting of the Boston Symphony Orchestra made his name a legend. That year also saw the demise of Aaron Copeland, "the dean of American composers."[1] And no one has ever matched the ageing Jewish genius with the violin, Yehudi Menuhin. With such musical talent liberally poured out upon the Jewish people, what majestic praise will be composed, played and sung for the LORD when they are gathered into Israel and redeemed according to promise!

In Israel during the decade of the 1970s, as has been mentioned previously, there were only a handful of Jews believing in Messiah Jesus. At that time there were some English hymns that had been translated and bound into books. Apart from these old hymns, of which many when translated into Hebrew never quite fitted the melodies, there was no modern, indigenous language of praise that could be sung in Hebrew. As the body of believers began to grow and realise the need for this language of Hebrew praise a great deal of prayer was offered up regarding it. In October of 1980 a "music conference" was held in Tel-Aviv, where members of the body of Christ submitted songs that the Lord had given them. Spirited songs came forth with beautiful Middle-Eastern melodies that expressed the heart of an emerging body. That movement continues today and many of David's psalms have also been put to expressive Israeli rhythm. By 1988 five books, of indigenous,

Hebrew worship songs, had been published in Israel by the believers in Messiah Jesus. The books were subsequently followed by a number of professionally produced music cassettes. One of these cassettes, an orchestrated choral tape, containing a number of the most popular songs sung today in Israeli congregations, is by my wife, Zipporah, who has been one of the most prolific composers of Israeli congregational worship songs (the cassette is available to readers and purchasing details are given at the end of this book).

In the United States, some extremely talented Jewish-believing-artists perform at concerts and also produce recordings of praise and worship. In 1991, the group "Lamb" had a song among the top ten Christian songs in America. Marty Goetz, a highly talented and exceptionally anointed singer and composer, who has written a number of songs for Debbie Boone, ministered at the huge gathering in New York where Billy Graham addressed some 400,000 people.

As Jews around the world are entering the Kingdom of God, an increasing amount of accomplished praise and worship is ascending to the Holy One of Israel. It is still a small sound with few voices compared to what it will be in future years. The restoration of the Kingdom of Praise is, as yet, perhaps the least noticeable of all the events concerning the Jewish people. But of those that experienced the barrenness of past decades not one would deny that the restoration has begun.

Dear LORD,
Restore the Davidic kingdom of praise and worship. Let the musical abilities of Your people create and perform for Your pleasure alone. Oh, let a glorious sound ascend to Your throne; may You fill the temple of *"living stones"* with the cloud of Your glory! And grant also, LORD, that I might be a worshipper like David. Amen.

19

THE KINGDOM OF POWER

Looking at David's kingdom of power and the present military might of Israel we see clear similarities between the two. Interesting parallels are found between ancient and modern Israel right down to the miracles.

Regarding David's might: In the twentieth century it is difficult for us to comprehend the warfare of 3,000 years ago. With the exception of those with "long-range weapons," the archers and sling-shot experts, the combatants fought hand to hand in close contact. Prolonged hand to hand combat, clad in some form of armour, called for physical fitness that few today could obtain even with the aid of gymnastic equipment. Extreme agility, great stamina, muscular power and superb physical condition were essential if a man were to survive more than an hour or two of his maiden battle. Such a man was King David. Because of the picture-book portrayal of David's slaying of Goliath, the giant Philistine, we often picture David as a skinny kid, barely into his teens. How far from the truth this actually is!

As a shepherd David showed his fearlessness when confronting lions or bears that attacked his lambs:

"When it arose against me, I caught it by its beard, and struck and killed it" (1 Sam 17:35).

And it is as a shepherd, before he slew Goliath, that David is described by one of King Saul's servants:

*"I have seen a son of Jesse the Bethlehemite, who is ... **a mighty man of valor, a man of war**"*   (1 Sam 16:18).

Our picture-book David is here described as *"a mighty man of valour—a man of war."* David was obviously young compared to a professional soldier, but he was certainly not "wet behind the ears," neither was he little. According to Biblical evidence, the young David was above average height and build. Hence, shortly after killing Goliath, David was placed over Saul's fighting men:

*"And **Saul set him over the men of war**, and he was accepted in the sight of all the people and also in the sight of Saul's servants"*   (1 Sam 18:5).

Saul was not the wisest of the kings of Israel, but he would certainly have been the most foolish had he put a young inexperienced lad in charge of his fighting men! Just as Saul had put David over his *"men of war,"* so David led them into battle:

*"All Israel and Judah loved David, **because he led them in their campaigns**"*   (1 Sam 18:16 NIV).

David became a mighty man of war and always gave credit to the LORD for his prowess:

*"**He teaches my hands to make war, so that my arms can bend a bow of bronze**"*   (Psalms 18:34).

DAVID'S MIGHTY MEN

David's army was made up of extremely proficient fighting men, of whom the leaders were almost supernatural in strength and ability:

*"Josheb-Basshebeth the Tachmonite, chief among the captains ... because he had **killed eight hundred men at one time**"*   (2 Sam 23:8).

It is a little hard for us to imagine one man killing 800 of the enemy in hand to hand combat in a single battle!

"Eleazar the son of Dodo, the Ahohite, one of the three mighty men with David when they defied the Philistines who were gathered there for battle, and the men of Israel had retreated. **He arose and attacked the Philistines** *until his hand was weary, and his hand stuck to the sword. The LORD brought about a great victory that day; and* **the people returned after him only to plunder**" (2 Sam 23:9&10).

Israel had retreated before the enemy, and one man, concerned for the honour of his king, attacked the enemy single-handed! How he must have fought! The Philistines were all around him, and he killed them on all sides! The Israelites returned to the scene of the battle only to strip the dead of anything valuable.

"Three of the thirty chief men went down at harvest time and came to David at the cave of Adullam. And the troop of Philistines en- camped in the Valley of Rephaim. David was then in the stronghold, and the garrison of the Philistines was then in Bethlehem. And David said with longing, 'Oh, that someone would give me a drink of the water from the well of Bethlehem, which is by the gate!' So **the three mighty men broke through the camp of the Philistines, drew water** *from the well of Bethlehem that was by the gate, and took it and brought it to David"* (2 Sam 23:13-16).

David, not realising the consequences, verbalised a longing for *"a drink of the water from the well of Bethlehem"* that was some distance away. Three men ran to Bethlehem and fought their way through the entire Philistine camp just to get some water for their king. Having gotten the water, they fought their way out of the camp and returned to the stronghold in Jerusalem to give it to David! There are other examples of great bravery and prowess recorded in the same chapter from which these were taken. From all these stories we get an understanding of the quality and might of David's fighting men. Adding together *"the numbers of the divisions equipped for the war"* from all the tribes of Israel (1 Chr 12:23-38), we find that the total number of men that established David in his Kingdom were 340,822. In those days this was a relatively small army; however, after the establishment of his power, the numbers swelled noticeably until it was a formidable force:

"Joab gave the sum of the number of the people to David. All **Israel had one million one hundred thousand men** *who drew the*

*sword, and **Judah had four hundred and seventy thousand men**
who drew the sword"*   (1 Chr 21:5).

David's army, even though it was small at the beginning of his
power, was undefeated in battle. Such was the fighting prowess of the
men that the army could divide its ranks and strength against multiple
opposing forces and still gain complete victory:

> *"**If the Syrians are too strong** for me, then you shall help me; but
> **if the people of Ammon are too strong** for you, then I will come
> and help you"*   (2 Sam 10:11).

Even 3,000 years ago Syria and Jordan (Ammon) had Israel fighting on
two battle fronts. David's army conquered all opposition and
established Israel as a powerful military force, paving the way for a
reign of peace and prosperity under Solomon.

THE KINGDOM

The kingdom that David ruled was extensive for that time:

> *"He reigned over **all the kings from the River** to the land of the
> Philistines, **as far as the border of Egypt**"*   (2 Chr 9:26).

David had several "kingdoms" within his kingdom. These were vassal
states that he had conquered. David did not go to war against these
smaller kingdoms for the sake of building an empire. He merely took
back land that belonged to the Israelites in former years that had been
appropriated by enemies of Israel:

> *"David also defeated Hadadezer the son of Rehob, king of Zobah,
> **as he went to recover his territory** at the River Euphrates"*
>   (2 Sam 8:3).

Once subdued, these "kingdoms" paid tribute and homage to David
in return for his protection. David's kingdom extended from the great
river Euphrates in the north down to the brook, or wadi, of Egypt, which
was the Egyptian border. It contained all of modern Syria, all of modern
Jordan, part of the Gaza strip and some of the lower portion of modern
Lebanon.

RETURN OF THE KINGDOM OF POWER

We know from Chapter Seventeen that any restoration of the Kingdom of David could not be possible for a considerable period of time
after the ascension of Jesus. Approximately one hundred years after the
ascension, thousands of Jews had fled the country and some three
million had died by starvation or the sword. Thousands more had been
taken captive, the land had been renamed and Jews were not allowed
into Jerusalem. Israel was only a memory for several decades, and then
even the memory faded with time. Israel became just a hope – a dream.
Obviously, a restored Kingdom could only arise from a restored Israel.

The United Nations partitioned Palestine between the Jews and the
Arabs on November 29, 1947. And on May 14, 1948, the new State of
Israel was born. The very next day, following the declaration of the
State of Israel, Arab armies attacked the new state in a bid to annihilate
it. Restoration of the Kingdom of Power began on Saturday, May 15,
1948, with this first war waged against the new state. It was the first in a
long line of humiliating defeats for armies opposing Israel.

In her first military conflict, the new State of Israel found herself
embroiled in all-out war with seven Arab nations. Those nations were
Syria, Iraq, Trans-Jordan, Lebanon, Egypt, Yemen and Saudi-Arabia.
The Arab armies had been trained and equipped by the British. General
Sir John Glubb commanded the Jordanian army against Israel, and there
were also British officers commanding the Syrian forces. The British
gave the Arabs their full support and even encouraged them to attack.
Just as the Jews had challenged the might of Rome on several
occasions, so they had been humiliating the British Imperial lion by
stepping rather heavily on its tail. In an attempt to stop Jewish resistance
to their rule in Palestine and also to stem the flood of Jews being
smuggled in, the British began hanging the leaders of the growing
Jewish resistance movement. The Jews responded in kind by hanging a
higher ranking British officer for each of their own that were executed.
They also dynamited the headquarters of the British housed in
Jerusalem's famous King David Hotel, killing eighty British officers
and wounding seventy others. This type of retaliatory action finally
drove the British to relinquish their mandate of Palestine to the UN. A
serious wound had been inflicted on British pride, and, as they licked
that wound, the *New Statesman* reflected the mood of the nation by

publishing a full front page editorial entitled, **"War for the White Paper?"** which stated *inter alia*:

"... in fighting the Jews, the Government had the help of the B.B.C. and probably most of the widely-read papers, and there would be a flood of anti-Jewish 'atrocity' stories and editorials on **the righteousness of liquidating the obstinate survivors of Hitler's gas chambers** [bold emphasis added]."[1]

The offensively conspicuous anti-Jewish hostility displayed here by the British press has really changed very little since this editorial was published in 1946. The humiliating blow dealt to British pride, during the mandate period, gave both reason and impetus for the full British backing of the Arab armies attacks on the new-born state of Israel:

"On paper they [the Arabs] should have conquered Palestine in a week; they were regular troops, trained, well organized, properly supplied, fully equipped, and they held the initiative."[2]

Conversely, the Jewish forces were mostly untrained, and a large percentage of their rifles were "home-made." Against the invading Arab armies:

"The Israelis mustered about 18,000 fighting men with 10,000 rifles, 3,600 sub-machine guns, four elderly mountain guns smuggled in from Mexico, some bazookas, and two tanks which had been 'liberated' from a British depot ... ."[3]

Israel was hopelessly outnumbered and she did not even possess sufficient guns for each fighting man to have his own! Against full-fledged air-forces, Israel had next to no air power:

"Four aircraft represented the whole of Israel's fighter-bomber force."[4]

Nevertheless, with two of her aircraft destroyed on the first day of the war and her poorly equipped men fighting on five fronts, by the time the UN managed to arrange a cease-fire between the opposing sides, Israel was holding nearly three times the area of land that she had been allocated in the partition!

Let us look at a Scripture that we have used previously concerning the land and the state and, also, the verse that follows in its context:

"Who has ever heard of such a thing? Who has ever seen such things? Can a country be born in a day or a nation be brought forth in a moment? Yet no sooner is Zion in labor than she gives birth to her children. 'Do I bring to the moment of birth and not give delivery?' says the LORD. 'Do I close up the womb when I bring to delivery?" says your God'" (Isa 66:8&9).

The country had been born by a vote that took minutes. The nation came forth when the land allocated by the vote had been declared to be the State of Israel. The LORD says that He will not bring Israel to the moment of birth without delivering. He will not bring her to the point of delivery and then close up the womb, preventing the birth. In other words, the LORD is saying that He will ensure Israel's entry as a nation into the world. Put that into a war situation, and we find that those opposing Israel actually oppose the LORD. Hence, ill-equipped and outnumbered Israel defeated the seven armies aligned against her.

In June 1967 the Six-Day War broke out between Israel and the Arab nations. Israel again found herself fighting larger and more powerful armies from several nations. Israel struck hard and fast:

"On Monday night, the end of the first day's fighting, some four hundred warplanes of five Arab nations had been obliterated. Egypt alone lost three hundred, Syria sixty, Jordan thirty-five, Iraq fifteen, Lebanon at least one. The cost to Israel's four-hundred-fighter air force: nineteen planes and pilots, mostly downed by ground fire."[5]

At the end of six days of fighting, when a cease-fire was negotiated, Israel was in possession of huge areas of land. Israel had captured all of Jerusalem, the West Bank, the Gaza Strip, the entire Sinai desert and the Golan Heights. Again, as in 1948, she now had nearly three times the area of land that she had before the war! And as David ruled over "vassal" states so Israel now found herself ruling over the one million Jordanian, Egyptian and Syrian inhabitants of the conquered territory.

The Arab armies had been devastated by Israel in 1967. With the help of the Soviet Union, the Arabs began to rearm and retrain under the watchful eyes of Soviet advisers. In 1973 they were ready for war, but the timing must be right. On October 6, *Yom Kippur*, the holiest day of the Jewish year, the Arabs struck. The Jews were fasting in their synagogues, dressed in white clothing. There were no newspapers published, televisions and radios were off the air. No one would answer a telephone if it rang, and the only vehicles on the streets would likely be ambulances.

The Arabs swamped the unsuspecting Israeli troops that had been left on duty during the high holy day. Syria's initial assault contained 1,200 tanks, more tanks than Britain and France had combined, more than Germany used against Russia in 1941, and more than that at the battle of Al Alamein. Egypt, according to Abba Eban, attacked with 3,000 tanks, 2,000 heavy guns, 1,000 aircraft and 600,000 men. During the days following, these two Arab nations were joined by armies from Jordan, Saudi-Arabia, Kuwait, Yemen, Iraq, Sudan, Libya, Morocco, Algeria and Tunis. North Vietnam sent pilots to Egypt, and North Korea sent pilots to Syria.

Israel took three days to complete her mobilisation. The invading Arab hoards were driven out of Israel within days but at a dreadful cost of Israeli lives. Huge losses were inflicted, in return, upon the Arab armies. Only 240 tanks returned to Syria, and the body of the Kuwaiti commander was found among the many corpses on the battlefields. The greatest tank battle in the history of warfare took place in the Sinai desert on Friday, October 19, 1973, when there were so many tanks that it was impossible to manoeuvre. Once more a cease-fire was arranged, and once again Israel was in possession of further large areas of land. At the time of the cease-fire Israeli troops were advancing upon both Damascus and Cairo!

Israel does not fight for an ideology like other nations, she fights for survival. Nevertheless, while the Israeli troops have a determination not to lose, it is not her prowess that brings the victory:

*"For they did not gain possession of the land by their own sword, nor did their own arm save them; but **it was Your right hand, Your arm, and the light of Your countenance, because You favored them***" (Psalms 44:3).

A very conservative estimate of the Arab troops aligned against Israel in 1973 would be well in excess of 1,200,000. Anwar Sadat, the Egyptian president, whose idea it was to start the war, said that Egypt was willing to sacrifice a million men! The number of Israeli defending troops were never officially made public. However, a brother in Christ, the sole survivor of an élite Israeli unit that was wiped out on the Golan Heights early in the war, told me, "Israel had about 300,000 men." And this can be substantiated by calculation:

Israeli Jewish population figures for 1973 were less than 3,000,000.

Fifty-five percent of the population were under the age of eighteen, the minimum age for conscription.

Half of the forty-five percent over eighteen were females who do not participate in combat (contrary to popular overseas opinion).

Half of the male twenty-seven and one half percent were over the age of fifty-four, the maximum age for military service at that time.

Thus we have: $3,000,000 - 55\% = 1,350,000 - 50\% = 675,000 - 50\% = 337,500$

Approximate Israeli fighting force in 1973:   337,500 men.
David's force at the beginning of his power: 340,822 men.

As David's fighting force greatly increased throughout the years of his reign, so has Israel's during the years of her population increase. The maximum age for conscription for military service has been reduced by nearly ten years from what it was two decades ago.

And as David and his men were superbly fit so, too, are the men of the IDF. Many desire to enter the "élite of the élite" units, and these men are said to be required to run sixty kilometres (thirty-seven miles), non-stop, in full battle kit in order to be considered! Singapore invited Israel to train her country's military forces but, after a brief period of time, requested that the level of training be lowered. The Singaporean men were unable to arrive at the standards required by Israel.

Each time Israel has been attacked she has expanded her borders, bringing back the land that was given to them by the LORD and which they had conquered under Joshua. Another prophecy finds its double fulfillment in the new State of Israel:

*"I will not drive them out from before you in one year, lest the land
become desolate and the beast of the field become too numerous
for you. 'Little by little I will drive them out from before you,
until you have increased, and you inherit the land'"*
(Ex 23:29&30).

The literal fulfillment of this prophecy fits better in the second Israeli
conquest than it does in the first. The first conquest of Canaan was
mostly over within the space of five years under Joshua. The Israelites
would not have *"increased"* greatly during that time, certainly not
enough to *"inherit"* the land. The second conquest has taken from
1948, when there were approximately 650,000 Jews in total, until the
present day when there are over five million in the land. *"Little by
little"* they have taken the land and settled in it.

David's army began with a small group of discontented men (1 Sam
22:2) and grew into a mighty force (1 Chr 21:5). The Israel Defence
Forces also began with a small group of discontented men. Men who
were looking for a "better deal." They were looking for a Jewish
homeland away from the continuous anti-Semitism of the world. This
small group of untrained, ill-equipped men has proven to be a mighty
force:

"In something like thirty years the Israeli Armed Forces have
apparently progressed from nothing to being one of the most efficient
and battle-hardened forces in the world and, though they have suffered setbacks, they have never suffered defeat."[6]

ISRAEL IS CHALLENGED

Israel does not have to contend with just the Arab nations. As she did
in 1948, when Britain gave a helping hand to Israel's enemies, so Israel
continues contending with others who desire to see her crushed. In a
rare exposure of Soviet military activities, an article in a Soviet
magazine reported:

"Soviet Air Force units and Anti-Aircraft troops took part in armed
clashes between Egypt and Israel from late 1969 to early 1971 ...
Soviet anti-aircraft units, using rockets, had succeeded in shooting

down a number of Israeli Skyhawk, Mirage and Phantom warplanes, but had suffered heavy casualties from Israeli bombing raids."[7]

Israel was certain that the Soviets were not only arming Israel's enemies but actually taking part in combat against her. The article confirmed it. And in the 1973 *Yom Kippur* war Israel downed a number of Soviet jets manned by Russians.

PLO terrorists, based in Lebanon, had infiltrated Israel on many occasions, killing numbers of Israelis, mainly women and children. And the persistent firing of *Katyusha* rockets from southern Lebanon into Israeli border-towns caused many deaths and kept much of the population of northern Galilee confined to bomb shelters. Israel reached the limits of her patience in 1982, and, on June 6, launched an invasion into Lebanon to destroy the PLO infrastructure. The operation was called "Peace for Galilee," and the object was to establish an Israeli patrolled "safety zone" in southern Lebanon which would place the Israeli border towns beyond the reach of *Katyusha* rockets. The Israelis stormed over the border and day by day, week by week, emptied the countryside, villages and towns of the terrorist presence, methodically driving the PLO before them until they were finally bottled in Beirut. Israel wanted to finish the job but, as in all of her other wars, outside interference prevented this, and the PLO terrorist forces were evacuated by sea, jubilantly holding their guns aloft as if they had themselves won the war.

The interesting fact of the Lebanese War was, not that Israel succeeded in her mission, but that in capturing the Lebanese city of Sidon, she unearthed the preparations for a massive Soviet-led invasion of Israel. In seeking out the terrorist PLO and its supply dumps, Israeli forces entered underground facilities which contained submarine bays showing signs of recent use. A hasty effort had been made to destroy records, but Israel gathered a great deal of information from partly burnt documents. The Israeli government has never made public the details of this information nor of that concerning the submarines, but, with thousands of troops having taken part, secrecy did not long prevail. All that was officially made public was information about the enormous cache of weapons captured. So great was the haul that it took three months to transport the weapons to Israel. There were insufficient army vehicles available for the job of shuttling back and forth. So the army, as it has the right to do in times of need, commandeered large numbers of private vehicles to accomplish the task. The **4,330 truckloads**[8] of weapons brought back to Israel would have sustained a million-man invasion originating only a short distance from her border! The Israeli invasion of Lebanon was an act of Divine intervention.

When the Israelis moved into Lebanon against the PLO terrorists on June 6, 1982, Syria challenged Israel for supremacy of the air. Syrian forces in the strategic *Beka'a* valley began firing Soviet SAM (Surface to Air Missile) missiles at the Israeli planes flying overhead but registered no hits. On June 9, three days after the operation had begun, the IAF (Israeli Air Force), having spent the previous seventy-two hours monitoring the radar frequencies of the Syrian missile batteries, attacked. Wave after wave of Israeli warplanes hit the SAM batteries destroying all but two of the batteries the first day (these were destroyed the following day). During Israel's initial attack on the missiles the Syrian air force attacked with its Russian MiG-25 interceptors. They fell prey to the Israeli pilots like ducks to a shotgun. After losing ninety-six planes without bringing down a single Israeli aircraft in return,[9] they refrained from any further attacks upon the Israelis. Israel then attacked the Syrian ground forces who were now extremely vulnerable. Having no air cover or defense against the rockets fired from the Israeli warplanes, the Syrian troops were forced to withdraw completely from Lebanon back beyond the Syrian border and remained there for the duration of the war:

"In a single twenty-four hour period the Israelis had obliterated more SAM batteries than during the entire 1973 Yom Kippur War. They had all but knocked the Syrian air force out of the skies ... without cost to the Israelis."[10]

SUPERPOWER

In 1986, Mordechai Vanunu, a former technician at Israel's nuclear plant in Dimona, "leaked" (for a "gratuity" of £60,000) information about the country's nuclear arsenal to the British Press.[11] That which many had suspected for years became known: Israel possessed large quantities of nuclear and atomic weapons.

Within weeks of the public disclosure concerning her nuclear capabilities, Israel test-fired a missile named "Jericho II" which has a greater range than the initial "Jericho" series that had been developed.

The Soviet Union tracked the trajectory of the new missile and found that it had the capability of carrying a nuclear warhead into the Black Sea area where the Soviet Union kept masses of military equipment and troops. The Soviet Union had been feeding the unrest in the Middle East for decades and, realising the seriousness of this new threat, made an appeal to Israel in a full page newspaper article saying *inter alia*:

"We three superpowers, the Soviet Union, the United States and Israel, must sit down and talk."[12]

Israel was recognised as a superpower! And in 1987, Leonard Spector, of the Carnegie Endowment, said that Israel —

"... had enough nuclear weaponry to level every urban centre in the Middle East with a population of more than 100,000."[13]

And concerning chemical weapons:

"Israel, incidentally, also has a chemical weapons stockpile, one far larger than that of Iraq, according to knowledgeable authority, as well as the potential for far more efficient means of delivery."[14]

Israel continues to develop weapons and defence systems, but testing them in a country the size of the state of New Jersey (in America) is problematical. Anything tested is immediately reported in the foreign press since Jerusalem is unfortunate enough to have the third largest concentration of journalists in the world, next only to Washington and Moscow.

Israeli sources have consistently refused to reveal technical details about the "Arrow," the country's anti-missile system currently being developed. However, reports in the foreign press, including Jane's Defence Weekly, suggest that —

"... it will be able to destroy hostile short range missiles at a distance of ninety kilometres [fifty-six miles] from the defended position. To that end it will be able to develop a velocity of 11,000 kph (nearly two miles per second), and to climb to an altitude of up to 30,000 metres (almost twenty miles). In order to remain operational under those conditions, the Arrow's component systems are said to be capable of withstanding accelerations of up to two hundred gravities."[15]

The 1991 Gulf War brought missiles raining down upon Israel. They kept millions of mask-wearing Israelis sealed into rooms prepared for gas warfare. These missiles upon Israel were described by an insensitive Norman Schwarzkopf as —

"Nothing greater than a thunderstorm in Georgia."[16]

The Israeli government's response to the missiles was quite different:

"If Tel Aviv absorbs missiles again, Damascus and Baghdad will be obliterated."[17]

Due to the American policy of arming both sides of the Israeli-Arab conflict, and the rest of the world arming the Arab nations, concern is often expressed about Israel's capability to stay ahead in the arms race. Moshe Arens, Israeli Minister of Defence from 1988-92 replies to this concern:

"We do have a qualitative edge. We have it because our defense industries have succeeded in developing weaponry that in many areas is more advanced than anything that exists. If we had to go to war now, the enemy will find the I.D.F. with technological surprises, with weapons systems that are superior to anything they have, and I think that they don't even know about."[18]

A HELPING HAND FROM THE LORD

Israel has fought and won every war waged against her. These have been major wars with overwhelming odds in favour of the enemy. Only supernatural intervention has prevented her defeat. The LORD has intervened on many occasions because He is fighting to ensure the maturing of baby Israel whom He brought to birth in 1948.

Many stories circulate about miracles on the battlefield. For example: Two Israeli tanks topped a sand dune in the Sinai campaign in 1967 and found themselves facing a complete Egyptian tank unit. The Egyptians stopped, opened their turrets and jumped out. They took off their boots and ran through the desert. Captured Egyptians said there were "hundreds of Israeli tanks"! Because of this, in the 1973 *Yom Kippur* War, Israel found many of the Egyptians chained inside their tanks. This had caused needless deaths as they were unable to leave burning vehicles.

There is a parallel in the Bible to this miracle. If you remember, the king of Syria was waging war against Israel, and each time he planned his camp the LORD told the prophet Elisha the location, who in turn told the king of Israel. After this had happened a number of times, the king of Syria informed his people that there was a traitor in the camp. But they replied that Elisha knew what the king said even in his bedroom! The king of Syria then ordered Elisha's capture and sent a large force of chariots and men to surround Dothan, where Elisha lived. Elisha's servant arose one morning, saw the Syrian Army surrounding the city and expressed his great dismay to Elisha. In the prophet's response we have the parallel:

> *"'Do not fear, for those who are with us are more than those who are with them.' And Elisha prayed, and said, 'LORD, I pray, open his eyes that he may see.' Then the LORD opened the eyes of the young man, and he saw. **And behold, the mountain was full of horses and chariots of fire all around Elisha"** (2 King 6:16&17).*

A great miracle took place early in the *Yom Kippur* war. Syria stormed across the unprotected Golan and should have been in the city of Haifa within twenty-four hours. The entire army stopped on the ridge overlooking the city of Tiberius and remained there for three days. This gave the Israelis time to muster their forces and to engage and destroy the Syrians in battle. Why did the Syrians remain on the ridge? In the words of a non-religious Israeli general:

"There was a great, grey-white hand pressing down onto the Syrians from out of the sky."

A reliable brother, known to me personally, described seeing the frightening red trace of bullets coming towards him in 1973. He said —

"… they just parted and went around me."

Another brother, also known to me personally, described how, in 1982, in Lebanon, he turned the corner of an apartment building and found himself looking down the barrel of a terrorist PLO machine-gun:

"The terrorist opened fire, crossing me both ways in the form of an 'X,' but nothing hit me. He looked at me with his mouth gaping wide open, and I took him prisoner with my *Uzi*."

Many such experiences are indelibly impressed upon the minds of believers in the IDF, and a parallel is found here between the early Church in Jerusalem and the early Church in re-created Israel. Eusebius, the first historian of the Christian Church, left us an historical record stating that in the terrible famine and destruction of Jerusalem by the Romans, "There is not evidence that a single Christian perished in Jerusalem."[19] And, similarly, there is no evidence available or any knowledge within the community of believers in Israel, that a single Israeli believer in Jesus has perished or even been seriously wounded in any war since the founding of the modern state.

Miracles abound for Israel. A small force, divided on several fronts, totally devastates massive armies many times its own size. Israel is a nuclear power and recognised as a superpower. It has been stated in foreign publications that, "Man for man, Israel has, perhaps, the best army in the world,"[20] and that, "They are the fourth most powerful fighting force in the world (only behind America, Russia and China).[21] The Kingdom of Power has returned!

For Israel part of her destiny is to fight and keep on fighting. Many Christians, because they have a pacifist mentality, do not understand Israel's calling. The LORD desires to focus the eyes of the world upon one tiny nation and, through that nation, eventually bring all attention to where it should be—upon Himself. The Arab nations are part of the plan and, because of bellicose threats, some, like Ammon and Moab (making up modern Jordan), will become extinct:

"*'Therefore, as I live,' says the LORD of hosts, the God of Israel, 'Surely Moab shall be like Sodom, and the people of Ammon like Gomorrah—Overrun with weeds and saltpits, and a perpetual desolation; the residue of My people shall plunder them, and the remnant of My people shall possess them. This they shall have for their pride, because they have reproached and made arrogant threats against the people of the LORD of hosts. The LORD will be awesome to them, for He will reduce to nothing all the gods of the earth; people shall worship Him, each one from his place, indeed all the shores of the nations'"* (Zeph 2:9-11).

But it is not just Arab nations who are to suffer through military conflict with Israel's Kingdom of Power:

"At that time, when I bring back the captives of Judah and Jerusalem, I will also gather all nations, and bring them down to the Valley of Jehoshaphat; and I will enter into judgment with them there on account of My people, My heritage Israel, whom they have scattered among the nations; they have also divided up My land" (Joel 3:1&2).

A multitude of nations are to come against Israel in the valley just outside of the Old City of Jerusalem. And the time set for this is in the not-too-distant future. *"When I bring back the captives ... ."* The LORD is doing this today, and, no doubt, this will continue for a number of years. It is the gathering of the nations against Israel that makes the "New World Order" of 1990 so dangerous. This could be the very alliance that will confront Israel in the future, perhaps even in an effort to drive her out of, what is termed today, "the occupied territories." The above passage of Scripture clearly links the division of the LORD'S land to the assembling of all the nations against Israel. Whenever that confrontation comes, the fire-power witnessed in the Gulf War in 1991 will seem like a fourth-of-July fireworks display in comparison:

"This is the word of the LORD concerning Israel. The LORD, who stretches out the heavens, who lays the foundation of the earth, and who forms the spirit of man within him, declares: 'I am going to make Jerusalem a cup that sends all the surrounding peoples reeling. Judah will be besieged as well as Jerusalem. On that day, when all the nations of the earth are gathered against her, I will make Jerusalem an immovable rock for all the nations. All who try to move it will injure themselves ... . On that day I will make the leaders of Judah like a firepot in a woodpile, like a flaming torch among sheaves. They will consume right and left all the surrounding peoples, but Jerusalem will remain intact in her place. The LORD will save the dwellings of Judah first, so that the

*honor of the house of David and of Jerusalem's inhabitants may
not be greater than that of Judah. On that day the LORD will
shield those who live in Jerusalem, so that **the feeblest among
them will be like David, and the house of David will be like God,
like the Angel of the LORD going before them. On that day I will
set out to destroy all the nations that attack Jerusalem"***
(Zech 12:1-3, 6-9 NIV).

It will be a display of destruction such as never witnessed in history's
war arena. The outcome has been pre-determined. Israel wins, and the
other nations lose. Israel is a destroying weapon in the LORD'S hand:

*"**You are my war club, my weapon for battle—with you I shatter
nations, with you I destroy kingdoms"***   (Jer 51:20 NIV).

*"**Rise and thresh**, O Daughter of Zion, for I will give you horns of
iron; I will give you hoofs of bronze and **you will break to pieces
many nations"***   (Micah 4:13 NIV).

Israel is the bait set in a trap for the nations. The bait is irresistible, and
the LORD waits patiently—He waits to spring the trap upon *"all the
nations of the earth,"* both the small and the great. Israel is bait, but she
remains precious to the LORD:

*"**For the LORD'S portion is His people; Jacob is the place of His
inheritance"***   (Deut 32:9).

It is **in** Jacob, the Jewish people, that the LORD has His inheritance.
The nations of the world and the New World Order are apparently
blissfully ignorant of what awaits them in Zion.

Just as David's conquests ushered in a reign of peace under Solomon,
so Israel's conquests will, finally, usher in King Jesus and His eternal
reign of peace.

Dear LORD,
You have kept Your promise to raise up David's Kingdom in the physical
realm. You have established the might of Israel again and raised up a
force to bring judgement upon the nations. Oh, LORD, in judgement
remember mercy. Open the eyes of our leaders before it is too late.
Even so, come, Lord Jesus! Amen.

20

THE
ETERNAL
CAPITAL

For the purposes of this book, the beginning of Jerusalem's history begins with the Israelite capture of the city as part of the conquest of Canaan around the year 1407 B.C. The Israelites did not, however, capture the *"Stronghold of Zion"* which was the fortified village of the Jebusites:

> *"As for the Jebusites, the inhabitants of Jerusalem, the children of Judah could not drive them out ..."* (Josh 15:63).

Every campaign undertaken by the children of Israel to dislodge the Jebusites was repulsed and the fortress appeared to be impregnable. The Jebusites became so confident that they ridiculed the efforts of the children of Israel. Some 400 years after the conquest, King David, Israel's warrior king, determined to change the status quo. He marched to Jerusalem with his army and laid siege to the fortress but was, like others before him, mocked by the men of Jebus. The Jebusites, however, had never faced the fighting power or tenacity for which David and his mighty men were famous. The following passage of Scripture says it all:

> *"And David and all Israel went to Jerusalem, which is Jebus, where the Jebusites were, the inhabitants of the land. Then the inhabitants of Jebus said to David, 'You shall not come in here.' Nevertheless David took the stronghold of Zion (that is, the City of David)"* (1 Chr 11:4&5).

No city or army withstood the might and ingenuity of David's men. The fortress was captured, and David, impressed with its ability to withstand would-be conquerors, established his headquarters there:

*"Then **David dwelt in the stronghold**; therefore they called it the City of David."*   (1 Chr 11:7).

David's kingdom continued to expand as he established his power and influence, *"from Dan to Beersheba—from the River to the land of the Philistines, as far as the border of Egypt,"* by means of his sword and bow. And it is recorded that in approximately 1000 B.C. he made Jerusalem capital of his kingdom.[1] It was not only David that made Jerusalem his headquarters, so too did the LORD:

*"**I have chosen Jerusalem**, that My name may be there ..."*
                                                    (2 Chr 6:6).

David, as Israel's most famous king, is remembered by Jews more for three great peaceful accomplishments than he is for his many wartime triumphs: He made Jerusalem the capital of the Jewish people, he brought up the Ark of the LORD to the city, and he made the preparations and gave the provision for building the temple.

Jerusalem became the seat of political government—*"the City of David"*—and it became the seat of religious government—*"the City of the Great King."* It remained Israel's political and religious capital throughout the Babylonian exile and the years of repressive occupation by foreign powers. Jerusalem ceased to be the capital of the Jewish people in 135 A.D. when the Romans renamed it *Ælia Capitolina* and banished the Jews from its precincts.

DIVIDED CITY

During the War of Independence in 1948, Jordan gained control of the Old City of Jerusalem, and, after the Arabs had sued for peace and a cease-fire was arranged, the Jordanians subsequently expelled all remaining Jewish residents of the Old City[2] and dynamited fifty-eight synagogues.[3] They also refused Jews access to Judaism's holiest site, the Western Wall, which was a betrayal of the negotiated cease-fire agreement that guaranteed the privilege.[4]

After the war Israel controlled what had become known as the "New City" which is the surrounding areas containing the more modern buildings and the commercial centre. It was a wholly divided city. Israel, nevertheless, established her government there, and, in 1950, formally declared Jerusalem as the "capital" of the State of Israel.

REUNIFICATION

In 1967 Jordan joined forces with four other Arab nations in another bid to obliterate the State of Israel and "rid the land of the Zionist presence." Israel defeated the five opposing armies and gained her greatest prize—the Old City of Jerusalem. Israel annexed this portion of captured territory and, in 1980, declared the entire unified city of Jerusalem to be the "undivided eternal capital of the Jewish people."

Nearly 3,000 years ago David's mighty men conquered the almost impregnable fortress of Zion and paved the way for it to become the capital of a great kingdom. The IDF conquered the ancient walled city on June 7, 1967, making way for the re-establishment of the ancient capital of King David. Jesus is *"the Root and the Offspring of David"* (Rev 22:16), and soon He is coming to rule and to reign in Jerusalem. His kingdom will be the greatest of all kingdoms.

NINE RE-ENACTMENTS

Each of the nine important events in Israel's history are, today, in the process of re-enactment. The land is being restored to the people, and the people are being restored to the land. The people are, also, being restored to the LORD. Jerusalem is restored to Israel, and the status of capital is restored to the city. And David's Kingdom is returning, too. When all things are fully restored Jesus, the Jewish Messiah and King, will return. Time, for this world and its inhabitants, is running out.

Dear LORD,
Once more Your city is preparing to receive her King. I long for that day, LORD. Surely You are *"coming quickly. Amen. Even so, come, Lord Jesus!"* And grant that I may be ready to receive You, also. Amen.

PART IV

PEACE!
PEACE!

"They have seduced My people, saying, 'Peace!' when there is no peace"

(Eze 13:10).

21

THE CONFLICT

The Arab-Israeli conflict has been the cause of great suffering. Many thousands of lives, of both Arabs and Israelis, have been lost. Between one and two million Jews and Arabs have been deprived of their personal property. Parents, wives and sweethearts grieve for loved ones, and a multitude of children mourn the loss of their fathers. The conflict has raged for decades, and an ever widening ripple effect brought the world to the brink of nuclear war in 1973. More sophisticated weapons with greater lethality are being introduced into the area each year in the millions of tonnes. The only ones who prosper are the weapons manufacturers and dealers who support the conflict, plus the newspapers, magazines and television networks which report the conflict; others just suffer. Millions of bullets have been fired, thousands of articles have been printed and hundreds of diplomatic "peace" missions have been undertaken, but the conflict goes on. It is time to seriously ask ourselves two questions:

a) What is the cause of the conflict?

b) Why have efforts to end the conflict failed?

A: THE CAUSE

If a survey were to be made among European, Western, Eastern and Asian nations as to the cause of the Arab-Israeli conflict, overwhelming public opinion would be that disputed ownership of the land is the cause of the trouble. This is the apparent reason, and scarcely a day passes without the news media propagating and enforcing this line of reasoning into the minds of the world's masses. No one will deny that there is a violent dispute between Israel and the Arab nations over land, the land that the LORD covenanted to give Israel as an inheritance. Chapter Ten gives Scriptural proof that the ownership of the land belongs to the LORD and possession is vested in Israel by deed of covenant—which other nations reject. Those that do not recognise the covenant attack the one who is party to it, and the party to the covenant ends up possessing more of the land that is subject to the covenant.

Thus the world's news media publishes interviews with both sides of the conflict. From the Arab point of view:

"The Arab states want a 'complete Israeli withdrawal' from occupied territories, including Jerusalem."[1]

And from the Israeli point of view:

"Where in the world would you find people who are ready to give up territory of their land, their homeland?"[2]

Therefore we promptly conclude that territorial dispute is the obvious reason for the conflict. It is the apparent reason but not the real reason. The real and actual is not always obvious to the mind or eye, especially if it is of a spiritual nature.

The Arab nations hold territory of 11,800,000 square kilometres (4,600,000 square miles). Israel, with captured territory included, holds only 88,000 square kilometres (34,000 square miles)! Israel is content to live on what land she holds and will not attack Arab states in order to regain what was given thousands of years ago. The Arab nations on the other hand are not content for Israel to live in their midst, and they continually attack her. Analysing the outcome of the Arab-Israeli wars we find that the territorial dispute is merely the chosen route by which the LORD is restoring the covenanted land back to Israel.

When rightly related to the LORD, even Palestinian Arabs understand the territorial dispute as a Christian-Palestinian-Arab publication demonstrates:

"Israel will very likely conquer the northern one-third of the Kingdom of Jordan and march all the way to the Euphrates River in Iraq."[3]

The LORD is after more from the Arab-Israeli conflict than restoration of the land, and this will become clear as we proceed.

With the help of both Arabs and Jews, Britain captured Palestine from the Turks in December 1917. The land was partitioned between the Arabs and Jews in November 1947. The Arabs received seventy-seven per cent of Palestine, and the Jews received only twenty-three per cent even though they outnumbered Arabs almost two to one in many areas. As the Jewish presence rose so did the intensity of the violence against them. War did not break out until the day following the declaration of the State of Israel in May 1948. There was great opposition to a larger Jewish presence in Palestine, but full-scale war came when the State was declared, which tells us that the actual State of Israel is a bigger contention than the land. Follow this conclusion with the famous speech by Anwar Sadat, the President of Egypt, who initiated the *Yom Kippur* War:

"I promise to crush Israel and return it to the 'humiliation and wretchedness established in the *Koran*.'"[4]

In that one short statement we have the real reason for the Arab-Israeli conflict—*Islam*! Israel raised her head once more on May 14, 1948, and now she must be returned again to the humiliation and wretchedness written of her in the *Koran*.

Anwar Sadat was a devout Muslim who spent his early years attending the village *kuttab*, an Islamic school —

"... where he learned to read and write and studied the *Koran*. It was the beginning of the lifelong religious faith that, in later years, left the familiar Muslim mark on his forehead from touching the floor in frequent prayer."[5]

Muslims believe that Christianity superseded Judaism and that *Islam* superseded Christianity. The Islamic people believe, beyond all else, that the *Koran* is the final and true revelation of God and that

Muhammad is His prophet. To say otherwise is to bring a mandatory death sentence in countries under *Sharia* (Islamic) law. Jews especially, but also Christians, are portrayed in the writings of the *Koran* as ignominious, and here lies the secret of the conflict.

The *Koran*, believed by Muslims to be the final and true revelation of God, holds Israel as non-existent and the Jews as an insidious people worthy only of contempt and punishment. The Bible, on the other hand, in both the Old and New Testaments, has the sure promise of a restored and vital Israel. The prospect of a Jewish state within Palestine, looming on the horizon during the time of the British mandate, caused Muslim hate to rise against the Jews as shown in these statements by Arab leaders:

"The Muslim world is duty bound to prevent a sovereign Jewish state from springing up in its midst."[6]

"The Arabs will launch a *Jihad* to prevent the establishment of a Jewish state in any portion of 'sacred Palestine.'"[7]

Jihad commenced, bullets flew, bombs exploded and Jews began to die in Palestine. An economic boycott against the Jews began in 1946 and continues with ever-intensifying pressure until the present day.

The advent of the re-created State of Israel in 1948 created the ultimate challenge to the Islamic world. It struck at the very heart of Islamic theology and undermined it. A re-created Israel proves the Bible to be true and the teaching of the *Koran* to be false. Not only does a re-created Israel thrust a sword through the heart of Islamic belief, but it also adds insult to the injury by being re-created in the very centre of the Islamic heartland! The size of the State of Israel is immaterial. This tiny speck on a world map is an affront to *Islam*, and no true Muslim will rest until Israel is obliterated. The honour of *Allah* has been sullied. *Allah* has been dispossessed of a portion of his land. Israel must be annihilated to restore that honour:

"The Arab nations should sacrifice up to ten million of their fifty million people, if necessary, to wipe out Israel. Israel to the Arab world is like a cancer to the human body. And the only way of remedy is to uproot it."[8]

ISLAM EXPOSED

Many people are under the impression that Jehovah, God of Jews and Christians, and *Allah*, god of the Arabs, are one and the same—this is incorrect. Jehovah is ridiculed by Muslims even in high school text books:

"If you knew the attributes which they attributed to their God, those which they wanted and those which they have adorned him with, then you would certainly be astounded. Jehovah, Lord of Hosts, Lord of Israel, commands them to smear their houses with sheep's blood in order to save their sons and let the Egyptians perish. He is a God who feels remorse for creating Adam and for setting Saul on the throne. He is bloodthirsty, fickle-minded, harsh and greedy ... he is loquacious and passionately fond of long speeches ... ."[9]

If we go to Arabia, to the roots of *Islam*, we find that in Mecca in a square, stone building called the *Kaabah* which, according to the *Koran*, was built by Adam, there were 360 *jinn* (idols, angels and demons), one of whom was named *Al-ilah*. Muhammad was exposed to the belief in *Al-ilah* from childhood. This deity commanded Muhammad to destroy all the idols in the *Kaabah*, and *Al-ilah*, "the god," became *Allah*, "God," and *Islam* ("submission"—to the will of *Allah*) was born. *Islam* is the only post-Christian religion and now the world's second largest religion. It is also the world's fastest growing religion. But the spirit behind it is demonic.

The holiest place for Muslims is the Great Mosque in Mecca. This mosque was built around the *Kaabah* which houses an occultic "black stone" said to have been given by the angel Gabriel to Ishmael. The second most holy site is the mosque in Medina, built upon the house of Muhammad after his death in 632 A.D. The third holiest place in the world is the mosque of *El Asque*, built over the site of the porch of Solomon on the Temple Mount in Jerusalem.

The porch of Solomon is the place where Jesus taught His disciples, the place that gave birth to the Christian Church and the place where the 3,000 souls were saved at Pentecost:

*"And Jesus walked in the temple, **in Solomon's porch**"* (Jn 10:23).

*"Now as the lame man who was healed held on to Peter and John,
all the people ran together to them **in the porch which is called
Solomon's**, greatly amazed"*   (Acts 3:11).

*"And through the hands of the apostles many signs and wonders
were done among the people. **And they were all with one accord
in Solomon's Porch**"*   (Acts 5:12).

The significance of this site for the Muslim world cannot be over-
estimated. It is of such exceptional value that it rates the world's third
holiest place for *Islam*. There are three extremely important reasons
why a mosque is built on this site for all the world to see. For the
Muslim, the mosque bears testimony that:

a)   Muhammad is greater than Jesus.
b)   *Islam* superseded Christianity spiritually.
c)   *Islam* defeated Christianity militarily.

The fourth holiest place for Muslims is the Umayyad mosque in
Damascus. Damascus was an important Christian city until Umar I
conquered it in the seventh century and defeated the Christian
Byzantines. It was in Antioch, in Syria, that the disciples of Jesus were
first called Christians (Acts 11:26). Antioch was destroyed by
earthquakes in 526 and 528 A.D. making Damascus the most important
Christian city outside of Jerusalem. Therefore, the fourth holiest Islamic
place, built on the site of the Basilica of St. John the Baptist, also
testifies to the Muslim of the superiority of *Islam* over Christianity.

In Jerusalem, only a matter of yards separate the *El Asque* Mosque
from the Mosque of Omar, the familiar golden-domed mosque that is
better known as the "Dome of the Rock." It is said that it was here that
Muhammad ascended up to heaven on his white horse. But here, under
the golden dome, stands the rock upon which Abraham, in a test of
obedience, was willing to offer Isaac as a sacrifice. It was through Isaac,
the son of promise, that all the world was to be blessed. It was on this
great rock on Mount Moriah that the sacrifice nearly took place:

*"**Take now your son, your only son Isaac**, whom you love, and go
to the land of Moriah, and offer him there as a burnt offering on
one of the mountains of which I shall tell you"*   (Gen 22:2).

*"Then **they came to the place of which God had told him**. And Abraham built an altar there and placed the wood in order; and he bound Isaac his son and laid him on the altar, upon the wood. And Abraham stretched out his hand and took the knife to slay his son"* (Gen 22:9&10).

The LORD was testing Abraham's obedience and stopped him from carrying out the sacrifice, providing a ram instead. But this is not the only significance of the rock under the golden dome. At the height of King David's power, a deadly disease was destroying the people of Israel, and the prophet Gad came to David with the remedy:

*"Gad came that day to David and said to him, 'Go up, **erect an altar to the LORD on the threshing floor of Araunah the Jebusite.'** So David, according to the word of Gad, went up as the LORD commanded"* (2 Sam 24:18&19).

*"Then Araunah said, 'Why has my lord the king come to his servant?' And David said, '**To buy the threshing floor from you, to build an altar to the LORD,** that the plague may be withdrawn from the people'"* (2 Sam 24:21).

*"And **David built there an altar to the LORD,** and offered burnt offerings and peace offerings, and called on the LORD; **and He answered him from heaven by fire on the altar** of burnt offering"* (1 Chr 21:26).

The rock upon which Isaac was almost sacrificed was part of Araunah's threshing floor which David purchased in order to build an altar for sacrifice to the LORD. After David had built the altar and offered the sacrifices, the LORD answered by fire from heaven. This meant, in real terms, that "This is the place of the LORD." And because the LORD answered by fire this site was chosen for the temple:

*"Now **Solomon began to build the house of the LORD at Jerusalem on Mount Moriah, where the LORD had appeared to his father David, at the place that David had prepared on the threshing floor of Araunah the Jebusite"*** (2 Chr 3:1).

Placing a great mosque over this rock has enormous significance for the Muslim world. Abraham had a son, Ishmael, by his wife's Egyptian maid, Hagar. This son is not recognised by the LORD—only Isaac was, the son borne by Sarah, Abraham's wife:

*"Take now your son, **your only son Isaac**, whom you love, and **go to the land of Moriah** ..."*   (Gen 22:2).

But Islamic theology teaches that it was Ishmael, not Isaac, through whom the promises were to come and that it was Ishmael, not Isaac, that was offered upon the rock on Mount Moriah! The Muslim feast of *El-Dahiya* (Feast of Sacrifice) commemorates Abraham's attempt to sacrifice Ishmael (not Isaac) and is the most important feast of the Muslim calendar. Having the rock under Muslim control signifies to the Muslim that this is fact. Having the site of the Jewish temple underneath the golden dome signifies to them that Judaism has been superseded and that *Islam* is supreme.

One belief that Christians and Jews hold in common is the coming of the Messiah to the Mount of Olives:

*"And in that day **His feet will stand on the Mount of Olives**, which faces Jerusalem on the east. **And the Mount of Olives shall be split in two**, from east to west, making a very large valley; half of the mountain shall move toward the north and half of it toward the south"*   (Zech 14:4).

Both Christian and Jewish tradition says that the Messiah will cross over from the Mount of Olives and come to the Temple Mount by way of the Golden Gate. The Golden Gate has been bricked up by the Muslims because *Islam* teaches that Muhammad was the great and last messenger. The Golden Gate is venerated by many Christians, and, to stop Christians from reaching the blocked up Gate, a Muslim cemetery has been established in front of the Gate to deny access to it. No non-Muslim is allowed into that cemetery on pain of death, and there are armed guards on the other side of the Gate to stop non-Muslims from approaching it from the Temple Mount area. This establishes, for the Muslim mind, Islamic supremacy over Christian and Jewish belief.

This belief in Islamic supremacy is manifested by the building of mosques on the high places or on sites holy to other religions. In England alone more than one hundred churches have now been turned into mosques. In 1989 New Zealand hosted a forty-five-nation Islamic conference. The spread of *Islam* today is as great as that during the seventh century, and spokesmen for the one billion Muslims around the world state plainly the objective desire of the Muslim world:

"Our goal is not an Islamic state but an Islamic World Republic."[10]

"The governments of the world should know that *Islam* cannot be defeated. *Islam* will be victorious in all the countries of the world, and *Islam* and the teachings of the *Koran* will prevail all over the world."[11]

And this can only be brought about by *Jihad*—holy war:

"To struggle in the cause of *Allah* with pen, speech, or sword is *Jihad*."[12]

The sword brings results faster than either the pen or speech; therefore, practically everywhere that Muslims are found in large numbers, violence is found also. Every country named in the following list have, within the space of just a few weeks, been reported by the world's news media as having outbreaks of violence involving Muslims: Afghanistan, Algeria, Armenia, Azerbaijan, Bangladesh, Egypt, Fiji, France, India, Israel, Jordan, Kenya, Lebanon, Libya, Morocco, Niger, Pakistan, the Philippines, Sudan, Tunisia and Turkey. Unrest is everywhere within and without the Muslim world. If an area is not under *Islam, Jihad* is waged to bring it under *Islam*. If it is already under *Islam,* the fanatical Muslim brotherhoods fight to bring a stricter *Islam.* There were over 800 international terrorist incidents that claimed 2,223 casualties in 1985 alone. The facts and figures indicate that most were sponsored by fanatical Muslim groups.[13] Casualty figures have not yet been released for 1991, but international terrorist acts exceeded 4,000. Again, everything indicates that the majority of incidents had Muslim involvement. It is called "The Sword of *Islam*" due to its mania to wage war and shed blood. The Ayatullah Khomeini, the fanatical leader who ousted the Shah and became the leader of Iran in his stead, said:

"The purest joy in *Islam* is to kill and be killed for *Allah*."[14]

He merely follows in the footsteps of Muhammad, the founder of *Islam,* who said, "A day and night of fighting on the frontier is better than a month of fasting and prayer." For a Muslim to die for *Islam* is to ensure immediate entry into paradise which holds the promise of —

"... abundant sensual pleasures ... perpetual luxury, physical comfort, food, clear water, mansions, servants, lovely maidens and virgins."[15]

For this most Muslims are quite willing to die, especially since the majority of them live in poverty, by Western standards.

B: FAILURE

Why have efforts to end the conflict failed? Because those trying to end the conflict do not understand the conflict! As long ago as December 8, 1947, it was reported:

"Last week the United Nations General Assembly after much anxious hesitation settled the thirty-year-old Palestine dispute. They voted, thirty-three to thirteen, to partition Palestine into two states, Arab and Jewish."[16]

Not understanding the dispute caused a presumptuous statement to be circulated throughout the world. On the contrary, the partitioning of Palestine led to worse and worse violence. Being aware of the underlying cause of the conflict, we are able to understand that any "peace" effort, including the "International Peace Conference," under the auspices of the world's great powers (all of whom have benefited tremendously from the conflict), cannot bring a lasting peace. What the Arab states hope to bring about from the so-called "Peace Conference" is to force Israel into handing back the land lost in their abortive wars. If the proposed "Palestinian" state could be set up next to a tiny Israel, which would have a long, narrow corridor only fourteen kilometres (less than nine miles) wide, then a full scale war would have the possibility of dividing Israel quickly by choking it at the corridor. This would make the likelihood of an Arab victory more likely than ever before.

Syria hopes to regain the Golan heights, but Egypt is avoiding any negotiations regarding a return of land as this would mean gaining back the Gaza Strip with another million mouths to feed. Israel would like to rid herself of the Gaza problem, but, when the Sinai was returned to

Egypt following the Camp David accords, **Egypt refused to take back the Gaza Strip** which had been under its control prior to the 1967 war! Egypt is playing the "peace" game, too, and the Egyptian Minister of Defence was publicly reported as saying, a few years ago:

"Israel is our only real enemy, and when Syria attacks we will give it all the help we can."

That statement was embarrassing to Egypt's President Hosni Mubarak, who was negotiating with President Reagan at the time for more U.S. economic aid, so he had the newspapers recalled. President Mubarak himself has since vowed ("peace treaty" with Israel or not) —

"... to support any Arab state in a war against Israel."[17]

Unarmed Israeli tourists have been gunned-down by Egyptian soldiers and others have been arrested and beaten by Egyptian police. Electric shocks were put in the mouths of some and they were told repeatedly:

"There is no peace between Israel and Egypt and you are Jews and you are dirt."[18]

The Arab purpose for the "Peace Conference" is to gain a launching pad for the next war against Israel. The more land Israel is forced to return the less there will be to fight for. There is no lessening of the desire to eliminate Israel; the Arabs are just getting more clever at the way they wage war. The following statements reflect current Muslim-Arab sentiments:

"Israel will exist and continue to exist until *Islam* eliminates it, just as it eliminated what preceded it" (referring to the defeat of the Crusaders).[19]

"What was taken away by force cannot be recovered except by force! ... we are committed to ... principles: no recognition of Israel, no peace with Israel, no negotiations with Israel ... ."[20]

"We shall never call for or accept a negotiated peace. We shall only accept war—*Jihad*—the holy war. We have resolved to drench the lands of Palestine and Arabia with the blood of the infidels or to accept martyrdom for the glory of *Allah*."[21]

"This will be a war of extermination and a momentous massacre which will be spoken of like the Mongolian massacres and the Crusades. No Jew will be left alive."[22]

"The Jews in Palestine must be exterminated. There can be no option for those of us who revere the name of *Allah*. There will only be *Jihad*."[23]

"The Zionist conquest of Palestine is an affront to Muslims. This colonialist barbarism cannot and will not be tolerated. There can be no compromise until every Jew is dead and gone."[24]

"The entire Jewish population must be destroyed or be driven into the sea. *Allah* has bestowed upon us the rare privilege of finishing what Hitler only began. Let the *Jihad* begin. Murder the Jews. Murder them all."[25]

How true today are the recorded words of the psalmist 3,000 years ago:

"They have said, 'Come, and let us cut them off from being a nation, that the name of Israel may be remembered no more"
(Psalms 83:4).

Thus far, since the creation of the state of Israel, there have been five major wars. As stated earlier, territorial conflict has been the means of restoring the Promised Land to Israel. Of necessity there must be more wars in the future because Israel is not yet in possession of all of the land promised in Genesis chapter fifteen. But the LORD is after much more than just restoring the land through the conflict.

As we saw in Chapter Nineteen, each war had a multiple of Arab armies pitted against Israel. One war had at least 1,200,000 troops facing Israel's 300,000. Israel has routed the enemy and won every single war. A call has been made for a "united Arab army to confront Israel." A united Arab army could involve up to 5,000,000 troops, a formidable figure indeed, but when it occurs Israel is still assured of victory because the LORD desires to use this conflict to accomplish something other than a return of Israel's land.

Let us not even think for one moment that the LORD desires to wipe out the Arab nations. This is so far from the truth. The Arab people are also very precious to God; He merely uses situations for His own ends, as we see in the following example:

"Now when Joshua was near Jericho, he looked up and saw a man standing in front of him with a drawn sword in his hand. Joshua went up to him and asked, 'Are you for us or for our enemies?' 'Neither,' he replied, 'but as commander of the army of the LORD I have now come.' Then Joshua fell face down to the ground in reverence, and asked him, 'What message does my Lord have for his servant?' The commander of the LORD's army replied, 'Take off your sandals, for the place where you are standing is holy." And Joshua did so" (Josh 5:13-15 NIV).

This is an interesting passage for a number of reasons. First, there is only one other passage in Scripture where a person is told to take the sandals from his feet:

"When the LORD saw that he turned aside to look, God called to him from the midst of the bush and said, 'Moses, Moses!' And he said, 'Here I am.' Then He said, 'Do not draw near this place. Take your sandals off your feet, for the place where you stand is holy ground'" (Ex 3:4&5).

As Moses was standing in the presence of Deity, so also was Joshua. Second, the passage is interesting because the Commander of the LORD'S army had nothing to say to Joshua, the commander of the Israelite army, except for him to take his sandals off! Third, we know that the LORD had promised to drive out the inhabitants of the land and to deliver them over to defeat by the children of Israel (Deut 7:2,20,22-24). Yet when Joshua, not knowing who He was, asked the Commander of the LORD'S army if He was on Israel's side or the Arab's side, He said "neither," (Hebrew *lo* meaning "no," but more idiomatically—"neither") even though He was there to ensure an Israelite victory! We see the total impartiality of the LORD in situations like the conquest of Canaan and the Arab-Israeli conflict. The LORD had every intention of helping the Israelites conquer Canaan and has every intention of helping Israel defeat the Arab nations, **but He was not then, and is not now, against the other side!**

The LORD is using the re-creation of the State of Israel to bring about a confrontation of major proportions. The spirit of *Islam* is the greatest evil force in the world today. The Spirit of the risen Christ is

the greatest force in the entire universe! The spirit of *Islam* is on a collision course with the Spirit of the risen Christ, and we need to remember one thing—**God never loses** in any confrontation. It is through the Arab-Israeli conflict that the LORD intends to bring the Muslim world to Himself.

One Arab leader, Anwar Sadat, President of Egypt, was tiring of the "wasteful confrontation" with Israel. Nevertheless, he launched the 1973 *Yom Kippur* war that caused terrible Israeli casualties. Although Egypt was beaten in the war and lost further territory, Anwar Sadat claimed a moral victory and felt that he had restored Egyptian self respect. A museum was built on the road to Cairo depicting the opening hours of the October war with the Egyptian infantry swarming over Israel's Bar-Lev line—the film footage of the dead or falling Israelis in the bunkers is authentic. Egypt is able to daily relive the crossing of the Suez Canal, its greatest military victory in the country's modern history. The museum implies that Egypt actually won the war! With some restored pride, Anwar Sadat formally made peace with Israel on March 26, 1979. He died in a hail of bullets from the guns of the Muslim Brotherhood on October 19, 1981. He died because he was a "traitor" to *Islam.*

Egypt's peace treaty enraged other Arab leaders who accused Sadat of treachery for abandoning the struggle against Israel. Egypt was thrown out of the Arab League, and eighteen Arab nations imposed economic and political sanctions against Cairo, most of which are still in force today. The only Arab leader to make peace with Israel died from the bullets of his own people. Egypt still has "peace" with Israel, a tenuous peace, a peace that will only last until a more opportune time. Only the Prince of Peace, Himself, can bring peace to the region. An exchange of territory will not bring peace; it will take the exchange of hearts. The LORD is patient, but the appointed time and season for the confrontation draws nearer with the passing of each day.

Dear LORD,
I do not understand Your ways, and I am grateful that I am not required to. Your ways are too lofty for one such as I. Bring the Muslim people out of darkness into Your light, LORD. Wash away the hate in their hearts with the blood of Your Son, Jesus. Grant that these cousins, the Jews and the Arabs, might soon embrace in the love of the Messiah—*"the Lamb of God Who takes away the sin of the world."* Amen.

22

THE PALESTINIAN QUESTION

This chapter contains some of the most important information regarding Israel and the "Palestinian problem" that you will ever read. It is essential that Christians understand the essence of the "Palestinian problem," and until we understand the nature of it our hearts cannot join with the heart and purpose of the LORD. He needs us. He requires our prayers. We have a responsibility to enlist as intercessors and engage in prayer. And it is my prayer that you might read this with a mind freely focused and that the Holy Spirit might enlighten your understanding.

It cannot be denied that there is a "Palestinian" problem today. Wherever one happens to be in the world, there is persistent assailment by the news media about either the plight or the right of the "Palestinian." We are going to examine some of the workings of this problem, but let it be stated at this juncture that it is not really a "problem" but rather a war, and it is a war that the Arab people are winning at this time. Each time the Arabs have taken up arms against Israel they have been severely beaten. Having learned from these experiences, they began, in December 1987, what has become known as the *intifada* (Arabic "to shake-off"). The strategy of the *intifada* has been to gain as much publicity as possible by keeping women, children and the elderly in the limelight while killing or maiming hundreds of Israeli civilians by using what is classed in Israeli war-protocols as "soft" weapons (guns, grenades etc. are classed as "hard" weapons). "Soft" weapons include rocks capable of crushing skulls to pulp, a stick or shortened broom handle with numerous sharp protruding nails which is used for slashing faces, petrol bombs, axes, knives etc. Until the law was changed in late 1992, Israeli soldiers and police were not able to retaliate or defend themselves against "soft" weapons. Even when being attacked by a knife- or axe-wielding Arab, the soldier or policeman had to first fire two bullets into the air and after that was only allowed to fire at the attacker's legs. Consequently, numbers of armed Israeli soldiers, policemen and policewomen died at the hands of Arabs. Had the Arabs taken up conventional arms against Israel the *intifada* would have been over within one week instead of dragging on violently for years.

The greatest and most powerful weapon that has been used by the "Palestinians" during the *intifada* (with devastating effect) is the foreign news media, against which Israel has absolutely no defence. It has been stated previously that Jerusalem has the third largest press bureau in the entire world. That means to say that the third highest concentration of journalists in the world reside in Jerusalem, and they are all looking for a story that might keep their employers happy. And we saw in Chapter Thirteen who the employers were and what pains are taken to trouble Israel. The anti-Israel media, therefore, has played along with the "Palestinians" and given the "problem" constant coverage according to "Palestinian" dictates. This has affected practically every nation in the world and caused many of them to distance themselves further from Israel. When Israeli authorities tried to counteract the damage by restricting the access of television camera crews in the "occupied territories" the major American television networks distributed "Super-8 video cameras" to the "Palestinians" themselves.[1] The reader can imagine for himself what type of "factual and balanced news" was beamed into millions of American homes! Jim Lederman, an American journalist with over twenty years of experience in living and reporting in the Middle East, writes:

> "Media news coverage is a marketplace. Those who participate in it behave no differently from farmers who come to town on Thursdays to sell their produce or brokers who work on Wall Street. Each is out to buy, sell, beg, barter, invest, or steal for his or her own defense or gain."[2]

Little close attention is paid by viewers to the news coverage of violent clashes between "Palestinians" and Israelis and the numbers of young children, teenagers and women involved go almost unnoticed. Males in their late twenties to late fifties are not involved. It is the women, children and elderly that bring sympathy for the "problem."

One American lady observed recently concerning the *intifada*: "I have seen the same Arab woman on television three times!" The reason for this is that some television crews are not at all embarrassed to treat the world's news as a cheap stage production by paying willing "actors, actresses and extras" in order to produce "news" for their employers. They produce and direct their own "scenes of violent protest:"

"First it was CBS's *60 Minutes* crew, an ingenious bunch. Back in the 1970s, years before the intifada, they were accused by Israeli police of paying Arab boys to set tires on fire for the cameras.
During the intifada, Japanese television crews in Gaza were caught staging a rock-throwing assault on passing jeeps. They paid even more than the German crews in Judea-Samaria."[3]

An Australian television crew was also observed asking young "Palestinians" not to throw rocks until they had their cameras in place. Numbers of crews from all over the world are guilty of the same things. No shame or embarrassment is expressed, only the newsman's famous line, "We just report the news as we see it."

The free publicity given by the media has been worth billions of dollars to the PLO terrorist organisation and has placed the "Palestinian problem" on the front pages of the world's major newspapers and magazines and also on the prime-time slots of television news programs. The minds of the world's population have been fed a pre-packaged, pre-cooked and pre-digested diet of "poor Arab-nasty Israeli" meals, and "brave David brings down Goliath the giant Philistine" has been replaced by "Jewish bully beats up Arab kid!"

It is a well known fact that the one who controls your information, controls your judgement and, ultimately, your actions. What has happened during the past few years with Israel bears out the truth of this. But the isolation of Israel by the nations and their rejection of her are necessary to the plan of God, and, whereas the media plays into the hands of the "Palestinians" to effect the nations, the nations are themselves playing into the hands of the LORD.

The "Palestinian" problem is really part and parcel of "The Conflict" which was dealt with in the last chapter. It is the continual struggle by Muslims for an "Islamic State" that causes the "problem." The great majority of "Palestinians" who have died during the *intifada* have been killed by their own people, not by Israel:

> "More than 80 percent of the [*intifada*] killings in the territories are perpetrated by Palestinians against other Palestinians."[4]

Hundreds of "Palestinian" Arabs have died brutal deaths at the hands of fellow "Palestinians." Radical Muslims have been executing drug dealers, prostitutes and any person considered a bad influence on society. The definition of a bad influence on society has been loosened to include people simply working in a government school or hospital. Even a nurse was dragged from a hospital's operating room into a corridor and beaten to death. A reign of terror operates and people fear for their lives:

> "A 37 year old Arab requested the Police to put him in prison. He told the judge that his house had been burned down and that a masked assailant had endeavoured to stab him. He had also been stoned. He preferred prison to a life of terror."[5]

Israel becomes the scapegoat for the killings. All the murder victims are placed under the rubric of "Israeli collaborators" and thus the blame is shifted to the Zionist enemy. It is not the purpose of this chapter to pay much attention to the Islamic nature of the "problem," but if the "problem" had to be filed under a single category, it would most certainly be placed in the slot marked "*Islam.*" Disregarding the religious aspect still leaves us with a complex situation, and we will work through the "problem" piece by piece.

PALESTINIAN?

In this chapter, thus far, "Palestinian" has been intentionally placed within inverted commas. We need to work the word out from between those commas by an understanding of the word "Palestinian." We bandy the word "Palestinian" around without much idea of what we are saying. First, "Palestine" is the Anglicised form of the Latin *Palæstina*, which means "Philistia," the country of the "Philistines." Therefore, when we say "Palestinian" we are really saying "Philistine." Second, "Palestinian" is a comparatively recent word and is used liberally now to capture our attention for the situation in the Middle East.

Throughout the British mandate, the Jews living in Palestine were always carefully referred to as "Palestinian Jews" by the British. This was done in order not to offend the Arabs. The Arabs, who came mainly from Syria, Egypt and what is now known as Jordan, scorned the name and were simply referred to as "Arabs." After the creation of the State of Israel in 1948, the "Palestinian Jews" became "Israeli Jews" and the name "Palestinian" became almost defunct. A few Arabs did pick up the name "Palestinian" as a way of laying claim to the land, but it was an unpopular practice.

During the 1948 war it was the Arabs of Trans-Jordan (now known as Jordan), that fought Israel for most of the area under dispute today. It was the Jordanians that had control of the West Bank after the war, and it was Jordan that annexed it in 1950, placing it under Jordanian sovereignty until it was lost to Israel in 1967. In 1968, King Hussein of Jordan first made his now famous statement:

"Jordan is Palestine and Palestine is Jordan."[6]

King Hussein was not the only Arab to make such a statement. Yasser Arafat himself, the leader of the PLO terrorist organisation and self-styled "President of Palestine," said in 1974:

"What you call Jordan is actually Palestine."[7]

However, as the Arab-Israeli conflict continued, King Hussein, suffering from a convenient, short-term memory loss, made another statement in 1989, in which he said:

"Israel seeks to solve its problem by saying that Jordan is Palestine."

Others, including the media, have since picked this up and use it as if it were their own original thinking and justified their anti-Israel statements. But the facts of the matter are that the same people—Jordanian citizens, living in the same areas that Israel captured from Jordan, have, for political and propaganda purposes, suddenly changed from Jordanian identity to Palestinian identity.

The following magazine excerpts reinforce the truths presented:

"In 1920, the League of Nations made Britain the mandatory power in Palestine, effective in 1922. The Mandate, in line with the Balfour Declaration, provided for the establishment of a Jewish national home in all or any part of Palestine. The British, in violation of the Balfour Declaration and of the Mandate, divided the country into two parts. They granted the area east of the Jordan River to the Hashemite tribes, thus excluding it from Jewish settlement. They limited the Jewish National Home to [within] the 23% remaining west of the Jordan River.

In its War of Independence, against overwhelming odds, the newly formed Israel Defense Forces, in what must be considered almost a Biblical miracle, were able to defeat five combined Arab armies. Transjordan, however, succeeded in pushing westward across the Jordan River ... occupying Judea and Samaria ... and they stayed in that occupation until they attacked Israel in 1967 and were defeated in the Six-Day War. During its 19 years of occupation, Transjordan, now named 'Jordan,' systematically removed all Jews from the territory. Jewish holy places were profaned and destroyed.

A homeland for Palestinians? Of course, they deserve one. They have such a country. It's Jordan (77% of the British Mandate). Jordan is Arab Palestine, just as Israel is Jewish Palestine. Never in history has there been an Arab state in Judea and Samaria, and there certainly was never any mention of it during the 19 years of Transjordanian occupation. King Hussein himself has said: 'The truth is that Jordan is Palestine and Palestine is Jordan.'"[8]

A correction needs to be made, however, to the number of attacking armies mentioned—there were actually seven Arab nations defeated and not five. A quotation from each of two authoritative sources should dispel any doubts on this matter:

"May 14 ... the whole world held its breath anticipating the entry of seven Arab armies into Palestine ... ."[9]

"And this day in 1948 as Israel faced its enemies there were seven nations opposing her ... ."[10]

The correct number of armies also serves to draw our attention to the LORD'S involvement in Israel's conflict. It directs us to a significant parallel with the conquest of Canaan, namely, that *"seven nations greater and mightier than you"* (Deut 7:1) would be driven out. And each of the seven nations in 1948 were larger and better equipped than Israel. But, returning to the magazine article, I concur whole-heartedly with the writer that there is a "Palestinian" state in existence, and that state is Jordan. And, when it suited them, both King Hussein and Yasser Arafat publicly made this known. I also agree that there has never been an Arab state in what Israel calls "Judea and Samaria" and what the world calls the "West Bank." Neither is there any provision in Biblical prophecy for one to be created, and if one is forced into existence I believe it will just as soon be annihilated. A prominent Israeli figure adds his comments on the issue of a "Palestinian" state:

"Jordan is the only Palestine there will ever be ... Jordan is 77% of Palestine, as it was under the British until they split it into Trans-jordan and the area that is our country now."[11]

As an interesting side-note, those seeking to bring forth a Palestinian-Arab state call themselves "Palestinians"—"Philistines." It was the Philistines that King David fought most often. They were a constant irritation to Israel, but in the end they were either destroyed or subjugated under Israeli rule.

REFUGEES

In exactly the same way as there is a Palestinian "problem" so, also, is there a refugee "problem." And as the Palestinian problem is part of the overall strategy of Muslim war against Israel so, too, is the refugee problem. By the constant barrage of extreme one-sided and distorted news items concerning the "plight" of Palestinian refugees world opinion is formed, and judgement rules in favour of the Palestinians while Israel is subjected to further criticism and penalties.

"When the world speaks of the inalienable rights of the 590,000 refugees that fled Israel in 1948 and 1967, they irrationally forget the more than 850,000 Jewish refugees that fled Arab nations from 1948-1973. Of the 850,000 Jewish refugees from ten Arab nations, not a one has received a penny in return for the inestimable properties left behind. While the Arabs who left Palestine were, on the whole, peasants from primitive and underdeveloped areas, some of the Jewish refugees left fortunes, businesses and lands in the countries from which they fled."[12]

These figures are substantiated in an article by a member of the editorial staff of the "Jerusalem Post." This publication, far from being biased, was featured by the BBC World Service program, "Great Newspapers of the World," in the summer of 1991. They described the "Jerusalem Post" as "one of the leading and most influential newspapers of the world." The article states:

"The losses by the expropriated Jews who left Arab countries were sudden and total; the Jews took next to nothing. In the Arab exodus, the rich Palestinians went in early waves, taking as much of their property as they could. No one was prevented from taking anything.

By the most conservative estimates, the value of homes, businesses, banks, real estate and other assets owned by the Jews of Iraq and Egypt alone amounted to billions of dollars. (In 1952, financial expert, Dr Edmund Roth, dispatched by the Jewish Agency, calculated Jewish losses in just the Maghreb countries as reaching seven billion dollars, which obviously would be much more today). There is no valid comparison in value with property abandoned by local Arabs in the wars (and duly registered by the authorities concerned).[13]

What is made clear from the above is that an irrevocable "de facto" exchange of population took place to the overwhelming benefit of the Arab countries. The Arab attack in 1948 created two concurrent refugee problems, but due to the Western news media everyone in the world knows only about Arab refugees. The refugees flowed in two directions, but justice is demanded only for the Arab. Arab "justice," however, does not demand only that the Arabs be compensated for loss of property but also that Israel be replaced by an Islamic state.

REFUGEE TREATMENT

Concerning the treatment of refugees, one is again constantly subjected to television film clips and newspaper and magazine photographs (some genuine and others not) of the squalid living conditions of the Palestinian refugees. Many refugees living in camps do, indeed, live in squalid rat-infested conditions, but that is not the fault of Israel. First, many Middle Eastern Arabs have little concept of health or sanitation, and open or no sewerage has been a way of life for generations. Second, Israel did not build the refugee camps—the Arabs did. Third, Israel has tried repeatedly to rehouse Palestinian refugees into better conditions. The following information is taken from an official information release in January, 1988, by the Israeli Embassy in Wellington, New Zealand. It was released to the public in an effort to counteract the negative New Zealand press:

"Recent events in the territories have cast attention on the poor conditions prevailing in the Arab refugee camps, especially in the Gaza District. When Israel entered Judea-Samaria and the Gaza District in 1967, the inhabitants in the camps were found, after 19 years of Arab rule, to be living in the same abject squalor and misery as had existed in 1949.

Since 1970, Israel has been engaged in a consistent effort to improve the living conditions there. Beginning in that year, plans were drawn up and steps were taken to improve the situation of the refugees, and provide them with proper housing and an infrastructure of services. Nine residential projects were built, housing some ten thousand families who chose to leave the camps. Each family was given a plot of land, and more than 70 percent of the families built their own homes according to their needs and preferences. The new neighbourhoods were built on State land within Municipal areas near the camps, and each was provided with its own network of electricity, water, sanitation, roads, paved sidewalks and developed surroundings. In each neighbourhood, public buildings – schools, health clinics, shopping centres and mosques – were built.

The policy continues. A refugee who wishes today to leave the camp is given a plot of land, chooses his own type of dwelling and construction plan, receives a building permit from the Municipal authorities who are responsible for supervising construction, and becomes the full property owner once the building is completed, his property being registered in the Land Register.

With the limited means and resources at its disposal, Israel cannot resolve this most difficult problem on its own. However, by initiating and going ahead with this refugee rehabilitation programme, Israel seeks to show that a solution to the problem is feasible.

Since 1971, a little-noticed U.N. Resolution on the Gaza Strip has
been annually adopted, most recently on October 30, 1987. The
resolution states *inter alia*:

> 'The General Assembly ... reiterates strongly its demand
> that Israel desist from the removal and resettlement of
> Palestine refugees in the Gaza Strip ...'.

This year's vote on the resolution was: 150 for; 2 (Israel, the United
States) against; 3 (Costa Rica, Liberia, Zaire) abstaining.

A similar annual Resolution on the West Bank, also adopted again on
October 30, 1987, states *inter alia*:

> 'The General Assembly ..., alarmed ... by Israel's plans to
> remove and resettle the Palestine refugees of the West Bank
> and to destroy their camps ... calls once again upon Israel
> to abandon those plans and to refrain from any action that
> leads to the removal and resettlement of Palestine refugees
> in the West Bank ...'.

On this resolution the vote was: 145 for; 2 (Israel, the United States)
against; 7 (Costa Rica, El Salvador, Equatorial Guinea, Central
African Republic, Ivory Coast, Liberia, Zaire) abstaining.

Is it not ironic that many of those who preach about the need to
overcome the plight in the camps have repeatedly lent a hand to U.N.
Resolutions which would, if implemented, perpetuate the
problem?"[14]

The UN does not want the refugees out of the camps, it wants Israel
out of the land. The Palestinian refugee problem is political. It is a
weapon used against Israel, and the suffering of refugees is of no concern to those who use that weapon. From time to time, Arab leaders
have a twinge of conscience and actually publish their part in the
conspiracy of suffering:

"The Arab armies entered Palestine to protect the Palestinians from
the Zionist tyranny [sic], but instead they abandoned them, forced
them to emigrate and to leave their homeland, imposed upon them a
political and ideological blockade and threw them into ghettos in

which the Jews used to live in Eastern Europe. For seventeen years, the Arab radio stations broadcast their intentions of returning the refugees to their homes. They did not throw the Jews into the sea, nor did they return the refugees to their homes."[15]

"Since 1948 it is we who have demanded the return of the refugees while it is we who have made them leave. We have rendered them dispossessed. We have accustomed them to begging. We have participated in lowering their moral and social level. Then we exploited them in executing crimes of murder, arson, and throwing bombs at men, women and children."[16]

"The Arab States encouraged Palestinian Arabs to leave their homes temporarily in order to be out of the way of the Arab invasion armies."[17]

The Arab people know full well what caused the refugee problem:

"For the flight—it is our leaders who are responsible. They instilled fear and terror into the hearts of the Arabs of Palestine until they fled, leaving their homes and their properties to the enemy."[18]

And the refugees themselves also know why they are in the camps:

"We, the refugees, have the right to address the members of the Arab League and to declare: We left our homeland on the strength of false promises by crooked leaders of the Arab States."[19]

Israel has repeatedly extended a helping hand to the Palestinians:

"Almost ten percent of all the Arabs who fled in 1948 were permitted to return under the family reunion scheme, as were about 70,000 of the approximately 200,000 1967 refugees. These refugees ended up in neighbouring zones where the same language, religion, culture, history and ethnic—even blood-kinship prevailed. Their fate was to be denied resettlement, to be consigned instead by their Arab brethren to camps and (with the exception of Jordan) refused even a vestige of citizenship. By contrast, the approximately 200,000 Palestinians who chose to stay in the Jewish state have citizenship and rights beyond that enjoyed by nationals of Arab lands. Today, they represent more than sixteen per cent of the voting population of this democracy. The refugees, meanwhile, have been callously allowed to rot in their camps by Arab decree, while offers by Israel to rehouse them more suitably in Gaza have been rejected."[20]

Israel has consistently lost the "war of words" concerning the refugee issue and is frustrated at every turn in her endeavour to help remedy the situation. Taking up the publicised admission of guilt from the Arabs themselves, an Israeli newspaper article addressed James Baker, the United States Secretary of State in the Bush administration. The article suggested that he say to the Arab nations:

"Friends, the plight of these Arab refugees was caused by you; and you, by your own admission, have perpetuated it:

By your consistent refusal to accept the existence of the State of Israel in what you regard as the 'abode of *Islam*;'

By waging five aggressive wars against Israel—and then demanding that she give up those very areas from which your aggression was launched;

By your inhuman refusal to countenance resettlement of your Arab brothers, in order to perpetuate their wretched conditions as a weapon against Israel. You have perpetuated their bleak despair, their hatred, their extremism and their terrorism; and the world has suffered, too.

You have contributed only a fraction—in 1985, less than two per cent—to Unwra's funds for the support of refugees."[21]

Indeed, it is a fact that Israel has contributed more to the UN and other relief funds than have Kuwait, Egypt, Iraq, Jordan or Syria."[22]

It is also fact that the large majority of Israel's 800,000 Arab citizens prefer Israeli rule to that of fellow Arabs. Even in the midst of the *intifada* madness, intimidated both by the terrorist PLO and radical Muslim fundamentalists, over half of them still voted for Zionist parties rather than for an Arab party."[23]

To see the discrepancy in the presentation of the news media one needs to take a drive through the "occupied territories." Unbelievable prosperity will be found among those employed by Israel. Many large two, three or four story homes have been built that only the most well-to-do Israelis could afford. The abundance of Mercedes Benz and BMW cars gracing the streets gives the lie to the news media's representation that those living in the Israeli administered territories are all poor and oppressed. One wealthy Arab contractor remarked to me nearly ten years ago that, "Under the Turks it was awful, under the Jordanians it was not much better, but under the Israelis we make money."

Despite how the press portrays the situation, Israel, even during the *intifada* and the continued murder of Jews in their own country, shows many acts of compassion towards the Arab people. And, facing the threat of missiles containing poison gas from Iraq, Israel even distributed gas masks to the Arab people who were urging Iraq to attack and "burn up Israel." Many who had murdered or injured Israelis actually received gas masks even before large numbers of Jews did. Israel administers a greater sense of justice than was ever found by Jewish people in Arab lands:

"The history of Jews in the Arab world varied by country and century but one thing was usually true: there was no real equality between Jew and Muslim, in theory or in practice. Jews were expected to recognise their inferiority. When trouble occurred, it was usually because the Arab thought the Jew had failed to keep his place. At times through history tyrannical Arab rulers invented ways to stig-matise the Jew. One Sultan ordered them to dress in black cloaks and pointed hats; an Egyptian ruler forced Jews to wear wooden blocks around their necks; in some countries they had to walk head downcast, or squat when they talked to a Muslim. The oath of a Muslim automatically nullified the oath of a Jew, so he was always at the mercy of hostile Muslim neighbours. Before the State of Israel was established, Jews in Arab countries were victims of occasional anger, but after 1948 they became hostages. Whenever Arab fortunes suffered a reverse, Jews under Arab rule paid a price."[24]

LIES: A WAY OF LIFE

Part of Arab culture is to lie. One lies to "save face," and this is very important for an Arab. Lying is not only part of the culture, it is entirely acceptable. Only when an Arab truly comes to know the Lord Jesus Christ does the battle to stop telling lies begin. Even as true "born-again" Christians, Arabs have problems with telling the truth because it is so foreign to them. Stories are made up and propagated because Arabs do not like to be thought inferior, as inferiority is "loss of face." Instead of Hebrew, Arabic becomes the original language of the Bible.

Instead of Isaac, Ishmael becomes the son that Abraham was going to offer as a sacrifice. To have it otherwise would mean that Arabs, as descendants of Ishmael, were inferior to Jews who are the descendants of Isaac.

A classic case in point is the claim of Hanan Ashrawi, the Palestinian spokesman for the "negotiating" team at the Peace Conference that began in Madrid in October 1991. Fending off a question from a reporter representing a Christian publication, she states:

"I am a Palestinian Christian and I know what Christianity is. I am a descendant of the first Christians in the world, and Jesus Christ was born in my country, in my land. Bethlehem is a Palestinian town."[25]

Ashrawi may or may not be an excellent negotiator, but she certainly knows how to tell "grandmother's tales." It is a very ignorant claim to make because:

a) All the first Christians were Jews. The early Church was exclusively made up of Jews or proselytes to the Jewish faith. The Church remained that way for almost a decade until Peter preached to Cornelius, the Roman centurion and his household (in Jewish Caesarea) and admitted them to the Church after their conversion (Acts 10:24-48).

b) Bethlehem was in "Judea" (Matt 2:1). Judea and Samaria (Acts 1:8) are the Biblical names of portions of Israel that are now termed "occupied territories."

c) Palestine did not even exist at the time of the early Church. In Egypt Joseph was instructed to take the infant Jesus to *"the land of Israel"* (Matt 2:21&22). The Romans did not rename Israel *Syria Palæstina* until more than 100 years after the resurrection, by which time the whole known inhabited world had been evangelised.

d) Arabs did not come into the land until *Islam* conquered the Christian Byzantine empire in 637 A.D.

Even Jews, who have no love for Christians or the New Testament, recognised Ashrawi's fraudulent statement and mocked her:

"It is almost as difficult to argue with anyone who claims to be a descendant of 'the first Christians in the world' as it is to dispute a claim of direct kinship to Adam. And one should have enough faith in Ashrawi's integrity to believe that her bragging about Jewish ancestry was done for the purpose of receiving an *aliya* [immigration] loan from the Jewish Agency.

One should also like to hope that her claim to progenitors who lived around Bethlehem 600 years before the Arab conquest – a claim tantamount to an outright confession that she is not an Arab – will not get her into trouble with the less gentle among her colleagues.

But chances are she will be forgiven. Her fellow-PLO proxies know that her family – like most Palestinian Arabs – most likely arrived in Palestine from Egypt or Syria after the terrible Zionists created jobs in the country."[26]

Ashrawi is not alone in trying to strip Jesus of His Jewishness and make Him into a Palestinian Arab of convenience. Canon Naim Ateek, of St. George's Cathedral in the Arab sector of Jerusalem, makes the same claims in his book, *Justice and Only Justice: A Palestinian Theology of Liberation*:

"Jesus was born in Bethlehem, grew up in Nazareth, was baptized in the Jordan river ... Therefore, the first witnesses to the Resurrection were Palestinians; the Church was born in Palestine as the early disciples and followers of Jesus were Palestinians ... The Palestinian Christians of today are the descendants of those early Christians."[27]

Lies, if told often enough, will eventually be believed to be true, and this one has now spread throughout the entire "Christian-Arab" population in the land.

Another Palestinian-Arab "Christian," Greek-Catholic priest, Gerrie's Khoury, has also written a book entitled: *The Intifada of Heaven and Earth: A Palestinian Theology*. In his book Khoury propounds that the *intifada* (which has claimed over 1,100 deaths and multi-thousands of injuries and disfigurements) is divine and from God. His "divine *intifada*" doctrine states *inter alia*:

"Any believer who tries to justify through his theology the religious right of Israel in Palestine is an infidel who denies God and Christ."[28]

Anglican priest Elias Khoury was convicted for transporting explosive devices in his car that killed two people and injured eleven others at the British Consulate in Jerusalem and at a city supermarket.[29] Khoury is now on the executive council of the PLO terrorist organisation in Amman, Jordan.

Greek-Catholic Arab, Archbishop Hilarion Cappucci, was caught gun-running for the PLO terrorist organisation, with large quantities of weaponry and explosives hidden in his Mercedes. Cappucci said, "Jesus Christ was the first *fedayeen* [terrorist]. I am just following His example."[30]

A well known "charismatic" Palestinian-Arab-Christian in Jerusalem, funded by Western Christians, is involved in reconciliation work between Jews and Arabs, yet he sat in the writer's house and told him and his wife privately that, "Terror is the only answer to Israel—we will beat you in the end!" Other similar sentiments have been expressed both publicly and privately by respected and active Palestinian-Arab pastors. Egyptian, Lebanese and Syrian-Arab-Christians have proved to be delightful brethren, but most Palestinian-Arab-Christian's lips speak peace while the heart plans war. And if the stance of the Palestinian Church is almost one of war it should, therefore, come as no surprise that Arabs in general hate Israel and lie about everything pertaining to her.

JEWISH MINORITY?

Jews were not quite the minority in the land that the Arab nations claim they were. In the cities Jews greatly outnumbered the Arabs. In the villages Arabs outnumbered the Jews. Accurate, country-wide population figures are non-existent but it is a moot point whether the Arabs even had a majority at all. It is reported that in 1850 the entire population of Palestine was less than 200,000 persons![31] Remember, Mark Twain wrote of his touring of the land in 1867, that he "never saw a human being on the whole route."[32] And, in 1889, an American newspaper also reported:

"Thirty thousand out of forty thousand people in Jerusalem are Jews."[33]

The great majority of Jerusalem's population, and also that of other cities, was Jewish, and as Jewish presence throughout Palestine increased so, too, did the Arab presence. They came from far and wide attracted, like bees to a honey-pot, by jobs created by Jewish expertise in agriculture, manufacturing and settlement. The Arabs came to Palestine and attached themselves to the Jewish population in order to partake of the benefits that the Jews were, and still are, willing to share with them.

LAND FOR PEACE?

Tremendous pressure is put upon Israel to hand back land in return for "peace." Israel knows, however, that simply giving land back to the Arabs will not bring lasting peace. But Israel today has a very large problem with over a million Arabs within her territory, making the prospect of a "fifth column" (an organisation that works within a country to further the military and political aims of the enemy) in time of war, a real and grave danger. High level discussions have taken place concerning the possibility of returning almost the entire land as part of a planned military exercise to rid themselves of the Arab problem.

The certainty of another war being launched against Israel after the return of land would then allow the Israeli army to use a type of "bulldozer" operation to drive everything out before them. This would leave the land empty of Arabs and firmly in the possession of Israel. This is a strategy that Israel may yet adopt and perhaps might be uppermost in the mind of Yitzak Rabin, the present Prime Minister of Israel, who, since taking office in July of 1992, has appeared to be obsessed with an exchange of territory for peace. Rabin was a highly respected general in the IDF and also Chief of Staff in 1967 when the brilliant Six Day War was executed. In addition to being the current Prime Minister he is also the Minister of Defence.

Many Israeli generals are against returning land under any circumstance, especially land that was won with the blood of Israel's sons and considered necessary for the defence of Israel:

"Urging Israel to give up control of Judea and Samaria, from which the Arabs have attacked her three times, is an invitation to suicide."[34]

"The West Bank figures prominently in Israel's reserve call-up calculations. The distance from Iraq's westernmost border with Jordan to the West Bank is two hundred and ten miles [three hundred and eighty kilometres]. It has been estimated that an Iraqi division could cover this route in about thirty-five hours. Thus, an Israeli ground force in the West Bank is critical for holding an initial defensive line in the event of an Iraqi assault."[35]

Israel took these disputed lands in wars waged against her. She did not instigate these wars and, therefore, won this land in an act of self-defence. A former legal adviser to the U.S. State Department wrote:

"Where the holder of territory has seized that territory in the lawful exercise of self-defence it has, against the prior holder, better title. As between Israel, acting defensively in 1948 and 1967, on the one hand, and her Arab neighbours, acting aggressively in 1948 and 1967, on the other, Israel has better title in the territory of what was Palestine, including the whole of Jerusalem, than do Jordan and Egypt."[36]

That is the considered opinion of an expert on international law. Notwithstanding, almost every nation is trying to force Israel's hand on the issue. We do know, however, that, even if Israel is forced to make concessions under extreme pressure, that same land will return to her sometime in the near future. Here is an interesting passage of Scripture:

"Thus says the Lord GOD: 'These are the borders by which you shall divide the land as an inheritance among the twelve tribes of Israel ... I raised My hand in an oath to give it to your fathers, and this land shall fall to you as your inheritance. On the east side you shall mark out the border from between Hauran and Damascus, and between Gilead and the land of Israel, along the Jordan, and along the eastern side of the sea'"
(Eze 47:13,14&18).

This passage of Scripture refers to a second division of the land of Canaan. The prophecy was given through Ezekiel just before the Israelites went into exile to Babylon, and it was given by the LORD to let the Israelites know that they would be coming back to their land. The importance to us is that we are told that the new eastern border will be *"between Hauran and Damascus."* In the writings of Josephus the Jewish historian, written in Greek in the first century A.D., he makes mention that *"Hauranitus"* incorporates *"Gaulanitus* (Golan)." This means that the border of Israel in the new division will run between Damascus and the Golan—which is the current border resulting from the 1967 war!

Our passage also informs us that this eastern border will be *"along the Jordan,"* again, exactly where it is today! Whether, as this indicates, Israel will make no concessions regarding the Golan Heights and the West Bank or whether they will be forced to concede territory and then recapture it again at a later date is impossible for us to tell. The LORD knows the answer, and only time will reveal it, but it is most important that we see Israel's right and Biblical connection to the land if we are ever to understand Israel's present or future position.

CAUTION

Even for Christians, rejecting Israel's right of possession can have far-reaching results. A highly respected and delightful Christian-Arab leader, Alex Awad, was bringing a short message at an Arab-Israeli reconciliation meeting for Christians in Jerusalem several years ago. These meetings were designed to bring Arab and Jewish Christians together in an effort to break down barriers, especially doctrinal ones. Arab Christians hold to the "Replacement Theology" discussed in Chapter Four, and the Jewish believers firmly believe that the LORD has restored Israel back to her land. Alex was reading from the book of the prophet Isaiah and he read a passage stating that Israel would come back to her land. As Alex read the passage, the significance of what he was actually reading struck him and, looking up, he said, "Let me say that I am not happy about this."

Had it not been so tragic, it would have been funny. For the first time Alex understood that the LORD intended to restore the Jews back to their land, and before him were a large group of Jews bearing out the truth of what he read. Alex, however, for reasons known only to himself, held to his former belief and went against what the LORD had clearly revealed to him. Within a matter of months, due to some minor problems (that he chose to ignore) involving the Israeli military authorities, and despite the support and advice that many of us gave him, he was expelled from Israel—from the land of his birth. Alex had the revelation of God and ignored it. As a consequence he was removed, not only as a leader from among his people but also from the land.

Israel has a willingness to share the benefits of her technology and higher living standards with all the Arab people. A Palestinian deported from Kuwait after the 1991 Gulf War created a stir when he said:

"It's absurd ... rather than all the Arab states, the place we feel most wanted is here [in Israel] ... the worst situation here is still better than the best situation in the Arab states."[37]

Israel has also given Israeli citizenship to thousands of Arabs which allow them the same rights as Jewish Israelis. Bearing this in mind, we need to be aware of the following:

*"Thus says the LORD: '**Against all My evil neighbors who touch the inheritance** which I have caused My people Israel to inherit—behold, I will pluck them out of their land and pluck out the house of Judah from among them. Then it shall be, after I have plucked them out, that I will return and have compassion on them and bring them back, everyone to his heritage and everyone to his land. And it shall be, **if they will learn carefully the ways of My people, to swear by My name**, "As the LORD lives,' as they taught My people to swear by Baal, then **they shall be established in the midst of My people.** But if **they do not obey, I will utterly pluck up and destroy that nation,**' says the LORD"* (Jer 12:14-17).

We have stated elsewhere that ownership of the land belongs to the LORD, and the possession belongs to Israel. The LORD refers to His *"evil neighbours"*, the nations that surround His land. The LORD says that these *"neighbours touch the inheritance"* which He gave to Israel, obviously meaning the land. Because the neighbours took His land and divided it up the LORD plucked them out of it and created enormous problems in the Middle East. The LORD says that He will allow His neighbours back into the land *"if they will learn carefully the ways of His people."* Palestinians will be allowed to live in Israel's land if they choose to turn from their current violent path and accept the ways and conditions of Israel.

ARABS AND VIOLENCE

"Arab spokesmen tell Westerners 'if it were not for the Israelis, all would be peace and harmony in the Middle East.' This is the 1990 equivalent of the anti-British and anti-French diatribes American diplomats and pressmen heard from Arab contacts in the 1940s and 1950s. One does not have to be an imperialist to recognise that the Middle East has been a bloodier and more insecure region since the departure of the British and French than it was during their brief stay there. And one does not have to be a Zionist to understand that most of the coups, conflicts and killings in the Arab states and Iran in the last forty years have not been connected to Israel.

Since 1950 there has, at some time, been tension with fighting or the trading of threats along almost every important inter-Arab frontier: Syria-Lebanon, Syria-Iraq, Saudi Arabia-Oman, Saudi Arabia-Yemen, North and South Yemen, Libya-Egypt, Libya-Sudan, Libya-Tunisia, Algeria-Morocco ... Israel was involved neither in these incidents nor in the Middle East's worst war, that between Iraq and Iran; and it did not intervene when King Hussein of Jordan ordered his security forces to crush Palestinian activists who were trying to subvert his regime. Many Palestinians then fled to Israel, fearing their 'Arab brothers' far more than they feared the Jews."[38]

It is generally believed that the Arab problem has its roots in the union of Abraham and Hagar, the Egyptian maid of Sarah, Abraham's wife. This is not true and there are nations described today as "Arab" that are not really Arab at all. The name "Arab" was given to those who lived in Arabia. Iran, which is a very troublesome spot, is not even distantly related. Iran is ancient Persia; *Islam* is her only common denominator with the Arab nations. The founding father of Egypt, the leader of the so called "Arab" nations, was a grandson of Noah as were the fathers of Libya, Canaan and Ethiopia (Gen 10:6). Obviously, if Ishmael, the son of Abraham, had an Egyptian mother, he certainly did not father that nation. From Egypt (Hebrew: *Mizraim*) came the Philistines (Gen 10:14). Lot, Abraham's nephew (Gen 12:5), fathered Ammon and Moab in an incestuous drunken spree (Gen 19:36-38), and these are the fathers of modern-day Jordan. The father of the nation of Yemen (Hebrew: *Teman*) was the grandson of Jacob's brother Esau (Gen 36:11&34).

From the genealogies we can see that most of those living in the Middle East are indeed blood relations. But it is as incorrect to say that the problem was caused by Abraham as it is to say that all the nations are Arab. Ishmael had twelve sons, who no doubt have contributed to the mixing of the pottage, but Arabs were Arabs, Jordanians were Ammonites and Philistines were Ashdodites back in the days of Nehemiah:

*"Now it happened, when Sanballat, Tobiah, the **Arabs**, the **Ammonites**, and the **Ashdodites** heard that the walls of Jerusalem were being restored and the gaps were beginning to be closed, that they became very angry"*   (Neh 4:7).

All three nations were blood relatives, but each was distinct and separate. They were, however, united in their anger toward Israel even then.

Ishmael's temperament has probably had an influence on the volatile nature of the Middle Eastern people:

*"He will be **a wild donkey** of a man; **his hand will be against everyone and everyone's hand against him**, and **he will live in hostility toward all his brothers"***   (Gen 16:12 NIV).

"A wild donkey of a man" means that he would be untamed, lawless, rebellious, fleet and sure of foot. He was to *"live in hostility toward all his brothers,"* and the truth of all this has been borne out by history. An interesting note is found concerning this passage in the *Midrash Rabbah*, a renowned, ancient Jewish commentary on the Hebrew Old Testament. Ishmael is described there as a "highwayman." A highwayman robbed people at gunpoint, and much of the world's hijacking has, in fact, been carried out by Arab extremists.

There are additional reasons for the violent nature of the Arab people:

*"The **Nephilim** were on the earth in those days—and also afterward—when **the sons of God went to the daughters of men and had children** by them. They were the **heroes of old, men of renown**"*   (Gen 6:4 NIV).

Nephilim is often wrongly translated as "giants" in some English translations. *Nephilim* is the plural of the Hebrew word *nephil* meaning "bully." It has its root in the Hebrew word *naphal* which means "fall," and from that root comes *nephel* —"a miscarriage." Hence, *nephilim* can literally mean, "fallen bullies who are the product of a miscarriage."
    These are the "fallen angels," *"the sons of God,"* procreating with human females of which the result is "half flesh-half spirit" beings. They became the *"heroes of old, the men of renown."* Is it really

surprising that these "beings" obtained pre-eminence in battle? We need to remember that the "flesh" dies, but the "spirit" lives on, manifesting itself in men like Abu Nidal, the most wanted man in the world. He is an Arab man to whom assassination and murder is commonplace and who also thinks nothing of blowing capacity-loaded, jumbo jets out of the skies.

There are also other descendants of Biblical "heroes" living in the area of the Arab-Israeli conflict:

> *"Yet again there was war at Gath, where there was a man of great stature, who had **six fingers on each hand and six toes on each foot**, twenty-four in number; and he also was born to the giant"*
> (2 Sam 21:20).

A Muslim-Arab man named Abu Fuchti showed me where he had had his sixth finger removed from each hand and it was unmistakable! A shiver ran down my spine as my memory recalled Biblical passages of Goliath the Philistine and his brothers. Abu Fuchti said that his son's fingers, and also those of his father had been removed, but those of his grandfather were intact. The blood that flows down through the generations may have become mixed and, therefore, a little weaker, but the passion for violence and battle has not diminished with time.

CURSED BE CANAAN

When the children of Israel came out of Egypt they were opposed and denied help by the Ammonites and the Moabites, the ancestors of the present nation of Jordan:

> *"They did not meet you with bread and water on the road when you came out of Egypt, and ... they hired against you Balaam the son of Beor from Pethor of Mesopotamia, to curse you. Nevertheless the LORD your God would not listen to Balaam, but the LORD your God turned the curse into a blessing for you, because the LORD your God loves you. **You shall not seek their peace nor their prosperity all your days forever"***   (Deut 23:4-6).

Just as the LORD turned the curses of Balaam into blessings for Israel, so does the LORD turn today's curses by "hired prophets" into blessings for them, too. And the LORD forbade peace! This should give us a clearer perspective on the present turmoil.

The lot of the Palestinian Arab has not been easy. They were made *"woodcutters and water carriers"* under both Joshua and David. Now, in the newly re-created Israeli state, wealthy Arab contractors employ their own brothers cheaply, on a daily basis, on Israeli building sites. How true have been the words of Noah:

"Then he said: 'Cursed be Canaan; a servant of servants he shall be to his brethren.' And he said: 'Blessed be the LORD, the God of Shem, and may Canaan be his servant"   (Gen 9:25&26).

We looked at *arar,* the Hebrew word for "curse" in Chapter Eight. It has a long and dreadful effect. Canaan still serves the offspring of Shem. It is not by choice, it is by decree.

The "Palestinian" problem is both a political and military weapon created and disguised specifically to win sympathy for the Arabs who are in a declared state of war with Israel. The sole intention of the Arab cause is to wipe out completely and permanently the entire Jewish presence in the Middle East.

The Palestinian refugees are denied basic human rights by their own people in order to foster the ideals of *Islam,* and the world's news media unashamedly contributes to the daily misrepresentation of facts.

Dear LORD,
Only You know the outcome of the Palestinian problem. Bring it to a place of peaceful rest, LORD. Oh, may they learn the ways of Your people Israel that the brethren may dwell together in unity. Protect the innocent ones, and wipe away all the tears from their eyes. Amen.

PART V

AN
UNFRUITFUL
CHURCH

"You did not choose Me, but I chose you and appointed you that you should go and bear fruit, and that your fruit should remain, that whatever you ask the Father in My name He may give you."

(Jn 15:16).

23

THE
GREAT
HATRED

It was Maurice Samuel that termed anti-Semitism "the great hatred," and it is something that has been with us for millennia. A harbinger of suffering and anguish for the Jewish people, it lies latent within the breast of many men and women. Anti-Semitism is a vent for the frustrations of life and will probably continue with us until that final day when the LORD of creation will Himself comfort His chosen people:

*"And the LORD God will wipe away tears from all faces; **the rebuke of His people He will take away from all the earth**; for the LORD God has spoken"* (Isa 25:8).

The worst anti-Semitism to hit our modern world came during World War II. It came because one man, Adolf Hitler, had an insane passion to rid the world of every living Jew. Fortunately, he never succeeded. But he did succeed, with the willing help of others infected with the anti-Semitic virus, in murdering six million Jews—one third of the entire race. That systematic murder, known to the Germans as the "Final Solution," is recorded in the annals of history as the "Holocaust." During the Holocaust the German people, who were employed by the thousands in concentration camps, sank to new depths in barbarism. They learned to pry dead lips apart and deftly knock out gold-filled teeth, collecting many tons of gold[1] from the murdered masses. They manufactured cloth and mattresses from the hair shaved from the heads of the dead women[2] and committed many other crimes too heinous to mention. Agony fills the soul of the believing Christian with every remembrance of the German belief in their own superiority as expressed through their blatant contempt for God's chosen people. And to this stark pain in the breast of the Christian is added unmitigated shame and humiliation because it is recorded that:

"Six days a week, the new elite worked in the concentration camps. On Sunday they rested, went to church with their wives and children, and after church ... ."[3]

Some people deny that the Holocaust took place. They seek not only to downplay the catastrophe but also to ease guilty consciences and, ultimately, to stir up further anti-Semitism by inferring that the Jews made the whole thing up. But no matter how much some would like to brush it under the rug and forget about it, we cannot, because great publications, like *National Geographic*, document it:

"Once they were many; now they are so few. Nearly three and a half million Jews lived in Poland in 1939, and their homes, synagogues, and schools throbbed with an exuberance that made Poland a center of world Jewish culture. Then came the Holocaust ... ."[4]

Wherever the Nazis rolled into town in their tanks, crushing its defenders, Jewish populations were all but exterminated. But it was the Polish Jews that suffered the most, almost three million died by the end of the war. The War ended and so did the Holocaust, but not so anti-Semitism. Some Polish Jews survived, and some returned to Poland hoping to link again with family, but:

"In the years since, anti-Semitism has driven thousands more from Poland. Today the remaining Jews number perhaps 5,000, nearly all of them old, scattered like withered straw across the Polish plain. Survivors bear death-camp tattoos and grim memories. Few want anything to do with strangers."[5]

Anti-Semitism is as relentless as waves crashing upon the shores of the seas. Ofttimes there is a calm when the fury abates, but every calm is eventually shattered by another storm.

The Jewish world-view has been molded by anti-Semitism. Today, thousands of Jews nightly relive the horror of the Holocaust. Unspeakable sights haunt their eyes; the screams of the dying echo and ring in their ears; and sleep, for the most part, eludes them. It is worse for some than others:

> "Jonasz Stern escaped death on July 20, 1943. It happened in the ravine at the end of Janowska Street, the site of mass executions of the Jews of the Lwow ghetto. Months earlier his wife had been shipped to Auschwitz, where she threw herself onto the electrified fence. Now it was his turn.
>   Miraculously, as SS bullets hit rows of people, he fell unhurt. Corpses covered him. He fainted. When he came to, the Germans had left. He lay there until the bodies around him became cold and stiff. In the night he crawled out. Smeared with the blood of strangers, he ran into the depths of the forest, then fled to Hungary. After the war he moved to Krakow and became a celebrated painter. His work, much of it abstract composition using fish skeletons and animal bones, is clearly obsessed with death. Stern comments, 'A man who has lived through his own death could hardly tell the world anything else.'"[6]

Volumes have been written and many more volumes could yet be written on the inhuman treatment of Jews by Gentile people in "Christian" nations. But the purpose of this chapter is to focus on anti-Semitism within the Church herself. Anti-Semitism in the Church has delayed, and is delaying still, the purposes of God. But let us look at the actual deed before we assess the damage or propose a solution.

CHRISTIAN ANTI-SEMITISM

Unfortunately, the Church has an unenviable record of anti-Semitism, of which Jews are painfully aware because it is such a large part of their actual, recorded history. Christians, however, even highly educated ones, are all but totally ignorant of these sins. As Edward Flannery, the leading authority on anti-Semitism, explains,

> "They are ignorant of it for the simple reason that anti-Semitism does not appear in their history books. Histories of the Middle Ages—and even of the Crusades—can be found in which the word "Jew" does not appear, and there are Catholic dictionaries and encyclopaedias in which the term "anti-Semitism" is not listed. There seems to be only

one conclusion: The pages Jews have memorised have been torn from our histories of the Christian era."[7]

Perhaps the pages of this chapter will, in part, replace some of those missing from our Christian history books. It is necessary, even essential, that we deal with this painful subject as it is not only a key to restoring wholeness to the Church but also a key to the successful evangelism of the world. We dare not, as some Christians recommend, say that the past is past and claim that we live under grace. The grace of God becomes actual to us only when we repent of our sin, and today the Church stands naked before God, bereft of His grace because of her sin of anti-Semitism.

Before we can repent we must be aware of our sin. A few anti-Semitic academicians have, over the years, pieced together an entire account of anti-Semitism, but, unfortunately, none of these works are readily available (all are out of print). Recently, for the express purpose of helping to document this chapter, I was fortunate to purchase, through an out-of-print book-search specialist, a copy of, perhaps, the definitive work on anti-Semitism. It was a signed first edition of *The Anguish of the Jews* by Edward H. Flannery. It was offered for sale by a city's public library in the United States because the book had never once been checked out of the library in twenty-six years! From this, and other sources, we shall see how the Church changed her holy days to exclude the Jews, established doctrines to exclude the Jews from the covenants of promise and also how they excluded them from mercy by killing and torturing hundreds of thousands, even millions, of them. This latter, dreadful form of anti-Semitism excluded the Jew from finding hope in Jesus. Jesus, for the Jews, is a totally unmentionable name, He is the "God of the Gentiles" and the founder of the religion that persecutes their people.

CHURCH FATHERS

Some have said that those who killed and persecuted Jews were not real Christians. But can we charge some of the greatest church fathers with not being real Christians? For example, John Chrysostom (347 – 407), is recognised by some as the greatest of all Christian preachers, greater even than Spurgeon, the "prince of preachers." Chrysostom's powers of oratory were exceptional. His eloquence earned him the name "golden-mouthed."[8] He was bishop of Constantinople and a "Doctor of the Church,"[9] a rare title given to "Christian theologians of outstanding merit and acknowledged saintliness."[10] Even though he was recognised as an outstanding theologian, preacher and saint, Chrysostom was a rabid anti-Semite! Throughout Church history, Chrysostom is without peer or parallel in his hatred of the Jews. And, being in a high position with distinguished theological works credited to his name, he used his oratorical powers to lay the foundation for much of the Church's future anti-Semitism:

"How can Christians dare 'have the slightest converse' with Jews, 'most miserable of all men,' men who are '… lustful, rapacious, greedy, perfidious bandits.' Are they not 'inveterate murderers, destroyers, men possessed by the devil' whom [sic] debauchery and drunkenness have given them the manners of the pig and the lusty goat. They know only one thing, to satisfy their gullets, get drunk, to kill and maim … ."[11]

"The Synagogue? Not only is it a theatre and a house of prostitution, but a cavern of brigands, a 'repair of wild beasts,' a place of 'shame and ridicule, the domicile of the devil, as is also the souls of the Jews.' Indeed Jews worship the devil; their rites are 'criminal and impure;' their religion is 'a disease.' Their synagogue, again, is 'an assembly of criminals … a den of thieves … a cavern of devils, an abyss of perdition … I hate the synagogue also.'"[12]

"God hates the Jews and always hated the Jews … I hate the Jews also."[13]

It is no wonder that after some of Chrysostom's sermons in 388, his "flock" went out and burned down synagogues.[14] But what caused his great hatred of the Jews? In Chrysostom's own words:

"Their odious 'assassination' of Christ … for this deicide, there is 'no expiation possible, no indulgence, no pardon … vengeance is without end."[15]

Thus Chrysostom cemented into the mind of the Christian his own stereotype of the Jew—"Christ-killers." His anti-Judaic onslaught lit a fire within the Christian Church to which others constantly added more fuel. Augustine, a contemporary of Chrysostom said:

"Judaism, since Christ, is a corruption; indeed 'Judas is the image of the Jewish people;' their understanding of the Scriptures is carnal; they bear the guilt for the death of the Saviour, for through their fathers they have killed the Christ. The Jews held Him; the Jews insulted Him, the Jews bound Him, they crowned Him with thorns, dishonoured Him by spitting upon Him, they scourged Him, they heaped abuses upon Him, they hung Him upon a tree, they pierced Him with a lance."[16]

Though he may have been a great saint, Augustine's knowledge concerning the crucifixion of Christ appears to be sadly lacking, whether by ignorance or design we shall never know. But it was the Romans that "crowned Him with thorns," and it was the Romans that "scourged Him, abused Him, hung Him upon a tree and pierced Him with a lance." Chrysostom and Augustine were not alone in their anti-Semitism. Other great and influential men had their own particular versions of the great hatred:

Ephraim called the Jews:

"Circumcised dogs."[17]

Jerome, while asking Jews for Hebrew lessons, denounced them as:

"... Judaic serpents of whom Judas was the model."[18]

Gregory of Nyssa, in delivering a homily on the resurrection, said the Jews were:

"... adversaries of grace, enemies of God, devil's advocates, brood of vipers, Sanhedrin of demons."[19]

The list of prominent anti-Semitic Church fathers is overly long for our purposes here. Suffice it to say, only rarely do we find one that was really sympathetic to the Jew. And the ferocity of the Church's anti-Semitism did not cease with the passing of time. A millennium later we come to a man that had tremendous impact upon the Church: Martin Luther. As a reformer, Luther had no equal. As an anti-Semite, Luther fell only slightly short of Chrysostom. Just as Chrysostom lit the fire, so Luther rekindled it when the flames were dying down. Martin Luther (1483 – 1546) courted the Jews as he founded his new faith, confident that Christianity stripped of "popery and monkery"[20] would soon win them to Christ by the "pure" gospel. But Luther, who reminds us of the apostle Paul in his zeal for Christ and his persecution by the religious of his day, lacked both the patience and Christlike spirit of the great apostle and also the prophetic light and insight into God's plan and purpose for this unique people. Because the Jews were not converted in masses but rather persisted in opposing the gospel, Luther turned against them in a most terrible way:

"He raged at them in a language that at least equalled in violence anything uttered against them before or after. With biting sarcasm and occasional scatological insult, he renewed all the old charges of the past: Jews are poisoners, ritual murderers, usurers; they are parasites on Christian society; they are worse than devils; it is harder to convert them than Satan himself; they are doomed to hell. They are, in truth, the anti-Christ. Their synagogues should be destroyed and their books seized; they should be forced to work with their hands; better still they should be expelled by the princes from their territories."[21]

In his last sermon, delivered only days before his death, he called for their expulsion from all of Germany. His assault against the Jews was long, continuous and virulent. Adolf Hitler, in his drive to eradicate all of Jewry, used some of the words of Luther to justify his actions. Of Martin Luther, Flannery wrote:

"The devil the reformer would have exorcised from the Church seemed to have taken full possession of him."[22]

CHRISTIAN COUNCILS

Christianity became the state religion in Rome in 312 A.D. Emperor Constantine was tolerant of the Jews for a brief three years. In the year 315, the Council of Nicaea was convened and the more than 300 attending bishops gave to the Church one of the most beautiful of all Christian statements, the Nicene Creed, given here in part:

"We believe in one Lord, Jesus Christ, the only Son of God, eternally begotten of the Father, God from God, Light from Light, true God from true God, begotten, not made, of one being with the Father..."[23]

This first Christian Council that history records, which came forth with perhaps the greatest statement of faith ever presented to the Church, also resolved to break the ties of relationship with the Jews. Among other things, Easter was to be observed on a fixed date, away from the Jewish calendar. Constantine addressed the bishops:

"We desire to have nothing in common with this so hated people, for the Redeemer has marked out another path for us."[24]

The edicts made against the Jews by the Council of Nicaea were the forerunners of many that were to follow from subsequent councils. At the Council of Vienna in 1267 it was decreed that:

"'No Jew should be admitted in a public bathing establishment, an inn, or a house of call for journeymen'—in short, the Jew was to be shunned 'like one plague-stricken, whose very breath is infectious, like a dangerous seducer whose speech harbours the poison of scepticism and unbelief.'"[25]

The third and fourth councils of Orleans enacted laws that forbade Jews the right to appear on streets during Christian festivals:

"... since their presence would be a species of offence to Christianity."[26]

The climax of the great hatred on the part of the Church found expression in the Lateran Council of 1215. The whole of Western Christianity was represented: 71 archbishops, 412 bishops, 800 abbots, and a host of Church dignitaries and priests. Its decrees were embodied in seventy canons, four of which dealt with the Jews. The one that has had the most terrible consequences for the scattered people for centuries was the one that put upon them the badge of outlawry. From this time on, all Jews:

"... in all Christendom and at all times were ordained to wear a distinctive dress or badge."[27]

In some countries they wore a badge in the shape of a wheel—red, yellow or parti-coloured—fixed upon the breast. In others it was a hat—a pointed yellow hat or a horn-shaped head-dress, red, green etc. As a result:

"The Jews everywhere cringed in abject humility and slavishness of spirit; but at heart they became ever more and more embittered against Christians, and more intense in their hostility to Christianity. Utterly helpless in themselves, they were condemned by the leaders of Christianity to be the outcasts of mankind, and were compelled to endure contempt and hatred, plundering and banishment, blows and murder, from all the world. From this time especially the Jewish people became the martyr nation of the earth, and of mankind; and its tormenters were the Christians."[28]

After the first council of Nicaea, the decrees had come in relentless succession. Finally, they left the Jews nowhere to turn. Marriages between a Jew and a Christian were punishable by death.[29] Jews were excluded from all public offices.[30] They could not practice professions or handcrafts nor could they engage in agriculture, since ownership of land was forbidden them everywhere.[31] Some countries allowed Jewish physicians, but it was often a hazardous occupation; if the patient was cured the Jew had used sorcery; if the patient died the Jew had poisoned him.[32] On each Good Friday for 300 years, Christians were told to hit Jews in the face in retribution for the crucifixion.[33] Christians were forbidden to sell or rent property to a Jew or to trade with them.[34] The Jews were denied food and shelter, the basic necessities of life.[35]

During the first two Christian Crusades to the Holy Land, Jews in Germany and Italy sought protection from Henry IV and Conrad III. The crown then made them "imperial serfs" reducing them to:

"... the status of pieces of property that could be—and were—bought, loaned and sold as any other merchandise."[36]

Denied any craft, Jews were confined to money-lending and usury, forcing them to become financial leeches. This became an additional cause of ruin as they were often treated by the rulers as sponges which were rung out when full and then given over to the hatred of the people.[37] They were forced into conditions that made money as important as life itself:

"Every step and every act of daily life of a Jew were subjected to payment of a tax. He had to pay to come and go, to buy and sell, to enjoy his rights, to pray in common, to marry, to beget children, indeed for the very cadaver he carried to the cemetery."[38]

If the Jews of a particular country did prosper through trading, money-lending or usury, they were often expelled from the land and their goods and chattels confiscated by the crown. One such expulsion was carried out by France, but, after the treasury finances suffered through lack of Jewish taxes, the Jews were readmitted. After a few years, they were expelled yet again and once more suffered the loss of all their possessions.[39] Often, according to Flannery, "the poison that killed the Jews was their goods."[40]

BAPTISM OR DEATH

One of the most devastating ordeals—worse than death itself for the Jew—was forced baptism. In most parts of Christendom this was practiced at one time or another, and thousands of Jews chose death rather than succumb to the rite. The Toledan Councils of Spain ruled that:

"Whoever is led to Christianity by violence, by fear and torture receives the imprint of Christianity and can be forced to observe the Christian faith."[41]

Throughout Christendom, Jews were tortured and maimed in an effort to enforce the "true faith" upon them, and the results were catastrophic:

"Jewish mothers took their infants, and, loading themselves with stones, sprang with them from the bridge [into the Moselle river] to certain death."[42]

"... Jewish women killing themselves and their children for dread of what would come upon them. Jews lay dead in their own blood everywhere."[43]

In Portugal, a decree was issued that all Jewish children under fourteen years of age must be baptised before, or on, Easter Sunday, 1497. The misery caused to Jewish parents cannot be described:

"Some killed their own children, some threw them into rivers and wells to prevent what they feared for them more than death. Many parents and children were torn from one another by the whip and scourge, and then dragged by the hair to the baptismal font, the poor children being afterwards distributed among Christians to be brought up as such."[44]

In Poland, in 1648, at Tulzin:

"... fifteen hundred Jews were done to death who would not receive baptism, ten Rabbis were spared for the sake of the ransom which might be wrung from their communities."[45]

In Homel, during the same period:

"... the Jews were driven naked into the fields and 1,500 men, women, and children, who would not be baptised, were put to barbarous deaths. Hundreds and thousands of Jews perished in numerous other towns. On one occasion a hundred Jewish children were killed and thrown to the dogs."[46]

MARRANOS

Forced baptism was not a short-lived phase; it lasted for many centuries. It was so prevalent in Spain during the fifteenth century that thousands of Jews were forcibly "converted" against their will. Many regretted the step that they had taken and continued to practice their Jewish faith, either secretly or openly. This angered the Spanish Church, which was contemptuous of the double standard of the Jews; and the new converts were referred to as *marranos*—swine. The Church rose against the *Marranos*, and the Inquisition was born. The Inquisition was operative throughout Spain, Portugal and all their colonies, and it terrorised the *Marrano* Jews for years until all Jews were expelled from these areas. A list of thirty-seven clues to ferreting out the "Judaizers" was published, including failure to wear one's best clothes on a Sunday or omission of the *"Gloria Patri"* in prayers.[47] Baron quotes the Jesuit historian, Mariana:

"The net total of *Marranos* for the first year of the Inquisition amounted to 2,000 victims burnt alive and 17,000 sentenced to loss of property, loss of civil rights, or incarceration."[48]

In Granada, in early 1492, the decree was signed by King Ferdinand and Queen Isabella of Spain that all Jews of Spain, Sicily and Sardinia must quit those countries within four months or die. They could take their property with them with the exception of gold, silver, coins or such articles as were forbidden to be exported. It was, for all practical purposes, the confiscation of their property:

"... a piece of cloth was offered for a vineyard, an ass for a house."[49]

The Jews offered an enormous amount of money to the king, who had a reputation for being rapacious. As Ferdinand reconsidered his decision, Torquemada, the first, and cruellest Inquisitor General, rushed onto the scene, holding a crucifix aloft, and cried:

"Judas Iscariot sold Christ for thirty pieces of silver; will your highness sell Him for 300,000 ducats? Here He is, take Him and sell Him."[50]

This outburst caused the king to hold to his decision, and the Jews left the land which they had occupied for 1,500 years.

COMPULSORY SERMONS

Examples of compulsory attendance for Jews at sermons are available from the ninth century, and the practice was made law in 1278 by a decree of Pope Nicholas III, who laid down rules for the delivery of the sermons. The reformers continued the practice until it was finally abolished in 1848. Flannery writes:

"One can imagine the few conversions these enforced sermons obtained and the chagrin of the reluctant listeners, who in some places had to have their ears inspected for removal of cotton placed there for obvious reasons. Others required an excitator to keep them awake throughout expositions on the truth of Christianity and the falsity of Judaism that sometimes lasted two hours."[51]

CHILDREN

Not only were the Jews' civil and religious rights violated but so, also, were their parental rights. As mentioned earlier, decrees were enacted to seize the children of unbaptised Jews and raise them as Christians. This practice began in the early centuries and, as Flannery informs us, continued for more than 1,500 years, with examples even up to the nineteenth and twentieth centuries. Church authorities justified the misery inflicted upon Jewish families by their conviction that the forced baptism of the children made them Christians:

"Whoever did not openly manifest his opposition to baptism at the very moment of its administration was not truly forced—even if it meant death itself awaited such opposition—and was therefore validly baptised, incurring all the rights and duties of Christian life. Baptised children were ... the dominion of the Church civically as well as spiritually."[52]

THE CRUSADES

A fateful year for Jewry was 1096, the beginning of the Crusades, all of which had dire consequences for Jews. Swarms of knights, nobles, monks and ill-equipped peasants set out in that year to free the Holy Land from the Muslims, but the leaders of the crusade said:

"We desire to combat the enemies of God in the East; but we have them under our eyes the Jews [sic], a race more inimical to God than all the others. We are doing this whole thing backwards."[53]

The crusaders turned against the Jews, and, with the cry "God wills it" on their lips, massacred them and destroyed their communities along with Muslim communities across the length and breadth of Europe as they travelled to free the Holy Land. No crusader from the first crusade survived to reach Jerusalem; they succumbed either to disease or to the Muslim sword. The second and third crusades followed a similar, but less intensive, pattern of misery for Jewish communities under the same battle cry. And, as an incentive to help recruitment for the Crusades, all debts owed to Jews by those who enlisted were cancelled. Many signed up just to rid themselves of mortgages, etc., and large numbers of Jews were ruined financially. The success of the second crusade was little better than the first. A remnant did reach Damascus but failed to dislodge the Muslims there, and the crusade was abandoned. The third crusade was led by Godfrey de Bouillon, and about one fifth of the crusaders reached their goal and —

"In 1099 at journey's end in Jerusalem the soldiers of Godfrey de Bouillon found the Jews assembled in a synagogue and set it ablaze."[54]

Afterwards, the crusaders went to the Holy Sepulchre and gave thanks for their great victory. They had driven the Muslims from the Holy Land and had driven the Jews even further from Christ.

HOST DESECRATION

When the Church was not murdering the Jews, it was libelling them. Besides the usual charges of ritual murder and crucifixion of Christian children, usually emanating from the finding of a drowned child, an unexplained death or a missing person, the Jews were accused of "desecrating the Host" (Communion wafers). Christians with a belief in trans-substantiation of the wafer into the literal body of Christ were passionately aroused against Jews when it was broadcast that:

"… the Jews had stolen and desecrated the Host. It had actually been seen that 'as they pounded the wafer in a mortar, blood spurted up from it.'"[55]

This libel, combined with the inbred hatred of the Jew, justified, in the eyes of the Christians, the turning of synagogues into churches, the killing and terrorising of Jews and the confiscating of their property. Once more, we read of Jewish mothers killing their children and then destroying themselves rather than falling into the hands of "demon-possessed" mobs.[56] And, in France, a town's entire Jewish community was burned at the stake.[57]

THE GHETTO

As Church decrees went forth the Jews were seen to be more and more pernicious, and in some lands they were separated from the Christian population into ghettos:

"By confining the Jewish population in the narrow quarters of a ghetto whose space never widened, though the families within it increased, where they were shut within gates every night, they were kept like a caged beast who can be slaughtered at will."[58]

The ghetto was, for Christians, a place to confine the most odious of people in conditions befitting them. The ghetto, for the Jew, despite the conditions, became a refuge, a haven of rest away from the violent mobs.

ANTI-SEMITIC LITERATURE

Just as some Christians fabricated libels against the Jews, in the past, so some Christians, today, publish anti-Semitic articles. Of late, even radically anti-Semitic videos have been produced and circulated among thousands of pastors within the United States. There is, however, one notable piece of anti-Semitic literature that has enjoyed wide readership in several countries among Christians and non-Christians alike, *The Protocols of the Learned Elders of Zion.* This work, by twentieth-century, Russian anti-Semites, has been called "The Hoax of the Century."[59] *The Protocols of Zion* is a series of twenty-four supposed lectures by the "Elders" detailing Jewish plans for subjugating the world. Translated into at least seven other languages, this work has had tremendous influence both before and after it was exposed as a "crude forgery" in 1921. According to Flannery, three editions appeared in America where it enjoyed the widest circulation due to Henry Ford's publication, *The Dearborn Independent,* which had a circulation of 700,000. Even after they were proven to be a forgery, Ford resolutely continued to use the *Protocols* and compounded the damage by re-issuing all his anti-Semitic material in four volumes.[60]

Ford formally denied the genuineness of the *Protocols* in 1927 when brought to account by a law suit. He declared his mortification and expressed a desire to make amends, but the damage had already been done. Thus Carey McWilliams could say:

"In one sense, Hitler began where Ford left off."[61]

An American priest, Charles E. Coughlin, who had a radio ministry during the 1930s with a listening audience of some 3,500,000, and who possessed considerable influence, became increasingly anti-Semitic with the passing of the years. He took up the cause of the *Protocols of Zion* and suggested that their reliability was unimportant as —

"... we can't ignore the news value of their strikingly prophetic nature."[62]

The Protocols of Zion is still circulating widely in America and its popularity has increased of late with the noticeable rise of anti-Semitism there.

SCAPEGOATS

In Chapter Five it was stated that the Jew became the scapegoat for every ill-wind of misfortune that came upon certain countries. It is historical fact that:

"If sickness prevailed, it was because the Jews had poisoned the wells; if a Christian child were lost, it had been crucified at a Jewish ceremony; if a church sacristan was careless, it was the Jews who had stolen the Host from the altar to stab it with knives at the time of Passover. In many periods, in almost all lands, whoever sinned or suffered, the Jews were accused, and the occasion straightway made use of for attacks in which hundreds or thousands might perish."[63]

It is dreadful to realise that the situation is little better today than it was yesterday with regards to blaming the Jews for the tragedies of life.

The virulent anti-Semitic tradition in Christendom stems from the fourth century when certain Church fathers, especially Chrysostom, re-interpreted Biblical passages as divine punishment for Israel's sins. It is not surprising, therefore, that in the Christian chronicles and histories of the ages:

"No sign of compassion, not a word of indignation, is to be met with in their reports of the outrages against the Jews. Many of the clerical chroniclers even manifest their pleasure in them. Thus, for instance, the monk of Waverly relates in a triumphant tone the slaughter in London at the coronation of Richard I, which had taken place without any cause being given by the Jews, and concludes by exclaiming: 'Blessed be the Lord who hath delivered up the wicked.'"[64]

How has all this affected the modern Jew? Baron quotes a German theologian of renown, Franz Delitzsch:

"'Go to Jerusalem,' Delitzsch writes, 'and there you can see it. On the south-western side of the Temple hill, where the tremendous ruins of the area of Solomon's Temple stand, is the 'Wailing Place of the Jews.' As their fathers of yore by the waters of Babylon, so the elders of the daughters of Zion mourn here every Friday, laying their hoary heads low in the dust by the crumbling Temple wall and their tears fall in torrents on the open page of the Book of Lamentations, which they hold with their trembling hands. Youths, lying on their faces, moisten the penitential Psalms of David with their tears. Maidens, with dishevelled hair, bow their heads to the ground, kissing the ancient stones, and weeping for the misery of their people.'"[65]

Like Delitzsch, I have personally witnessed the tears of the Jews at the Wall and other places—a most disturbing experience.

SUMMATION

Christian anti-Semitism stems from the election of the Jews to be a *"set-apart people"* solely for the purposes of God. The isolation of the Jew, says Flannery, "originated in his sense of divine election, his dedication to the Law, his worship of Yahweh."[66] The Jews have clung tenaciously to their election as a unique nation of people and this, together with their gifting in many areas, has earned them the wrath of the nations. **Christian anti-Semitism is rooted in the rejection of Jews as a divinely chosen people**. And it is also this rejection of Jews as the divinely chosen people that forms the basis of the widely accepted, but nevertheless blasphemous, doctrine that rejects Israel and replaces her with the Church.

The suffering and death portrayed in this chapter tells but little of what the Jews have endured at the hands of the Church. Flannery makes the following observation at the close of his tremendous work:

"For the believing Christian this tale of horrors ends in the deepest chambers of the spirit. The sin of anti-Semitism is many things but in the end **it is a denial of the Christian faith, a failure of Christian hope and a malady of Christian love**. Nor is it the least of sins. The agony of the Jews is one, Jacques Maritain has pointed out, in which Christ participates. **And was not this the supreme defection: that the most severely and persistently persecuted of Christian history were not those to whom persecution was promised by the Master (John 16:2-4) but rather the people from which He came?**

Maritain saw this clearly when he wrote: '**The passion of Israel is more and more clearly taking the shape of the Cross** [bold emphasis added].'"[67]

As has been made clear in these few pages, there are parts of Church history which we Christians should be justly ashamed of. My hope and prayer is that a new understanding and compassion might open for the Jew in the heart of the reader. The Jewish people are excruciatingly aware of our history; and even when Saddam Hussein threatened to "burn up half of Israel" in 1991, they simply equated him with Christianity, with sentiments similar to those expressed by Chrysostom, Luther and other men of influence.[68]

The Church must repent of her anti-Semitic sins. We might not have personally committed them, and we can never atone for them, but we can, and must, repent of them. The LORD will call us to account:

*"Whatever is has already been, and what will be has been before; and **God will call the past to account**"*   (Eccl 3:15 NIV).

In the next chapter we shall see three righteous men, Ezra, Nehemiah and Daniel, identifying themselves with the sins of their people. We need to emulate them and follow their examples of repentance. The Jewish people are still the elect nation of God, *"for the gifts and calling of God are irrevocable"* (Rom 11:29). They are still *"beloved for the sake of the fathers"* (Rom 11:28). And we, the Christian Church, have abused them in the most repulsive way.

Dear LORD,
Grant me the grace to repent of the sins of the Church of which I am a member. Oh, LORD, what horror we inflicted in Your name—what suffering we forced upon Your people. Root out anti-Semitism from the Church, LORD. Cast it into the pits of damnation where it belongs. Cleanse us, LORD, cleanse us with the precious blood of Jesus. Wash away our shame. Wash away our reproach. Grant us love, genuine love, for Your Jewish people, and help me in some small way to expiate the horrendous sins committed. Amen.

24

THE ROOT
OF
THE PROBLEM

The importance that Israel plays in world events cannot be over-estimated nor over-emphasised. Israel is a key to every major happening in the plans and purposes of God. The observation was made in Chapter Six that, from the context of the original Greek, "Salvation proceeds from, and is completed in, the Jewish people." We need to develop this subject and see the role that Israel plays in world evangelism and how essential it is for the Church to be rightly related to Israel.

For centuries, the Christian Church has felt secure in her belief that her doctrine was in order, and, anticipated that, at any moment, the world would fall at her feet. But, after almost 2,000 years, the Church is shockingly divided, opposed from within and without, and being challenged by a younger, more militant religion for supremacy. If the Christian Church has the true Word of God, and if Jesus is, in fact, the Son of God who defied the grave and holds the keys to death and hell, and if the Holy Spirit really came at Pentecost to empower us to disciple all nations, why have we not carried it out? Obviously something is wrong!

The Church has generally held to the belief that she replaced Israel and has become the light to the world, but she is wrong in her assumption. The Church, influenced by an anti-Jewish mood that has existed within her ranks since the second century, corrupted the exegeses of Scriptures pertaining to Israel and the Jewish people.

Doctrines came forth that were anti-Semitic in nature. Thus the Church, believing herself to be the "True Israel," has persistently boasted of her superiority over the Jewish people who are natural Israel according to the flesh. In truth, however, the "True" Israel was actual eons before the Church came into existence but this truth has never been a part of Church doctrine. Neither has the fact that this "True," wholly Jewish Israel, supports, maintains and nourishes the entire Church. The Apostle Paul, primarily addressing Gentile believers, makes an important point concerning natural Israel:

> *"If the **root is holy**, so are the branches. And if **some** of the branches were broken off, and **you**, being a **wild** olive tree, were **grafted in among them**, and **with them** became a **partaker of the root and fatness of the olive tree**, do not boast against the branches. But if you do boast, **remember that you do not support the root, but the root supports you***"   (Rom 11:16-18).

Paul uses the metaphor of an *"olive tree"* to describe natural Israel. The *"branches"* that were *"broken off"* are the unbelieving Jewish people. Paul cautions the Gentile Christians against the very thing that they have been guilty of for nearly 2,000 years—boasting of their favoured position over the unbelieving Jews. The Church must acknowledge and accept the established fact that not all Jews were unbelieving and neither were all the Jewish *"branches"* broken off. The Gentile Christians, branches from *"a **wild** olive tree, were grafted in **among them**"*—**among the Jews**, into natural Israel, the **natural** *"olive tree,"* and now share the nourishment, the goodness, and the blessings of that tree. It is very important to see that it is the Gentiles who are grafted in among the Jews and not vice versa. When a Jew comes to faith in Jesus he is grafted back into his own olive tree, among his own people. Abraham and the patriarchs are *"the root,"* the parent-stem of *"the olive tree"*—the Jewish nation. From this olive tree the unbelieving branches were broken off leaving a vigorous remnant of believing branches growing from a holy stock and supported by a *"holy root."* And it is this *"root"* and *"stump"* (Isa 6:13), that *"supports and nourishes"* the Church. Unfortunately, the Church fell into the same trap as Elijah, who felt that he was the only true believer in the LORD:

> *"**God has not cast away His people** whom He foreknew. Or do you not know what the Scripture says of Elijah, how he pleads with God against Israel, saying, 'LORD, they have killed Your prophets*

*and torn down Your altars, and **I alone am left**, and they seek my life'? But what does the divine response say to him?· **'I have reserved for Myself seven thousand men** who have not bowed the knee to Baal.' Even so then, **at this present time there is a remnant according to the election of grace"***   (Rom 11:2-5).

The Scripture is clear: *"God has not cast away His people."* He has always kept a *"remnant"* for Himself, and this Jewish *"remnant"* is nourished and sustained by a Jewish *"root."* In the book of Ephesians the Apostle Paul presses the point that the Jews were also the first to believe in Christ and only later did the Gentiles believe:

*"**We who first trusted in Christ** should be to the praise of His glory. In Him **you also** trusted, **after you heard** the word of truth, the gospel of **your** salvation; in whom also, having believed, **you** were sealed with the Holy Spirit of promise"*   (Eph 1:12&13).

That the *"we"* were Jews should be quite clear. The very early Church was exclusively Jewish. Only after Peter went to the house of Cornelius the Roman centurion, in obedience to a heavenly vision some eight years after the ascension of Christ, did the gospel spread to the Gentiles (Acts chapter ten). The Jewish leadership of the early Church grasped the plan of God and made room for the Gentile believers among the Jewish *"branches."* It is a lamentable fact, however, that the great majority of Gentile believers, past and present, through erroneous teachings that began in the second century and continue until today, did not grasp God's plan for the Church and ostracised the Jews for being Jews. Gentiles are Gentiles and Jews are Jews even as Paul made clear:

*"Therefore remember **that you** ... **Gentiles** in the flesh—who are called **Uncircumcision** by what is called **the Circumcision** ..."*
(Eph 2:11).

The Jews, obviously, are the *"Circumcision"* and the Gentiles are the *"Uncircumcision."* Paul also said that *"there is neither Jew nor Greek [Gentile] ... male nor female"* (Gal 3:28). But he meant that Jews and Gentiles, males and females, all stand equal in Christ before God. He did not mean that Jews ceased to be Jews when they come to faith. Baptised Jews do not become Gentiles any more than turkeys immersed in water become chickens.

The point that I want to make very clear is that the holy, Jewish, patriarchal *"root"* nourishes the holy, Jewish, believing *"remnant"* which, together, form the true *"Israel of God"* (Gal 6:16) into which the Gentile believers are grafted. Paul, a learned Rabbi, has introduced us to an aspect of Rabbinical exegesis known as *remez*, or "hints." Paul's use of *"holy root"* hints at prophecies in the book of Isaiah. Desolation was about to come to the cities and villages of Israel. Only a small portion of the people were to survive the rape of their land:

> *"But yet a tenth will be in it, and will return and be for consuming, as a terebinth tree or as an oak, **whose stump remains** when it is cut down. **So the holy seed shall be its stump**"*   (Isa 6:13).

A *"tenth"* of the people would survive the Babylonian destruction. Within that *"tenth"* was the believing *"remnant"*of that time, *"the holy seed,"* of which Daniel, for example, was a part. The *"tenth"* would return from exile and again be subject to a *"consuming,"* which was the Roman conquest that took the lives of millions of Jews. The ten northern tribes of Israel never returned to the land after the Assyrian and Babylonian captivities, only a remnant of Judah:

> *"And **the remnant** who have escaped of the house of Judah **shall again take root downward, and bear fruit upward**"*   (Isa 37:31).

After the Jews returned from their exile, the temple was rebuilt, and there was again a *"holy remnant"* of true believers in the land. After a period of time had elapsed, however, the majority of the nation turned away from the LORD, and once more it was time for discipline. We know that the following passage was referring to the Roman destruction, as the prophecy concerns Jesus and was fulfilled on the night of His betrayal (Matt 26:31):

> *"'Awake, O sword, against **My Shepherd**, against **the Man who is My Companion**,' says the LORD of hosts. '**Strike the Shepherd, and the sheep will be scattered;** then **I will turn My hand against the little ones**. And it shall come to pass in all the land,' says the LORD, 'That two-thirds in it shall be cut off and die, but **one-third shall be left** in it: I will bring the one-third **through the fire**, will refine them as silver is refined, and test them as gold is tested. They will call on My name, and I will answer them. I will say, 'This is My people'; and **each one will say**, 'The LORD is my God'"*
> (Zech 13:7-9).

We also know from history that during the great revolt that ended with the destruction of Jerusalem in 70 A.D., together with the Bar-Kochba revolt, over three million Jews died at the hands of the Romans. Altogether, the greater part of the Jewish presence in the land was destroyed. *"One-third"* was to be left, and, like the passage from Isaiah, these survivors were to be *"brought through the fire and tested and refined as gold."* The LORD says that He will *"turn His hand against the little ones."* This is not *"turning His hand against the little ones"* in a destructive way. On the contrary, the Hebraism used is that of protection, not of harm. The LORD'S hand is being brought back "over" the *"little ones"* as a protective shield. The *"little ones,"* no doubt mean the more than 60,000 Jewish believers that fled to Arabia and found refuge in and around Pella at the outbreak of hostilities with the Romans. Jesus warned His disciples in Matthew chapter twenty-four to *"flee to the mountains,"* and history records:

"The Christians, warned by these predictions, fled from Jerusalem to Pella, and other places beyond the Jordan; so that there is not evidence that a single Christian perished in Jerusalem."[1]

The *"one-third"* were the surviving Jews who were then taken through the *"fire"* of world anti-Semitism which culminated in the Holocaust. As in every past generation, there is today a *"remnant"* of *"holy"* (*"if the root is holy, so are the branches"* Rom 11:16) Jews who believe. And the promise is that every surviving Jew will come to know Messiah Jesus: *"I will say, 'This is My people'; and **each one** will say, 'The LORD is my God.'"* Today, the *"holy root"* continues to nourish the *"holy branches."* And it is *"among"* these *"branches,"* the *"remnant,"* that today's Gentile Christians are being grafted. It is the Jewish *"holy root"* and the Jewish stock—the long, thin line of believing Jews throughout the ages, beginning with Abraham—*"the Israel of God,"* that *"supports"* the Gentile believers and from which they receive their *"nourishment."* The Gentiles *"**now share in the nourishing sap from the olive root**"* (Rom 11:17 NIV). Let us make no mistake. Let us look again and confirm whose *"root"* and *"tree"* it is:

*"For **if you** [Gentiles] were cut out of the olive tree which is wild by nature, and were **grafted contrary to nature** into a cultivated olive tree [Israel], **how much more will these** [Jews], **who are natural branches, be grafted into their own olive tree?"***

(Rom 11:24).

The Gentile Christians are *"wild olive"* branches *"grafted"* into Israel, the *"cultivated olive tree"*—an unnatural horticultural act. The Jews are the *"natural branches,"* and the cultivated olive tree is *"their own."* The importance of seeing this essential doctrine cannot be over em- phasised. It is absolutely vital to the health of the Christian Church. Paul tells us that *"some of the branches"* were broken off *"because of unbelief"* (Rom 11:20). He then goes on to say:

> *"And they also, **if they do not continue in unbelief**, will be grafted in, for **God is able to graft them in again**"*   (Rom 11:23).

If the *"branches broken off,"* the unbelieving Jewish people, *"do not continue in unbelief they will be grafted back into their own olive tree."* We know from Chapter Eleven that the LORD promises to make a new covenant with the entire house of Israel:

> *"**They all shall know Me, from the least of them to the greatest of them**, says the LORD"*   (Jer 31:34).

Obviously, the currently unbelieving Jewish people are not going to remain in *"unbelief"* and will, at some point in time, in their *"appointed season,"* be *"grafted back into their own olive tree."*

CUT OFF FROM THE ROOT

In the previous chapter we looked at the role played by the Church with regard to anti-Semitism. The hatred deep within the bosom of even many professing "born-again" Christians brought forth a long and fearful nightmare for Jews, the chosen people of God. The LORD purposed to bring the Gentiles into His salvation in order to make the Jews jealous and desire Him:

> *"I say then, have **they stumbled** that they should **fall**? Certainly not! But **through their fall, to provoke them to jealousy, salvation has come to the Gentiles**"*   (Rom 11:11).

Notice that the Jews did not *"fall,"* they merely *"stumbled."* They *"stumbled at the stumbling stone"* (Rom 9:32), which was the Lord Jesus Christ, but they *"certainly"* never fell beyond recovery. And, because they *"stumbled,"* salvation came to the Gentiles. It was God's purpose for the Gentile believers in Christ to live and act in such a manner that the Jewish people would be provoked to jealousy. Being jealous of the Gentile's acceptance, the Jews would be stimulated into action to seek after the LORD, find Him, and, ultimately, usher in the the greatest of all events, namely the second coming of the Lord Jesus:

> *"For if their being cast away is the reconciling of the world, what will their acceptance be but life from the dead?"* (Rom 11:15).

But what happened, in fact, was that the Jews were not provoked to jealousy by the Gentile Church, they were actually persecuted, tortured, maimed and killed, and thus pushed even further into *"unbelief."*

The Church is most often portrayed by the metaphor of a "fruit bearing" tree. For example:

> *"Every branch in Me that does not bear fruit He takes away; and every branch that bears fruit He prunes, that it may bear more fruit"* (Jn 15:2)

To bear fruit, and especially to bring fruit to maturity, a tree must have a healthy root system. The roots of a tree not only give stability to the tree itself, but also take the necessary food from the ground in which it is growing and transfers it to the branches by means of the tree's sap. If the sap is hindered in its flow, by disease or interference with the tree's rooting system, the result is a mixture of stunted and withered fruit and the shedding of that fruit from the branches that bore it.

After research has been carried out by different members of the Church with regard to evangelism, some startling facts come to light:

a: The Western Church has steadily decreased in numbers since 1968.[2]

b: From over 4,000 decisions for Christ, registered with nearly 200 churches in America, less than three percent continued in church membership after a few months.[3]

c: Of 18,000 registered decisions from the ministry of the greatest living evangelist,[4] who has the highest percentage of ongoing commitments among major ministries, less than seven percent were continuing in church membership after several months.[5]

Most pastors in the West experience the same phenomenon. The majority of their new converts do not travel very far along the Christian road before falling away, usually within weeks, or, at best, a few months.

The truth of the thesis being advanced in this chapter becomes apparent. The Jewish root and stock of the true Israel—*"the Israel of God,"* is that which supports, sustains and nourishes the Church. But, by its anti-Semitism, which includes the various brands of "Replacement Theology," the predominantly Gentile Church cuts herself off from the the *"nourishing sap,"* thereby causing the Church's fruit to drop from her branches. And a restricted sap flow is possibly the chief reason why there is such an abundance of weak and sickly "church members."

Generally, the Charismatic and Pentecostal streams of the Protestant Church are guilty of being "evangelastic" rather than evangelistic. The truth is "stretched" and the claim is made that the Church is advancing throughout the world "like a storm." The oft reported figures by western Christians of nearly one hundred million Chinese embracing Christianity in China are disclaimed by the Chinese Christians. They themselves claim only forty million. The same holds true for South Korea. Westerners claim that thirty to thirty-five percent of the total population of South Korea is Christian. South Korean pastors claim twenty percent or less. Constantly, one hears the quoted figure of 64,000 people being born daily into the Kingdom of God. Even if this were true, what is that compared with a daily population increase of nine humans born each second? In just one day the world population increases by some 777,600 people. Subtracting our assumed 64,000, leaves an additional 713,600 unreached people. Adding this number daily to the billions that we have never reached only proves that, at the present rate of success, we have absolutely no chance of winning this world to Christ. We have to be honest concerning the daily 64,000 commitments, too. These 64,000 people may or may not be making commitments to Christ, but how many of those who make them actually keep the commitment?

I have been involved personally in evangelism on five continents and also throughout Australia, New Zealand and the Pacific areas. The fall-away rate in those areas differs little from that in America. The research figures quoted previously gave us an average ongoing-commitment-rate of less that six and a half percent. Supposing that, in order to be more than fair, we quadruple that amount to twenty-six percent, we still only manage a daily total of less than 17,000 souls added to the Church, and from this figure we must subtract the ever-increasing fall-off from established Christianity. The Church, therefore, is growing at a rate less than 17,000 daily while the unbelieving world grows by more than 750,000. The gap between saved and unsaved grows wider and wider.

Prominent Christians in America proclaim that, at the present rate of growth, nearly all the world will be Christian by the end of the decade. And throughout America great claims are being made of revival and tremendous increase in church congregations. The following statement from a group of research specialists says it all:

"Eighty percent of all U.S. church growth is 'transfer growth'— people moving from one church to another, instead of the unchurched people coming into church [bold emphasis added]."[6]

The truth, as can readily be seen, is that at the present rate of growth the Church is in danger of becoming displaced as the leading religion by the end of the decade. All is not lost, however, and the rate of the Church's growth need not stagnate at the present level, but a change of heart-attitude toward Israel is absolutely essential. A change of doctrine is necessary regarding the place of Israel in the overall scheme of things and a recognition that it is the Jewish *"root"* and stock that supports the mass of Gentile *"branches."* When the Church gets Israel into the right perspective the rate of evangelism will accelerate and the results will be lasting, not temporal.

INDEBTED TO THE JEW

The Bible tells us that Gentile Christians are indebted to the Jews and encourages Gentiles to minister material blessings to the Jews as a *"duty,"* in exchange for the spiritual blessings received from them:

*"For it pleased those from Macedonia and Achaia to make a certain **contribution** for the poor among **the saints who are in Jerusalem**. It pleased them indeed, and they are **their debtors**. For if **the Gentiles have been partakers of their spiritual things, their duty is also to minister to them in material things"***
(Rom 15:26&27).

Before Gentiles came to faith in the Lord Jesus, they were not in an enviable position:

> *"Therefore, remember that formerly **you who are Gentiles** ... were **separate** from Christ, **excluded** from citizenship in Israel and **foreigners** to the covenants of the promise, **without hope and without God** in the world"*   (Eph 2:11&12 NIV).

Gentiles were once *"separate"* from both *"Christ and Israel"* and *"without God or hope."*

The Church was never meant to be separate or divorced from Israel. Neither was the Church called to replace or displace Israel. The Church was **joined into** the commonwealth of Israel by being *"grafted in among"* the Jewish *"branches,"* and, as a consequence, partakes of the spiritual blessings of *"the Israel of God."* Ministering material blessing to today's Jewish *"remnant"* not only helps repay the debt but also helps propagate the gospel among the Jewish people. Gentile Christians should seek an indigenous Israeli-Christian ministry to support prayerfully and financially and, as we saw in Chapter Eight, *"in blessing, they shall be blessed."* And genuine Christian love needs to be shown to all Jewish people simply because they are the beloved of God.

REPENTANCE

The Christian Church must enter into a time of deep repentance, both individually and corporately, for the sin of anti-Semitism that has been so much a part of her history and is still in her midst today. It is irrelevant whether one personally committed acts of anti-Semitism or not. If we belong to the Church we share in the sins of the Church as well as in the blessings. Ezra was an extremely righteous man, as were both Nehemiah and Daniel, but all three holy men identified themselves with, and repented of, the sins of their people:

> EZRA: *"At the evening sacrifice I arose from my fasting; and having torn my garment and my robe, I fell on my knees and spread out my hands to the LORD my God. And I said, 'O my God: I am too ashamed and humiliated to lift up my face to You, my God; for **our iniquities** have risen higher than our heads, and **our guilt** has grown up to the heavens"*   (Ezra 9:5).

NEHEMIAH: *"Please let Your ear be attentive and Your eyes open, that You may hear the prayer of Your servant which I pray before You now, day and night, for the children of Israel Your servants, and confess the sins of the children of Israel which **we have sinned** against You. **Both my father's house and I have sinned"***   (Neh 1:6).

DANIEL: *"And I prayed to the LORD my God, and made confession, and said, 'O Lord, great and awesome God, who keeps His covenant and mercy with those who love Him, and with those who keep His commandments, **we have sinned and committed iniquity, we have done wickedly and rebelled**, even by departing from Your precepts and Your judgments. **Neither have we heeded Your servants the prophets**, who spoke in Your name to our kings and our princes, to our fathers and all the people of the land'"*
(Dan 9:4-6).

These great men leave us an example. They never personally committed the sins they confessed, but they did belong to the nation of Israel; therefore, they identified themselves not only with the people but also with the sins of the people. In the same way, Christians must repent for the sins committed against the Jewish people by the Church. Failure to do this will only further delay the evangelisation of the world.

VEILS OF BLINDNESS

"Salvation is of the Jews." This statement is as true today as when Jesus made it. The LORD has one simple strategy for evangelising the world's population—win the Jew! Win the Jew to Christ, and the world is won. We know that a *"veil of blindness"* lies over the heart of the Jew:

*"But **their minds were blinded**. For until this day **the same veil remains unlifted** in the reading of the Old Testament, because **the veil is taken away in Christ**. But even to this day, when Moses is read, **a veil lies on their heart**. Nevertheless **when one turns to the Lord, the veil is taken away"***   (2 Cor 3:14-16).

"The veil is taken away in Christ." It was, and still is, God's purpose for the Gentiles to provoke the Jew to jealousy and bring them to Christ.

If, in the heart of a Christian, there is a love for a lost world, it is essential to understand that the Jews must first come to the knowledge of Christ before the great mass of the Gentiles can be effectively reached. For it is not only the Jews that have their hearts covered by a *"veil of blindness:"*

*"He will destroy ... the covering cast over all people, and **the veil that is spread over all nations**"*   (Isa 25:7).

The *"veil"* that is spoken of here is a "mist of ignorance." This *"veil,"* or shroud, is a symbol of the spiritual blindness of the nations, like the *"veil"* upon the heart of Israel. Just as the *"veil"* that lies over the Jewish heart *"is taken away in Christ,"* so also the *"veil that is spread over all nations"* will be *"taken away in Christ."* The Jew will be won by Gentiles provoking them to jealousy. The world will be won by Jew and Gentile yoked together in the love of Christ. It is not possible to evangelise this world apart from the Jew, and efforts to do so have thus far borne little fruit.

Dear LORD,
Thank You for showing me the root of the problem. Help me to get rightly related to the holy stump of Israel that supports me. Grant that I might connect to the root so I may be nourished from its sap. Oh, LORD, we have sinned and acted wickedly towards Your people. We repent and pray for Your peace to be upon the Israel of God. Amen.

25

A DISMEMBERED BODY

There are two main reasons why, in two thousand years, the Church has not accomplished her God-given task. One of these reasons, anti-Semitism, has already been looked at. The other is a lack of desire on the part of the average Christian to take his faith seriously. There have always been, and always will be, those who are totally committed to the Lord Jesus. There are, however, many who are only *lukewarm* (Rev 3:16) in their faith, and there are, also, many committed more to the "Lord's work" than to the Lord, Himself—committed to programs and projects; and, while all these activities might be valid, the "good" will always remain the enemy of the "best." Generally, we need the revelation that the Christian faith involves more "being," than "doing"—that Christianity is a living relationship with a living Saviour.

In another Biblical metaphor, the Church is the Body of the Lord Jesus Christ:

*"He is the **head of the body, the church**"*   (Col 1:18).

Every person, Jew or Gentile, that yields his life to Jesus becomes a member of that Body of which Jesus is the head.

Many modern churches evangelise with a view to getting "decisions" for Christ. But, as we saw in the previous chapter, these "decisions" are, for the main part, of the same ilk as New Year Resolutions which rarely last longer than a month or two. There is a common endeavour to present the gospel in such an appealing way that it will cause the unchurched to "choose" Jesus over the way of the world. It is even suggested that these unchurched people "try" Jesus. Only the preaching of Jesus Christ as the crucified Son of the Living God brings lasting results. When we lift Jesus up as the Eternal Son who died and rose from the dead on the third day and who makes the way back for man to relate again to his Creator as in the beginning, the Holy Spirit ensures results that glorify God. The Holy Spirit does not sanction the presentation of Jesus dying in our stead merely so that we might go to heaven, because that is a travesty of the gospel. God's redemption of man is so much more wondrously comprehensive than that. Gimmicky presentations of Jesus are not necessary, and suggesting that people "try" Jesus is an insult to the Son of God. He is not on trial—we are. And "choosing" Jesus is no more a Scriptural term than "deciding" for Him:

*"**You did not choose Me, but I chose you** and appointed you that you should go and **bear fruit, and that your fruit should remain, that whatever you ask** the Father in My name He may give you"*   (Jn 15:16).

We, ourselves, are chosen by Jesus, not vice versa. We are also appointed to bear fruit, and this fruit is to remain—to become mature. Fruit is a natural result of a life lived in Christ and is also a condition for answered prayer. The average Christian does not *"abide"* in Christ (Jn 15:4) and, of a consequence, cuts himself off from Christ (Jn 15:2).

Anti-Semitic acts and doctrines resulted in the Church being cut off from the *"root,"* and the lack of abiding cuts the individual off from Jesus, the "head" of the Body. Thus, the average Christian is cut off from the *"root"* that supports and nourishes and also from the *"head"* that instructs.

The Body of Christ is divided mainly by doctrine and, for the most part, cannot find any common ground on which to meet. Slander, libel, name-calling and outright hate are nowadays commonplace even within the same denomination or stream of Christianity. The Body of Christ is a dismembered body with vital limbs and organs severed from each other. No "head" is able to command or instruct that which is not attached. Unity will come between born-again Christians when there is a fixation with Jesus—a radical and absolute identification with Him.

JESUS IS LORD?

The pulsating, vibrant early Church, in general, has become a "Christianity of convenience," especially in the West. The risen, Biblical Jesus—the One who healed the sick, gave sight to the blind, raised the dead, fed the thousands and quieted the winds and seas—has now become a "prayer-room" Jesus. And, even among the relatively few who enter the prayer-room, some bring petitions that closely resemble a shopping list. The Church is the only known body which gives orders and directions to its head—to its own brain.

The early Church was radical in her commitment to the living Christ, and practically everywhere the Gospel was preached signs, wonders and miracles accompanied it. The average Christian today, having never personally experienced the miraculous, accepts the teaching that the miraculous ceased with the close of the Apostolic era. It is true that there has been a dramatic lessening in the miraculous acts of God as demonstrated through the members of His Church, but the reason for this lies with man, not with God. The LORD says clearly enough: *"I am the LORD, I do not change"* (Mal 3:6). And there is full assurance also that His Son, the Lord Jesus Christ—the head of the Church—*"is the same yesterday, today and forever"* (Heb 13:8). No! God has not changed! It is man that has changed!

The average Christian's faith rests upon experience and upon what his intellect can justify rather than upon what is written in the Bible. There is little commitment to the Lord or dependency upon Him. The dependency has been transferred to governmental, social-welfare schemes, retirement funds, insurance, assurance, hospitals, doctors, etc. None of these, of themselves, are wrong, but the focus of Christian dependency has shifted onto them and off of Jesus, who is the All-Sufficient One. The average Christian relies heavily upon the ways of the world to protect himself, his health, his goods and his property, all of which rightfully belongs to a supernatural kingdom. Normally, this property, belonging to a supernatural realm, will also be protected supernaturally if the faith for this exists. Millions of Christians pour billions of dollars into the coffers of the world's insurance companies when, with the exercising of just a small amount of faith, they would have little need for insurance and would receive the peace given by Jesus, Himself, rather than the peace offered by the world (Jn 14:27). The peace of mind than comes from insurance and assurance may be very beneficial to those who do not know the victorious Christ, but Christian insurance people that target other Christians are prostituting themselves.

The average Christian is content to be a Christian provided this does not interfere too much with his life-style. His behavioural pattern does not differ greatly from the unchurched,[1] and his children are being raised with the same low standards as his own. A number of Christian youth organisations have sponsored research into youth behaviour, and the results reveal that the **only** major difference between Christian and non-Christian youth is a **verbal** one: "The Christians answer 'no' when asked if they would lie, cheat, steal or go to bed with someone, while the non-Christian youth say, 'Of course, if it's to my advantage.'"[2] The Church is not called to shine in the sunlight of Christian gatherings but in a world darkened by sin.

The average Christian is now caught up in the pursuit of the good-life: houses, cars, trailer-caravans, boats, televisions, video players—the list is endless. What used to be luxury has become necessity. He needs to go through a baptism of bereavement concerning his possessions. Most often, the things which we possess possess us, and we become slaves to our materialism. Even if the Church got her doctrine concerning Israel corrected today she would still be too busy with her own comforts to be overly concerned about the billions of people sliding into the pits of hell. It is time we stopped blaming the devil and let the blame lie at our own feet where it belongs:

"The cares of this world, the deceitfulness of riches, and the desires for other things entering in choke the word, and it becomes unfruitful"   (Mk 4:18&19).

This was part of the explanation of the parable of the sower that Jesus gave to His disciples. And through this we learn that we are directly responsible for being personally unfruitful. We are caught up with *"the cares of this world"* instead of trusting in Him. We are misled by *"the deceitfulness of riches"* and have *"desires for other things"* rather than for Him. So caught up are we with our endless pursuit for the elusive good-life that we have not time for this One whom we call Lord. The cry of pastors, elders, deacons and lay church members throughout Christendom is "I have no time." The LORD will not make more time available to man—we have all there is to be had. We find time for our favourite recreations, but we cannot find time for God. We will always find time for what is most important to us, and whatever takes precedence over the Lord Jesus is, ultimately, our god.

A survey was taken among Christians at a conference. Each participant was given a slip of paper and asked to write down how much personal, private devotional time was spent daily with the Lord. They were also requested to indicate whether they were ministers or lay people. The result of the survey was that the average pastor spent ten minutes each day with the Lord and the average church member only five minutes. I have personally conducted the same type of survey amongst missionaries on the field, and many of them admit to only five, ten or fifteen minutes a day in prayer and private devotion to the Lord Jesus. As God does nothing except in answer to prayer it is hardly surprising that we have a weak and impotent Church. We loudly declare in our songs that "Jesus is Lord," and we speak among ourselves constantly of the "Lord," but we are only fooling ourselves. If we give only five, ten, fifteen or twenty minutes to the Son of God, while spending the remaining 1,440 minutes of each day pursuing our concerns and interests, how can He be Lord? Were we to individually analyse our own personal faith, actions and motives the greatest fraud in all the world would be seen to be ourselves. And, seriously, if we were to *"prosper just as our souls prosper"* (3 Jn 1:2) many of us would be classed as living below the poverty level.

God has no favourites in this world. Jew and Gentile, male and female are all equal in His sight; each has a specific role, but all stand on an equal footing before Him. The Jews are not God's favourite people but His chosen people. Jesus is not God's favourite Son but His beloved Son. The LORD responds to those that seek Him, and some people find Him in a way that others do not. The difference lies with the individual, not with God. Our personal revelation of God depends upon our character—not upon God's.

The average Christian, in order to relax after a days work, turns to the world's entertainment system and fills his mind with ungodly images and sounds that, within a relatively short space of time, bring forth a multiplied harvest. I would challenge my readers to abstain from watching any television, videos or movies for one whole month and also to abstain from reading anything other than the Bible during that period of time. The time that would usually be given over to television

(Christian or secular), magazines (Christian or secular), and newspapers, is to be used solely for Bible-reading and prayer. Readers are guaranteed that many changes will take place in their spiritual, emotional and physical lives as well as in the lives of those with whom they are in contact. It is my firm opinion that television is today's number one cause of defeated Christian lives. It takes the place of God in a Christian's home and affects his Christian walk and also that of every member of his family. Television affects a Christian's pattern of behaviour, his relationships, career advancement, finances, marriage, children's behaviour, children's school grades and much, much more.

Our dire need is to be truly born again. We are born with the Adamic nature which demands its right to itself. We must be born again, from above, with the sinless nature of God that seeks the welfare of others. The way we overcome the flesh, the world and the devil is by the force of our love for God regulating all our passions. We need to feed our new nature, but this cannot be done in front of secular television or by pursuing our own pleasures. We must, of necessity, reconnect to the "Head." We must learn to tithe our time, as well as our finances, to the King. Only by sitting quiet and still in His presence will we hear His voice and receive His instructions. God is a God of silence, and He is found only in a quiet setting. There is a time for worship, for song, for Bible study, and for reading the Bible in a meditative way, and there is a time for silent devotional worship when we simply concentrate and wait upon Him. We need to get alone with God. We need to recognise who He is and recognise who we are. When our minds and surroundings are still and quiet the LORD will communicate. May our hearts ever say to Him, *"Speak, for Your servant is listening"* (1 Sam 3:10).

Dear LORD,
I have sinned against You by neglecting my relationship with You. I have cut myself off from the Head of the Body of which I am a part, and I repent. I ask that You forgive me, Father, and help me to begin afresh from this moment. I want to know You. I want to serve You but do not know how. I want to love You but do not know how. Hear an honest cry from an honest heart, Father. Draw me into times alone with You where all may be still and quiet. Rebuke me when I want to skip those times in order to pursue other "things." Encourage me that my soul might pant for You *"as a deer pants for the water brooks"* in a dry and thirsty land. Amen.

PART VI

THE ETERNAL PURPOSE

"For He Himself is our peace, who has made the two one and has destroyed the barrier, the dividing wall of hostility, by abolishing in his flesh the law with its commandments and regulations. His purpose was to create in Himself one new man out of the two, thus making peace, and in this one body to reconcile both of them to God through the cross, by which he put to death their hostility. He came and preached peace to you who were far away and peace to those who were near"

(Eph 2:14-17 NIV).

26

ONE NEW MAN

One of the main reasons for world evangelism is to provoke the Jews to jealousy, thereby promoting the salvation of Israel. Until the Jewish people are brought into the knowledge of their Jewish Messiah the Church cannot obtain its objective of world redemption. The Church can no more fulfill her dreams today than she could yesterday.

Because of Christian behavioural patterns toward Jews since the early years of the Church, Jesus is not a religious "option" for the Jewish people. A Jew will be accepted by his own people if he believes that there is no God, and he will be accepted even if he becomes, say, a Buddhist or a Hindu. But he will not be accepted if he turns to Christ, simply because of what has taken place in the name of Christ. There is a great void in the souls of Jews, and I postulate again the statistics given in Chapter Thirteen, that between fifty and seventy percent of all members of religious sects and occultic groups are Jewish. The Jew is ever seeking to fill his soul's vacuum—his soul's mournful cry for God.

Great Jewish minds, like Albert Einstein, are attracted to Jesus:

"I am a Jew, but I am enthralled by the luminous figure of the Nazarene.
Jesus is too colossal for the pen of phrase-mongers, however artful. No man can dispose of Christianity with a '*bon mot.*'
No one can read the Gospels without feeling the actual presence of Jesus. His personality pulsates in every word."[1]

Such sentiments! Expressed from perhaps the greatest scientific mind the world has known. Other thinking Jews are also drawn to the "luminous figure" of Jesus, but His followers turn them away. Jews do not seek after Jesus due to the suffering experienced by their people at the hands of those who claimed to have been His disciples. Jesus, to the Jewish mind, represents the principal cause of two thousand years of Jewish suffering.

RIGHTLY DIVIDING THE WORD

It is important for the Church to read the Bible in the way God intended it to be read, and we are admonished to be:

"Rightly dividing the word of truth"   (2 Tim 2:15).

We are to know, and to correctly divide or explain, the word of God. A concentration on God's point of view allows us to see things through the eyes of the LORD. It is essential that both God and the Church walk the same path together, and we cannot unless we first agree:

"Can two walk together, unless they are agreed?"   (Amos 3:3).

The LORD has a distinct purpose for the Church. To fulfill her destiny the Church must accept God's purpose as her own. He has made His purpose known to the Church:

"His purpose was to create in Himself one new man out of the two, thus making peace, and in this one body to reconcile both of them to God"   (Eph 2:15&16).

God's Great Purpose *"was to create in Himself,"* that is, in *"His body, which is the Church"* (Col 1:24), *"one new man,"* Jews and Gentiles worshipping together in the love of Christ. And through this *"One New Man,"* this reconciled body, God would bring about the reconciliation of the world.

Tragically, the Church has opposed God's purpose for nearly two millennia and has almost sought to undo the work accomplished on the cross at Calvary:

*"For He Himself is our peace, **who has made the two one** and has destroyed the barrier, the dividing **wall of hostility**, by abolishing in His flesh the law with its commandments and regulations. **His purpose was to create in Himself one new man out of the two,** thus making peace, and in this one body **to reconcile both of them to God through the cross,** by which **He put to death their hostility**"* (Eph 2:14-16 NIV).

Jesus *"made the two one,"* the two being the Jew and the Gentile. Jesus made them one, but the Church made Jew and Gentile as far apart as the dawn is from the dusk. Jesus *"destroyed the barrier, the dividing wall of hostility,"* but the Church re-erected barriers and rebuilt her own walls of hostility. Jesus *"put to death their hostility,"* but the Church revived it. The medium through which the purpose of God was to be accomplished became an insurmountable obstacle:

*"His **purpose** was to create ... **through the cross**"*
(Eph 2:15&16 NIV).

The LORD purposed to reconcile both Jew and Gentile *"through the cross."* Today, for many Gentiles, the cross is worn as an ornament as a symbol of God's love, but, for the Jews, it is the symbol of the persecution of their people—a despised and hated thing.

WALKING WORTHILY

God's part for Gentile believers in the Great Purpose was to provoke the Jews to envy. The way to accomplish this is spelled out for us by the apostle Paul, who became *"all things to all men, that he might by all means save some"* (1 Cor 9:22). He admonished the early Church repeatedly concerning daily conduct, and those same admonitions apply to all who name the Name of Christ today:

*"I, therefore, the prisoner of the Lord, beseech you to **walk worthy of the calling with which you were called**"* (Eph 4:1).

*"**Let your conduct be worthy of the gospel of Christ**"* (Phil 1:27).

*"**Walk worthy of the Lord**"* (Col 1:10).

*"**Walk worthy of God**"* (1 Thes 2:12).

Had the Gentile Church, walked in a manner worthy of her calling, worthy of the gospel of Christ, worthy of the Name that she bears, she could have accomplished her particular purpose. She could have provoked the Jew to jealousy and brought about the salvation of Israel and, ultimately, the salvation of the world. The majority of Jews will not now accept Jesus until they again see Him (that is, His body, the Church) on the cross, dying for them.

The *"One New Man"* that the LORD purposed is nothing less than the "New Israel." The difference between God's "New Israel" and the Church's "New Israel" is that the LORD made provision for the Jew to have an active, vital role.

After nearly two thousand years of Christian persecution, the Jews have become the most difficult of all peoples to win for Christ. But they can be, and are being, won by those who truly love them with the love of Jesus. These "lovers" *"are to God the fragrance of Christ"* (2 Cor 2:15), and they walk worthily of His name. Despite the Church having slid from her foundation which is Christ, and despite her past and present history of anti-Semitism, God's purpose has not altered one fraction of one degree. And we need to remember also that the LORD, as the architect of all creation, is sovereign over His creation. He may allow us sufficient rope to hang ourselves, but he does not allow His purposes to be thwarted:

"The LORD of hosts has sworn, saying, 'Surely, as I have thought, so it shall come to pass, and as I have purposed, so it shall stand'" (Isa 14:24).

"Indeed I have spoken it; I will also bring it to pass. I have purposed it; I will also do it" (Isa 46:11).

These are but examples of many Scriptures that expound God's sovereignty of purpose. *"His purpose was to create in Himself one new man out of the two."* Since His purpose cannot be thwarted, then, the *"One New Man"* will certainly come to pass, but we need to remember:

*"To everything **there is a season, a time for every purpose** under heaven"* (Eccl 3:1).

No matter what past or present glories the Church may have seen, all of them combined will never equal the glory of the Church when she triumphs as the *"One New Man."* Think of it! Jew and Gentile, the most bitter of all enemies, reconciled to God and to each other. This is the Church that the LORD foresees, and it is in this Church that this Scripture will find its fulfillment:

"To Him be glory in the Church"   (Eph 3:21).

The Lord Jesus will have glory in the Church because it is decreed to be so. Presently, there is more glory in the Church for man than for Jesus. Even apart from anti-Semitism, the Church has liberal amounts of idolatry, racial and doctrinal bigotry, fornication, greed, envy, jealousy, lying, etc. Also, many church leaders, instead of being shepherds to their flock, are, in reality, guilty of spiritual abuse—spiritual assault and battery, *"lording it over those entrusted to them"* (1 Pet 5:3). There is often more "worldly" spirit manifesting than there is "Holy" Spirit, and what we see when we look at the world is what God sees when He looks at the Church. But a new day has dawned, and, as we have seen with Israel, the LORD is busily working His purposes without many being aware of it:

"The LORD has done what He purposed; he has fulfilled His word which He commanded in days of old"   (Lam 2:17).

Just as the LORD is fulfilling His word to the descendants of Abraham, Isaac and Jacob, so He is fulfilling His word concerning the Church, *"the One New Man."* The following chapter will introduce us to a new and exciting move of God. As we shall see, a new day has dawned for the Church; a new era has begun for our world.

Dear LORD,
Forgive us for not walking worthily of Your great Name. Forgive us for opposing Your purposes. Forgive us for our bigotry and worldliness. Oh, God, wash from us the religious dirt of past generations. Cleanse us, and we shall be clean, save us, and we shall be saved. Do it, LORD, for the glory of Your Name. Amen.

27

A NEW
ERA
BEGINS

Having studied the history of ancient Israel, I find it apparent that, due to the obstinacy of the Jewish people, she never fulfilled her appointed destiny. The unique survival of the Jews, however, and the unprecedented re-creation of the nation in their ancient homeland bear witness to the fact that her destiny still awaits her.

Turning our attention to the Church, it is also apparent that, due to the obstinacy of her people, she has not fulfilled her appointed destiny either. The Church of the first century was predominantly led by Jewish apostles and evangelists, and, with the exception of Luke (who may yet have been a proselyte to Judaism), the Jews wrote the New Testament. Within a period of approximately seventy years the gospel had been taken to the whole known inhabited world—and then anti-Semitism reared its ugly head. Today the Church survives but in a weak and relatively impotent form, challenged on every front, both by the world and also by a younger religion. The modern Church is, at best, only a hazy shadow of the first century Apostolic Church and, at worst, a mere social institution under the patronage of God. That the Church survives testifies that her destiny awaits her also.

An account of the parallels between ancient Israel and the Church concerning their respective glory, idolatry, adultery, lack of faith, bigotry, corrupt and greedy leadership, etc., would take the space of an entire volume and is not the subject of this work. There are, however, two parallels that do pertain to our present study. The first parallel is that there has always been a holy remnant:

> *"I have reserved seven thousand in Israel, all whose knees have not bowed to Baal ..."*   (1 Kings 19:18).

Just as the LORD reserved a remnant of faithful souls in Israel, so He reserved a remnant of God-fearing men and women in the Church. From Israel's remnant came the "deliverers" who led Israel back to the LORD. And from the Church's remnant came the "champions" who prayed or preached down revivals and brought forth the reformation.

The second parallel of interest here is that of time. Both Israel and the Church have had exactly the same period of exclusive "rights" to the LORD, although neither has fulfilled her destiny.

Locating the exact year of Abraham's birth is nigh impossible for any scholar, but 2111 B.C. falls about in the middle of the estimates. We do know, however, that Isaac was born to Abraham when Abraham was one hundred years old (Gen 21:5), and Jacob was born to Isaac when Isaac was sixty years of age (Gen 25:26). Jacob became the father of the twelve tribes of Israel. We know too, that Jesus was not born in the year 1 A.D., but 4 or 5 B.C. The death and resurrection of Jesus is placed in His thirty-fourth year which would be 28 or 29 A.D. We therefore calculate thus:

$$2111 - 100 - 60 + 28 = 1979$$

This is the period of time that Israel had exclusive "possession" of the LORD as her personal God: from the time of Jacob's birth until the ascension of the Lord Jesus Christ—1,979 years.

The Church actually existed prior to Pentecost, but it was at Pentecost that the power of the Holy Spirit came to dwell exclusively with the Church. We can therefore calculate thus:

$$1993 - 28 = 1965$$

This is the period of time that the Church had exclusive "possession" of the LORD as her personal God—1,965 years, from Pentecost until and including the year 1993.

The fourteen year difference between the time of ancient Israel "possessing" the LORD, and the time of the Church doing so is negligible, especially as we are uncertain of exactly when Abraham was born. And Jacob, of course, could not have had any real knowledge of the LORD for some number of years after his birth. However, the period of time that Israel enjoyed the LORD was one era, and the period that the Church enjoyed Him was another. We are presently at the end of that particular era while, at the same time, another is being ushered in.

AN OVERLAP OF ERAS

The beginning of the Christian Church birthed a new era for mankind. In the early years, as the good news of redemption and reconciliation spread across the known world, nations and cultures underwent transformation. As the Gentile nations moved into the grace of God, so the Jewish nation moved out of that grace into their longest and worst period of suffering.

Today there is a modern, re-created State of Israel to which the LORD is gathering the scattered remnant of the descendants of ancient Israel. The LORD is also working miracles on a daily basis, establishing Israel again as a people, a nation and a formidable military force. Conversely, many Gentile nations now face economic collapse, continuous incidents of murder, violent and non-violent crimes, euthanasia, drug abuse, immorality, abortion, sexually transmitted diseases, AIDS and various other dreadful diseases. Each of the evils is also increasing in frequency or gravity.

Apparently the Jews are moving once again into the grace of God, and the Gentile nations are moving out. We are in an overlap of two eras, the end of one and the commencement of another. It is obvious that a new day dawned for the Jews and the nation of Israel some years ago. We can expect economic and physical catastrophes among some Gentile nations simply on the basis of the curse discussed in Chapter Five, as God has a definite contention with those nations. And we can also expect great and dramatic changes throughout the world as the LORD manoeuvres all nations, both great and small, into position for that final "showdown," the timing of which is known only to Himself.

The new era will do more than just bring the Jewish people back into grace. As mentioned, both the Jews and the Church had an era apiece to fulfill their destiny, and both failed. The new era will be the one that sees the fulfillment of both destinies. Israel will capture the attention of the world and get it focused on the LORD, and the Church triumphant will reap the massive harvest.

Throughout many chapters of this book we have seen what God is currently doing with Israel and what He intends to accomplish in the future. The eyes of the inhabitants of the nations are already focusing on Israel; all that is needed is a little more time. The LORD is also moving to fulfill the destiny of the Church. To some this new move is quite apparent, but to most it is not. Let me lay a foundation that will allow the reader to see the new move within the Church.

SIGNS

The Jewish people usually requested a "sign" to confirm a prophet or a spiritual teaching:

*"**What sign will You perform** then, that we may see it and believe You?"*   (Jn 6:30).

Millennia have passed but the Jewish desire for "signs" has not. They still seek them, and the Gentiles still want to work things out by their own "intelligence":

*"The **Jews** ... **want a sign** from heaven as proof that what is preached is true ... the **Gentiles** ... **believe only what agrees with their philosophy** and seems wise to them"*   (1 Cor 1:22 TLB).

Most often the LORD gave a "sign" to make a particular point. The object of the "sign" was to get the attention of the people, to make them question the "sign" and think about it. He gave many and varied "signs" to Israel:

*"**The LORD Himself will give you a sign:** Behold, the virgin shall conceive and bear a Son, and shall call His name Immanuel"*
(Isa 7:14).

*"My servant Isaiah has walked naked and barefoot three years **for a sign and a wonder** ..."* (Isa 20:3).

*"In their sight you shall bear them on your shoulders and carry them out at twilight; you shall cover your face, so that you cannot see the ground, for **I have made you a sign** to the house of Israel"* (Eze 12:6).

Many times the "signs" were so obvious that they elicited a response from the Israelites, and the prophet would have an attentive, listening audience:

*"And the people said to me, 'Will you not **tell us what these things signify** to us, that you behave so?'"* (Eze 24:19).

Even today, the Jewish people have not abandoned their quest for "signs," and the LORD has retained His particular freedom to furnish them.

During the past decade in Israel, as the LORD moved spiritually in the land and the Israeli Body of Christ emerged and grew, the Jewish believers had a unique propensity to marry Gentiles. This seems to be peculiar to Israel and is relatively rare among Jewish believers outside of Israel. Many Jews outside of Israel married Gentiles while they were unsaved and uninterested, but those having met the Messiah while single are usually very particular in choosing another Jew as their life partners. The LORD has given a "sign," not only to Israel as a nation but also to the Church in general, that this is indeed the "New," or "True," Israel: Jew and Gentile together, loving and living in harmony. This is not to be taken as a "sign" that Gentiles should marry Jews or anything of that nature. It is a "sign" to say that the *"One New Man"* of Chapter Twenty-six is emerging. The young Christian Gentiles that travel to Israel do so because they have a love for Israel and for the Jewish people. Many of them perform the most menial tasks for Israelis as a token of their love offering. The LORD has joined a sizeable number of them in covenant relationship to His people to be a "sign" to this present generation. In Chapter Twenty-Six, we looked at *"His purpose,"* which was *"to create in Himself,"* that is in *"His body which is the Church, one new man."* The *"One New Man"* is Jew and Gentile worshipping together in the love of Christ, with every *"barrier"* down and every *"hostility"* dead, and the dawning of a new era has brought the dawning of a new day for the Church.

FROM JERUSALEM

It was mentioned in the previous paragraph that the Israeli-Jewish believers had a propensity for marrying Gentiles. The truth of this is borne out by the fact that the great majority of weddings in the believing community have been mixed. And there are today a number of Israeli couples who travel out as teachers, evangelists and missionaries. They cover the Germanic countries, Europe, the Eastern Bloc countries, Scandinavia, North America, Mexico, the Far East, Australia, New Zealand and the South Pacific. At the time of this writing, my wife and I alone hold invitations to minister in more than forty countries. What is unique about all these couples, including us, is that we are all, without one exception, Jew and Gentile couples, and we all emanate out of Jerusalem. It is the *"One New Man"* that is bringing *"the word of the LORD from Jerusalem"!* The LORD first establishes natural Israel with the object of establishing spiritual Israel:

> *"The spiritual is not first, but the natural, and afterward the spiritual"* (1 Cor 15:46).

I shared in Chapter Eleven how the gospel proceeded forth from Jerusalem until it reached Christchurch, New Zealand—the end of the earth. I mentioned the prophetic word that came forth in that city concerning the "Olympic Torch" returning, and how that "Torch" finally arrived back in Jerusalem in 1986.

The Church was born in Jerusalem. And, in the last analysis, it is from Jerusalem that the world received the good news concerning the Lord Jesus Christ. It is Jerusalem that now houses the largest *"One New Man"* congregations in the world, and it is from Jerusalem that the latest move of God is flowing:

> *"For **out of Zion** shall go forth the law, and the word of the LORD from Jerusalem"* (Isa 2:3).

The *"One New Man"* has emerged as a sign and is *"going forth from Jerusalem,"* taking the word of the LORD to the nations. The sign signifies that God is going to move throughout the entire Church and join Jewish and Gentile hearts in the Spirit. An increase of over two thousand per cent in the body of Christ in Israel within the past few years seems to indicate that the LORD will move soon.

Obviously, the LORD is doing a new thing in the earth with Israel, but churches—traditional, evangelical and charismatic—are turning their backs on her in ever increasing numbers. In the near future we will likely see a definite polarity in the Church between those that stand with Israel and those that stand against her. Every church leader and every church member must choose which side of the fence he wants to be on—will it be *"blessing"* or will it be *"cursing"*? The LORD has already made His choice and stands on the side of His ancient people:

*"I will **bless those who bless you, and I will curse him who holds you lightly in esteem"*** (Gen 12:3 Lit. Trans.).

Examine the evidence of God's present involvement with Israel as presented throughout this book. Meditate, pray and choose whether to accept or reject it. Hopefully your choice will be to go along with the LORD'S plans for Israel and the Church. It may be the necessary key for your survival. The *"Church,"* we are told, will not have *"spot or wrinkle or any such thing"* (Eph 5:27). How the LORD will clean up His *"Bride"* remains to be seen, but one gets wrinkles out of a rug by laying it down and letting people walk on it.

Dear LORD,
Thank You that we are moving into a new era, an era that will see You glorified in the Church. And thank You that Your *"purpose"* is being implemented and Jews and Gentiles are being welded together to form the *"One New Man."* Thank You for establishing the *"natural"* that the *"spiritual"* may finally come forth. Grant that I, my church and my church leaders may stand with You and with Israel at this crucial time. Amen.

28

THE
FINAL
ANALYSIS

We began in Chapter Five to look at the history of Israel as the LORD foretold it to Moses more than 3,500 years ago. There were six main areas of events that were to take place. Each of these has been, or is currently being, completed.

In Chapter Nine, we looked at the nine main events of ancient Israel's past that needed to have a modern re-enactment prior to the second coming of the Lord Jesus Christ. Again, each event either has been, or is currently being, re-enacted.

The Great Purpose of God for the Church is also coming to pass, with Israel taking a leading role. Israel, in reality, is a "clock" by which we can tell the Biblical "time," and the present hour in which we live is a decidedly late one.

Fulfillment of Biblical prophecy occurs daily in Israel without an apparent awareness that it is happening. With the LORD so involved with Israel at this time, many prophecies are simply tumbling into fulfillment. Apart from any mentioned thus far, let us look at just a few of the more obvious prophecies currently being fulfilled.

Perhaps the most obvious prophecy being fulfilled is that concerning the Hebrew language:

*"I will change the speech of my returning people to **pure Hebrew** so that all can worship the Lord together"*   (Zeph 3:9 TLB).

From the time of the commencement of the first exile the Hebrew language underwent many changes. Words and idioms from the languages of the conquering nations were constantly being added to it. Hebrew remained, however, the language of religion, and, even today, many pious Jews will only speak Hebrew when discussing something pertaining to the Scriptures, preferring to keep the language "holy" by using *Yiddish* or other exilic languages for common conversation. During the early centuries of the second exile, Hebrew was used less and less as a spoken language as the dispersed Jews took up the languages of their host countries. The reading and pronunciation of the Scriptures and Prayer-books became increasingly difficult. In the seventh century, the Jewish scribes living in the city of Tiberius, studying *Masora* (the accumulated Jewish tradition concerning the correct Hebrew text of the Old Testament), developed a system of vowel points called *nikud* (points). The Masoretes, the name by which these scribes were known, painstakingly applied *nikud* to every letter of the Hebrew Scriptures and Prayer-books. This vowel system preserved the correct pronunciation of Hebrew and the most commonly used Hebrew text for Bible translation today is called the Masoretic Text.

While the Masoretic Jews had preserved the pronunciation of Hebrew for posterity its use was confined to synagogue worship and prayers. Hebrew had become a "dead" language. Anti-Semitism, and, later, Communism, forced greater and greater numbers of Jews to grow up without even exposure to the printed Hebrew.

The son of a Lithuanian rabbi, Eliezer Ben-Yehuda, suffering from acute tuberculosis and while furthering his studies in Paris, conceived the idea of reviving the Hebrew language. He promptly set out for Palestine and, after his arrival in 1881, sent for a young woman, Deborah, the daughter of a benefactor. Before marrying Deborah, he made her promise never to speak any language other than Hebrew. In 1882 Deborah gave birth to a son, Ben-Zion, the first of four children that she was to bear to Eliezer. Ben-Zion's mother tongue was Hebrew—as was that of all his future brothers and sisters—and Deborah was "the first Hebrew mother in nearly two thousand years."[1]

Ben-Yehuda was "possessed" with his task. Arising promptly each day at 4:00 a.m., he worked until midnight. His children were never, ever, allowed to play or mix with other children for fear that they might be exposed to "disgusting" languages of the exile. All visitors to the

Ben-Yehuda home had to agree, before entering the house, to speak only Hebrew, and if they could not speak any Hebrew they were to remain silent.

In 1891 Deborah died of tuberculosis, contracted from her husband, and in 1892 Eliezer married Hemda, Deborah's younger sister, who bore him five more children (five of the nine Ben-Yehuda children died from various diseases and hardships characteristic to that region). Eliezer did not live to see his dream entirely fulfilled. He died in 1922 after having published only six volumes of his Hebrew Dictionary. Eleven posthumous volumes were pieced together from his notes and the thousands of slips of paper that were found, some even in the pockets of his clothing hanging in the closet. The present, seventeen-volume Ben Yehuda Hebrew Dictionary is said to contain every word in the Hebrew language and is a legacy to the nation of Israel. Eliezer took the Hebrew Scriptures and adapted the individual words to make thousands of modern words that were never before in existence. For example, the Hebrew word *chushmal* (electricity) is taken from the "burnished bronze," or " glowing amber," seen by the prophet Ezekiel in a vision (Eze 1:4). The Ben-Yehuda family lived, ate and slept Hebrew and spoke, perhaps, the purest Hebrew that was possible to be spoken. The LORD used a completely non-religious man and made him the father of modern Hebrew. Hundreds of *Ulpanim* (language schools) are dotted throughout Israel, teaching millions of immigrants, from more than 140 nations, the language of the Hebrew Bible and uniting them with a common tongue—the tongue of the ancient prophets.

In order to fully grasp the fulfillment of our next prophecy we should understand beforehand that dense forest once covered much of Israel:

*"The battle spread out over the whole countryside, and **the forest claimed more lives that day than the sword**"*   (2 Sam 18:8 NIV).

But the Bible prophesied that those forests would be reduced to a very small number of trees:

*"**The splendor of the forests** and fertile fields it will **completely destroy**, as when a sick man wastes away and **the remaining trees** of his forests will be **so few that a child could write them down**"*
(Isa 10:18&19 NIV).

The great forests were destroyed by the Turks of the Ottoman Empire. The Turks instituted a system of taxation that was based on the number of trees growing on a particular parcel of land. Consequently, all trees that could not produce more than the amount of required taxes were felled to escape payment of the taxes. The number of trees remaining at the time of the British Mandate was so small that the British actually re-corded every single tree that grew in the land!

Trees, of course, play a major part in a country's rainfall and air purification, as well as providing supplies of food. The Bible, foretelling the return of the Jewish people, gives us our prophecy:

> *"But you, O **mountains of Israel**, you shall **shoot forth your branches and yield your fruit to My people Israel**, for they are about to come"*   (Eze 36:8).

The barren mountains were to put forth branches and yield fruit for the re-created state. Since 1947, Israel has planted more than 700 million trees, abundantly fulfilling that prophecy.

Palestine, as Mark Twain wrote of her in the 1890s, was:

> "A desolate country ... a silent mournful expanse."[2]

It was a deserted wasteland, almost devoid of trees and inhabitants, a barren land waiting for her people. But the Scriptures give us another prophecy:

> *"The **wilderness and the wasteland** shall be glad for them, and the **desert shall rejoice and blossom as the rose**"*   (Isa 35:1).

The Israelis drained the malarial swamps, ridding themselves of the infectious disease, and utilised the rich alluvial soil of the swamps for agriculture. And, through the pioneering and developing of the famous "drip-irrigation" systems, what was once wasteland and sandy desert is now lush with green vegetation. High yields of fruit and flowers are now being extracted from that land. And, true to the LORD'S words to Abram: *"I will make you a great nation ... and you shall be a blessing,"* Israel exports and installs her "drip-irrigation" in many countries of the world. Countries as diverse as Australia, Fiji, New Zealand, Asia and some in Africa are turning formerly parched and unproductive land into fertile oases and increasing productivity in low yield areas.

Since the collapse and breakup of the Soviet Union even Muslim states of the C.I.S. have invited the Israelis to install irrigation systems. Uzbekistan was one cotton-producing state that invited the Israelis to install a "drip-irrigation" system. Cotton production requires a great deal of water and Israelis maintain that their "drip" systems will lower water consumption while raising cotton production. Uzbekistan took them up on their claim, albeit with some scepticism, as expressed by the Uzbekistan minister of agriculture to an Israeli entrepreneur and reported in the Israeli press:

"'We've been growing cotton for 2,000 years and you've only been growing it for 40 years. What can you teach us?'

Nevertheless, the Uzbekis signed a contract and an Israeli team of mostly kibbutz members from Bait Hashita began working on a 10,000 dunam [approx 1,000 hectares – 2,500 acres] site early last year.

The results astonished the Uzbeks; cotton production increased by 40 percent, water usage was reduced by two-thirds, and there was 10 to 20 percent less use of fertilizers and pesticides.

Thousands of officials and agriculturalists flocked to the site from all over Central Asia to look at the spectacular size of cotton and hear the statistics. Contracts for similar projects were subsequently signed for this year with Kazakhstan and Tadjikistan ... and again with Uzbekistan ... ."[3]

The LORD greatly gifted the Jewish people and prophesied to the world at large that:

*"In days to come **Jacob will take root**, Israel will **bud and blossom and fill all the world with fruit"*** (Isa.27:6.NIV).

"Jacob" (the Jewish people) is changing the face of the world through his expertise in irrigation and is literally filling it with fruit. And *"Jacob"* has, himself, *"taken root"* in his ancient homeland causing it to bud and blossom in such profusion that everyday, except the Sabbath (Saturday), specially prepared jumbo jets carry flowers, fruit and vegetables to the world's markets. The land of the Dead Sea area, the lowest elevation on earth, has been de-salinated; and, even when Europe

is blanketed under heavy snow, produce from this natural "greenhouse" is flown to overseas markets. Israel today, is one of the principal fruit and flower-exporting nations of the world—even exporting tulips to Holland!

A notable Biblical Encyclopaedia applauds the Israeli effort with the following observation:

"These determined settlers have produced the most marked advance of cultivation over waste that has occurred since Roman times, bridging centuries of misuse and neglect."[4]

Surely, "the most marked advance of cultivation ... since Roman times" clearly points to the fulfillment of the following:

*"For the LORD will comfort Zion, he will comfort all **her waste places; he will make her wilderness like Eden, and her desert like the garden of the LORD ...**"*   (Isa 51:3).

*"**The desolate land shall be tilled** instead of lying desolate in the sight of all who pass by. So **they will say, 'This land that was desolate has become like the garden of Eden ...'**"*
(Eze 36:34&35).

But this "most marked advance of cultivation" has not been accomplished merely by Israeli strength of arm and back:

*"**I, the LORD, have rebuilt the ruined places and planted what was desolate ...**"*   (Eze 36:36).

Some say that modern Israel is of the flesh and not of God. Remember, Jesus was rejected, crucified and resurrected nearly two thousand years ago. Because some choose not to believe in His resurrection does not in any way invalidate the truth of it. Israel has been rejected, crucified and resurrected, too, and the evidence demands a verdict. It is not coincidental that it is written:

*"... with the Lord **one day is as a thousand years, and a thousand years as one day**"*   (2 Pet 3:8)

Israel was rejected and crucified both by the world and by the Church two thousand years ago. Now she has been resurrected and we have the testimony of Scripture:

"After two days He will revive us; on the third day He will raise us up"   (Hosea 6:2)

After two days—two thousand years—the LORD revived Israel and resurrected her on the third day.

WATERS OF NOAH

The Jewish people are moving back into the grace of God. For Israel, it is a time of reacceptance and comfort. For the LORD, it is like the waters of Noah:

"'For your Maker is your husband, the LORD of hosts is His name; and your Redeemer is the Holy One of Israel; He is called the God of the whole earth. For the LORD has called you like a woman forsaken and grieved in spirit, like a youthful wife when you were refused,' says your God. 'For a mere moment I have forsaken you, but with great mercies I will gather you. With a little wrath I hid My face from you for a moment; but with everlasting kindness I will have mercy on you,' says the LORD, your Redeemer. 'For this is like the waters of Noah to Me; for as I have sworn that the waters of Noah would no longer cover the earth, so have I sworn that I would not be angry with you, nor rebuke you. For the mountains shall depart and the hills be removed, but My kindness shall not depart from you, nor shall My covenant of peace be removed,' says the LORD, who has mercy on you. 'All your children shall be taught by the LORD, and great shall be the peace of your children'"   (Isa 54:5-10&13).

The LORD has sworn that He will not be *"angry"* again with Israel. He is her *"Husband"* and her *"Redeemer."* He will gather Israel, plant her in His land and establish the covenant of Jeremiah thirty-one, and all of Israel's children *"shall be taught by the LORD."*

Jesus was God manifest in the flesh. He chose this incarnation for one purpose—to pull the entire human race back to where God designed it to be. Israel is being "manifested in the flesh" because she is part of that purpose. The nations that will come against Israel will not be sent by the LORD as a means of judgement against Israel but as judgement against themselves. Every nation that comes against Israel will fall because of her, and some of my readers, or those near and dear to them, may actually die in battle on Israel's soil.

UNITED STATES

Israel continues along her pre-determined path, fulfilling both prophecy and herself. Various nations are affected in different ways, depending upon their past relations or present attitudes toward her. One nation in particular that is playing a significant role in determining the pace of events is the United States. The United States, as mentioned in Chapter Ten, is playing the field in an effort to emerge a winner in the oil stakes. In moves designed to align herself closer to the Arab nations and distance herself from Israel, she has not only sided with the enemies of Israel in denouncing Israel but has, in fact, even taken the initiative. The Bush administration used stronger language in condemning Israel than did even the PLO![5] And may the following journalistic observation not be found written on the tombstone of the United States:

"... Bush and James Baker ... constituted the most hostile US administration to Israel since the Eisenhower-Dulles duo of the 1950s."[6]

The entire economy and welfare of the United States took a decided plunge downward due to the Bush administration's anti-Israel posture. President Bush did, however, foster a marked improvement in US-Israel relations in mid-1992 not, as most would have us believe, because of the change in Israel's Prime Minister, but because both Bush and Baker desperately needed the American-Jewish vote in the November elections to help them remain in office. Bush, himself, had said that he would "do anything to get re-elected," and Baker, resigning as Secretary of State – turning his back on the Middle East Peace negotiations to run Bush's re-election campaign – gave an indication of how desperately this pair tried to preserve their headship of the New World Order.

A basic miscalculation on the part of the Bush administration was the size and strength of the United States. With a confidence bordering on arrogance, it took to threatening Israel with a big stick. But the more it stood against Israel, however, the more precarious its own position became. The internal debt of the United States now exceeds anything ever before recorded, and the entire financial structure is that of a house of cards waiting for the first "puff" of God's breath to bring it all down. The former Soviet Union, with the world's largest oil reserves, the world's most powerful military machine and a population seventeen percent greater that that of the United States, opposed the purposes of the LORD concerning His covenant people and collapsed in ruins. If President Clinton does not drastically alter the posture of the United States toward Israel from that established by his predecessor, her demise will be sooner, rather than later, and is as certain as that of the Soviet Union. The greatest threat facing the United States today is not Japan, balancing the budget or AIDS; it is the God of Israel.

THE HARVEST

Most Christians subscribe to the doctrine that there will be few in heaven compared to the number of those in hell. This doctrine tends not only to discourage Christians but also to disparage the LORD. First, the LORD created Satan, and the LORD kicked him out of Heaven. Second, Satan can operate only within the parameters allowed him by the LORD (see Job 1:6-2:7, Lk 22:31&32). Third, the LORD is absolute Sovereign over heaven and earth, and *"No purpose of His can be thwarted"* (Job 42:2 NASB). Fourth, there are more people living today than have lived collectively from Adam until the present time! One big move of God today would outbalance hell even if it should contain every previous person, which it most certainly does not. And Jesus, being God manifested in the flesh, must have emptied hell when He descended there during the days between His crucifixion and His subsequent resurrection, and *"preached to the spirits in prison"* (1 Pet 3:19).

The Bible tells us that God came to earth:

*"In the likeness of sinful flesh, **on account of sin:** He condemned sin in the flesh"*   (Rom 8:3).

God came *"on account of sin"* and then *"condemned sin in the flesh."* He pronounced judgement upon sin, and, hanging on the cross, He said:

"It is finished!" (Jn 19:30).

"It is finished!" What a statement! It was not just Jesus' part in history that was *"finished."* The whole plan of redemption was finished! There is nothing more for God to do! Mankind has been redeemed! But only a small fraction has been regenerated. It is now entirely up to individual action. God took full responsibility for sin and bore it away in His body on the cross, opening the way for us to return to the place of fellowship that man enjoyed before the fall. And simply believing does not redeem us; that only enables us to realise that we are redeemed! Embracing His atonement, yielding our lives up to Jesus—giving to Him our "right to ourselves"—causes us to enter into God's salvation.

The LORD intends that the great majority, not the small minority, of mankind should know Him:

*"Look to Me, and **be saved, all you ends of the earth!** For I am God, and there is no other. **I have sworn by Myself; the word has gone out of My mouth** in righteousness, **and shall not return**, that to Me **every knee shall bow, every tongue shall take an oath"***
(Isa 45:22&23).

The LORD will use His great power to ensure that every individual knee will voluntarily bow before Him in worship. The veil of blindness that lies upon the heart of the Jews will be removed in Christ, as will the veil of blindness that covers the nations. All the earth shall worship Him:

*"Through the greatness of Your power **your enemies shall submit** themselves to You. **All the earth shall worship You and sing praises** to You; they shall sing praises to Your name"* (Psa 66:3&4).

*"They shall not hurt nor destroy in all My holy mountain, for **the earth shall be full of the knowledge of the LORD as the waters cover the sea"*** (Isa 11:9).

The ability to hurt and destroy will still exist but will not be exercised because, *"the earth shall be full of the knowledge of the LORD"*. *"All the earth shall worship"* Him. It is on **all flesh** that the LORD will pour out His Spirit:

" 'All flesh shall come to worship before Me,' says the
LORD "   (Isa 66:23b)

"I will pour out My Spirit on all flesh; your sons and your
daughters shall prophesy, your old men shall dream dreams, your
young men shall see visions. And also on My menservants and on
My maidservants I will pour out My Spirit in those days"
                                                           (Joel 2:28&29).

His Spirit will be poured out on **all flesh** and **also** on *"My mens-*
ervants and on My maidservants," which is the Church! This is pre-resurrection, not post-resurrection! And yes, the Church will indeed come to true unity:

"I do not pray for these alone, but also for those who will believe
in Me through their word; that they all may be one, as You,
Father, are in Me, and I in You; that they also may be one in Us,
that the world may believe that You sent Me"   (Jn 17:20&21).

The Lord Jesus never prayed a prayer that would not be answered! This prayer has already been answered to the letter. We may not see it now, but we shall see it before too many more years pass us by. We are probably living in the most exciting period of all of history, even though there are troubles looming on the horizon.

DECISION TIME

Do not be disturbed today by thoughts about tomorrow. Leave to-morrow alone in confidence of God's ability. Yesterday has gone and cannot be recalled—there is no road back to it. Tomorrow is not yet and cannot even be assured. Only today is ours. If you love eternity, make use of today while it is still today:

"Today, if you will hear His voice, do not harden your hearts as
in the rebellion"   (Heb 3:15).

Felix, the governor of Caesarea, listened to the apostle Paul concerning faith in Christ. At a certain point he became alarmed:

*"Now as he reasoned about **righteousness, self-control, and the judgment** to come, Felix **was afraid** and answered, '**Go away for now; when I have a convenient time I will call for you**'"*
(Acts 24:25).

If you have a decision to make concerning faith in Christ, or a decision regarding the legitimacy of the place of Israel in your heart or doctrinal beliefs, you need to make that decision now, today. To put off making that decision until a tomorrow of *"a more convenient time"* means that you have already *"hardened your heart."*

As we have seen in the pages of this book, Israel is an instrument in the hand of the LORD, an instrument of war and an instrument of salvation. Those that love her are *"blessed,"* and those that despise her are *"cursed."* Israel was called to the purposes of God that He might effect His salvation to the ends of the earth:

*"This is **the purpose that is purposed against the whole earth**, and this is the hand that is stretched out over all the nations. For **the LORD of hosts has purposed, and who will annul it? His hand is stretched out, and who will turn it back?"***   (Isa 14:26&27).

That there is a storm ahead cannot be denied. The Bible declares it, and the daily news broadcasts it. The LORD is the Rock of our salvation (Psa 95:1), and we can dwell in His shadow. But if we prefer the cruel sun of this world to the refreshing shade of the Rock we will get burnt. There is a sure promise for every true believer:

*"**I also will keep you from the hour of trial which shall come upon the whole world, to test those who dwell on the earth**"*
(Rev 3:10).

Having an intimate, vital, personal relationship with Jesus and being obedient to His commands ensures that we shall be *"kept from the hour of trial which shall come upon the whole world."* If we desire anything instead of Jesus we shall suffer and be disillusioned. Jesus does not give us "overcoming life," but He will give us "life" as we "overcome." Cling to Him, and He will take you safely through the storm.

The LORD is looking for men and women who will walk and work with Him, agreeing with His purposes. And in the timeless words of Oswald Chambers:

"One individual life may be of priceless value to God's purposes, and yours may be that life."

He is looking for men and women who will stand between holy God and sinful man and intercede. And He is waiting for the individual that would dare to enter in beyond the second veil and gaze upon the majesty that is to be found there—the majesty that is Almighty God, Himself. Perhaps you are that individual.

Dear LORD,
I come to You today trusting like a little child, believing that You are Who You say You are: the Almighty Creator, LORD of heaven and earth—my Heavenly Father Who loves me so very much. I come to You, my Father, repenting of my sin and repenting of living my own way. I come to You for the forgiveness of all my sins and ask that You might wash me clean in the blood of Your dear Son, Jesus, Who died on the cross that I might live and Who rose from death that I, too, might rise on That Day.

I come to You, dear Father, promising that, with Your help, and to the best of my ability, I will, from this very hour, live only for You. Please teach me, Father, how to love You more than myself. Thank You for loving me. Thank You for being so patient with me, and thank You for accepting me just the way I am. Amen.

"Your name O LORD, endures forever, Your fame, O LORD, throughout all generations"

(Psa 135:13).

CHAPTER NOTES

Chapter 2

1. Richard Wurmbrand, in *The Voice of the Martyrs: Christ to the Communist World,* August, 1990.
2. Information for this section taken from Encyclopaedias including *Encyclopedia Britannica, Grolier's Illustrated Encyclopedia* and *The World Book.*
3. Calculations throughout are based on the American system of numbering.
4. See note 3.
5. Figures for the most part have been rounded to nearest appropriate unit.
6. See note 5.
7. Celsius = centigrade.
8. "Voyage of the Century," *National Geographic,* Vol.178, NO.2 August 1990.
9. "Spacecraft launched," *The Jerusalem Post,* Wednesday, October 4, 1990.
10. "Voyage of the Century," *National Geographic,* Vol.178, NO.2 August 1990.
11. Ibid.
12. See note 3.
13. "Galactic Birth?" *Time Magazine,* September 11, 1989.
14. Readers Digest *"Atlas of the World,"* (London: Toucan, 1990).
15. Thomas a Kempis, in *The Imitation of Christ,* (14th Cent.).

Chapter 4

1. *Thompson Chain-Reference Bible,* (Kirkbride: Indianapolis, 1988.

Chapter 8

1. Elmer A. Josephson, *Israel: Key to World Redemption,* (Kansas: Bible Light Publications, 1978).
2. *Webster's New Universal Unabridged Dictionary,* (New York: Simon & Schuster, 1989).

Chapter 10

1. *NIV Study Bible,* notes on Gen 15:17, (Michigan: Zondervan, 1985).
2. *The Oxford English Dictionary (Second Edition),* (New York: Oxford University Press, 1989).
3. *Complete Works of Flavius Josephus,* (Michigan: Kregel, 1980).
4. Ibid.
5. Ibid.
6. Mark Twain, writing in *The Innocents Abroad.*
7. William L. Hull, *The Fall and Rise of Israel,* (Michigan: Zondervan, 1954).
8. The Balfour Declaration, London, 1917.
9. Hafez al-Assad, President of Syria.

10. Hafez al-Assad, quoted in "Syria: War with Israel to last forever," *The Bangkok Post,* Saturday, March 10, 1990.
11. "Study tracks $163 billion in arms sold to Mideast," *The Cedar Rapids Gazette,* Monday, May 6, 1991.
12. "American military aid to Israel," *The Jerusalem Post:* Friday, October 19, 1990.
13. "Favoring Arabs," *The Leaf-Chronicle,* Saturday, January 18, 1992.
14. "Study: Anti-Semitism low, but potential for increase exists," *Nashville Banner,* Friday, January 17, 1992.

Chapter 11

1. Verbally estimated by *Messianic Jewish Alliance of America,* October 1988.
2. Ibid.

Chapter 12

1. Broadcast on *The Voice of Israel Radio,* Wednesday, September 16, 1992 as the 750th Russian Jewish child under the age of 10 years arrives in Israel requiring treatment for exposure to radiation.
2. "Chernobyl fires spread radiation," *The Tennessean,* Tuesday, May 5, 1992.
3. "Soviets seek $1.5 billion emergency grain credit," *The Cedar Rapids Gazette,* Friday, April 19, 1991.
4. Ibid.
5. "In Moscow, panic buying and non-stop baking," *USA Today,* Thursday, November 14, 1991.
6. Ibid.
7. Ibid.
8. "Russians fuming over gas prices," *The Tennessean,* Tuesday, April 21, 1992.
9. "In Moscow, panic buying and non-stop baking," *USA Today,* Thursday, November 14, 1991.
10. "In Soviet Union, even Santa's sack is empty," *The Bangkok Post,* Tuesday, December 25, 1990.
11. "Soviet Union is finished," *The Cedar Rapids Gazette,* Friday, September 6, 1991.
12. "Mopping up after the cold war," *U.S. News & World Report,* Monday, April 27, 1992.
13. "This is how it feels to come home after 2,000 years," *The New York Times,* Monday, June 25, 1990.
14. "Thousands of Soviet Jews flood into Israel," *The Bangkok Post,* Saturday, December 22, 1990.
15. Ibid.
16. "A Million Immigrants by 1992?" *Dispatch from Jerusalem,* 4th Quarter, 1991, Vol. 16 No.4.
17. Steve Lytle, with Eberhard Muhlan and Katie Fortune, *Exodus II* (Bulwark: Bridge Publishing, 1983).

Chapter 13

1. Steven Katz, professor of Jewish Studies at Cornell University: in "Talking to God: An Intimate Look at the Way We Pray," *Newsweek,* January 6, 1992.

2. "Special Editions: Ex-Israel extras at Time and Newsweek," *The New Republic,* October 8, 1990.
3. Ibid.
4. Ibid.
5. Ibid.
6. Ibid.
7. Ibid.
8. Ibid
9. *Battle Lines: The American Media and the Intifada.* New York: Henry Holt, 1992).
10. "TV news fabrication," *The Jerusalem Post,* Friday, October 12, 1990.
11. Quoted in a letter by Teddy Kolleck to the editor of *Commentary,* April, 1991.
12. "'60 Minutes' & the Temple Mount," *Commentary,* February, 1991.
13. Ibid.
14. "Faking it with pictures," *The Jerusalem Post,* Friday, August 21, 1992.
15. Alan Ray, "That Mideast Peace," *The New Leader,* Monday, October 29, 1990.
16. Ibid.
17. "Foreign media dance to piper-payer's tune," *The Jerusalem Post,* Friday, September 4, 1992.
18. Ibid.
19. Ibid.
20. Ibid.
21. David Bar-Illan replying to a letter from Jonathan Ferziger, *UPI* Bureau Chief, published in *The Jerusalem Post,* Friday, October 23, 1992.
22. "The Myth of UN Fairness to Israel", *Dispatch from Jerusalem,* 3rd Quarter, 1991, Vol. 16 No.3.
23. "Commentary," *Dispatch from Jerusalem,* 3rd Quarter, 1991, Vol. 16 No.3.
24. "The Myth of UN Fairness to Israel", *Dispatch from Jerusalem,* 3rd Quarter, 1991, Vol. 16 No.3.
25. "Visiting Team," *The New Republic,* November 5, 1990.
26. "Temple Mount, Haram Sharif, and the UN," *National Review,* November 5, 1990.
27. "Visiting Team," *The New Republic,* November 5, 1990.
28. "Anatomy of a dangerous leak," by William Seamans, recently retired as ABC-TV news correspondent, quoted in *The Jerusalem Post.*

Chapter 14

1. Office of Israeli Ministry of Absorption, 1985.
2. Ibid.
3. Ibid.
4. "14,400 joyful Ethiopian Jews reach Israel," *The Miami Herald,* Sunday, May 26, 1991.
5. "This is how it feels to come Home after 2,000 years," *The New York Times,* Monday, June 25, 1990.
6. "14,400 joyful Ethiopian Jews reach Israel," *The Miami Herald,* Sunday, May 26, 1991.
7. "Albanian Jews land in Israel," *The Cedar Rapids Gazette,* Friday, April 12, 1991.
8. Ibid.
9. Ibid.
10. "A new chapter in Israel-China relations," *In Jerusalem,* Friday, October 2, 1992.

11. Jewish Agency figures quoted by *Christian Friends of Israel: Watchman's Prayer Letter,* September, 1992.
12. "U.S. maintains world's highest living standard," *The Cedar Rapids Gazette,* Saturday, September 21, 1991.
13. Reported in *Dispatch From Jerusalem,* 4th Quarter, 1991, Vol.16 No.4.
14. Anti-Defamation League, reported in *The Birmingham News,* Friday, February 7, 1992.
15. The Jewish Agency, reported on *Voice of Israel Radio,* Tuesday, July 7, 1992.
16. Edward H. Flannery, *The Anguish of the Jews* (New York: Macmillan, 1965).
17. Simcha Dinitz, Jewish Agency head, quoted in *The Jerusalem Post,* International Edition, Week ending January 11, 1992.

Chapter 15

1. "State of Israel," *Time magazine,* April 19, 1948.
2. "Israel at War," *Time magazine,* June 16, 1967.

Chapter 16

1. *Complete Works of Flavius Josephus,* (Michigan: Kregel, 1980).
2. "State of Israel," *Time magazine,* Monday, May 24, 1948.
3. Saddam Hussein, speaking on *Radio Baghdad,* January 27, 1991: Quoted in *The Jerusalem Post International Edition,* Week ending April 6, 1991.

Chapter 18
1. "Top American composer Aaron Copeland dies at 90," *The Cedar Rapids Gazette,* Thursday, September 12, 1991.

Chapter 19

1. "War for the White Paper?" *The New Statesman,* Saturday, June 22, 1946, reprinted in *The Palestine Post,* Sunday, June 23, 1946.
2. *Israeli War Machine: The Men; The Machines: The Tactics,* Ian V. Hogg, (London: Hamlyn, 1983).
3. Ibid.
4. Ibid.
5. "Israel at War," *Time magazine,* June 16, 1967.
6. *Israeli War Machine: The Men; The Machines: The Tactics,* Ian V. Hogg, (London: Hamlyn, 1983).
7. "Soviets say their units downed Israeli planes in War of Attrition," quoted from *Ekho Planety,* and published in *The Jerusalem Post,* Friday, July 7, 1989.
8. *A History of Israel, Volume II: From the Aftermath of the Yom Kippur War.* New York: Oxford University Press, 1987.
9. Ibid.
10. Ibid.
11. *The London Sunday Times.*
12. *The Jerusalem Post,* 1986.
13. "Dropping the Big One," *The Nation,* September 10, 1990.
14. Ibid.

15. "Successful First Flight of Arrow missile defense system," *Innovation,* November, 1990.
16. Norman Schwarzkopf, quoted in *The Jerusalem Post,* International Edition, Week ending January 18, 1992.
17. "A trauma unlike previous traumas," *The Jerusalem Post,* International Edition, Week ending January 18, 1992.
18. Moshe Arens, in an interview with *The Jerusalem Post,* Friday, September 21, 1990.
19. Eusebius, *Ecclesiastical History,* quoted in *Barnes' Notes,* (Michigan: Baker, reprinted from 1884 edition).
20. *Battle Lines: The American Media and the Intifada.* New York: Henry Holt, 1992.
21. *Tishrei,* Vol 1, No. 1 – Autumn 1992.

Chapter 20

1. "Jerusalem," *The Software Toolworks [Grolier] Illustrated Encyclopedia* 1990.
2. "City of Peace, hornet's nest," *U.S. News & World Report,* March 26, 1990.
3. From a letter by Teddy Kollek, Mayor of Jerusalem, to the editor of *Commentary,* April, 1991.
4. "City of Peace, hornet's nest," *U.S. News & World Report,* March 26, 1990.

Chapter 21

1. *The Boston Globe,* October 25, 1991.
2. Yitzak Shamir quoted in *The Cedar Rapids Gazette,* July 25, 1991.
3. Dr. Anis A. Shorrosh, writing in *Anis Shorrosh Evangelistic Association, Progress Report,* Winter 1991.
4. Anwar Sadat, April 25, 1972. Quoted in *History and Hate: The Dimensions of Anti-Semitism.* David Berger, (New York: The Jewish Publication Society, 1986).
5. "He Changed the Tide of History," *Time magazine,* October 19, 1981.
6. Azzam Pasha, Secretary of the Arab league in 1946, quoted in *The Blood of the Moon,* George Grant (Tennessee: Wolgemuth & Hyatt, 1991).
7. Grand Mufti Ammin Husseini, 1946, quoted in *The Blood of the Moon,* George Grant (Tennessee: Wolgemuth & Hyatt, 1991).
8. King Abdul Aziz Ibn Saud, quoted in *New Dimensions Magazine,* January, 1991.
9. The Hashemite kingdom of Jordan, text book for second-year high school Art Students: *General History, Ancient and Medieval Civilisations.*
10. Quoted in *Signs Following,* official Newsletter of Mahesh Chavda Ministries International, Spring, 1988.
11. Ayatullah Khomeini, quoted in *The Blood of the Moon,* George Grant (Tennessee: Wolgemuth & Hyatt, 1991).
12. *Islam at a Glance,* a brochure distributed in Birmingham, England, in July 1985.
13. United States State Department's Office of Counter-Terrorism, quoted in *Islam Revealed: A Christian Arab's View of Islam,* Dr. Anis A. Shorrosh (Nashville: Thomas Nelson, 1988).
14. Ayatullah Khomeini, quoted in *Islam Revealed: A Christian Arab's View of Islam,* Dr. Anis A. Shorrosh, (Nashville: Thomas Nelson, 1988).
15. *Islam Revealed: A Christian Arab's View of Islam,* Dr. Anis A. Shorrosh (Nashville: Thomas Nelson, 1988).
16. "State of Israel," *Time magazine,* December 8, 1947.

17. "Syria: Back to the Military Option?" *Middle East Intelligence Digest*, June 12, 1992.
18. "Egypt frees four Israelis," *The Jerusalem Post*, International Edition, Week ending May 16, 1992.
19. Imam Hassan al-Bana, former leader of Egyptian Muslim Brotherhood, quoted in *Holy War for the Promised Land*, David Dolan, (Nashville, Thomas Nelson, 1991).
20. Gamal Abdel Nasser, quoted in *Time Magazine*, December 1, 1967.
21. King Abdul Aziz Ibn Saud, quoted in *The Blood of the Moon*, George Grant (Tennessee: Wolgemuth & Hyatt, 1991).
22. Azzam Pasha, Secretary of the Arab league in 1946, quoted in *The Blood of the Moon*, George Grant (Tennessee: Wolgemuth & Hyatt, 1991).
23. King Farouk of Egypt, quoted in *The Blood of the Moon*, George Grant (Tennessee: Wolgemuth & Hyatt, 1991).
24. King Idris of Libya, quoted in *The Blood of the Moon*, George Grant (Tennessee: Wolgemuth & Hyatt, 1991).
25. Haj Amin el Husseini, Muslim Mufti of Jerusalem 1946, quoted in *The Blood of the Moon*, George Grant (Tennessee: Wolgemuth & Hyatt, 1991).

Chapter 22

1. *Battle Lines: The American Media and the Intifada*. New York: Henry Holt, 1992.
2. Ibid.
3. "Senseless, mind-blowing journalistic punditry," *The Jerusalem Post*, Friday, September 11, 1992.
4. "Herzog: Amnesty report not credible," *The Jerusalem Post*, Friday, July 10, 1992.
5. "Unusual Request," *A Word From Jerusalem*, July/August 1992.
6. Quoted in "Is Jordan Palestine, or Not?" *Dispatch From Jerusalem*, 1st Quarter, 1993.
7. Yasser Arafat, speaking to Orina Fallacei. Quoted in *The New Republic*, and reprinted in *The Jerusalem Post*, Friday, September 11, 1992.
8. "Judea and Samaria (the 'West Bank')," *Cahera*, February, 1990.
9. *A History of Israel: From the Rise of Zionism to Our Time*, New York: Alfred A. Knopf, 1991.
10. William L.Hull, *The Fall and Rise of Israel*, (Michigan: Zondervan, 1954).
11. Ariel Sharon,"Never! Never! Never!" *Time magazine*, April 17, 1989.
12. "Handbook of the Israeli-Arab conflict: Jewish Refugees," *Maoz*, Texas, May 1988.
13. *The Jerusalem Post*, International Edition, Week ending January 11, 1992.
14. Information Section, *Embassy of Israel*, Wellington, New Zealand, January, 1988.
15. Abu Mazen, quoted in *Falastin al-Thawra*, the official PLO journal, March 1976.
16. Khaled al-Azzem, former Syrian Prime Minister, in his memoirs, 1973.
17. The Jordanian daily, *Falastin*, February 19, 1949.
18. The Jordanian daily, *Al-Urdun*, April 9, 1953.
19. The Jordanian daily, *Falastin*, May 30, 1955.
20. *The Jerusalem Post*, International Edition, Week ending January 11, 1992.
21. *The Jerusalem Post*, International Edition, Week ending April 6, 1991.
22. *The Jerusalem Post*, International Edition, Week ending January 11, 1992.
23. "Pull this racist show out of the Knesset," *The Jerusalem Post*, International Edition, Week ending November 28, 1992.
24. Bernard Dineen, Literary Editor of *The Yorkshire Post*.

25. "A Palestinian version of the New Testament, *The Jerusalem Post,* International Edition, Week ending January 18, 1992.
26. Ibid.
27. Quoted in *Dispatch From Jerusalem,* 1st Quarter 1992.
28. Reported in *Middle East Intelligence Digest,* Vol. 3 No.4, October, 1992.
29. Ibid.
30. Ibid.
31. Charles Gulston, *Jerusalem: The Tragedy and the Triumph,* (Michigan: Zondervan, 1978).
32. *Pittsburgh Dispatch,* July 15, 1889.
33. Mark Twain, in *The Innocents Abroad.*
34. *The Jerusalem Post,* International Edition, April 6, 1991.
35. *Israel Defense Forces Journal,* January-February 1991.
36. Stephen Schwebel, *American Journal of International Law,* May, 1970.
37. "350,000 Palestinian Deportees and the World is Silent," *Dispatch From Jerusalem,* 1st Quarter, 1992.
38. "The Old Villain," *The New Leader,* October 29, 1990.

Chapter 23

1. Max I. Dimont, *Jews, God and History,* (New York: Simon & Schuster, 1962).
2. Ibid.
3. Ibid.
4. "Remnants: The Last Jews of Poland," *National Geographic,* Vol. 170, No.3, September, 1986.
5. Ibid.
6. Ibid.
7. Edward H. Flannery, *The Anguish of the Jews* (New York: Macmillan, 1965).
8. *The Oxford Dictionary of the Christian Church,* (New York: Oxford University Press, 1990).
9. Ibid.
10. Ibid.
11. Flannery, *The Anguish of the Jews.*
12. Ibid.
13. Ibid.
14. David Baron, *The Shepherd of Israel: A Solution of the Enigma of Jewish History,* (London: Morgan & Scott, 1915).
15. Flannery, *The Anguish of the Jews.*
16. Ibid.
17. Baron, *The Shepherd of Israel:*
18. Ibid.
19. Ibid.
20. Flannery, *The Anguish of the Jews.*
21. Ibid.
22. Ibid.
23. *The Book of Common Prayer* of the Episcopal Church, (New York: The Church Hymnal Corporation, 1979).
24. *Eusebius' Ecclesiastical History,* (Michigan: Baker, 1991).
25. Baron, *The Shepherd of Israel:*
26. Ibid.

27. Ibid.
28. Ibid.
29. Ibid.
30. Ibid.
31. Ibid.
32. Flannery, *The Anguish of the Jews.*
33. Baron, *The Shepherd of Israel:*
34. Ibid.
35. Flannery, *The Anguish of the Jews.*
36. Ibid.
37. Baron, *The Shepherd of Israel:*
38. Flannery, *The Anguish of the Jews.*
39. Ibid.
40. Ibid.
41. Ibid.
42. Baron, *The Shepherd of Israel:*
43. Ibid.
44. Ibid.
45. Ibid.
46. Ibid.
47. Flannery, *The Anguish of the Jews.*
48. Baron, *The Shepherd of Israel:*
49. Ibid.
50. Flannery, *The Anguish of the Jews.*
51. Ibid.
52. Ibid.
53. Ibid.
54. Ibid.
55. Baron, *The Shepherd of Israel:*
56. Ibid.
57. Ibid.
58. Ibid.
59. Flannery, *The Anguish of the Jews.*
60. Ibid.
61. Ibid.
62. Ibid.
63. Baron, *The Shepherd of Israel:*
64. Ibid.
65. Ibid.
66. Flannery, *The Anguish of the Jews.*
67. Ibid.
68. *The Jerusalem Post,* International Edition, Week ending April 6, 1991.

Chapter 24

1. Eusebius, *Ecclesiastical History,* quoted in *Barnes Notes,* (Michigan: Baker, reprinted from 1884 edition).
2. A.L. Johnston, *The Advancing Church* (Birmingham: Broadway Press, 1988).
3. John Wimber with Kevin Springer, *Power Evangelism* (New York: Harper & Row, 1986).

4. Billy Graham.
5. John Wimber with Kevin Springer, *Power Evangelism* (New York: Harper & Row, 1986).
6. The Barnea Research Group, quoted in *National & International Religion Report*, January 13, 1992.

Chapter 25

1. John Wimber with Kevin Springer, *Power Evangelism* (New York: Harper & Row, 1986).
2. Quoted by Howard Hendricks in *Teaching To Change Lives,* (Portland: Multnomar Press/Walk Thru The Bible Ministries, 1987).

Chapter 26

1. Albert Einstein, quoted in *The Saturday Evening Post,* Saturday, October 26, 1929.

Chapter 28

1. Robert St. John, *Tongue of the Prophets,* (Hollywood: Wiltshire, 1952).
2. Mark Twain, in *The Innocents Abroad.*
3. "Israel's benign, business-oriented march into Central Asia," *The Jerusalem Post,* Friday, August 21, 1992.
4. *The Zondervan Pictorial Encyclopedia of the Bible,* (Michigan: Zondervan, 1976) vol 4.
5. "What Aridor should have said," *The Jerusalem Post* International Edition, Week ending, January 18, 1992.
6. "For referendum on the territories," *The Jerusalem Post,* Friday, September 18, 1992.

SELECT BIBLIOGRAPHY

Baron, David.
The Shepherd of Israel: A Solution of the Enigma of Jewish History. London: Morgan & Scott, 1915.

Berger, David.
History and Hate: The Dimensions of Anti-Semitism. New York: The Jewish Publication Society, 1986.

Dimont, Max I.
Jews, God and History. New York: Simon & Schuster, 1962.

Dolan, David.
Holy War for the Promised Land. Nashville: Thomas Nelson, 1991.

Eban, Abba.
Personal Witness: Israel Through My Eyes. New York: G.P. Putnam's Sons, 1992.

Eusebius, Pamphilus.
Ecclesiastical History. Michigan: Baker, 1991.

Evans, Mike.
Israel: America's Key to Survival. Plainfield: Logos International, 1981.

Flannery, Edward H.
The Anguish of the Jews. New York: Macmillan, 1965.

Grant, George.
The Blood of the Moon: The Roots of the Middle East Crisis. Tennessee: Wolgemuth & Hyatt,1991.

Gulston, Charles.
Jerusalem: The Tragedy and the Triumph. Michigan: Zondervan, 1978.

Hogg, Ian V.
Israeli War Machine: The Men; The Machines: The Tactics. London: Hamlyn, 1983.

Hull, William L.
The Fall and Rise of Israel, Michigan: Zondervan, 1954.

Insight Team of the *Sunday Times.*
Insight on the Middle East War. London: André Deutsch, 1974.

Johnston, A.L.
The Advancing Church. Birmingham: Broadway Press, 1988.

Josephson, Elmer A.
Israel: Key to World Redemption. Kansas: Bible Light Publications, 1978.

Josephus, Flavius.
Complete Works of Flavius Josephus. Michigan: Kregel, 1980.

Lederman, Jim.
Battle Lines: The American Media and the Intifada. New York: Henry Holt, 1992.

Lightle, Steve, with Eberhard Muhlan and Katie Fortune.
Exodus II: Let My People Go. Bulwark: Bridge, 1983.

Peters, Joan.
From Time Immemorial: The Origins of The Arab-Jewish Conflict Over Palestine. London: Michael Joseph, 1985.

Sachar, Howard M.
A History of Israel: From the Rise of Zionism to Our Time, New York: Alfred A. Knopf, 1991.

Sachar, Howard M.
A History of Israel, Volume II: From the Aftermath of the Yom Kippur War. New York: Oxford University Press, 1987.

Shorrosh, Anis A.
Islam Revealed: A Christian Arab's View of Islam. Nashville: Thomas Nelson, 1988.

St. John, Robert.
Tongue of the Prophets, Hollywood: Wiltshire, 1952.

Wimber, John, with Kevin Springer.
Power Evangelism. New York: Harper & Row, 1986.

FOR YOUR INFORMATION

The author resides in Jerusalem and may be contacted through *Arm of Salvation* whose address for service is:

P.O. Box 32381, Jerusalem 91322, ISRAEL
Fax: 972 2 250-532

Ramon Bennett also writes in the *MINISTRY & PRAYER UPDATE*, the periodic newsletter of the *Arm of Salvation Ministries*. The *UPDATE* keeps its readers informed on the ministry and movement of the Bennetts and also on current events in Israel. An annual donation of $10.00 is requested toward production and postage costs.

If you have enjoyed reading *When Day and Night Cease* and would like to be advised of forthcoming books by the same author, please indicate this to *Arm of Salvation* and you will be notified immediately new books are available.

Copies of *When Day and Night Cease* are available by mail and can be purchased by sending $13.95 plus $3.00 shipping and handling.

Some of the messages contained in this book are obtainable on audio cassette. A list of these and other available titles will be sent upon request.

Please mail your check/money order in U.S. currency to:

ARM of SALVATION
P.O. Box 32381, Jerusalem 91322, ISRAEL

DAVID'S KINGDOM OF PRAISE BEING RE-ENACTED!

THE HEART OF ISRAELI WORSHIP

AUTHENTIC HEBREW SCRIPTURE IN SONG!

Some of the most popular worship songs sung in Israel today appear on *GATES OF ZION* a skilfully arranged choral praise tape, in Zipporah Bennett's uniquely Hebraic style.

An excellent way to learn your first Bible verses in Hebrew. Full Hebrew texts, English translations and transliterations are printed inside the cassette's cover.

Zipporah, a Jerusalemite, works from the original texts of the Hebrew Bible setting them to melody.

$9.95

Plus $2.25 shipping and handling

Please mail your check/money order in U.S. currency to:

ARM of SALVATION
P.O. Box 32381, Jerusalem 91322, ISRAEL

Theology Today

THEOLOGY TODAY

Reflections on the Bible and
Contemporary Life

Patrick D. Miller

WESTMINSTER
JOHN KNOX PRESS
LOUISVILLE · KENTUCKY

Book design by Sharon Adams
Cover design by Night and Day Design

First edition
Published by Westminster John Knox Press
Louisville, Kentucky

This book is printed on acid-free paper that meets the American National Standards Institute Z39.48 standard.

PRINTED IN THE UNITED STATES OF AMERICA

06 07 08 09 10 11 12 13 14 15—10 9 8 7 6 5 4 3 2 1

Library of Congress Cataloging-in-Publication Data is on file at the Library of Congress, Washington, D.C.

ISBN-13: 978-0-664-22992-4
ISBN-10: 0-664-22992-1

To
Craig Dykstra, Tom Long, and Ellen Charry
with thanks

Contents

Foreword

"Make of it what you will."

That's what Reuben Land, the eleven-year-old narrator of Leif Enger's stunning debut novel, *Peace Like a River*, says whenever he describes a miracle he has seen.[1] *Peace Like a River* is possessed of many virtues—finely drawn characters, a deeply moving narrative style, and breathtaking descriptions of the north country landscape—but mainly it is a bold novel about miracles, miracles that most folks, their heads bent down with the grind of ordinary living, either miss entirely or run from out of fear of having their world turned upside down. But Reuben Land has seen miracles and doesn't shy away from describing them. In fact, his own birth was a miracle, since he went for the first twelve minutes of his life without breathing, his poorly developed lungs refusing to fill. The doctor had given him up, but Reuben's father, Jeremiah Land, lifted up the lump of newborn clay that was Reuben and said, "Reuben Land, in the name of the living God I am telling you to breathe."[2] And he did.

Make of it what you will.

Reuben is persuaded that it takes two things to make a miracle. First, miracles are intrusions. They aren't ordinary greeting card niceties, like the return of spring or a pretty sunset. Miracles are like Lazarus getting up out of the tomb. They upset people because, as Reuben says, they "rebut every rule all we good citizens take comfort in."[3] Second, real miracles always have at least one witness. "Someone to declare, Here's what I saw. Here's how it went. Make of it what you will."[4]

For twenty years at *Theology Today*—six years as book editor followed by fourteen years as editor—Patrick D. Miller was a reliable witness. A witness to trends in theology, twists and turns in biblical scholarship, ripples in culture and the arts, yes. But he was also a witness to what can only be called miracles, divine intrusions into our world that "rebut every rule all we good citizens take comfort in." Mind you, Pat is no friend of simplistic theological discourse or easy chatter about the miraculous. In his *Theology Today* editorials, some of which are collected in this volume, he was always critical of literalism and of all theological language that flattens God-talk into the mundane, the manageable, the cheaply magical. More than once in these pages he points to poetry as a necessary genre for doing the work of theology. Moreover, he has a sophisticated knowledge of the complex *pas de deux* between theology and science that is both impressive and, to many of us who are his colleagues, downright intimidating.

But finally, Pat Miller's God is a God who acts. Indeed, Pat's boldness as an editor sprang from his refusal ever to stop at the level of mere description. He was never content to stand at an emotional or convictional distance from the primary object of theology. "If it is not possible," he wrote in one editorial, "to speak of God's doing anything, even 'intervening' in our world to accomplish things that matter, then the reality of God is not very important or significant for human life." Later in the same piece he said, "Miracles are a symbol of, or a testimony to, the fact that God is at work and active in the world, and one lets go of such symbols reluctantly."

Make of it what you will.

One of the great assets that Pat Miller brought to his editorial duties is that he is a superb specimen of that rarest of creatures in the theological zoo: a working biblical theologian. Time and again in these pages, we see Pat spotting places where the theological discussion has become less vibrant, or even an ideological echo chamber, because the multivoiced biblical witness has been ignored or reduced to a single note. We see him bringing surprise and delight into the conversation by shining his flashlight on the gems, treasures, and unexpected wonders to be found in the scriptural cave. For example, in "Hallelujah! The Lord God Omnipotent Reigns," an essay in which he notes the current tendency in theology to reject images of God as king, warrior, and judge, Pat expresses both understanding and empathy for the need to step over heavy-handed and potentially domineering depictions of divine power. He also notes, however, that the rejection of these biblical metaphors "happens all too often without attention to their complexity," and he points to Isaiah 40's mixed metaphors, the "conjoining of the pastoral, royal, military, and maternal in a single complex of images," as a clue to the complexity and intricacy of the biblical depiction of divine power. "That God's rule can be both powerful and tender," he writes, "is regularly a claim of the biblical text."

In that same editorial, which appeared in an issue of *Theology Today* devoted to the theme of divine sovereignty, Pat urged his audience to read the essays in the volume "on the way to worship." It is an important remark, a sign not only that Pat considers theological discourse to be finally a churchly activity but also, and even deeper, that he views the proper telos of theology to be eschatological praise.

An unmistakable churchly interest and vision runs through these essays, as it does through the journal that gave them birth. Once himself the pastor of a congregation in South Carolina, Pat is an excellent academic scholar who remains a committed churchman, and he is unsatisfied until he knows what theological claims mean to the church, how theological arguments finally play out in the pastoral and missional life of the community of faith. For seven years I served with Pat as coeditor of *Theology Today*, and, under Pat's influence, the journal maintained and strengthened its ecclesial ethos. Our editorial conversations focused as often, if not more often, on the needs of our pastor-readers as on those of academic theologians. Our wondrous and loyal business manager, Nancy Pike, employed the latest computer technology in administering the mailing list of subscribers, but she also diligently kept a file of thousands of 3x5 cards, one for each subscriber, with churchlike notations not translatable into "computerese" (e.g., "received note . . . liked the issue on hope," "gave a gift subscription to his daughter when she was ordained"). *Theology Today* did not have mere subscribers; it had a kind of congregation.

I will never forget a lunch meeting we had one day with officials of the New York company that managed our subscription renewals and solicitations. At the time, *Theology Today* had about 14,000 subscribers, but Pat and I were convinced that we were missing a lot of intelligent ministers, priests, and laypeople interested in theology. As dessert was served, we turned to business. "We have a strong number of subscribers," Pat began, "but we'd like to reach more."

One of the company guys pushed a piece of apple pie across his plate with his fork. "How many more do you want?" he asked. Pat and I looked at each other, nonplussed. What should we say? How many more *did* we want? A thousand? Two million?

"It's all math," the company guy said. "We buy mailing lists from other magazines and send out the introductory subscription offers. We play the percentages. It's a formula. Buy enough mailing lists, mail out enough letters, cut the new subscriber price low enough, and you can get almost any number of new takers. So, how many do you want?" We sat there in silence. Did he really think we wanted him to buy mailing lists from *Rolling Stone* and *Guns and Ammo*? Would he suggest that Girl Scouts sell subscriptions to *Theology Today* door-to-door along with boxes of Chocolate Mint Supremes?

"No," said Pat. "It's not really about sheer numbers. We don't have a number in mind; we have pastors in mind."

And so it always is with Pat Miller. He has the church and its ministry in mind. The child of a Presbyterian manse, Pat loves to cite the first entry in the Westminster Shorter Catechism, namely, that the "chief end" of human beings is to glorify and enjoy God forever, and that's where Pat's eschatological thinking comes into play. He considers the praise of God not only to be a description of where human life is headed, our "chief end," but also to be subversive of where we are now. Praise, he says, undercuts "all human structures and every human being as pretenders for ultimacy or absolute devotion. . . . Any community that sings with conviction 'All people that on earth do dwell, sing to the Lord with cheerful voice. Him serve with fear, his praise forth tell' cannot give its ultimate allegiance to a Hitler or a Kennedy or a Reagan or a political party of any stripe."

The idea that the praise and worship of God cuts through human pretension is not, for Pat Miller, simply a piece of theological rhetoric. It is a way of life, a faithful affirmation that yields the spirit of humility so evident in his living and in his writing. Regarding humility, here is a thing that happened: Many years ago, Pat and I found ourselves late one Friday evening standing in a nondescript industrial building, improbably tucked off a side street of an Amish village in Pennsylvania farm country. We were in the main press room of the plant where *Theology Today* was printed, huddled there among the grimy pressmen and mechanics of the midnight shift. Like a couple of amateur interior decorators, we were there to pick colors.

At the time, *Theology Today* had been publishing for nearly fifty years and was among the largest circulation theological journals in the world, but Pat had become concerned that it had begun to look and feel its age. He had been urging us to brighten up our content, to include more poetry and art, and to freshen up our appearance with more appealing graphics, including new and colorful covers. As coeditor, I agreed that these were good ideas, so we had tinkered with the editorial formula, redesigned the interior, and decided on a rainbow look for the four annual issues, each sporting a different color. Now we had come to the printing plant in off hours to select just the right shades for the covers of a theological journal that wanted to come across as alive and current but not flashy and trendy. We sought striking, attractive, and yet still appropriately subdued and dignified hues of green, blue, purple, and magenta.

Nowadays, specifying the right cover colors would no doubt be done with rapid precision by computer, but back then trial and error was the only way. It worked like this: The head pressman would mix inks until he achieved something like the color we said we wanted. Then he and the others would slather the blended ink into the press and print a test batch of covers. We were told to work carefully at the mixing stage to identify exactly the right color because, if the trial run turned out wrong, the pressmen would have to go through the laborious process of cleaning the rollers on the big press, re-inking, and printing a whole new trial batch.

We started with the most challenging of the four colors, the magenta. Pat and I pointed to near-miss tints in the ink catalog. "Somewhere between this brick red and that rosy cinnamon," we said. The pressman began mixing the two inks. "A little more brick," we urged. "Make it darker. That's it! That's exactly the color we want!" The new color in the pot was now perfectly matched to the one in our imaginations. "Try that," we said, and the pressman looked at us warily.

"Sure this is what ya' want?" he asked, his brow wrinkled like Regis Philbin's, inquiring about the final answer.

"Yes; that's it exactly."

The pressman primed the press, pushed some controls, and the massive gears meshed and spun. Pat and I waited anxiously until, a few seconds later, the first of the brand new covers spat out of the press. It was the color of . . . Pepto-Bismol. The sample cover said *Theology Today*, but it looked like the in-house magazine of Mary Kay Cosmetics or maybe a manual on the care and feeding of poodles.

"How's that?" grunted the pressman, watching our faces. "Ya' like it?"

"Ju-u-ust a tad pink," grinned Pat, giving me a wink. With a weary sigh, the pressman pulled a rag out of the back pocket of his overalls and lumbered over to clean the press.

Eventually that night we got the correct tints, but for a couple of years afterward that first oh-so-pink cover was tacked to the bulletin board in our editorial offices. It was the office joke, of course, but it was more than that. It was a theological symbol, a reminder of the profound truth of our theological anthropology, a truth that prevails in the offices of *Theology Today* as well as in the White House or the halls of the university, that the most creative, imaginative, and well-intentioned of human actions can lead to foolish results. As human events go, that putrid pink cover was a small disaster for sure, but in its own context it was a disaster nonetheless, and as Pat comments in these pages, disasters small and large "remind us both of how wonderfully we are made when we reflect on our geniuses and minds . . . but also the limits of our finitude." The human creature, Pat Miller knows, is "as much a bumbler as a genius, as much a dominator as a governor, vulnerable to our own inventions, not safe on our own nor able to 'fix' our situation in any ultimate way, capable of effecting a genuine progress that sows the seeds of our own destruction."

Such a sober and realistic assessment of the human prospect leads Pat Miller not to despair but to hope, not to cynicism but to renewed trust in the God who saves. One cannot read very far in these essays without encountering Pat Miller's faith in the God who lavishes grace and redemption upon human beings in unfathomable measure. "God outruns our imagination," he beautifully observes.

Near the end of *Peace Like a River*, Reuben asks, "Is there a single person on whom I can press belief? No sir. All I can do is say, Here's how it went. Here's what I saw." As for Pat Miller, he points to the New Testament image of the "cloud of witnesses," saints who do not press belief on us but who remind us of "God's enduring work in the world," and who "tell us where we have been, and . . . make it clear that we have a long way to go."

Pat Miller is among those witnesses, and this collection of essays gives strong voice to his testimony. "Here's how it went. Here's what I saw."

Make of it what you will.

Thomas G. Long
Candler School of Theology

1

The W/Right Space

There is little argument that Frank Lloyd Wright was America's greatest, most original, and most influential architect. Though he often went for long periods without significant architectural assignments, the body of his work—including houses, public buildings, business establishments, churches, and hotels—is substantial and, in many respects, revolutionary. His work and his writing have shaped American architecture in large ways. The renovation of the Guggenheim Museum, his last major building, has called attention once more to the individuality and impact of his vision. And while several biographies of Wright have appeared through the years, the front page of the *New York Times Book Review* recently featured yet another one.

Among the latest studies of Wright's work is one by Grant Hildebrand entitled *The Wright Space: Pattern and Meaning in Frank Lloyd Wright's Houses.*[1] The author applies to the analysis of Wright's houses a pattern or theory of landscape aesthetics first set forth by Jay Appleton. Hildebrand claims, persuasively, that the houses Wright designed reflect a group of features human beings innately prefer in natural and man-made environments, features he finds present in Wright's houses in rich fashion. They are *complexity and order, prospect and refuge, hazard,* and *mystery.* The body of his book seeks to demonstrate through a large number of examples the prominence of these features.

Hildebrand's analysis is confined to private houses. One may ask, however, to what extent such features, if indeed in any sense innate or preferred by human beings, belong to the shape of a church, both architecturally and congregationally. That is, do church buildings and church communities manifest—or seek to do so—the characteristics that Hildebrand finds fundamental

1

to family buildings and the communities that inhabit them? Whether or not they do, one might argue that Hildebrand suggests an angle of vision on the "shape" of a "church"—with all the ambiguity that both terms carry.

Even a casual perusal of Wright's houses reveals great complexity within and differences among them. Yet it is clear that several basic patterns governed his plans, and that beneath the complexity of any given house there is much order. What they suggest for church structures is the possibility that surprise and novelty can coexist with a fundamental sense of coherence, that one who enters the building or the community may find difference, incongruity, even at times or in various modes, disorder and irregularity. There is an openness and freedom that means not everything is predictable and simple. Yet within and underneath the surprises and differences there exists a fundamental order, so that a sense of the whole is discernible, a way of characterizing and seeing how novelty and irregularity are not chaos, but the interaction of freedom and rootedness. It may not be the case that surprise and novelty are set before the architects of our contemporary churches as necessary ingredients anymore than they are prized in congregational life. But there is something in our human being that desires to encounter the novel and the more complex as long as it does not seem to undermine the stability that keeps us from falling apart.

The joining of prospect and refuge in a single structure is powerfully realized in Wright's houses, as Hildebrand demonstrates and any visitor to a Wright house will soon perceive. The fireplace occupies a central place in the house as a center of refuge. Entrances may be invisible or cavelike, and walls loom large and dominant. But upon entry, one always finds openness, the release of high ceilings along with the intimacy of low ones, visibility out and up and down, views of the outside world and of other rooms in the house. The world and nature are drawn in as much as they are shut out. Hildebrand's claim is that the combination of strong refuge signals with strong prospect signals makes a house pleasurable for human habitation. If so, the same combination suggests a way of being in the world that belongs to the "shape" of our churches. They are refuge in design and function. The sense of retreat for worship and prayer and from the cares of the world is a large part of their function and often visible in their design. What is true of the building is true also of the community. It is the mix, however, of both refuge and prospect that makes a house pleasurable and perhaps makes a church more human and inviting. Its refuge from the world joins with a way of seeing and viewing that same world, of being open to the outside as much as hidden from it. So in a small church I served as pastor, a visitor would encounter a simple brick-walled structure, inviting as a refuge or retreat from the world outside. Entry into its sanctuary, however, presented the visitor or member with one of the main walls as a mass of windows and doors opening visibly and actually to the world outside. (It also provided a regular mix of order and complexity, routine and surprise, as the familiar service of worship might be interrupted with the appearance of a neighbor's guinea hens in the trees outside the wall of windows.)

Hildebrand mentions two other features that are more minor and less frequent in Wright's houses. In his discussion of Fallingwater, the Edgar Kaufmann house built over a waterfall and arguably the most famous house in American architecture, he analyzes Wright's incorporation of *hazard* or *threat* into the architecture. It is seen especially in the flowing waterfall but also in the dizzying balconies that soar over the water and look, by Wright's design, permanently precarious. Hazard conditions may seem to have nothing to do with the "shape" of the "church," but the point ought not be dismissed too easily. For it has to do with the capacity of the design of the church, structural and congregational, to deal with societal intrusions and natural hazards. The incorporation of hazard conditions is an indication of the willingness of the church to be daring and to risk, to let the blending of prospect and refuge be a way of not simply retreating and viewing the world, but of encountering and being reminded of its threats and realities.

The dimension of *mystery* seems foreign to most private houses. But Hildebrand suggests it is present in a number of Wright's houses in the way in which their inhabitants sense that "spaces lie beyond spaces," "the suggestion but not the immediate revelation of distant spaces," and the recognition that "if more information about that sensed but unseen space is sought, it cannot be had without investigation." Where in the church are there such spaces beyond spaces, realms suggested and intimated but not immediately accessible, territory that must be investigated if one is to know more? What is true of Wright's houses belongs to the "shape" of the church in a far more fundamental way, to its shape *architecturally*, so that the structure itself suggests possibilities that must be explored and that give one a sense all is not self-evident, and to its shape *congregationally*, so that the life of the people does not assume a certitude without intimations of unexplored and unknown territory or a familiarity that is sure the discernible in space and time is all that matters and everything is in hand. The challenge is larger than the one Wright saw and constantly overcame. It is not only human space that is unseen and to be explored. It is the reality and mystery of God our structures are to intimate in what they show and do not show.

Architecture is the art of shaping space. The church in its architecture and architectonics—and we are still talking about both concrete and human structures—declares something about its identity and how it lives in the world. The argument here is that the Wright sense of space tells us something right about the space of the church. In the way we build the church, we "shape" its character and its life. It is one way we say who we are, what we are about, and what one may expect within our bounds or walls.

2

Whatever Happened to the Soul?

A book with the title *Soul: God, Self and the New Cosmology* has just come into the office of this journal for review.[1] I was struck by the title. Then I was struck with being struck by the title. What is so unusual about a book titled *Soul* being sent to a theological journal for review? Not much in theory. But in practice or "in actual fact," as we are accustomed to say, we don't hear very much about the soul in theological circles these days. One of the most theological of all terms is somewhat out of favor. The only person I know giving serious attention these days to the soul is not a theologian but a sociologist of religion. I confess that, like Karl Menninger when he wrote *Whatever Became of Sin?*, I am both surprised and a little dismayed at this state of affairs.

One would expect that contemporary Christian anthropology would give some attention to the soul as a traditional rubric of Christian theology, but that seems to be little the case if my nonstatistical perusal of recent theological literature, including this issue of *Theology Today* on anthropology, is any indication. A recent conference on the Bible and theology devoted a weekend to a discussion of "The Whole and the Divided Self" without any reference to the soul except in a paper on the dualism of Pauline thought about human nature. The book on the soul referred to above is a notable exception. While it is by a theologian, it grew out of research for a television series by the BBC. It may be a comment on the modern scene that television gives more attention to the soul than theology does, or that it is a popular, nonreligious rock singer who labeled his recent album *Soul Cages*.[2]

The most extensive reference to the soul I have encountered in recent times is not in theological conversation or reading but in Joyce Carol Oates's play *The Perfectionist*. A comedy satire of little significance but much amusement,

5

Oates's play has frequent references to the soul. A photographer speaks of primitive peoples being afraid of the camera stealing their souls, while contemporary young people let her photograph them because they hope the camera will give them souls. Whichever category of persons you choose, the soul here is a pointer to a dimension of depth in human existence that other terms convey with less directness or clarity. That defining the soul is not easy to do does not necessarily mean the term fails to denote and connote to its hearers.

Oates has clearly perceived this, as her easy and frequent use of the term, even in a comedy, demonstrates. Another of her figures speaks of his colleague's currying up to persons of questionable reputation in order to try to get their money as being "corrosive to the soul." The colleague sees it simply as necessary "kissing ass." One of the main characters is a teenager who is stricken with guilt and speaks of his own experience of "the dark night of the soul" or, as he goes on to say in his more colorful vernacular, "There's some heavy shit in my soul." Whichever cliché one prefers, the sense of sin and guilt and the feeling of despair express themselves in this sort of language in a way far different from the language of psychotherapy and sociology. The triumph of the therapeutic over the struggle of the soul may mask some authentic differences between the conceptuality of self and that of soul. In fact, it would be a significant gain for the therapeutic endeavor if it were to recover a sense of the soul. The modern sensibility knows about "kissing ass" without being sufficiently aware of the corrosion to the soul, the eating away of the moral fiber of one's being, that dimension of one's personhood that has, at least potentially and often actually, a sense of transcendence and of oughtness.

Years ago a colleague, writing about T. S. Eliot's *The Cocktail Party*, described the psychiatrist Sir Henry Harcourt-Reilly as a "soul doctor." While my colleague was not himself a religious person, indeed more Freudian than theological in outlook, he correctly described the way in which Sir Henry comprehends the religious depth of Celia Coplestone's behavior that leads to a horrifying martyrdom out of a strange sense of the need for atonement. The rest of the characters, precisely because of their modern sensibility, fail to see the need of the soul in Celia's journey, a failure that leads Sir Henry, in response to their sense of her fate—murdered in an African insurrection while treating "plague-stricken natives"—as "waste," to claim that "it was triumphant."

The disappearance of the soul from theological talk about the human is not without its positive reasons or justifications. Language changes, and fundamental notions get reconceived in different words. That happens and can be helpful. In this instance, however, the shift from *soul* to *self*, which seems to be the primary substitute word to talk about some of the same substance, is not simply a linguistic change. It represents in part, and certainly among theologians, a move toward a more unified understanding of the person. Certainly that development is to be applauded. The sense of our selves as wholes rather than component parts is a proper apprehension. The mind-body or soul-body dualism does not ring true in a phenomenology of the self that does not know minds without bodies. It is possible for bodies to exist, even to be born, without minds if the brain is dead or missing. But it is difficult to attribute personhood to such.

Even this last example, however, raises questions about the disuse of the soul language and the assumption that dualistic language has no connection to reality. There are those who are brain dead and seem to be merely body who, in fact, are loved, treated, fed, talked to, and to whom some personality is attributed by parents or others who love them. One can hardly speak about the presence of mind in these bodies, and perhaps with difficulty of the spirit. But to understand such individuals as "endowed with a soul," however inaccurate and imprecise such language may appear to be, is to say something significant about their existence as human beings.

Angela Tilby, author of the book *Soul* referred to above, articulates a contemporary perspective when she notes that many believe that science has "made the notion of the soul redundant." (For those who are not familiar with British expressions, "made redundant" means "rendered unnecessary" or, in its most common usage, "fired.") Tilby, however, judges this dismissal of the notion of the soul as a mistake. She sees in science a new book of nature emerging that speaks "very directly to peoples' sense of God and of themselves."

Whether or not that is the case, it is this dimension of soul language and soul conceptuality that is in danger of being thrown out with the bathwater as we relegate this term and this notion to the linguistic and conceptual wastebasket. The soul is a way of speaking anthropologically not simply about an outmoded personal dualism but of that dimension of human existence that is addressed by God and understands self and person as features of a God-human relationship. To speak about the soul is to speak about something that is part of us—in a nondefined and nonempirical fashion—that has to do with God, with the moral and religious dimensions of our being, in a way that no other anthropological term quite brings off. Clearly *the self*, which seems to be a more holistic and accurate term, does not carry the connotations of the term *soul*. Its psychological roots make it a rich term or notion for thinking about personhood, but it is able to stay firmly within a notion of the human that takes no account of either morality or transcendence. It is surely no accident that we speak about a "soul brother [or sister]" but not a "self brother." A "soul brother" is one who connects with me in the things that matter most in my being and activity.

In his *Church Dogmatics*, Karl Barth speaks of the "Thou" as the self created and addressed by God. "This 'Thou-I,'" he says, "is the human 'soul,' the

[one] who lives by the Spirit of God." He is careful to resist dualistic anthropologies and to insist of human beings that "they themselves are their souls, for their souls are the souls of their bodies." But, for Barth, to speak of self or of subject with reference to human beings is precisely to speak of soul, for one's soul is "in direct relation to God's awakening and sustaining Spirit."[3]

If, therefore, in distaste for dualistic and idealistic categories for speaking about the human, the soul is lost, something more than a linguistic change has occurred. We have relinquished the primary word for identifying our creatureliness as something more than natural. As John Leith has put it aptly in his *Basic Christian Doctrine:* "The soul is the human being in his or her knowledge of God and in the awareness that human life is not simply animal existence of instinct and impulse. The soul hears the word of God."[4]

Attention to the soul historically has focused on the question of ultimate personal destiny, the fate of "departed souls." The immortality of the soul has been the primary doctrine associated with the distinction between body and soul. There is no doubt that soul language has fallen in disrepute to no small degree because of the emphasis in current New Testament theology on the resurrection of the body over against the immortality of the soul. It is worth noting, however, that this distinction has come under vigorous criticism in a recent book by James Barr titled *The Garden of Eden and the Hope of Immortality.*[5] His emphasis is less upon the soul than it is upon the notion of immortality, which, he argues, is indeed a biblical concern. But along the way, he challenges current ideas about the way in which the Bible speaks of the soul and suggests that one can indeed speak of the soul in Scripture as distinct from the body, as that "superior controlling centre which accompanies, expresses and directs the existence of that totality, and one which, especially, provides the life to the whole."

All of this is to suggest that currents in biblical theology together with developments in psychology and related fields that have caused us to drop soul language and soul notions from our vocabulary and our theological formulations may not have served us well. Whether the question is who we are or what we are to become, the notion of the soul conveys in powerful ways a sense of human existence as God-given and God-addressed, morally freighted in our very beings, and transcending all natural categories even if we are also thoroughly natural. It is a strange sort of paradox that while the soul is the one anthropological term that is truly theological and does not fit the secular mentality, it seems to have its continuing viability more in secular usage than theological. Perhaps we need to take a cue from the realms of art and literature and restore the soul to a place of significance in our thinking and speaking, theologically, about the human.

3

Poetry and Theology

While this journal, like any other periodical with a fifty year history, has undergone numerous changes, one feature that has perdured is the regular publication of poetry. That does not make us unique among theological journals; there are others that include poetry with their essays. Yet it is safe to say that poetry is not typically what one expects to encounter when opening a theological periodical. We are not altogether sure what the reaction of our readers is to the presence of poetry in these pages or to the particular poems that we include. We get too few specific reactions to any feature of the journal to generalize about them, though occasionally a note from a reader indicates appreciation of a poem that we have published. What is evident, however, is the interest of poets in appearing in these pages. We receive as many or more unsolicited poems as unsolicited theological articles.

Inasmuch as the editors cannot justify the publication of poetry on the basis of demonstrable reader appeal, it may be worthwhile to give some attention to the rationale for its inclusion or, better, to the contribution we believe poetry makes to the ongoing enterprise of the church's theological activity.

If one starts with some reflection on the place of poetry in the Christian tradition, then the combination of poetry and theology is not all that surprising. From Milton and Dante to Donne and Herbert, from Hopkins to Eliot and Auden, there is a powerful and highly influential strain of poetic articulation of religious and specifically Christian sentiments and tradition. In our own time, there have been virtual poetic icons articulating succinctly the sense of an age in a way that whole tomes of theological analysis can suggest only in a much more cumbersome manner. One thinks, for example, of Eliot's "The

Hollow Men," with its ending that seemed to speak in a paradoxical way of the fate of an atomically destined world:

> This is the way the world ends
> This is the way the world ends
> This is the way the world ends
> Not with a bang but a whimper.

In similar fashion, one of the greatest of modern poems has become almost a cliché because of its capacity to fix in our minds, in metaphor and rhythm, an image of a world undoing and to suggest with the language of Christian faith the very thin line between the redemptive and the demonic possibilities for life on this planet. The very title of William Butler Yeats's poem "The Second Coming" draws upon one of the cardinal tenets of Christian eschatology and holds it before us with all the awe and terror and wonder that the doctrine is meant to convey but rarely does in its more dogmatic and homiletical articulations. How often has one heard that "things fall apart; the center cannot hold" or been confronted with that haunting and disturbing image with which Yeats concluded his poem and turned the Christian gospel into a terrifying image of the future of a world that believes its God has died and gone to hell:

> And what rough beast, its time come round at least,
> Slouches toward Bethlehem to be born?

Only in Scripture and poetry can one find such comparably vivid and disturbing pictures of the apocalyptic possibilities buried in religious faith and often resurrected.

Indeed, the justification of poetry in a theological context receives its first and most obvious ground in the example of Scripture, where poetry is one of the significant modes of expression. While the appeal of the Psalms is manifold in character, it rests in no small measure on the lyric, poetic form of these songs and prayers. One can talk much about human pain but hardly hear it as sharply as in the voices of those who cry out in the Psalms. The powerful images of the Psalms, whether of God or of the wicked or of the human predicament, express in nondiscursive form the glory of God and the plight of the human. Such matters can be talked about more rationally, exegetically, and systematically, but hardly with the same power and certainly not in the same way. Chapter 2 of the Westminster Confession of Faith is very good on the attributes of God. I use it with some regularity in my teaching of the Old Testament. But I am confident that neither my mother nor Karl Barth—to take two quite different theologians—turned to that chapter as often as they did to Psalm 103 to hear and think about the God who made them. Nor am I ever surprised to find people of faith and of no faith responding more to the way

God speaks in the poetic dialogues of Job than to that same voice in the narrative prose of the prologue and epilogue of the book. There may be theological reasons at work in that preference, but I doubt they are any more influential than the differences in genre. The poetic form of the dialogues conveys the issues of the book and the struggles and conflicts depicted therein with an imaginative power that grasps both heart and mind.

This is not to suggest that somehow poetry is the superior medium for faith or theology. Quite the contrary. Theology requires the kind of rational, logical, inductive, and deductive thinking—with attention to historical data, hermeneutical principles, and theological method—that characterizes most of the writing in this journal. Further, the narrative mode of Scripture has caught the attention of many and carried over into contemporary theological expression. Story and narrative are big items theologically, affecting even confessional theological formulations and appearing in these pages as both media of expression and subjects of discussion. Indeed, story has been the foundational form of the church's faith from the Scriptures to the present.

Poetry, however, more obviously perhaps than story, gives us theology and the expression of faith in a different voice. One of the things that is implicit in our setting up a regular section of poetry (admittedly, it is not always present because we do not always have poetry to print) is the desire for the poetry to be perceived as a form of theological expression in its own right rather than merely a light touch, a diversion, in an otherwise heavy and academic mode of theology. As in the poetry of the Bible, faith comes to expression in a different way. The language is more open. The play of poetry allows a play in theology that is less permissible in theology's more discursive forms. The ambiguity of expression that is intrinsic to poetry permits paradox, contradiction, multivalency, and open-ended articulation of matters of faith. The elliptical style of poetry, which means it may leave out as much as it includes, also gives room to play and resists finality, completion, and closure at every point. That is why poetry is often "difficult." What eye and ear perceive and hear make us aware that there is more here than meets the eye and ear. The images of poetry speak to startle and puzzle us, to provoke us and cause us to think. They set the imagination free, opening the reader to theological possibilities that might be less acceptable or even unthinkable in the essay mode. Images, dreams, personal experiences, sensual realities—all these aspects of our life that are often filtered out of theological work are front and center when poetry is the medium of faith's expression.

If the poetry of these pages is theology *in* a different voice, it is also theology *by* different voices. While occasionally one of our poems is by an author recognizable from essays in this or other theological literature, most often our poets are not theological essayists or even persons who identify themselves as theologians. In other words, poetry tends to articulate dimensions of religious faith through the voices of nonprofessional theologians, lay men and women, persons who spin out a form of theology that arises from a fragment of conversation, a visit to a cathedral, a memory of a friend or a family member, a biblical figure or text. The perspective is not that of the formal theologian. It is the vision of ordinary things seen more deeply, etched, imaged, and "rhythmed" rather than argued and exegeted.

The editors of *Theology Today* continue to wish for more essays by women theologians, but we are glad that the poetic theology appearing in these pages is often the powerful voice of women and that women in history and the present, known and unknown, are frequently the subject. From the articles published in *Theology Today*, for example, one would have little sense of the impact on religious faith of Mary, the mother of Jesus, but it is very evident in the poetry. The feminist voice may be more experimental, dramatic, and visionary, more risky in nonpolemical ways, in poetic form than in the more discursive articles and books. To take a single recent example, the following verse or strophe from the poem "Salome" by Elizabeth Creamer that we published in October 1994 joins the biblical and the contemporary, the experience of women and the tradition of Scripture, in a highly imaginative and even humorous way, but with a very serious edge (pun intended):

> No, all I would say was not said in the dance
> but the bump and grind was my mother tongue,
> breasts and hips an ingenue's scripted part.
> The Baptist risked his neck to exhort a wasted king,
> but for me, the daughter, he offered not one sermon.
> If the man had only thought that I might think,
> I would have chosen a different veil.
> As it was, I danced.
> It was the only way I knew
> for a girl like me
> to get a head.

While much is written in contemporary feminist biblical interpretation to provide another perspective on women who are portrayed negatively in Scripture, Creamer's poem does that in eleven lines (there is a prior verse of the same length in her poem) that belie the necessity of some complex hermeneutical method to overcome a presumed hermeneutical gap between the biblical text and the contemporary world. And we see Salome in a whole new way. The poem is fictive and truthful. It is story become poetry. It is Salome as sister, and, most clearly, it is woman as woman. The artful way in which the poem dances and narrows down to its conclusion and climax simply precludes articulation in any other way than the voice of the poet.

4

Whither the Church?

The church in North America, if not elsewhere, exists today in a strange kind of tension—precarious, anxious, and uncertain about its future, on the one hand, and assertive, thriving, and active, on the other. Perhaps it has always been that way. But the more obvious features of church life in this part of the world suggest why this manner of being should be the case. The changing character of the church in our culture evokes various kinds of response. A few indicators of that change will illustrate.

The energy and loyalty of church members are shifting—or have shifted—away from the denominational structures that have for so long been the visible representations of church life in the public eye and toward congregational life and local mission. Thus, supportive and missional structures that have been dependable and central are no longer either. The financial implications of that fact have been felt in distressing ways in virtually every major denomination. The latest headline in a denominational paper on my desk reads, "Unrestricted mission giving continues to decline."

This shift, however, is precisely a shift of energy and not simply a decline. The investment of people—convictional, financial, and personal investment—in the work of the church as represented in their local congregation and its mission, is, in many cases, amazingly diverse and significant. Our congregation began its stewardship season with two lay members reading, in rapid-fire fashion, a two-minute rehearsal of all that goes on in that congregation for its own life and the life of the world. The effect was both formally and substantively breathtaking.

New congregational structures and experimentation with various styles of worship suggest a kind of uncertainty and laissez-faire attitude toward the visible marks of the church as discerned in liturgy and congregational life. Familiar liturgical orders are being replaced by new official versions in the denominations and by all sorts and varieties of contemporary forms of worship in the congregations themselves. Neither at the denominational level where the worship resources are developed nor at the local level where worship is carried out can one assume that what the church has done is what it is going to do. Is this a major erosion, or a sign of powerful renewal? It is probably both.

So also the powerful educational impetus that denominations have found in the development of major curricular resources seems now to have evaporated. The excitement generated by a church-wide engagement in biblical and theological study around a common core of educational materials is not likely to occur again. There is neither the financial base nor the interest of the membership that such an enterprise requires. Yet educational programs in local churches are varied and lively. Theology and the Bible have not disappeared from the church. Indeed, the spate of Bible translations and commentary series is itself an indicator of our situation. The church can no longer count on a normative and thus familiar and reliable version of the Bible as a base for its pastoral, preaching, educational, and devotional life, but the multitude and variety of translations and resources, seen in its best light, testifies, among other things, to some kind of commitment to the Word of God in the church's life.

In the theological realm, the church is fraught with conflict over various issues, some of which threaten to create major splits. Indeed, division, both formal and informal, has already taken place in some denominations. The Re-Imagining Conference and the debates over the church's stance on sexual ethics, particularly same-sex relationships, are the most obvious and immediate examples of these theological controversies. How such conflict will shake out or shake the church remains to be seen. Many of us wish that we could get past such theological problems. Yet, the debates have forced church bodies, individual theologians, and anxious and troubled lay people to a kind of theological and moral discussion that might not be going on if we had more theological harmony. The church may not look very pretty when it engages in vigorous theological debate, but any therapist knows that anger is a sign of life. Theological anger that precipitates theological argument is at one and the same time a sign of a church troubled and a sign of a church alive. Indifference and lassitude may be the symptoms to be feared the most.

Whither, then, the church? It may not be self-evident to the reader who first picks up this issue and glances at the table of contents that its focus is the church and that we have asked our writers to speak about the church in this changing context. The very different angles they take is indicative of our situation. In one case, the focus may be theological; in another it may be cultural. For one, the need may be theology; for another, practice; for another, vision.

Is this an issue on the church, or on the culture? I am not sure which, but then that is in some sense the issue of the issue.

Since the editors have a self-granted permission—if not indeed a job requirement—to wade into the discussion, let me suggest two or three things that ought to belong to the church's directional search.

Attention to ecclesiology as a primary topic of theological conversation, teaching, and writing is a prime desideratum. It is symptomatic of our time that we have a continuing spate of sociological and historical studies on the church, but not as much theological study. In the early 1960s, two significant and influential works appeared that sought to look closely at the church as a social institution, Peter L. Berger's *The Noise of Solemn Assemblies* and James M. Gustafson's *Treasure in Earthen Vessels: The Church as a Human Community*.[1] I particularly remember reading Gustafson and being refreshed and delighted at a study that took so seriously the social and human dimensions of the church without forgetting its theological character. As a sociologist, Berger addressed the cultural establishment of American religion in powerful terms. Since that time, we seem to have given far more attention to the social and sociological study of the church than to developing a theology of the church that is fully aware of its "earthen" character but takes its starting point from what the church was called and called out to be. The study of the church as a social institution is inevitable and necessary. But when "voluntary association" governs our thinking about the church more than does "body of Christ," then something is askew. There is a crying need for the church and its ministry—both pastors and teachers—to ask as sharply as possible about who and what we are and what we are about in a way that expects to be informed by voices of Scripture as well as and as much as from cultural analysis.

The church is constituted by the grace of God. In practice and in theory, therefore, the church is a community of grace. This means the congregation knows itself to be redeemed sinners who join their lives together in the service and obedience of the Lord of the church. Its gospel is truly good news. The purpose of its preaching, in the words of George Buttrick, is to share a joy. The church is open and welcoming. In the tension between tightly defining its borders for the sake of faithfulness or clarity of identity and opening wide its arms at the risk of fuzzy self-consciousness, the church needs to remember there is one criterion for participation, and that is the awareness of the redemptive grace of God. We are in a time when the language and the notion of inclusion is increasingly criticized and dismissed. There may be grounds for qualifying inclusiveness in other institutions and arenas of public life—though it is difficult for me to conceive where that could be significantly so—but the openness of the church in all its facets is finally and simply an indication of the power of God's grace in our midst, or of our resistance to it.

Even as it is a community of grace, the church is also a community of conviction and commitment. Its shaky status in the contemporary world may have much to do with its failure to declare itself—as a corporate entity and as individuals—clearly as the people of God. That rubric, somewhat in disrepute in our time, is worth recovering. For it was used originally in order to identify the community's ultimate commitment, its binding obligation to live in this world as a people that is in every way tagged with the name of the Lord of Israel—in praise, worship, and obedience, in the quotidian and mundane as well as in those deep and transcendent moments when there is the profoundest awareness of a larger dimension to our lives than we ever dreamed. The church was first called the Way (Acts 9:2; 18:25–26). In our time, that image also bears recovering as a means of identifying a particular reality that is not simply consonant with the culture. "The people of the Way" is not a bad handle for the church unless our common life makes it meaningless. It is probably a telling sign of the church's contemporary plight in North America that such a rubric would seem more applicable, in the minds of some, to the political right of this country than to the church.

The church may not find it easy to be at the same time both fully open and fully committed. We have tended to stress either one or the other, either to be very welcoming, unrestricting, and undemanding, or to require specific modes of conduct and tests of devotion for both members and leaders. The tension between the two is real, but there is where the church lives—graced and commanded.

Such a mode of existence may be possible as the church lives also between memory and hope, remembering the story and stories of its saints and sinners and anticipating without doubt the power of God to vindicate the divine purpose. There is a powerful New Testament image that bears witness to the memory and hope of the church. It is the picture of the "cloud of witnesses" who surround us, reminding us of God's enduring work in the church through the ages and instilling in us the energetic hope that the future requires. The reality of the church has no surer ground than this cloud of witnesses. They encircle us as our past and as our future. They tell us where we have been, and they make it clear we have a long way to go.

5

Hallelujah! The Lord God Omnipotent Reigns

It seems built in to the nature of God, at least as Jews and Christians have learned about that, to be omnipotent, all-powerful, in charge of the cosmos. Reinforced by powerful biblical images of creator, ruler, warrior, and judge, the God of Christian faith wears the epithet "Lord" appropriately (apart from its possible gender associations). The only thing more obvious than that is the way in which human experience of the world seems to contradict such assumptions all the time. A traditional and central tenet of Christian theology generally and especially of the Reformed tradition, the sovereignty of God stands on relatively shaky ground in our time. The challenges, and they are not peculiar to our time, are several.

Theologically, the reality of great evil, identified so inescapably in the Holocaust, undercuts claims that God is in charge and rules in justice and mercy over the cosmos. Divine rule and divine power increasingly seem to be abstract and unreal notions. It is not only massive human evil, however, that raises theological questions about divine sovereignty. Much more personal and intimate experiences evoke theological questions and revisions. In his bestseller *When Bad Things Happen to Good People*, Harold S. Kushner argued that God's power is limited; he did so out of his own experience of the loss of a child.[1]

Pastorally, of course, God's effective rule of the universe is under suspicion in all the "why" questions that human experience raises in the face of tragedy, evil, and suffering, large or small. Few Christians do not find themselves at some time confronted with occasions that raise perplexing and disturbing doubts about God's power, particularly in relation to human suffering. That means we continually face both a theological responsibility and a pastoral one:

We need to find a more adequate understanding of God's power than those that have been around but have failed or foundered on the rocks of human experience and theological analysis, and we need to discover means of communicating such an understanding in ways that enable Christians to comprehend, that is, to understand and to overcome, the darkness that suffering and evil inevitably bring down upon us.

Furthermore, a different kind of challenge to God's sovereignty has arisen in our time. One might characterize it as a resistance to notions of power, control, and rule over others, to hierarchical relationships in general, and thus to their manifestation in divine-human relationships in particular. Several things seem to have evoked this resistance. A major factor, of course, is the oppressive domination experienced by individuals, nations, communities, and races who have lived under some controlling power. Power is not simply *assumed* to be an oppressive weapon. The heavy hand has in fact been felt over and over again when some have been under the control of others. The very image of ruler is laden with negative connotations in the face of the history of tyrannical leaders, monarchical or otherwise. Feminist theology has made this point vigorously and challenged theological positions and systems that focus on divine power and sovereignty, sliding lightly over the implications for such theologies of the fact that, as Catherine Keller wrote in these pages in July 1995, "The abuse of power . . . can be seen at every level of the social orders dominating the planet." The latest book in feminist theology to arrive on our review shelves titles its chapter on God "By Whose Power? The Problem of Divine Authority for Feminist Prayer."[2]

That this rational and visceral reaction to divine sovereignty as a kind of divine domination should be deeply felt in feminist theology is not surprising. The Bible itself sets forth notions of husbandly rule over wives and male rule over women and then tells us stories about such rule that curl the hair. Perpetuation of ecclesial male domination in hierarchical modes in the Roman Catholic Church and elsewhere simply reinforces the conviction of women that notions of sovereignty carry with them patterns of domination that suppress full and mutual responsibility, opportunity, and reward. It is to be expected that out of such encounter with human sovereignty, theologians, female and male, would seek to discover or construct a kind of theology that reveals a God in whose nature and activity mutuality or some other kind of relationship replaces hierarchical control of the world and its creatures and whose imaging is more appropriately set by images that are more open, gentler, vulnerable to others, and preserving of freedom in the creation in all its forms.

Other factors have pressed this challenge to divine sovereignty and power in contemporary theology and culture. The individualism that pervades our society resists relationships in which one's freedom and control are compromised. The desire for autonomy is as old as the Bible, but it has hardly ever been so thoroughly exalted and made a political and cultural slogan as is the case in much of Western society, especially in the United States. The "revolution" being talked about in the halls of the U.S. Congress in these days is at base a renewed quest for individual autonomy and the resistance to political systems that place any kind of control over one's life, finances, decisions, and values except on some matters, such as abortion. Such long-standing libertarian and individualistic forces in the ethos of our society permeate religious thinking as much as they do the social and political realm. Acknowledgment of a power over our lives and a power in our lives that is not ours to control (of course it has always been subject to question and challenge, at least in the biblical tradition) cuts against the grain, and so we seek theological directions that exclude or do not accent notions of sovereignty that might impinge on the world and on our particular lives.

Alongside such cultural and social factors—but not separate from them—there is within many of us a desire for a softer-edged God, "a kinder, gentler" deity, to use a recent presidential expression. The many depictions of the serene Jesus in popular Christian art confirm the preference for a "Lord" who will not dominate us. Positive responses to the use of maternal imagery for the divine are not simply due to the reclaiming of the feminine. They are seen as preferable to the aura of controlling power that is so often associated with paternal imagery. So also, the biblical image of the supporting arm grabs us, while the ruling arm of the Lord connotes domination and subjugation (Isa. 40:10–11; cf. Deut 1:30–31).

Finally, in behalf of this challenge to an image of divine sovereignty that focuses upon ruling and controlling power are the many indications from the Scriptures themselves that the ruling power of the God of the Bible is not solely to be defined by the most common perceptions of kings and rulers. Thorny crowns are as oxymoronic theologically as they are absent from the palaces of all human rulers, and they suggest, at least the only one I know of, a radically different kind of ruling power. Vulnerability may be the most popular new attribute of God, but it is in fact as old as Scripture, if vulnerability involves the pathos of God, the openness of the divine decision to human intercession, and the execution of God's anointed.

What then belongs to the ongoing enterprise of discovering and constructing what it means that God rules? Two or three things are fairly obvious. One is the need for continuing attention to the nature of power, its various manifestations and especially its relation to powerlessness. For one of the things that Christian faith maintains is that power and powerlessness are peculiarly joined together in the Godhead. So Paul hears a word from the Lord, "My grace is sufficient for you, for my power is made perfect in weakness," and says himself to the Corinthian Christians that Christ "was crucified in weakness, but lives by the power of God" (2 Cor. 12:9; 13:4). One of the meanings of the social character of God as manifest in the Trinity is the interaction of power and powerlessness in the nature and work of God. But that interaction, so often manifest in the Scriptures, tells against simplistic notions of power and domination as the nature of divine sovereignty.

So also, reflection on the nature of power and particularly divine power needs to discern and work out its relational character. As James Luther Adams often noted in his various essays on divine and human power, power involves both the expression of God's law and love and the exercise of human freedom in response to that law and love. One of the contributions of feminist theology is to press a relational notion of power rather than a unitary understanding. Both the social character of God and the reality of the world as creation invite a notion of power and sovereignty as a complex of interdependence and mutual dependencies.

The other large item on the agenda is the continued wrestling with—not dismissal of—the images of God in Scripture. The rejection of monarchical, judicial, and military metaphors in the depiction of deity in Scripture happens all too often without attention to their complexity. For example, it is rarely recognized, theologically at least, that one of the dominant royal images of Scripture is that of the shepherd. Indeed, the conjoining of the pastoral, royal, military, and maternal in a single complex of images in the text from Isaiah 40 mentioned above is an important clue to the biblical depiction of divine rule. The images speak in various ways about the fact of creation's standing under a divine governance and about the character of that governance. That God's rule can be both powerful and tender is regularly a claim of the biblical text. That God's rule can and will be just and merciful is also a claim of Scripture in direct statement and by its images for the divine rule. So also, the biblical texts know an encounter with the rule of God that is inscrutable in its outworkings (thus Job) and as painful for God as it ever has been for humankind (visit Golgotha on the way to Auschwitz and Dachau).

In the essays that follow in this issue, these and other matters are taken up by persons for whom the issues of divine sovereignty are important both theologically and personally. Read them on the way to worship. That is the only real check we have on these matters—at least until we finally bow before the throne. And remember that the early Christians went to their deaths out of the conviction that Jesus is Lord. They thought that was good news. It still is.

6

Teaching the Faith

The central feature of this issue is a symposium on the new *Catechism of the Catholic Church*. The appearance of this catechism, which has received much attention in the Catholic Church—some negative and some positive—comes at a time of renewed interest in catechetical instruction in some of the Protestant denominations as well. A recent special issue of *The Presbyterian Outlook* devoted to the subject of Christian education contains articles almost entirely on catechisms and the history and contemporary possibilities of catechetical teaching. Such a focus would hardly have been expected twenty years ago or even a decade ago, so out of favor has been the catechetical approach in many Christian education circles. That does not mean that catechisms have disappeared from the churches. On the contrary, a number of churches use catechetical instruction in a variety of ways. Further, the custom of giving awards and public recognition for recitation of one of the Catechisms, no small motivation in this writer's learning of the Westminster Shorter Catechism at an early age, continues even in a theological school such as Princeton Theological Seminary, where students who learn the Shorter Catechism receive a substantial enough monetary award that some faculty, perhaps only half-jokingly, have remarked that they wished they were eligible for the award.

Yet, it is certainly the case that, in general, catechetical instruction has fallen out of favor as a part of the church's teaching practice for most of this century. Its muted but serious revival is well worth considering. The ambivalent response of many persons to a return to catechisms is not surprising. In our time, it may be more difficult than it once was to use them as teaching tools, inasmuch as memorization generally has fallen on hard times not only because of the criticism by educators of rote learning but also because of the effect of sweeping technological advances from television to Xerox machines to calculators to computers, all of which have contributed to a move away from slower and less efficient modes of learning. Catechetical instruction has been an obvious mode of learning as it has often focused more upon committing to memory than it has upon understanding. Some have found that there are indeed other ways of studying the catechism to learn about church doctrine than simply memorizing it, but it may be worth asking if the return to memorizing may not have some usefulness if the material is such that comprehension and recall happen more easily for those who take the trouble to learn the catechisms. The form of a catechism, its style and level of presentation, will have much to do with how it is used in the Christian communities for which it is created. The new Catholic Catechism, running some six hundred pages, is a good example of one that is meant to be an extended doctrinal statement for study and understanding as well as for defining the circle of faith rather than for precise appropriation and commitment to memory.

The Catholic Catechism reminds us of the essentially conservative character of catechisms, as of creeds and doctrinal statements generally. That is appropriate in that part of their function, at least, is to conserve the tradition as it has been handed down, as it has been previously agreed upon. The church does not generally fix in doctrinal form matters that are under much debate or contemporary currents and trends in theology unless it does so precisely to assert the tradition against other voices and currents it deems unacceptable. The conservative nature of the catechetical form is one of its chief virtues and reasons for being. It may be most helpful just at the point of providing a kind of mooring, a formulation of the tradition of Scripture and theology in a time when things are loose and many voices are in the air. In a recently published and valuable study of confirmation and the catechetical tradition, Richard Osmer reminds us of the positive achievements of the catechetical movement in the time of the Reformation:

> The catechism was acknowledged as an indispensable tool in promoting theological literacy and Christian unity. It provided Christians with a basic doctrinal framework, enabling them to reflect theologically on their work in the church and ordinary life. The church did not seek to control every aspect of a person's life; only to provide a sure foundation on the basis of which liberty and conscience could be exercised. At the same time, the catechism was seen as promoting unity among Christians. Confession based on such instruction was of the church's one, true faith, not the individual's particular, idiosyncratic beliefs. The catechism thus was viewed as promoting both individual freedom and church unity.[1]

That capacity to advance theological literacy and to provide a shared under-standing of the faith continues to attract us to the possibilities of catechetical teaching.

There are, of course, some dangers in the conservative character of cate-chisms. They are more backward looking in general than forward, as one can see, for example, in the heavy-handed and tendentious use of masculine lan-guage in the Catholic Catechism. They tell us more about where we have been and what we have believed than where we are going and how to formulate the faith in our own time. That there are genuine verities that can be set forth is one of the things catechisms make clear, but they also reveal their highly time-bound character. A contemporary Reformed confession, for example, might not set the decrees of God so firmly to the fore as do the Westminster Cate-chisms and would surely talk about creation in other ways than as a six-day event.

Thus it is that catechetical instruction and the documents on which such teaching is based need to be both informing and inviting, that is, transmitting the faith and inviting persons to think further about it. The resistance to mem-orizing and perhaps to catechisms in general is sometimes because memoriza-tion seems to rule out discussion. But as a teaching tool, the catechism is much like the Shema of ancient Israel. It was to be learned, preserved, and recited. But it was to be talked about and discussed as well. Its implications and con-temporary force were and are always under discussion. So also the catechism is not meant to be so defining that there can be no discussion. The danger of catechetical formulations is that they may be dogmatic in tone and not just in substance, formulating the perimeters of faith as sharply as the center. The center should be fairly clear, but the periphery should be more open. One does not define the faith attested in the Scriptures primarily through such canoni-cal works as Job and Ecclesiastes, but that faith cannot be defined without including them and what they attest as a part of the circle of faith.

Along with Scripture, catechisms provide touchstones for growth in faith, formulations to which one can return again and again in a world where super-ficiality and rapid change are the order of the day. One of the tests of a cate-chism's ability to do the job is whether it provides for the journey at least a few pieces of theological coinage that do not tarnish or decrease in value as time goes by, theological "texts" that are there to turn to in the face of life's exi-gencies and uncertainties, its upheavals and crises. Most of those who have memorized the Westminster Shorter Catechism, one of the better-known cat-echisms of the Reformed tradition, will always remember its questions about what is sin ("Any want of conformity unto or transgression of the law of God") or who is God ("God is a Spirit, infinite, eternal, and unchangeable, in his being, wisdom, power, holiness, justice, goodness, and truth"). But the appeal of those questions and answers is their simplicity—indeed, excessive simplicity—in dealing with the largest of issues. The first question of the Shorter Catechism, however, works in a different way. As it asks about our "chief end" as human beings and answers that we are here "to glorify God and to enjoy him forever," we are given a fundamental definition of a tradition and the kind of foundation that lasts and lets us know in a defining way who we are and what we are about. So also the first question of the Heidelberg Catechism has carried many souls along their way and to their rest in a kind of fundamental assurance that goes very deep, even when they can only remember the first couple of lines:

> Q. What is your only comfort, in life and in death?
> A. That I belong—body and soul, in life and in death—not to myself but to my faithful Saviour, Jesus Christ. . . .

One can go a long way with simply that conviction and the 103rd Psalm. As one reads on in the catechism, it will give further definition and aid faith's search for understanding. But that beginning word is one that is always there. One comes to count on it.

In the end, the test of the catechetical tradition and its continuing viability in the churches may be its capacity for aiding the theological education of the young. Some of us may tend to think too much that catechisms are child's play, theologically speaking. One has only to take a glance at the new Catholic Catechism to demolish that assumption. But the education of the next generation is where the catechetical tradition begins in Scripture:

> When your children ask you in time to come, "What is the meaning of the decrees and the statutes and the ordinances that the Lord our God has commanded you?" then you shall say to your children, "We were Pharaoh's slaves in Egypt, but the Lord brought us out of Egypt with a mighty hand." (Deut. 6:20–21).

That first account of a child's catechism is instructive in several ways. For one, it sets an expectation that the questions and answers of faith are a part of the agenda of the future among the people of God. It acknowledges that both faith and practice will not always be self-evident and there need to be provisions made, responses anticipated for when the queries about faith and life come up, as they inevitably will. In ancient Israel as well as in the Reformation, catechetical instruction arose out of the needs of the community.

Second, if the catechism is to take the form of question and answer, the questions should not always be shaped by the one who creates the answers. Moses' words in Deuteronomy recognize that there are predictable questions that children (of whatever age) will ask. The community in its familial and in its congregational forms needs to anticipate those questions, but they should be, at least in part, questions that the children want answered and not only questions that the adults want asked. It is not difficult to anticipate such questions. What parent has not been asked some version of the child's question, "Who is God?" or "What does God look like?" The teaching of the young in our catechisms or in other forms can and should anticipate and address such questions, letting faith seek its understanding where that faith is.

Finally, we should ask if there is not a clue to the shape of our catechisms in the response that the parents of Israel were to give to the queries of their children. The answer to what and why and who in this Deuteronomic context is not a formulation of rational and abstract theological statement, though such means of teaching have value and place. Here the answer to the question is a story, a story of a people and of how by the grace of God they came to be and to be free. If catechisms are to tell us something of who we are and what we are to believe, they may need to begin in the story that does that. Further inferences may be drawn, as indeed they are in the Deuteronomic account (see Deut. 6:24–25). The biblical tradition seems to start everything in the experience of the grace of God and the calling of the one and the many into a new identity. We celebrate that at baptism. We should not forget it at confirmation. The catechism that will teach the next generation will be one that takes them back again to the questions of who they are and what it is that God has done for them. If that is tended to, then we may go on to the further theological elaboration that one regularly expects from the church's creeds and catechisms.

7

Remembering Our
Theological Past

We forget where we came from. It happens all the time. Theology is no less vulnerable to the common human tendency to forget than any other sphere of life. Powerful voices come on the scene, shaping our way of believing and living and then moving on to become episodes in historical and comparative studies but only dim memories or little more than names for the next generation. This issue of *Theology Today* is an exercise in recall and remembering some of those voices, both their lives and their theology. The choice is eclectic and quite varied. There are some here who are and will be remembered more than others, and there are other voices now stilled who also need to be recalled. For this reader, the lessons in remembering, at least those offered in these pages, are several.

The interplay of theology and *personality*—in the largest sense of the term—is evident all the way through, what William Stringfellow perceived as the incarnational and parabolic character of theology. Most theologians are remembered primarily for their writings, but even in the case of Karl Barth, the person of the theologian exercised powerful impact on others and became the focus of attention in a way comparable to his thoughts and writings. The writings of Dietrich Bonhoeffer and Stringfellow will endure and be recalled and reread, but surely their personal stories of radical commitment are the primary lessons they teach us. Bonhoeffer's life is the more familiar, known and reflected upon by countless persons, many of whom would never regard themselves as in any way theological. Stringfellow is far less known, but those who met him, even casually, and those who worked with him in the student Christian movement and in his passionate pursuit of justice for the poor and the oppressed were marked by his personal witness as much as or more than by his writings. Like Bonhoeffer, the integrity of his life confirmed the truthfulness of his theology.

Tom Driver's often humorous recall of a theologian not easily associated with light humor, Paul Tillich, is an acknowledgment of the personal factors that led him to come under Tillich's spell. But the "spell" of a theologian is often conveyed more in the person than in the thought. Like others I know, I had studied Christian ethics in a quite formal way only to find the whole matter becoming clear and terribly important, for the first time, through a single lecture by Paul Lehmann. It was as if the scales had fallen from my eyes. As significant as his writings remain, there was something about a lecture by Lehmann that communicated in the most powerful way, including enabling one to think that his often obtuse way of formulating a matter was in fact clear. Indeed, I would argue there was a clarity that broke through specifically in the oral presentation that is not always apparent in the written form. One of the inherently ephemeral dimensions of theology is in its being taught and not simply being written. Georgia Harkness, Paul Tillich, and Nels Ferré were incomparable teachers. As Tom Driver writes of Tillich, "He was the kind of teacher you never get over." Something happens in the classroom, at the podium, and in conversations that cannot be recaptured, although it can be recalled and intimated to others. Such intimations effect in us a longing for such contact and remind us afresh of those theological instructors, often less famous, who have shaped our minds and hearts in indelible fashion.

The teacher-student relationship often blossoms into friendship. The significance of friendship for the transmission of theology and for the theological enterprise in general is a marked feature of the essays on these theologians of our recent past. One has only to think of the dedication of Eberhard Bethge to the preservation of the Bonhoeffer legacy, a commitment borne out of early and deep friendship. But Bonhoeffer had many friends who were marked by their acquaintance with him and who influenced him in his thinking and his action. His early friendship with Paul Lehmann is recalled in the letters published here. William Stringfellow's sometimes abrasive personality did not inhibit the development of lasting friendships, particularly that with Anthony Towne, who joined with him in his theology of praxis and became the focus of some of Stringfellow's "biographical" theology.

That students become friends is no secret to any teacher, but we do not often recognize what impact that has on the legacy of a theologian. In friendship, the incarnational dimension of theology becomes sharply etched. The devotion to the work of a theologian by those who study and then become friends is not necessarily hero worship. Indeed, understanding may be more clear-eyed precisely because it has come up against and incorporated the humanity of the theologian. In the overcoming of simplistic dualistic understandings of human life—separating the formal thoughts and ideas from the life of the thinker—theology becomes richer, more revealing, and complex. These human relationships that carry out theology in so many ways are varied beyond description. So, for example, the reader of these pages will hear how a son and daughter (of Nels Ferré) came to understand their father more fully as his students than they would have if they had known him only in the intimacy of the parent-child relationship.

One cannot read these essays without also reflecting on the *locus* of theology, the context in which we receive it. Most often that is in theological books and essays. The theologians represented in these pages contributed their share. But even in that mode, the range is astonishing. Tillich addressed the whole world in his *Systematic Theology*, seeking to effect a theological coherence that would incorporate all of culture as well as religion and addressing the intellectual and artistic figures of his time, such as Karen Horney, Erich Fromm, and Berthold Brecht. But with equal vigor and desire for influence, Georgia Harkness, surely as self-conscious a Christian apologist as was Paul Tillich, set some of her sharpest theology in small college textbooks and denominational curricula, seeking in those vehicles to reach directly the minds and hearts of the next generation and the church, whose living out of the gospel is the chief rationale for the theological task.

But formal theology is by no means the only context in which theology is developed. Harkness put her theology into poetry and hymn as well as into theological textbooks. Her hymn "Hope of the World," written for the 1954 Assembly of the World Council of Churches, has become one of the beloved hymns of contemporary Protestantism. So also, one of the persons who appears in the following essays is a novelist, short story writer, and essayist, not a theologian. But it would be difficult to find a more complex, serious, and realistic understanding of human sin, a *theological* understanding of sin, than in the stories and novels of Flannery O'Connor. This is not accidental. She was highly self-conscious in her writing about her orthodox Christian, and more specifically, Catholic, perspective. Sin and redemption are the great realities of human existence, but they are talked about in O'Connor's stories and novels in a very different way than by most theologians. Little wonder that a contemporary theologian like Gregory Jones (*Embodying Forgiveness*) turns to O'Connor for guidance in thinking about sin and forgiveness, grace and redemption.

And then there are the letters, those private, ephemeral modes of communication that are not addressed to a larger public but sometimes become the most revealing and influential of all theological vehicles. Bonhoeffer's qualifications as a formal theologian are evident in many books and writings. But no work of his has had the impact of his letters and papers written to friends and family while he was imprisoned by the Nazis. His *Letters and Papers from Prison* may be the most influential theological work of the post–World War II period. The interaction of his life and his thought places a kind of validation upon the reflections in those letters that is compelling. But it is also the case that the life evoked the theology, that Bonhoeffer's great contribution is not simply to have been a martyr for Christ and for the human race but to have developed, precisely out of his life and times, a theological understanding that commands our attention. Could Bonhoeffer have left us that theological legacy in any other way or under any other circumstances? We cannot answer that question, of course, but we do know what he left us.

Finally, I have come away from these essays more sharply aware not only of the varied forms that theology takes but of its *manifold intentions and pluriform substance*. Some of the theologians represented here were highly apologetic in their purpose and in their content, engaging culture and seeking serious rapprochement between faith and culture (for example, Tillich, Ferré, and Harkness). Others set themselves against culture and saw in it demonic dimensions, a serious threat to the vitality and survival of Christian faith. Even more, they saw in the church a cultural Christianity that does not take seriously the lordship of Jesus Christ and its radical implications for those who would claim that Jesus is Lord and would live as Christ's disciples in this world (for example, Bonhoeffer, Stringfellow, and Lehmann). There is a sense also in which O'Connor identifies the radical character of Christian faith by spelling out so vividly the reality of evil but precisely in order to assert the centering of meaning in life in the redemption of human life by Christ.

The more radical forms of faith among the theologians visited in these pages seem to be manifest in those who are most orthodox in their identification with the biblical witness, while those thologians who, in the common understanding, seem less orthodox are less disturbing in their witness. Yet it is these same persons who saw in the world God made something to be taken account of theologically in all its forms and manifestations, a world that is to be engaged and not simply addressed or confronted. Bonhoeffer, in his own life and writings, reflects the coming together of these different theological styles—if one sets *The Cost of Discipleship* alongside the *Letters and Papers from Prison*, the former a powerful and influential identification of just what its title says, a warning against what we have come to call, in Bonhoeffer's terms, "cheap grace," and an insistence that "when Christ calls a man [*sic*], he bids him come and die," the latter an even more influential work that became the springboard for the whole secular Christianity movement that began in the 1960s.

We go back to these theologians, whose work and witness may have dimmed somewhat in our minds, to gain a handhold and some grist for the mill of our own personal and intellectual—and hopefully faithful—grinding of the same issues. In so doing, we discover in their lives and thoughts a biographical theology that reminds us that our own engagements with the issues of theology is powerfully interactive with who and what we are, the choices we make, the settings in which we live and think. The mix of timeliness and timelessness, of dated and perduring theology, that we encounter in seeking to remember our theological past is the best we can and should hope for our theological future.

8

Popularizing the Bible

Genesis is the book of the month—or rather of the autumn. Never in my lifetime has there been such widespread cultural focus on a book of the Bible. Books on Genesis are advertised all over the place—and few of them by biblical scholars. *Time* has done a cover story on Genesis (October 28, 1996) heralding "a spirited new debate over the meaning of Genesis." I do not know whether Bill Moyers has a kind of instinctive sense of what popular culture might be interested in at a more intellectual level, or whether his audience has instilled such a cultural confidence in him that he can create a wide interest simply by his skill at setting up a television series focusing upon something he thinks matters. I expect it is the latter, but whatever the case, he has done it again, and on a rather unlikely topic—a biblical book. By the time this editorial appears, millions of people will probably have watched a series of weekly conversations on the book of Genesis, extending from October through December. At the time of writing, I have seen only two of the episodes—conversations about Genesis 3 and Genesis 4. That small taste, however, evoked a number of responses, and not surprisingly. The Bible may be a holy book, but precisely because it is such an icon of our culture, any handling of it prompts varied reactions.

One of those reactions is gratitude for the possibility of sustained and intelligent conversation about a biblical book. Moyers has chosen well, even if his choice and format is in imitation of Burton Visotsky's living room conversations about the book of Genesis over the past several years in New York City. Genesis is not only the beginning of the biblical story. It surely is as formative, foundational, and influential as any biblical book, including the Gospels. Anyone who has spent time in its study knows that there are always further depths to

31

plumb, surprising discoveries, and sobering if not disturbing and abrasive resonances between its words, its stories, and our own life and faith. It speaks about who we are as man and woman, as individual and community, as chosen people and international community, and in our relation to God. It reminds us that the natural world is creation and so are we. Sin, sex, and social order are all to the fore in this book. Its scope is universal, but it also has a particularity that makes it the ultimate source of the story that Jews and Christians claim is the key to the meaning of our existence. Surely no book of the Bible better invites Christians and Jews into a conversation together as does the book of Genesis, and that conversation is one of the prime contributions of the television series.

It is also, of course, one of its problems. The universal scope of the book, which does not disappear when Abraham comes on the scene (see Gen. 12:3), can mask the particularity that is already indicated in the call of Abraham— the language of election is all through the Abrahamic traditions. Admittedly, the discussion so far has been confined to Genesis 1–11, where the focus is indeed universal, but already there one becomes conscious of the varieties of interpretations, for example, when the subject of death arises in discussion of Genesis 3. There is a particular angle on death in the story that Christians know. It begins in Genesis 3, but it includes the cross and the resurrection. Genesis 3 is part of why Christians believe that death is an enemy, but it is only part. Others, however, may view death simply as the natural conclusion to life. Indeed, there are parts of Genesis that fit such a natural reading of death. It is difficult to talk about such a topic under the best of circumstances. The conversations with diverse religious and nonreligious participants tend to let such more controversial and divisive matters slide by.

The Bible is so much a part of our culture, religious and otherwise, that discussions of it need to be widely inclusive, and that is one of the virtues of the format Moyers adopted. That diversity of participants also helps to create a lively conversation as very different voices and interests, for whom the book of Genesis may be sacred, a classic, foundational, or important in a variety of ways, bring their various perspectives to bear on the subject. If one doubted the capacity of the Bible to shape thinking and affect life, these conversations have provided confirmation of its continuing capacity for doing just that.

There is a certain amount of irony, however, in the fact that the more confessional approach to Scripture, which, one could argue, is the context out of which the Bible arose and for which it was created, is the dimension that is most in danger of being lost in the kind of popularizing that goes on in the serious and vigorous encounter Moyers' groups create. It is not simply that evangelical voices will not be heard. I assume that Bill Moyers's own background in the Southern Baptist Convention will ensure their inclusion. The wide diversity of participants almost guarantees that. But what it does not guarantee—and may preclude to some degree—is an uncovering of the power of the book as a testimony of faith, more specifically its revelatory character as the word of God. One comes away more aware of the rough manger in which the Word is cradled, if I may appropriate Luther's way of speaking about the Bible, and less in awe of the divinity it cradles.

At the same time, and at the risk of seeming contradictory, one of my impressions from the two sessions on Genesis 3 and 4 was the often uncritical approach to these texts on the part of some of the participants. The problem was not a matter of inattention to sources, such as the Yahwist or the Priestly source. Those are secondary concerns. What sometimes seemed ignored was the text itself and any sense that there is indeed a text in the house that must be studied carefully before one can be sure what it says. The perspicuity of Scripture is an important claim, but it has to do with the clarity of Scripture for faith and salvation and does not ever preclude careful reading of the text. All too often, the speakers in the Genesis conversations seemed free to read anything and everything out of the text. This was done at a very sophisticated level and so not subject to the criticisms of simplistic literalism. But the interpretive dangers are just as acute. Literalism, whose problems are real and insuperable, at least focuses upon the text. Preachers are constantly warned, and so constantly fearful, of springboarding from a text to say whatever they want. Such a criticism may be too strong for these conversations. But all too often I found myself saying, "Hey, where did that interpretation come from?" and unable to see any plausible connection to the text under discussion.

Contemporary theology and biblical studies have opened wide the door to a multivalent reading of Scripture. That is, in general, a good development. We have broken out of a modern concern for *the* meaning of a text—a concern that many of our interpretive forebears did not share—and have come to recognize that any text is rich and open toward a breadth of interpretive inferences and that readers and audiences have much to do with what is heard from the text. The Genesis conversations are a good example of that. But the openness of the text does not mean that there are no misreadings of the text, or more to the point, no possible misrepresentations and misunderstandings of the text. The aim of careful exegesis is as much to avoid misunderstanding as it is to elicit meaning from the text. The conversations on Genesis are helpful at the point of making us aware of the richness of the text. They are somewhat misleading as they lull us into a kind of anything goes mentality. The pastor's work at interpreting texts in preparation for their preaching is not the practice of an arcane discipline. It is careful meditation on a text to hear as much as one can and to avoid mishearing.

Other segments of the Genesis series may let the text itself exercise more control of the conversation than seemed to be the case in the treatments of Genesis 3 and 4. I am led to believe that some of the episodes will include a larger number of biblical scholars who will probably represent a more critical and canonical hearing of the text. Meanwhile, the segments I have viewed, despite my unease and maybe *through* my unease, remind me of the danger of reductionistic readings of the biblical texts and my own tendency, as theologian and exegete, to act in an imperialistic fashion with regard to the text, claiming in a careful and critical reading of it what really may be an effort at hegemony over the text and resistance toward the claims of others for an equal right to speak about its meaning. The authors, artists, and philosophers who do not speak as critical interpreters will uncover some dimensions of the text that my "discipline" misses.

In speaking about the Genesis series, Bill Moyers has stated as one of his intentions to present "a different kind of religious discourse . . . beyond the political rhetoric about God that's made it so difficult for us to hear one another." His model of that discourse is to be applauded, and the concerns above are expressed in the context of applause. Whether it will address those whose "political rhetoric" bothers him is quite uncertain, but many of those ears may be too stopped up to hear a different kind of discourse. It is important, however, that the large number of people who are bothered by such political rhetoric about God but care deeply about the Scriptures and see in them the rule of faith and practice be encouraged and led in helpful directions. The capacity of the mass media to contribute to that enterprise has never been indicated more markedly than in these conversations on Genesis. Their flaws do not diminish the significance of the effort.

Meanwhile, in the same week as the *Time* cover on Genesis, the front page of the business section of the *New York Times* confronted us with the headline "The Bible, a Perennial, Runs Into Sales Resistance," and we heard from the director of sales and marketing at Oxford University Press, for centuries a major publisher of Bibles, that the Bible is "no longer recession-proof." A poll conducted by Tyndale House Publishers was quoted as discovering that nine out of ten Americans own a Bible but less than half of them read it and that the major reason the Bible is not read is that it is hard to understand. So it really is more an icon than a rule. And anything Moyers can do to open it up is needed and welcome.

9

Revisiting the God Who Acts

Coming out of seminary in the late 1950s, having received a heady dose of Barth and under the strong impact of the biblical theology that was the center of seminary curricula, I had no difficulty identifying a graduate program in which to pursue Old Testament studies. With his influential and compelling monograph *God Who Acts*, which most seminary students read in those days, G. Ernest Wright's move to Harvard made that a natural place for one to study Old Testament theology. It was my habit to take a break from studies in the library by wandering into the periodical room and browsing through some of the current theological journals. On one such occasion, I picked up an issue of the *Journal of Religion*, where I spotted an essay by Langdon Gilkey with the intriguing title "Cosmology, Ontology, and the Travail of Biblical Language." Discovering that it was primarily devoted to an analysis of the work of Wright and Bernhard Anderson, I sat down for a moment and quickly read it. When I finished, I put the journal back and returned to my studies. But I did so with the disturbing, though not well-formed, sense that things would never be the same again.

That premonition turned out to be correct, although I had no idea how much so at that moment. One of the ironies of the history of theology and of biblical interpretation is that Gilkey's essay, often cited and republished, is now far more widely read than the larger and once dominating work of Ernest Wright. And the questions raised by Gilkey in that ten-page article have hounded biblical theology and biblical studies ever since. What does it mean when we speak and think of God's acting in the world? How in fact does God act, if at all? And especially, is it possible to speak of God's acting in special or even miraculous ways in a world that seems immune to interventions from beyond in the processes of nature and history? How does one identify God's activity or distinguish it from any other activity? What is the relation of God's activity to creatures in the universe, specifically, but not only, human beings?

These questions have consumed considerable theological energy over the last thirty-five years, though the discussion has moved much more into the systematic and philosophical side of the court than the biblical. That move is at least a signal that, while theologians have been critical of the way biblical scholars have spoken about God's acting, they have recognized that the issue is not simply a disciplinary concern but is of fundamental importance for Christian theology, broadly speaking. Whether or not Wright was correct in his analysis of God's acts, there is no getting away from the fact that the Bible, from beginning to end, speaks of God's acting in the world in various ways. Theology can no more ignore the question of how we are to understand that activity than can biblical interpretation. As Gilkey himself put it in his early essay, drawing on Wright's terminology in *God Who Acts*, while biblical theology concerns itself with "Hebrew recital," there is still the matter of "our recital," which is where confessional and systematic theology come into play.

There are both pastoral and theological concerns underlying the discussion, which means neither church nor academy can ignore the questions posed above. The *pastoral* dimension of this issue is rooted in the simple but fundamental question of every Christian: Can and does God do anything in our world and in our lives? The issue of God's acting is more complex than that question, which, in its simplicity, ignores such matters as double agency, special divine action, the mode of God's impingement on the world, and the like. But the pastoral concern I have identified suggests that the question of God's acting is seen by many as fundamentally the question about God, period. If it is not possible to speak of God's doing anything, of God's acting, even "intervening," in our world to accomplish things that matter, then the reality of God is not very important or significant for human life.

That was a fundamental conviction of ordinary folk in the Bible. While it is often said that there is no atheism in Scripture, the frequent and very elemental complaints about the abandonment and silence of God and about inactivity in the face of sickness, enemies, social oppression, and death that echo throughout the whole of Scripture are, implicitly and explicitly, questions that, without answers, make any assertions about the existence or reality of God meaningless. Things are little different now than then. The desire of most Christians to hold to some notion of miracle, some sense of special divine action, is not necessarily a reflection of a literalistic or simplistic faith unaware of the modes of reality that are uppermost in the mind and thinking of more philosophically or scientifically oriented persons. Miracles are a symbol of, or a testimony to, the fact that God is at work and active in the world, and one lets go of such symbols reluctantly in the face of secular encroachments at every turn. The resurrection serves as a kind of bottom line, even in its most "demythologized" interpretations.

The *theological* dimension of this issue, which is important for both the academy and the church, concerns whether we can speak about God's acting in an intelligible way that does not conflict significantly with our view of reality from other perspectives, whether scientific, philosophical, or common sense. This issue has occupied the attention of many in recent years in philosophy, theology, and science. For if there is not a coherent intelligibility to our talk of God's action, then the claims discussed above become very hollow. Theology has many aims, but in this enterprise, it is partly a matter of saving its soul (if not the jobs of its practitioners).

In this issue, we join the discussion, albeit in somewhat fragmentary form, convinced that there is much that has happened to aid our thinking since Gilkey tossed out the question and hoping that there are still resources to be tapped or angles of approach that will yet prove helpful in letting us speak about the God who acts. On the way into this issue, let me suggest a few of the possible avenues or directions that have been or ought to be pursued in the theological discussion about divine action.

Biblical theology itself has, to a large degree, shied away from the subject of divine action, even as theology has taken it up with some vigor. But the Scriptures have to remain a part of the discussion, not simply because they are the basis of the church's theology but because they offer a rich resource for thinking about the topic of divine action *theologically*. A careful look at the biblical material produces a picture of the activity of God that is extremely complex, a fact that often disappears in the "God-who-acts" theology as originally propagated and as sometimes disparaged. The interpreter renders a disservice to the text and to its understanding of God's activity if the complexity of either one is reduced. Even the exodus event as a mighty act of God, reduced by Gilkey and some of his sources to an east wind blowing over the Reed Sea, needs to be comprehended as a complex event told in a complex narrative structure, in which various accounts and portrayals have been woven together into a whole that cannot be treated historiographically or even theologically as if it were a simple narrative. The intricacy of the biblical stories and narrative complexes and the intricacy of God's activity within them—sometimes spelled out in detail, as in the exodus narrative, and sometimes inferred from the story, as in the Joseph narrative—correspond to the sense that we now have of the complexity of events and acts and their connectedness to things before and after. We do neither the biblical text nor reality as we encounter it justice by taking a reductionistic approach. The Bible is more realistic than we are sometimes in giving a sense of a complex web of events as the matrix of divine activity, definitely there but often hidden and mysterious or described in imagistic language that cannot be easily literalized, even if it clearly communicates, for example, "the hand of the Lord." Some of that complexity, as well as an indication of the significance of the narrative character of the material, is set forth in Terence Fretheim's essay revisiting the "God who acts" in the Old Testament.

The great new development is, of course, the engagement of science in the discussion of divine action. Much of the fresh thinking in the contemporary literature on this topic is in this area. While work along these lines is often—and necessarily so—somewhat technical in character, even a nonscientific reader quickly perceives that we are in something of a new ball game. Assumptions about the unbroken causal nexus that have so controlled our thinking about what is possible and what is intelligible fall before, again, a much more complicated and open situation. There seems now to be room, literally, for the divine action, but one may have to be pretty sophisticated scientifically to locate it.

But the paradigms and theories of science can only take us so far in defining the character of God's activity. There are other resources and other dimensions of the matter that should be brought into play. Let me suggest three areas that are not as prominently to the fore and one or two books that may be helpful to our thinking about God's activity.

(1) The work of the Spirit is often ghettoized in the church. But the third "person" of the Trinity is a way of speaking about God's work in the church and in the world. The public as well as private realm of the work of the Spirit and the involvement of the Spirit in the divine action to reveal the glory of God have been notably articulated and developed in Michael Welker's *God the Spirit*. Because the Spirit is a category that penetrates the divine but also touches human life as a dimension of our experience, one that we call "spiritual," and because we are accustomed to thinking about effects of the Spirit with less concern about modes of impingement or are able to conceive of those modes in nontheological and nonscientific categories (for example, the wind), God the Spirit may be an appropriate "image" by which we can view the divine activity. Welker suggests that it is through the "complex pattern of interconnected testimonies" to the Holy Spirit that one can get at the reality of God and God's power in richer forms.

(2) Some of the early criticism of the focus on revelation in history, which was a corollary of the theology of God acting, called attention to the degree to which revelation in Scripture happens through word as well as through deed. This is an important qualification of the tendency to absorb all of God's reality and God's work in the category of act. There is as much in the Bible about God's speaking as about God's doing. But this proper modification does

not eliminate the theological problems that need to be addressed. Indeed, it adds to them. For the phenomenology of divine speaking is no less elusive than that of divine action. What does it mean when the Bible says, "God spoke to Abram" (Gen. 12:1)? There are some accounts, particularly among the prophets, suggesting that divine communication takes place through visions. But they do not tell us why vision, dream, or hallucinatory experience should be perceived as a word from God or how that may be analyzed. As with our thinking about divine action, there is the further question about whether and how God speaks to persons or groups in the present. One may handle that question by simply referring to Scripture as the medium of God's voice and so keep the question out of the zone of contemporary experience. But that only pushes the issue back one stage. Furthermore, there are many in today's world who talk rather easily of God's telling them something or of God's informing them. The contemporary discussion about God's acting should incorporate a concern for this other kind of activity—speaking—and some theologians are doing so.

An important effort along these lines is the work of Nicholas Wolterstoff, *Divine Discourse: Philosophical Reflections on the Claim That God Speaks*. He is dissatisfied with subsuming God's speaking under a general notion of revelation. Drawing on various philosophical resources, particularly the work of J. L. Austin and John Searle on speech-act theory, Wolterstoff develops an argument for the possibility of God's speaking, the legitimacy of interpreting Scripture as seeking to discern what God as author has said in it, and the right—his more precise term is "entitlement"—of persons to believe that God has spoken either in Scripture or more directly. In so doing, Wolterstoff deals with some of the same issues that the discussion of divine action has taken up, but he broadens the subject matter in a way that suggests that we should not work out a notion of divine action without also giving attention to divine speech.

(3) Finally, I would suggest that scientific and philosophical modes are not the only ways into comprehending the activity of God. It may be that our most helpful language will turn out to be located in poetic speech and in images that belong more to poetry and story than to philosophical analysis. One is reminded of how effectively Gordon Kaufman draws upon the image of the master builder to create an analogy for speaking about God's acting (*God the Problem*). But his helpful analogy suggests other images that may invoke a picture as intelligible as any kind of analysis and as important to the contemporary believer as the discovery of science's openness. Thus, one may conceive of God's activity as similar to that of a conductor of an orchestra and thus think about divine acts as being directed by an agent in which other agents are brought into the process in a free and very complex way, requiring responsiveness on the part of the primary agent, but toward a rich and intended end.

Or one may think of an artist and so comprehend God's activity as incorporating nonhuman aspects of reality and evolving toward an intended goal that, although not clearly discernable, is in the mind at the beginning.

So it is that the reader should not deem the discussion in this issue to be finished when the last article is read. For surely the final contribution to our thinking about the God who acts is not a theological essay but Anthony Abbott's moving poem about "that strange emptiness/under the pain where God starts to work."

10

Life, Death, and the Hale-Bopp Comet

Hale-Bopp came through in the spring. Before it left to disappear into the reaches of space, it precipitated the largest mass suicide in American history and a possible revolution in our thinking about the origins of life. That is a lot to lay on the shoulders of one small and previously unknown comet. But if you were one of the millions who looked up night after night and saw it blazing its way across the sky, visible to the naked eye, you might not be all that surprised.

For many, certainly, this was the first and only encounter with a real, "live," and highly visible comet. We hear about the regular return of Halley's Comet and about other comets that have streaked across the sky, but many of us have never seen these earlier phenomena. They are for the experts, astronomers or highly knowledgeable and technically empowered laypersons who can tell the rest of us that something is going on. This time we saw it for ourselves.

The night my wife and I first saw it, our reaction was a mix of awe and ecstasy. It happened to be the same night of a lunar eclipse. It was almost too much for this earthbound creature to take in. The whole experience was somewhat revelatory, not in any concrete or religious sense but in the realization that the universe was a little more open to us, that something so distant as to be for all intents and purposes beyond our contact or interest was right there before our eyes.

The vastness of space is generally overwhelming. In Hale-Bopp, it touched us and seemed a little less cold and remote. Things go on out there, and one does not have to believe in aliens or UFOs to sense that. A comet putting on its show and inviting guests to take it in—as we did regularly from our back deck during the many days of its appearance—suggests a liveliness to the universe of which most us are unaware. We do not experience things going on out there in very direct fashion. Hale-Bopp, however, made the notion of the universe as "our home" seem not quite so silly and sentimental.

You cannot jump from the comet to God very easily, nor did watching it function for me as a religious experience. But further reflection takes me back to Psalm 8 with its words about the moon and the stars as "the work of your fingers," and I realize how easy it is to forget about that except as a kind of creedal statement about the "Maker of heaven and earth." If, as someone has suggested, Psalm 104 paints a picture of Leviathan as God's rubber duck for playing in the sea, maybe Hale-Bopp was a bit of heavenly fireworks, a kind of divine sparkler meant to enchant, to evoke delight and joy and wonder in the midst of the truly mundane. Throw in that lunar eclipse, and we got a lot for our money from the Creator last spring. I am not sure whether or not we learned anything from the performance. At least we paid more attention to the universe during those spring days than we usually do. That is not a bad idea for anybody.

It came through at Easter, by the way, and some, tragically—my judgment, not theirs—saw connections in that happenstance. They saw in the comet a sign of the new life and the new world that Easter has always promised.

So they staked their lives on that promise, literally. That is something many talk about but few, even in a life-staking movement such as Christianity has claimed to be and in some cases actually exemplified, have been willing to practice. Most of us are glad we do not have to risk our lives on the promise of the gospel. A few have showed us it is possible. Rarely has there been the kind of open, joyous, and catastrophically irrevocable gamble on one's conviction that we saw in the Heaven's Gate suicides.

It was a sobering event, by all accounts terribly sad and depressing for those left behind but not, apparently, for those who bet on a mixture of New Age, New Testament, and new technology to sign off from this life and, hopefully, this planet. Presumably, the vision of heaven is still able to capture the imagination even if it takes the form of a UFO and outer space. It may be, however, that the disappearance of heaven from much of theology and the religious imagination has played some part in the search for substitutes. Literalistic notions of heaven are no longer those of streets paved with gold. They have been replaced with more up-to-date pictures of spaceships, aliens, and cosmic rendezvous. Heaven is still up there and as material in our imagination as ever, if Heaven's Gate is any clue to the way we can take the metaphor and literalize it to death.

To whatever extent Heaven's Gate was indebted to the Christian faith for some of its strange notions—after all, Herff Applewhite was a Presbyterian preacher's kid, participated in Presbyterian youth work in Texas, and attended my seminary briefly—it caught hold of some of its worst parts, at least of a heresy that is as old as Gnosticism. William Temple argued that Christianity is the most materialistic of all religions, but you could not prove that by many of us. We are pretty hung up about that material we call our body and often want to indulge it extravagantly and dangerously or get rid of it any way we can.

I am not interested in arguing for or against asceticism. Nor does asceticism have to disrespect the body. But the strain within our theology and our practice that thinks of us as souls whose bodies are an incidental burden ignores the reality of the self as constituted by body, even when the body has become a kind of trap. We are not really here without it, and as long as it is here, we are here. If the body is simply a "container," as the members of Heaven's Gate saw it, then one can indulge it or disregard it. As with a lot of us in the Christian community, one of the problems with the followers of Heaven's Gate was that they knew too much about the "other world." We will find out about that soon enough. Yet even with all the mystery about what in the world can be understood by the resurrection, it always seems to include the body.

Hale-Bopp was not just about death, however. Some folks think it may tell us a lot about life, more specifically, how it came to be. Even the astronomers found this comet pretty spectacular and searched it extensively to get at the "uncanny link between comets and the first stirrings of life" (*New York Times*, April 1, 1997). The study of Hale-Bopp has confirmed other findings that some of the basic chemicals and gases presumed to be the precondition of life have come from the sky. Comets like Hale-Bopp may have been the bearers of life, so to speak, bringing to earth the mix of ingredients that provided the biological diversity that eventually sprouted or grew on this planet.

If so, of course, then such comets as Hale-Bopp could also have sown those same kinds of "seeds" on other planets and worlds. From Hale-Bopp to Mars to Jupiter's Europa, this universe may have a lot more going on than even the scientists have imagined (though probably not Arthur C. Clarke!). God's sparklers may be not just a big sound and light show for our amusement but part of the cosmic providence that brought us into being. That is a lot to ask of a comet, but if you saw Hale-Bopp, you did not have to be a member of Heaven's Gate to realize that it was something special, a once-in-a-lifetime experience that may ultimately tell us more about our life than about our death.

11

A Strange Kind of Monotheism

During his days of teaching New Testament at Harvard, Krister Stendahl enjoyed asking the Old Testament doctoral candidates in their oral exams, "What's so hot about monotheism?" It is a good question and one that becomes more acute when the one God is three. How does one do that without falling over into polytheism? For that matter, how does one do it period? The church has wrestled with this question for centuries, insisting as fully as any Jew or Muslim on the singleness of devotion to a single God yet talking constantly about three persons when doing so. It is difficult to imagine Christian faith or Christian theology being anything like what it is without the primacy of the Great Commandment: the obligation to give one's total and ultimate loyalty to one center of meaning and value whom we call God and who is revealed to us as one in whom all divinity is comprehended and who resists in every way any sharing of that loyalty, any assumption that there can be other ultimate claims on our lives or other forces at work in nature, history, and culture than the Lord of Israel and the church. It is also impossible to imagine Christian theology being Christian without the claim that God is not fully revealed apart from Jesus Christ or that one can exhaust what is to be comprehended about God without the work of the Spirit. This is no pantheon, but neither is it monolithic in the sense of "constituting a massive undifferentiated and often rigid whole" (so Webster).

Among the reasons why the Trinity is important for Christian faith is, somewhat paradoxically, because it undergirds the church's connection to Israel, and to the Lord of Israel, who has always been understood to be the same one whom Jesus called "Father." While the Trinity would seem to be so peculiarly Christian as to be perceived only as evidence of a break with the Old

44

Testament and Jewish roots of Christian faith, that is not the case. If one's exclusive and working sense about the Trinity is that it is the theological formulation that insists upon and guards the incarnation, the identity of Jesus with the God he called "Father," then the Trinity may serve to pull Christian faith away from its strong continuity with Israel. But if the Trinity also means that the God who is revealed in Jesus Christ is still one Lord, then it becomes a major piece of the church's understanding of its continuity with the Old Testament. The Trinity is as much a part of the church's insistence on the Shema and the oneness of God as it is a claim about the divinity of Christ. The latter could be claimed without the doctrine of the Trinity, but not the former.

The doctrine of the Trinity is largely a formulation of the early church and comes to expression in the creeds. That is so much the case that there is significant resistance on the part of modern biblical scholarship and criticism to talking about the Trinity as something that can be found in Scripture. In a recent effort to articulate an understanding of prayer in the New Testament, my speaking about "the Trinitarian character of Christian prayer" was questioned by a prominent and distinguished New Testament theologian on the grounds that there is no Trinity in the New Testament. If such an understanding of the New Testament could be argued, a Trinitarian dimension to the Old Testament would seem to be a moot question. But the Trinitarian development of Christian theology in the early centuries of the Christian era was pressed upon the church by its reading of the Scriptures—Old Testament as well as New. The way in which the New Testament pushed the church to speak about this threeness in oneness, a trinity or triunity that is God, is suggested by Donald Juel's contribution to this issue.

One of the strengths of his essay is his identification of the roots of Trinitarian thinking in an earlier understanding of the complexity of the divine world filled with heavenly beings, mediators and messengers of the divine world to the human, a picture that is well-attested in the Old Testament and Judaic literature. In a precritical age, the Old Testament was a source for discerning and thinking about the Trinity. Indeed, the scene of the three messengers who visited Abraham (Gen. 18) was for many centuries the only iconography of the Holy Trinity, and it is still the primary image for the Trinity in the Orthodox Church. While such an interpretation has largely disappeared in the critical age—except as an example of improper interpretation —one may well ask now if there is not a way of seeing, via a "postcritical naiveté," a Trinitarian rootage in the Old Testament. It is rather surprising, after all, that insistence upon an immanental as well as an economic Trinity, which would seem to be the large consensus of modern theology as well as ancient, has not led to more exploration of the way in which the God who is triune from the beginning is discerned as such in the Old Testament.

There are several ways in which the Trinitarian reality might be argued from the Old Testament alongside the New (not apart from the New, of course, but then why argue a New Testament perspective apart from the Old?). One is to recognize with the early church that such scenes as the appearance to Abraham, which is clearly understood as theophanic, point to a complexity and interaction within the divine world that Christians comprehend best within the specific revelation of the Trinity but that is also suggested in the many analogues to the appearance of the messengers to Abraham. The very notion of the "messenger of Yahweh," who often becomes—in the narratives of the messenger's appearance—the Lord and not just a messenger, is an indicator of agents within the divine world who may be identified with the Lord of Israel but also distinguished from that God. In the extensive Old Testament allusions to the divine council, Israel spoke about a unity in multiplicity, a oneness in complexity, and divine agents of the Lord's work in the world. It is this phenomenon to which Juel alludes in his discussion of heavenly intermediaries, and it produced indeed a strange kind of monotheism that insisted vigorously on both oneness and aloneness and also on the complexity and interaction.

Perhaps more important than this phenomenon of relationality and complexity in the divine world, however, is the revelatory continuity and consistency of the Old Testament and the New. If, as William Stacy Johnson has noted in a recent essay, "there is now a virtual consensus in trinitarian theology that God's reconciling act of grace in Jesus Christ must be more than an arbitrary and therefore potentially reversible deed; it must instead be a genuine expression in history (*ad extra*) of who God really is (*ad intra*),"[1] then one must ask for the ways in which that revelation in Jesus Christ is consistent with who God is as the Lord of Israel. It is as the Lord of Israel that God is God. So the revelation in Christ (*ad extra*) is demonstrably also God *ad intra*, God as known to Israel. The Trinity thus needs to be perceived as a feature of Old Testament theology if it is going to be a feature of Christian theology.

But there must be evidence that this is so. That is, the claim for the correspondence between *ad extra* and *ad intra* is not simply an a priori inference but an inference from Scripture—the whole of Scripture, not just part of it. So we search for the way in which such an inference may be drawn. If it cannot be inferred, then the doctrine may be up for question. The church has said in the past that such inference can be made. It may need to do so again, and perhaps in this postmodern age it can do so. One might start of course with the Spirit, whose work is as evident in the Old Testament as in the New. Indeed, an intelligible understanding of the Holy Spirit, much less a doctrine of the Spirit, can hardly be developed without significant inference from the Old Testament account of the work of the Spirit of the Lord, which by some readings, usually rejected in contemporary translations, is discernible from the very beginning, even in the work of creation (Gen. 1:2). The power of the Holy Spirit and its association with God's empowering of individuals and community to do the Lord's work is as much a dimension of the work of the Spirit in the Old Testament as in the New, even if there are aspects of that empowerment that came to expression in unique ways in the early church.

Equally important is the way in which the Old Testament tells us most about the first "person" of the Trinity but does so in a way that is fully consistent with the revelation in Jesus Christ. The revelation of the name of God in the Old Testament as a discernment of who the Lord of Israel is and what the Lord is like is carried forward in the names of the second person of the Trinity. The "I am" of Exodus 3:14 is best defined in Exodus 3:12 with the assurance "I am with you" or "I will be with you." "Immanuel," God with us, is what we learn about who this God is in the Old Testament and the New Testament. In those Exodus events, the character of the Lord of Israel is also revealed as the one who delivers and saves, a claim that is echoed again and again in the Old Testament and confirmed as the truthful word about the character of God through the one whose name "Jesus" means "He will save."

The Old Testament fills our understanding about the nature and character of the first person of the Trinity. It is only on this basis that the church can accept the claim that Jesus is one with God. Within the biblical story there is an identity between the words and deeds of the Lord of Israel and the Lord of the church that presses upon those who live by that story that they are truly one.

It is therefore unlikely that the church can hold its Scriptures together without a conviction that in the doctrine of the Trinity, we comprehend something of the fullness of God, who is with us and for us, who created us and goes with us, who redeems us and empowers us.

"'A' Is for Augustine, Aquinas . . ."

Have you noticed how many names of ancient theologians begin with the letter A? Five of these "A" theologians are the focus of essays in this issue of *Theology Today*, three from the patristic period and two from the medieval. And there could have been more: Anthony and Abelard, for example. Of course, there are many greats from our theological past whose names begin with other letters: Basil, Clement, Irenaeus, Tertullian, and others. Some of my kin would start the theological alphabet with C (Calvin, needless to say). And even Aquinas may belong under T instead of A.

So what's in a name? Not much perhaps, certainly even less in the first letter of a name. But our placing together the several theologians of the past whose names begin with A may serve as a kind of mnemonic device to help us remember or as a partial abecedary to help us learn our theological ABCs. Starting with the first letter of the alphabet is a simple device to take us back to the beginning. If nothing else, we hope in these essays to remind ourselves that theology is in no small part memory, and that it has a long history and deep roots. Sometimes we need to go back to the beginning to see a little more clearly where we are now and how we got here. Everyone who has taken a course in church history or the history of doctrine knows that. But it is very easy in our effort to articulate a theology for modernity and postmodernity to ignore antiquity and the unbroken line of theological work that has gotten us to this place. One who reads Ambrose's views on femininity and virginity may comprehend with new awareness the depth of the problem that women confront ecclesially and theologically in breaking out of assumed orders of creation and even of *new* creation. But Ambrose's Eve is an interesting character, as Kim Power reminds us, and the Eve-Mary connection is an example of an early crack in the seam of a centuries-lasting hierarchy of gender and virtue.

One of the aims of the essays in this issue is to ask in what ways these theologians are our contemporaries. And as these essays reveal, there are some obvious ways in which they are. Take Augustine's occupation with the self, which matches our modern *preoccupation* with the self, as Jean Bethke Elshtain reminds us. So also, his demythologization of evil is not only contemporary but, in the eyes of Elshtain and Andrew Delbanco,[1] our best bet for a nonrelativistic, nongenerative view of evil. Jeffrey Pugh notes how well Anselm's "faith seeking understanding," that is, reasoning as an act that takes place within the framework of beliefs and practices, fits within the nonfoundational character of postmodern theology.

But Thomas O'Meara echoes Otto Pesch in warning us against "instant fashionable applications of Aquinas" that ignore a basic distance between ourselves and the great medieval theologian. Maybe seeking to make these theologians our contemporaries, theologically, is a misplaced enterprise. Our best hope and greatest need may be found simply in being given, through theological recall of these significant voices of the past, a memory of where we came from and who we are, and thus a history of how we got here. Early on, Augustine called our attention to the place of memory in Christian formation in his extended discussion of the "fields and vast mansions of memory," which was for him a complex, wondrous thing, the vehicle of his search for God and the dwelling place of God (*Confessions*, book X). Few theologians have better comprehended the intricate connection between memory and mind and the way that memory shapes and guides us, even when it operates for storage of thought and perception, much like a stomach for food.

Augustine's phenomenology of memory bears little explicit connection to the Bible, but he echoes Scripture's own sense of the dynamic of memory, of its capacity to shape and direct the life of the community through the shaping and forming of individuals. It is the memory of the past that grounds the present moral life. A whole ethos of communal life and the relation to the other is created out of the memory of a people's experience in bondage and their deliverance: "You shall not deprive a stranger or an orphan of justice. . . . Remember that you were a slave in Egypt and the Lord your God redeemed you from there" (Deut. 24:17–18). Or perhaps one reads this text better as a call to a kind of moral life *in order to* bring back from the recesses of memory what the Lord has done for us. Remembering the Lord's goodness thus becomes not the ground of the moral life but its goal. So the community of faith gathers around a table and partakes of bread and wine in order to *remember* the death of our Lord.

Here I think we may be in the neighborhood of Augustine's fields of memory that provide the playing field of the search for God as well as the dwelling place of God in the mind of the believer. As Augustine seemed to have realized so well, the memory of the mind is not neutral territory. In a time of cultural exposure to so many stimuli and of the transiency of every moment accentuated in the rapidity of daily life and the rapidity of technological and social change, there needs to be within ourselves the possibility of holding and recalling the past, of living in the present and not simply by the present. Whether in the family, the community of faith, the political community, or simply the fellowship of friends, the remembrance of what has been done and said and experienced, whether in the immediate past or long past, will shape us now and in the future.

But what if there is little memory upon which to call? Scripture seems to know quite clearly that memory can be shared and given. So it tells and retells the story so that the next generations who were not there are given a memory. "Were you there when they crucified my Lord?" Oh yes, answers every Christian who has sat around the table and eaten the bread of Christ and drunk the wine of Christ. We use the rubrics of proclamation, education, nurture, and sacrament, but all of them tend to conceal the fundamental aim of the church's gathered life and often its more particular life in families, which is to create a memory, out of which prayer may come and praise is possible, out of which identity is discovered and purpose is developed.

"Remember who you are," said my father to me in my youthful days when I would engage in such risky affairs as going out on a date. That admonition arose out of a deep conviction that such memory, effected not only out of my immediate personal history but out of the memory planted in my mind and heart by my mother and father as they told the stories of the past I did not know, would work its power to control and shape my behavior—and indeed it did. So it was that the child in ancient Israel who asked about the statutes and ordinances, what they meant—and, implicitly, why they were kept—was given not a moral lesson but the story of the Lord's deliverance of the people from slavery. By this, the children came to know who they were and what God had done for *them*, not simply for their ancestors (compare Deut. 5:3). That memory is there to be called upon in every situation. So the psalmist says in time of exile and despair, "My soul is cast down within me; therefore I remember you" (Ps. 42:5).

Augustine, Ambrose, Anselm, Aquinas, and Athanasius are a part of our story. For better or for worse, and it may be some of both, they have helped to bring us to this point in faith's search for understanding. To listen afresh to them is to remember, and if we have forgotten or never known, it is to give us a memory so that we may know ourselves better in the present as we remember from whence we have come.

There is something else we see in these theological ancestors. In one of the most informative and helpful books on the classical theologians that has appeared in recent years, Ellen Charry has demonstrated their concern for the "aretegenic" or virtue-shaping function of Christian doctrine (*By the Renewing of Your Minds: The Pastoral Function of Christian Doctrine*). In some ways, her point is a rearticulation of the claim that truth is to goodness. But it is more fundamental than that. Charry's claim is that in the great theologians of the past there was a deep interest in demonstrating the salutary character of doctrine, in seeing how the divine pedagogy can lead us to dignity and excellence, to beauty and goodness as well as to truth. They did not engage in the struggles and conflicts, the revisions and reformations of theology, apart from a deep concern for the social, moral, and psychological implications of the divine instruction. Charry presses us to see in the theologians of the past not simply debates over matters of doctrine and formulations that may or may not fit in our constructions of theology, but to discern from them the necessity for theology to be instrumental in the most basic sense of all—identifying and encouraging a life that leads to God. Her reading of these same theologians ends in the hortatory conclusion that "theology must again become a normative and not simply a descriptive discipline. It must take a position on what an excellent life looks like."

Here, therefore, is yet a deeper dimension to the recollection, to the evocation of memory that a new encounter with the theologians of old elicits. We have assumed that such an enterprise is a part of faith seeking understanding. But it also may be faith's way of seeking goodness. Thus, the remembrance of our theological past, archaic and remote though its formulations and debates may seem to us, is like remembering who we are. It ought to tell us how to live and act in this world, what to value, what is good and excellent. If theology can learn from its distant past to move from theory and description to norming truth and shaping goodness, then remembering that past can render an incalculable service to the future of theology, and even more, to the living of the Christian life.

13

Good-bye *Seinfeld*

One of the most popular shows in the history of American television exited this spring from prime time in the prime of its life. Sitting on top of the ratings and raking in piles of dough, Jerry Seinfeld called it quits, taking with him his extraordinarily ordinary gang of George, Elaine, Kramer, and the other characters who have engaged our attention through the years. As an inveterate fan who is still trying to figure out the power and attraction of this show about nothing, I cannot resist the opportunity to say good-bye to one of the cultural markers of our time.

But a word of good-bye is hardly possible without some reflection on why this show has so claimed our attention and devotion. Any answers to that question will, of course, tell us as much about ourselves as about the show. (I am aware that there are many in American society who never watch this show and may be baffled by why there is so much fuss about it. So they can skip these remarks and go on to the more serious matters in the pages that follow.)

The most astonishing thing about the show is that it presented itself to us, quite self-consciously, as a show about nothing, a judgment with which any viewer would hardly quibble. There are plenty of television programs that are pretty much about nothing. But no other show has trumpeted that as its large intention. *Seinfeld* actually worked hard to underscore this point by creating a sequence of shows that had Jerry and George proposing to network executives an idea for a TV show about themselves that would be about nothing. How can you do a show about nothing? *Seinfeld* showed us how week after week.

Why would I watch a show about nothing? Whatever answers are given to that question cannot bypass the talented writers and actors who make up the show. A good line and good timing, a characteristic gesture—for example,

Elaine's two-handed shove or Kramer's stumbling all over himself—and the creation of consistent characterization (even of ostensibly uninteresting people) have always been able to arouse a laugh and hold the audience in their seats a few more minutes. Part of our good-bye to Seinfeld and his gang is a word of thanks for such marvelous talent. Critical kudos in the entertainment world are too often confined to upper-level entertainment—opera, dance, the stage, dramatic television, and art cinema. But surely the demands on actors to provide persuasive presentations of people and events that capture and captivate us week after week, through a different story line each time, are among the highest indicators of sheer talent. *Seinfeld* was loaded with it. Nor can one fail to appreciate the writing talent of a show that could begin an episode at the end, as happened one evening, and work back in time to the beginning—not by flashbacks but by literally moving backward in the story rather than forward.

But a show about nothing! Perhaps we are delighted to see the lives of others reflective of our own. The vacuity of the fictional lives of Jerry Seinfeld and friends—characters we have been told are based on real-life friends of his and of the show's cocreator, Larry David—is a mirror on our own, a reminder of the quotidian character of much—not all—of our life (what Jerry and George could do with the word *quotidian*!). But if the nothing of the show is about the nothing in their lives and ours, it is a nothingness that is transformed by making it interesting and making it funny.

How often one sat and watched while asking, through gales of laughter, Why am I watching this? It is not that surprising, however. The human predicament, theologically, is a large matter that requires us to speak about finitude, contingency, and sin—matters seemingly far removed from *Seinfeld*. But our experience of all of those things happens most often in the ordinariness of life, and that is precisely where George Costanza lived. Even Jerry, who is a glamorous stand-up comic in real life and on the show, rarely brought that glamor into the picture. It was his dealing with televisions that do not work, parents who show up unexpectedly, waiting in line at movies and restaurants, and neighbors who are hard to live with that occupied the time of the show. The "nothing" that was the entertaining—and moral—space of the show is where we live a large part of our lives, occasionally breaking out into "something," something that may be better—or worse—than the ordinariness of bathroom habits, work relationships, and buying food at the local market—all of which were regular staples of Seinfeld's comedy.

But we did not have to wait for our nothing to break into something. It happened every week for us through the lives—fictional or real?—of Seinfeld and friends. For half an hour, the ordinary became interesting and the nothing became something. And what may have been sad, uninteresting, or simply not worth talking about became incredibly funny.

The comic is often redemptive; in this case, however, not in any grand sense. After all, most episodes of the show ended by a climactic exacerbating of the problems raised rather than their resolution. No, the comic resolution on *Seinfeld* was very ordinary. It happened within us, within the viewers, as the simple, potentially meaningless dimensions of human existence were transformed into laughter. Most of the time, laughter, like music, is transformative. The situation comedies of television generally are about the laughter that transforms and elevates the ordinary. Their inanities are easy to put down, and the worst of them are easy to turn off. But when we encounter them at their best, as in *Seinfeld, The Cosby Show,* and M*A*S*H, the whole world watches and in odd ways is enhanced.

Theology has given insufficient attention to the place of laughter in human life. For laughter always either announces the reversal of our anxieties and tears into relief and joy, or in fact accomplishes that reversal. The Psalms know of the divine laughter that overcomes the dangers that threaten God's rule over our life (Ps. 2:4). More commonly, human life finds its loosening from the daily dimensions of our undoing in either play or laughter. *Seinfeld* gave us the latter as a weapon against the ego-bound self-centeredness that is manifest not in pride and assertion but in the inability to forget ourselves by letting go of all that worries us, that ties us up within ourselves. "Comic relief" is just what it claims to be, a relieving of what has become too heavy to bear. That does not have to be the weight of the truly tragic. For most of us, the relief from the strains of the ordinary day-in and day-out existence is found in the possibility of laughter at the end of the day.

Yet one is also left with some unease about these television friends and the life of nothingness they portrayed so well. Certainly, it was hard to ignore—between the bursts of laughter—the disturbing message *Seinfeld* conveyed about personal relationships and sexuality as a dimension of contemporary life. It is good to be past the time when a movie is censored for a single reference to women's underwear, as happened years ago in the innocent romantic movie, *The Moon Is Blue.* And while we are long since at the "anything goes" stage in the movies, a new level of directness about sex was achieved on *Seinfeld* in the famous "master of one's domain" episode, during which the cast spent the whole half hour talking about autoerotism (not as clever a euphemism as *Seinfeld*'s), never mentioning the taboo word while talking openly about the subject in ordinary restaurant conversation across gender lines. In our public presence, we are clearly no longer uptight about sex.

While I would argue there is some value in being able to talk about sex and laugh at it in a society whose Puritan influences have created a long-standing culture of suppression and repression it is certainly a mixed blessing. Most disturbing in remembering *Seinfeld* is less the direct or indirect references to sex than the superficiality of human relationships that were dominated by the pursuit of casual, undemanding, and uncommitted sex. The "nothing" of the lives of these characters carried over into relationships with persons of the opposite sex. Indeed, "opposite sex" was a kind of rubric for all the relationships outside the immediate "family." Sex with the opposite was the pursuit of happiness. But whenever that looked like it might lead to "something" instead of "nothing," everyone backed off. The only case where an outside relationship mushroomed beyond the casual level and involved a character with some definite personality of her own—George's fiancée, Susan—the writers killed her off.

Seinfeld is not the only show to purvey this particular understanding of the "chief end" of human life (to paraphrase the Westminster Shorter Catechism). But both the pursuit of sex as the operative practical goal of life and the insistence that it carry with it no commitment so dominated this show that it has to be seen as a major challenge to what Christian faith has claimed about both the locus of sexual activity in deeply committed human relationships and the divine intent that man and woman should find their life together in love and fidelity. Those two terms—love and fidelity—stand so forthrightly as code words for God's way with us and God's way for us that the explicit rejection of both loving and faithful relationships in a program with such powerful influence on the popular consciousness has to be not only recognized but decried. The church is struggling in a variety of ways with the need for a viable sexual ethic—viable in relation to the Christian tradition and in relation to the cultural context in which we have to live. It may have little chance against such powerful counter words from the entertainment media.

In the midst of this glamorization of casual sex and avoidance of the fundamental human experiences of love and fidelity, there was an ironic and to some degree paradoxical word about family. At its most obvious level, the show was as antifamily as it was antimarriage and anticommitment. Many episodes were built around unpleasant relationships between George and Jerry's parents or between George and Jerry and their parents or other members of the family. While one was never inclined to take all that too seriously, it was difficult not to cringe at some of the abrasive ugliness often manifest in those family relationships. Ironically, however, while existing family relationships were unpleasant and potential family relationships, through marriage, were resisted, Jerry, George, Elaine, and Kramer created, in the midst of a generally unfriendly and impersonal urban environment, a "family," a group of friends who cared about each other while never letting on that they did and who were painfully honest about each other's faults and foibles without ever letting go of one another.

Jerry and his buddies are gone now. The disappearance of *Seinfeld* was of little significance in the world of theology, but it was an epochal event in the lower realms of popular culture and the economics of the marketplace. The salaries paid to the stars and the income generated by even a few seconds of advertising on *Seinfeld*, especially during the final episode, may not break records, but they are emblematic of the impact of this show and, by example, of the power and influence of such shows and, more broadly, of television in general on our everyday life. We have had a sharp reminder of the dominance of the hot medium of television in both the economic and the moral market-places. Economics and morality have always been tightly connected. The rela-tively new thing in our world is the addition of a third force—a strong one and not a weak one, namely, television. The moral issues raised by the presence and absence of *Seinfeld*, therefore, outrun what that show may have conveyed about matters usually (and certainly within the worldview of this program) under-stood as having to do with personal morality. They confront us with a world where morality is shaped by the marketplace in the most direct way possible, while reminding us that the biggest single player in the marketplace is televi-sion and its entertainment congeners, whose moral yardstick, with few excep-tions, is purely economic. It is unlikely that any large attack on the moral looseness of our contemporary life will achieve anything until it has found out how to deal with this 800-pound gorilla who joins us in our living room each evening. His only real interest is in finding enough bananas to consume.

By the way, all this good-bye is really premature. In syndication we will be visiting with Jerry and his gang for years to come, listening again and again to the old lines, anticipating familiar scenes as a rerun appears for the tenth time. And a small bravo to Jerry for being able to foil the economic beast by walk-ing off and leaving all those further riches behind. We know he won't starve.

14

Theology and Science
in Conversation

In the latter half of the twentieth century, the conversation between theology
and science has picked up its pace considerably. Its tone is generally far different from the conflict waged between religion and science over much of
their common history and described in Andrew White's classic work *A History
of the Warfare of Science with Theology in Christendom* (1896). To quote a recent
issue of *Newsweek:* "Something surprising is happening between those two old
warhorses science and religion" (July 20, 1998). Further, one has only to think
of Teilhard de Chardin, or the work of Alfred North Whitehead and others
who, under the rubrics "process philosophy" and "process theology" have
taken the data of science as a major component of both philosophy and theology. The seriousness with which process studies have wanted to account theologically and philosophically for the world as science knows it has been one
of the attractive features of this enterprise.

Not everyone, however, has found the process route the best entrée into the
conversation between theology and science. In fact, that conversation is taking place on so many different levels and places and between so many different groups that a single systematic understanding is less and less the order of
the day. A number of essays and books have appeared, arising out of various
conferences and ongoing discourses at such locales as the Vatican and the Center for Theology and the Natural Sciences in Berkeley—to name only two of
the more prominent scenes of inquiry. The review shelves of *Theology Today*
are filled with far more books in this area than can possibly be reviewed.

The essays appearing in this issue grew out of an extended conversation
over several years at the Center of Theological Inquiry in Princeton involving
a group of theologians and scientists, not all of whom are represented in this

57

issue. These articles are varied, multidisciplinary, and interdisciplinary. All of the contributors are primarily either theologians or scientists save one—John Polkinghorne has made significant contributions in both fields, though his theological contributions are always fed by his deep scientific knowledge—but they are informed in various ways by the other discipline in the conversation.

One senses that for this group of discussants the conversation is not a side matter, worthy of an occasional foray out of one's normal scholarly confines. Rather, it is seen to be deeply important for both disciplines as well as for our thinking and living as human beings. Thus, the theologians do not believe that their work can be carried out either fruitfully or intelligibly—one might even say faithfully—apart from attention to and incorporation of the data, the theories and constructs, and the conclusions of the natural and human sciences. And increasingly, the scientists, as evidenced here, are dissatisfied with a limited perspective that does not push their disciplines into fielding the larger questions that fall over into theology and can hardly be handled without the implements of theology.

An unsystematic impression of the broader literature and the ongoing discussion, however, suggests that, at the moment, the sense of urgency in the conversation is felt more by theologians than by scientists. Certainly, the names most commonly encountered in the literature are more often theologians than scientists. One of the *desiderata* for a more intense and productive conversation, therefore, is the greater involvement of scientists who believe they cannot escape the larger questions their work ultimately evokes and who are eager to talk with theologians who believe they must be accountable to scientific understandings of reality.

As the conversation goes on, it has to reckon with the rapid pace of discoveries and developments in science and technology. Arguments and positions are constantly in need of revision. How will the world end? With a hot bang or a cold whimper? The evidence keeps shifting. As recently as January of this year [1998], new data from exploding stars have suggested to some experts—and contrary to much scientific thinking—that the universe "has been expanding at a slow steady rate since the beginning and is destined to expand forever."[1] In recent months, we have seen the first photographs of a planet outside the solar system and photographs of a star some twelve billion light years away that takes us back in time close to the Big Bang that started it all. Meanwhile, scientists worry about the "information paradox"—specifically, whether information disappears forever if it goes into a black hole—because the answer to that question has implications for our understanding of the structure of space-time and quantum mechanics. And the recent discovery of the existence of mass in neutrinos poses major consequences for the understanding and study of matter.

But if science does not stand still while it talks to theology, the other party in the conversation is not monolithic and static either, despite a fairly general impression—including among scientists—that it is. The history of theology shows it to be a dynamic enterprise, and research in every subdiscipline of the field continues to provide data for rethinking and reformulating positions. In the last half century, for example, postmodernism and the ecumenical discussion have had a large impact on theology, often challenging long-held assumptions and opening it up to new insights and fresh constructions of the Christian faith. So neither party can act as if the other is a closed system, a settled order in which the questions have all been answered once and for all. The rapprochement has to go on *in medias res* and in flux.

That is all the more reason some of the writers of these essays have favored what has been called "bottom-up" thinking, which is experience based and historically oriented, over against a more metaphysical "top-down" approach that seems to assume a more settled understanding of the nature of reality or of the theological and philosophical issues. Theology as much as science, however, builds upon a continuing examination of relevant data, for example, the exegesis of biblical texts and the investigation of historical sources. It cannot afford any more than science to assume a fixed order from which everything is to be deduced. Yet the reality of God means that top-down conceptuality is also built into the conversation. The tension between these modes of thinking about science and theology is one of the subtexts within these essays and a continuing feature of the conversation.

One of the challenges that has arisen generally but has been specifically identified in the conversations that brought about this collection of essays is the evaluation and warranting of truth claims in theology and science. In an informal paper following up the earlier conversations at the Center of Theological Inquiry, Polkinghorne and Michael Welker have suggested that a genuinely *theological* focus to the dialogue between science and theology is of fundamental importance for the following reason:

> In Western cultures, public expectation relies predominantly on scientific procedures and not much, if at all, on theology in the endeavour to get close to truth and evaluate evidence as well as to gain certainty and reliability in difficult and critical issues. Despite the crisis in scientific epistemology, and a growing suspicion with respect to the benefits of much technological progress, common culture in the West still sees the measure and model for truth claims as lying in the sciences.
>
> This can have many ideological side effects. But instead of complaining about this, theology has to rise to this challenge. Theology cannot give up seeking to make its impact on common sense and on contemporary mentalities. It has to put its theological truth claims into this arena of public discourse. It has to warrant its truth claims.

> At the same time, theology and science have to clarify the limits of scientific insights. However, all endeavors to score points for theology by simply opposing the sciences should be discouraged.

Such a weighty challenge, however, should not be read as demanding a focus on methodology. To the contrary, what is needed is more attention to particular theological *topics*, as exemplified, for example, in the decision of the Center of Theological Inquiry to follow up the dialogue reflected in these essays with a serious engagement with the subject of eschatology as a topic for the discourse of science and theology.

The identification of the dialogue partners as science and *theology* rather than science and *religion* is of more moment than some might recognize. While theology and religion overlap in obvious ways, the latter can fall over into more vague generalities and an exclusive attention to methodological and epistemological issues, issues that theology cannot, of course, avoid but always knows are prolegomena. By recognizing theology as a partner in the discussion, however, the conversation cannot avoid wrestling with the reality of God on the one hand and the topics of theology on the other. While the doctrines of creation and providence, and even anthropology, are obviously within the purview of any encounter between theology and science or between religion and science, the conversation cannot eschew attention to other doctrines, such as the person and work of Christ, pneumatology, the Trinity, and eschatology. Further, if the dialogue is to take place around *Christian* theology, Scripture and its interpretation will have to be among the partners around the table. A model for such interaction between scientific thinking and the specifics of Christian theology has been offered by Polkinghorne's book *The Faith of a Physicist* (also published as *Science and Christian Belief*), which takes the Nicene Creed as its framework.

Much of the dialogue between theology and science has taken place in highly academic ivory tower contexts and at a very sophisticated and complex level. Little of it has been carried out in a way accessible to the broader public or to the ministry and laity of the church. This despite the intense interest of the public in scientific matters, reflected in the degree to which scientific discoveries become front page news items and Stephen Hawking is a cultural icon, with his book *A Brief History of Time* one of the all-time best sellers. It has been suggested, however, that no book has sold more and been read less than this one. If that is so—and empirical verification is difficult in this instance!—it is symptomatic of the problem. A public intensely interested in things scientific and in scientific discovery is generally not well-equipped to deal with the topic and comprehend the discussion. The conversation, however, is so important for clergy and laity that it needs to be moved from the meeting rooms of conference centers and more into the life and thinking of contemporary Christians. To that end *Theology Today* presents these essays, fully aware that they are demanding but also believing they are important. If theology is going to matter, it cannot ignore its sister discipline. But if theology is going to matter broadly, that will come about, if at all, primarily from the pulpit, in the teaching and preaching of Christian ministers. Difficult as the task may be, theologically responsible preaching needs to take some account of the scientific world both preacher and congregation presume as the context of their life. Further, preaching that is truly *pastoral* as well as theological, touching the lives of Christian disciples in a way that explicates the faith intelligibly and provides tools for living and thinking in our world, will want to be informed about the conversation between science and theology and willing to struggle to grasp its various nuances. This is not an easy task; neither is it one to be avoided.

15

The Millennium Bug

The coming of the millennium is turning out to be less frightening than many have thought it might be. With its apocalyptic sound, the millennium would seem to be a moment to instill awe and fear, apprehension and dread. But it looks as if 2000 will be just another year. There will be various kinds of celebrations and commemorations. London is building a Millennium Dome to memorialize the moment. Rome is deeply worried about the number of visitors who will come to that great city in the year 2000 and what effect this will have upon its ancient monuments and its daily life. Jerusalem must surely have even greater concern as it anticipates the influx of the devout and the crazy. A friend of mine indicated she thought it would be neat to welcome in the new millennium in Babylon, a not inappropriate locale for apocalyptic visions and happenings. James Forbes, senior minister of the Riverside Church, has said he thinks that on New Year's Eve, December 31, 1999, there ought to be the biggest party ever in Times Square and all of us ought to come. It may be that there is no real difference between December 31, 1999, and January 1, 2000, but nobody really thinks that. With the year 2000—or Y2K, as we are now abbreviating this momentous year—only a year away, it still seems strange and a little awesome to speak about "2000."

Contemporary society in the West, which has nurtured apocalyptic visions of various sorts and has tied them to chronology and to millennial periods that would bring the end of the world and great judgment, seems not at all burdened by such spiritual anxieties as we approach 2000, not at all apprehensive about possible divine intervention that would destroy society and bring everything to an end. If there is some millennial danger, it surely will not be this one. Political events of the last quarter century, while certainly leaving the world no less likely a place for wars to break out and nations to fall, have taken our minds off the one apocalyptic element that modern society has taken seriously—the Doomsday Clock set up by atomic scientists to show us how close we are to midnight, meaning how close we are to an atomic holocaust that will end everything. The Doomsday Clock has by no means been dismantled—it took a step forward with the India and Pakistan nuclear tests—but the minute hand has been moved back some over the last two decades with the end of the Cold War and the efforts at disarmament, still meager but nevertheless positive signs about the future.

In the midst of this more relaxed and celebratory anticipation, there is one very discomfiting and disquieting feature of our life that bids fair to inject a more apocalyptic upheaval almost instantaneously with the turn of the millennium. It is the "millennium bug," an aptly named phenomenon that sounds at one and the same time like a minor pest and a horror movie beast. Overnight—indeed, with the stroke of midnight and the first minute of the new millennium—society may be turned into chaos. But our undoing will not be a self-evident divine judgment. Indeed, it can hardly be seen as a dimension of judgment at all. This is one we are not inclined to blame on God, nor are we likely to see it interpreted theologically. The millennium bug is our own problem, one of our own unwitting creation, a telltale indicator that human society is developing at a pace that may outstrip our capacity to handle the change and progress we achieve and celebrate. The "return to chaos" is no longer a mythic or eschatological rubric. It is a possibility of our own making.

Early announcements about the millennium bug brought forth both laughter and incredulity. How can the simple matter of a date formula on a computer, more absurdly, the shift from "19" to "20," be a matter of any consequence? Early computer programmers created the problem by not wanting to use up the extra memory that it would take to put two more figures (for example, *1973* and not just *73*) in the date formulas of computers. That seems laughable now when the memory of computers can hold whole libraries of information (though at the time it was a serious decision because, as one commentator has put it, "in the early days of computing, memory was luxury real estate"). The laughter has become very muted, however, and the efforts to squash this little bug have become massive as society has become aware of the potential breakdown of everything we do that is computer controlled if this "bug" is not fixed.

The possible scenarios run from the piddling—the experience of minor delays and inconveniences—to the catastrophic, as society engages in a massive meltdown because every aspect of our life is technologically controlled. The investment analyst Michael Bloomberg has called the Y2K problem "one of the greatest frauds of all time," while Edward Yardeni, chief economist of the Deutsche Morgan Grenfell investment bank, estimates that "the odds are strongly in favor of an economic recession as serious as the one triggered by the 1973–74 oil shock."[1] Fixing the "bug," if that is possible, will be the most expensive resolution of a problem in the history of humankind. A *Newsweek* columnist last summer referred to "that glitch in computer programming that threatens to shut down civilization at the stroke of midnight Dec. 31, 1999."[2] If ever there were a secular equivalent of the announcement of the end, of a final day when all would be destroyed, that is it. Both the serious press and the popular culture have produced essays and books on this topic with titles of truly apocalyptic character. Five years ago, Peter de Jager wrote an article in *Computerworld* titled "Doomsday 2000."[3] Among the spate of novels appearing is one by Jason Kelly, *Y2K: It's Already Too Late*, with a cover depicting a planet completely afire.[4] A less sensationalist book is Michael Hyatt's *The Millennium Bug*.[5] I do not know what the experts think about his prognostications, but this nonfiction book is scarier than any horror thriller.

Among the more scholarly and sane essays, Edward Tenner's recent article in the *Wilson Quarterly* suggests some of the possibilities of the effects of the millennium bug if allowed to run freely in our technological systems:

> Running the gamut from shifts of investment funds based in Internet-transmitted rumors about the Year 2000 readiness of particular companies, to depletion of bank and automatic teller machine currency supplies, to runs on bread and toilet paper, a late 1999 panic might be comical but also potentially deadly.
>
> Add potential sabotage to the equation. The Pentagon already worries about information warfare and terrorism. Hostile states, criminal organizations, and domestic and foreign radical movements can already attack vital networks. The beginning of the year 2000 is a perfect cover.[6]

This is pretty scary stuff. And if one adds to it the possible breakdown of air control systems, electric power distribution switches, traffic lights, elevators, pipeline controls for water, medical machines of all sorts, supply systems for merchandise inventories of every sort—nearly all of which have embedded microchips that control the systems—then the picture just gets worse. It did not help this writer to hear that educational systems are as badly exposed to Year 2000 problems as other organizations, or that the computer on which this editorial is being typed, without which I seem to experience a genuine feeling of anxiety and helplessness about my life and work, may be vulnerable to the "bug." What can be done about it?

One analyst, somewhat tongue-in-cheek, I think, suggested why not just go back to 1900? Would that be so tragic? Perhaps not, but I am not sure I want to relive the twentieth century. The excitement of the man on the moon is not worth the Holocaust. Our best hope—indeed, our only hope in the face of poor planning—is that the increasingly intense, vigorous, and anxious efforts to reprogram all the systems will be accomplished, at least sufficiently to hold disaster at bay until things can gradually be worked out. Meanwhile, as Y2K comes upon us and the possibilities of suffering greatly at the hands of this "bug" seep in upon us, we may find ourselves reflecting on what all this means down deep and over the long haul. I will start the ball rolling and see where it goes.

For one thing, having invoked the language of hope and planning, I am reminded afresh of what Jürgen Moltmann and others have taught us about the difference between the two. Our hope is not in what we can plan for the future, but in the God who comes to us. That is totally different from the planning of a future that can avoid disturbing shocks like the millennium bug and secular but real apocalypses such as the possible meltdown of Doomsday 2000. The difference is so complete that we may not be inclined even to talk about them together. But I would argue that the failure of planning is a reminder of our hope. The hope of God's redemptive coming has sounded in those moments when the human situation seems darkest. Maybe this is not one of those moments, but it is at least pretty shadowy, and if some of the worst scenarios should come to pass, there will be a huge sense of personal and corporate helplessness.

Y2K is also a reminder that planning is still a human responsibility, that the effecting of global means of cooperation, communication, mutual enhancement, and the handles for working together are so incumbent upon us that the failure to accomplish these means for the sake of human ends may mean the human end. For surely our human interconnectedness seems to come more sharply to the fore when it is reflected in our vulnerability to catastrophe, as in the case of the millennium bug and the global repercussions of financial problems in Thailand and Russia over the past year.

If some of our disasters can be catalogued readily among the consequences of the familiar systems of sin (financial disaster = greed; nuclear war and ethnic genocide = greed, hatred), others may not fit so easily into the realm of sin and evil, belonging rather to our capacities as human beings. They remind us both of how wonderfully we are made when we reflect on the geniuses and minds that have enabled computers, space travel, television, satellite communication, and the like, but also of the limits of our finitude, demonstrated again and again in our limited foresight, inadequate cooperation among persons and social units, governmental laziness, ineptitude at the personal and corporate level, and large social and cultural differences. These are not the seven deadly sins. But they are dimensions of our being human, and remind us of that strange paradox we read about in Genesis where the spread of the nations is viewed as both the outcome of the divine blessing of fertility and multiplication

(Gen. 10) and the judgment of God because of human breach of the creaturely limit (Gen. 11).

The *imago Dei* in Genesis 1, if I read it correctly, has to do with our creation and placement in this universe to rule and govern it, to keep and till the garden, even more the harsh wilderness. That is a fairly high anthropology, and I do not want to let it go. But the millennium bug reminds me afresh of the reality of the human creature that we are—as much a bumbler as a genius, as much a dominator as a governor, vulnerable to our own inventions, not safe on our own nor able to "fix" our situation in any ultimate way, capable of effecting a genuine progress that sows the seeds of its own destruction. We may fix the millennium bug, but we cannot finally save ourselves—technologically or any other way.

That sense of anxiety and finitude that the millennium bug brings, along with its other problems, cannot allow us to give up being human. So we persevere to till and to keep the garden, knowing that we have to use computers to do that now because we invented them for our convenience and for the betterment of life in this world. Cast out of the garden, we have discovered the snake has joined us. It is just a bug now, but it may undo us as thoroughly as the more threatening creature of Genesis. The snake was one of God's creatures. This one we have made ourselves. One hopes that our God-given human capacities are capable of overcoming this threat to life in God's good world as much as they have those of the past, that societal apocalpyse is not the order of the day on January 1, 2000. But the threats that lie ahead of us may be as subtle and seemingly innocuous as the snake and the fruit must have seemed at the beginning. Will they remind us afresh of our creatureliness even as we seek to assert our dominance over them? That remains to be seen. The computers seem to be in control now. Surely human beings can find ways to take control back from the th☐☐☐☐!☐'☐#☐$☐%☐&☐ (Maybe not!)

16

The State of the World

Most of us do not expect the world to come to an end or even to undergo any significant cataclysm or change at the turn of the millennium. (Of course, we may be surprised or caught off guard, since the millennium does not really turn until January 1, 2001, a date Arthur C. Clarke alerted us to sometime ago with his book *2001* and the movie that gave it such wide popularity.) Some stocktaking, however, is certainly going to take place and is already underway—witness the series on the American century on PBS this spring. From whence have we come and where are we going? We have thought about some theological stocktaking as an agenda for *Theology Today* but have shied away from it for various reasons, many of them good but some of them simply cover for fear of being wrong. It is a lot easier to say how one's mind *has* changed than it is to say how it *will* change, much less how the minds of others will change. One wonders what theological prognosticators might have expected for this century back in 1899.

Reticent to speak about the state of theology and its future, I will boldly suggest that an even more important enterprise at this chronological turning point is the state of the world. That would seem to be a far more presumptuous task than assessing the state of theology if it were not for the fact that there are a number of persons and institutions seriously engaged in just such large scale assessment in order to let us know what we are doing to the world, what is happening to it, and the probabilities and possibilities for the future. Among the more significant of such agencies is the Worldwatch Institute (www.worldwatch.org), which describes itself as "a nonprofit public policy research organization dedicated to informing policymakers and the public about emerging global problems and trends and the complex links between the world economy and its environmental support systems." It is under the leadership of Lester Brown but involves many persons who are knowledgeable in various aspects of the environment and environmental economics. Worldwatch is probably best known for its annual report issued each year for the last twenty-five years, titled *State of the World: A Worldwatch Institute Report on Progress Toward a Sustainable Society.* Its 1999 or "Millennial Edition" is well worth reading for those who are concerned both about the state of the world and the role that Christians and Christian thought and action can play in taking us to the next millennium.

One wonders about how we can possibly make it through the next millennium in the face of two factors: (a) the rapid pace of progress and (b) the slow but ever increasing self-destruction of the global economy through the destruction of nature's support systems. Worldwatch speaks of the former reality, the increasing pace of change, in terms of "the acceleration of history." There are many illustrations of that acceleration. One rather dramatic example is the fact that in the three years from 1995 to 1998 the growth in economic output exceeded that during the 10,000 years from the beginning of agriculture until 1900. Another is what has been called "the death of distance" in the twentieth century due to our increased mobility and the speed with which communication and information can move around the world. More chilling is the realization that there were three times as many victims of war in the twentieth century than in all the centuries since the first century. The increasing self-destruction of natural support systems is documented in detail by Worldwatch. In an article in the March-April 1999 issue of the magazine *World Watch*, Brown summarizes the situation:

> The Earth's forests are shrinking, fisheries are collapsing, water tables are falling, soils are eroding, coral reefs are dying, atmospheric CO_2 concentrations are increasing, temperatures are rising, floods are becoming more destructive, and the rate of extinction of plant and animal species may be the greatest since the dinosaurs disappeared 65 million years ago.

In his study of the prophetic movement in the Old Testament, *The Prophetic Imagination*, Walter Brueggemann calls attention to the way in which the prophets of Israel carried out a twofold task: *criticizing the present reality* and the systems and structures that corrupted human life while *envisioning and imagining a different future* characterized by blessing and shalom, by neighborliness and security, by wise leadership and just practices for the whole community. There is something of this prophetic stance in the work of Worldwatch and what they report to us. Their picture of the way things are and where we are headed contains an always implicit and sometimes explicit critique. But the report on the state of the world is not simply a handwringing despair or a standoffish indictment of the human community and especially the Western world, though such indictment is to be inferred. Their report suggests serious ways in which the future can be changed, things we can do to "build a sustainable society." That phrase, a catchword for Worldwatch, sounds very much like something the prophets were after when they talked about living by God's law, about turning swords into plowshares and providing security for each family unit, a security that included the provision for daily needs and protection from economic endangerment. Building a sustainable society is what the case law of ancient Israel was all about, that is, structuring into the systems of life and communal processes access to the gains of the community's productivity but also protecting the neighbor's means for life: animals for food and work as well as clothing and the tools and equipment for production. The producers of *State of the World* do not provide theological grounds for their critique, but they do expect communities of faith to contribute to and support the vision of a different future.

How can the church in its corporate and individual manifestations do that? The question is not a new one, and the good minds of Worldwatch, some of whom I suspect are participants in Christian congregations, have a few suggestions themselves. Let me identify some possibilities before us as a way of continuing the conversation.

1. Warning of the dangers of making goods into gods. The *State of the World* report itself suggests this is a task for the religious communities. The First Commandment may have its most concrete contemporary target in the conspicuous consumption that is characteristic of the way of life in the West, and especially the United States. The impossibility of serving both God and wealth is something Jesus taught us, and he made no qualifications. There is some relation between spiritual health and material health. There is an even clearer relation between my consumption and my neighbor's deprivation. The First Commandment has always had the neighbor in view, but never more clearly than now. The materials needed to meet the basic needs of persons on the whole planet will require a large reduction in the use of those materials by the world's heaviest consumers—in cars, homes, clothing, electronics, and the like. Reordering the center of meaning and value in human life from goods to God will have a large ripple effect on the health of the world and our own health.

2. Attending afresh to the theology of creation. Theology has staked its claims about God as creator heavily on notions of an absolute transcendence and a sharp distinction between God and creation. We may begin to change our ways of thinking about the natural world as habitat and resource as we become more aware of the interaction of God and nature and of creation as a complex of interdependent relations between different creaturely realms, to use the language of Michael Welker in his book *Creation and Reality*. Distinctions between nature and culture may be made, but the biblical-theological understanding of creation assumes continual and consistent interaction between nature and culture as a part of the creative work of God. So the knowledge of creation becomes an exploration of the interdependencies of nature and culture. The dominion of humankind has, in the terms of the *State of the World* report, "overwhelmed the earth," as the cultural realms have forgotten their interdependence on the natural realms and assumed a hierarchical structure of power that originates in notions of divine causation and carries forward in human domination of the earth. Rethinking creation with the help of Scripture will open up the very serious issues of power and powerlessness in cultural and natural realms, issues of immense importance to the building of a sustainable society, a secular way of talking about the creation that Christians should help to explicate both theologically and practically.

3. *Seeing the* oikumene *as encompassing natural, social, and cultural dimensions of human life so that ecumenical theology and ecumenical expression are not perceived as merely religious.* The cooperative spirit of the ecumenical movement and what has been learned there about how to live and work together in the face of deep differences in theological conviction should be carried over into other spheres where the church will need to work with national governments, nongovernmental organizations, and other religious movements to build a sustainable society or, in biblical terms, to provide blessing for all the families of the earth (Gen. 12:3).

4. *Molding a counterculture to the culture of violence that is reflected not only in our propensity for war and the prevalence of crime but also in our obsession with guns, our addiction to media violence, and our insistence on a primitive blood revenge in the form of execution.* The church will have to learn new ways to make plows out of swords if the conflicts that have made the twentieth century "the most violent of all human ages unprecedented in the scale and intensity of killing and destruction" (*State of the World*, 151) are not to be the wave of the future.

5. *Providing a model of action that is not dominated by self-interest and pragmatic acts, while working hand in glove with those for whom the impetus is always a pragmatic one.* The millennium bug in our computers has stirred up massive efforts and hundreds of billions of dollars because we are afraid our system will break down if we do not fix the problem. The state of the world is such that the whole system is breaking down fast, but we are slow to engage in the massive endeavors necessary to offset that breakdown because its effects are most immediately felt on others and less on ourselves. Once again, it is the task of the church to identify the neighbor with new clarity and think afresh about how I love my neighbor in the sub-Sahara and Indonesia. Protecting my neighbor from eco-

nomic endangerment is what is meant by the commandment, "You shall not steal." In a global community, how do we still leave grain in the fields for the hungry without land?

The *State of the World* report is by no means a jeremiad against contemporary society and its consumptive propensities. It recognizes important ways in which the last century has made life a blessing—the report's language—for millions of people and identifies significant indications of movement toward a sustainable society. Would you believe, for example, that in 1969 the world produced 25 million bicycles and 23 million cars, whereas in more recent years production of cars has averaged 37 million a year while bicycle production has averaged 105 million, most of which are for basic transportation? But the state of the world is precarious and the future as filled with danger as promise. We may do ourselves in long before cosmic catastrophes bring a screeching halt to the earth's future. Apocalyptic possibilities are present without much confidence about there being clear winners when the dust settles. We may all go under. Christian hope and Christian practice should say something about how the world ends up, or at least about its state when the next millennium rolls around.

17

The Church's First Theologian

There are many reasons why it is appropriate for a theological journal with a primarily Protestant setting to devote an issue to theological reflection on Mary, the mother of Jesus. They include the fact that under any reckoning she is a central biblical figure, and Protestant devotion to Scripture invites as much attention to her as a figure of faith as to any of the other biblical personalities. Her place in the historic creeds and the systematic discussions of major Protestant theologians underscores that need for major theological attention. The significance of Mary for ecumenical discussion, both as a historic source of divisions in the Christian family and as a more recent locus of new dialogue among Protestants and Catholics and new grounds for unity, makes her an appropriate topic for a journal whose ecumenical commitment is historic and whose readership includes a large number of Christians from other than Protestant denominations.

At least one reason for paying attention to Mary is that an argument can be made for her place as the first theologian of the church. While that may seem a dubious claim, I would urge its consideration on two grounds. One is found in Mary's silence, the other in her loud voice. The silence that contains profound theological contemplation is alluded to twice in the Gospel of Luke, in each case with similar language. At the conclusion of the story of Jesus' birth and the visit of the shepherds, the evangelist says that "Mary treasured all these words and pondered them in her heart" (Luke 2:19). In similar fashion, the account of Jesus' disappearance from his parents and his sitting at the feet of the teachers in the temple ends not simply with the parental anxiety, rebuke, and nonunderstanding but once again with the note that after the whole matter was over "his mother treasured all these things in her heart" (Luke 2:51). We do not know, of course, what went on in Mary's mind, and any proposals are simply guesswork. We do know that her story as the Lord's servant began with a mystery she could not comprehend (Luke 1:35) and that she would face many and painful puzzles about her beloved son and God's purpose through him—some at a wedding, some at his execution. And we may have some clue in the response of the people to the words and deeds of his predecessor, John the Baptist, for they also "pondered" those things and asked "What then will this child become?" (Luke 1:66). Surely that was at the heart of Mary's theological and maternal pondering: What then will this child become—and what then will become of this child? We can be confident that thinking about the meaning of this child, about what God was doing in him and about the mystery of how people (poor people, academics, and just plain "church" folk) responded to him in wonder and praise whether encountering him as a tiny helpless baby or as a precocious adolescent, was something that must have gone on all the time in Mary's mind. She was not one of the rabbis, not one of the persons called or appointed to the study of God's ways as found in Scripture and the story of Israel. We have no book of Scripture written by this woman. She was simply the mother of this child. But the first musings over his significance, the first christological reflection, began with the woman who brought him forth in pain and nursed him on her breast. While we do not know all she thought, we know that her theological reflection never ceased, for such is the way of mothers with their children. The treasuring of their words and deeds and the incidents of their childhood is not something that ever disappears. Nor does a mother ever stop trying to understand her child. According to the story, she realized, at least, that what had happened at his birth and the critical moment of his youth set this child as one whose mother's responses outran those of any other mother while also being very like those of any mother: "Child, why have you treated us like this? Look, your father and I have been searching for you in great anxiety" (Luke 2:48).

The story of Mary makes us wonder about how much other theological work has gone on in the silence of a mother's heart. This mother, of course, was different precisely because of the one who was her child. But there are surely untold reams of reflection about God's ways and purposes in the birth of a child that are part of a mother's quiet and unspoken treasure. As Jesus' birth and his death led Mary to think deeply about both events, so the birth and death of children sets their mothers into an unannounced and unrecognized theological enterprise. Fathers too, I believe, but Scripture seems to suggest that the primary theological work at those moments—certainly in birth, infancy, and childhood—belongs to the mothers. And it is not a public act. Rather, it comes with the territory, the often painful and anxiety-creating territory of mothering a child. Some may be vocal about it. Many will treasure their theological thoughts in their hearts, as did Mary at the beginning.

Mary's theological voice, however, is not altogether silent. Indeed, she has given the church its most sung hymn of praise and thanksgiving, the Magnificat (Luke 1:46–55). Mary's testimony to the powerful work of God has been a touchstone of the liturgy of the church as prayer, praise, and music have come together to echo her song again and again down through the ages and in every land. If Mary's theological ponderings about her child are kept in her heart, her witness is very articulate and worthy of our pondering as much as our singing.

From the start, one needs to acknowledge a kind of anomaly here. The song of Mary that is sung in great cathedrals and churches around the world, by choirs in beautiful robes and congregations of substantial means, is a song that reflects the piety and the faith of the poor. The song that is sung most often in established churches—I have probably heard it most often in the King's College Chapel in Cambridge, where it has been sung constantly since the days of King Henry VIII—is an antiestablishment song, one of the biblical texts that has founded and funded a theology of liberation whose primary base is among Christians of the poorer countries and peoples of our planet. So there is something ironic in the church's appropriation of this text, indeed something truly subversive in its singing such a song, for what it undercuts is not someone else's ideology and place in the scheme of things, but our own.

The Magnificat is a song of the poor and the downtrodden, and its character as an expression of the faith of the poor is seen in two particular ways. At the start is the self-understanding of the one who sings this song that she is lowly, and she identifies herself with the lowly in Israel, over against the proud, the powerful, and the rich. Those who sing this song have to find a connection with that voice or sing it to their own damnation. It is a song of praise and thanksgiving of one who is poor and lowly, and either we sing it as the poor and lowly or we hear it as a testimony (over against us?) in hopes that it is also the hope for us. The song also expresses the faith of the poor in its claim that God is the helper of the poor, the one who lifts up the lowly and gives food to the hungry. The song thus echoes one of the primary themes of the hymns of praise and the songs of thanksgiving of Israel: the activity of God in behalf of the weak, the needy, and the poor, an activity described in this poem as a reversal of fortunes. The political character of Mary's song is heard in the claim that the work of the Lord of Israel is literally a revolutionary one, turning things upside down in the most radical way possible, accomplishing the impossible in the socioeconomic world of that time and, indeed, of any time, utterly changing the structure of power and domination and economic access. Taking a cue from the words of the messenger to Mary—"For nothing will be impossible with God"—Walter Brueggemann has called this type of song a "song of impossibility," for it deals with things that we assume are too difficult, really impossible in this world. Perhaps we assume that in order to take comfort in it. The Magnificat as a song of the poor sees things differently in the world God rules.

The claim of the poor in the voice of Mary is that there is a power at work in the world where poverty and hunger are not the final word, where the powerful and the rich shall not always remain in control and have primary access to the necessities and goods of life. Thus, our customary assumptions that the poor are only in conversation with God at the point of crying out for help and petitioning is too limited. Here are the sounds of victory and triumph on the lips of the lowly. The divine savior is at work in the world and can be praised by the poor because the Lord delivers them.

An inevitable question arises, however, as we read this text, as we listen to Mary and her predecessor Hannah, whose song in 1 Samuel 2 is the progenitor of Mary's testimony: Does this mean simply a reversal, in which the powerless become powerful, the rich become poor, and vice versa? So, then, God has to keep on repeating the cycle? I doubt it. That is indeed the way we think of revolutions, for it is a typical pattern: The weak take power from the mighty, and the poor take the wealth of the rich. The end result may be simply more of the same, only the roles are reversed, and we have a new domination and control.

But that is the problem with our limited imaginations over against the impossible things God imagines. In the coming of Jesus and his purpose in our midst, God outruns our imagination. Mary's words are to be taken most seriously: When God's purpose is under way, things do not work in the customary fashion. The proud and self-sufficient, who show no need of God or of God's help, shall not rule and run things in the kingdom that is ruled by the stable-born, manger-laid, shepherd-watched baby. And the lowly, those who cannot trust in their own strength and might because they have none and so have to rely in utter confidence upon God, shall be exalted.

These revolutionary possibilities in God's way seem to be glimpsed primarily by women who in their own lowliness and need have testified to God's impossibilities (Hannah, Mary). They are certainly beyond my imagination, though I see a few clues that are given in the context of Mary's song. The primary one is Mary herself, unheralded, of no claim to fame, wife of a Jewish carpenter but pregnant before they are married, truly one of low estate who regards herself as a handmaid of the Lord and sees that in choosing her, God has exalted her to high estate. So future generations will call her blessed, beginning with Elizabeth's own greeting to her (Luke 1:42). Mary gains no wealth or power in the worldly sense. Yet in and through this humble woman, God's great purpose shall come to pass. Mary, not Herod or Caesar, is God's revolutionary, imaginative way. She is the demonstration that nothing is impossible for the Lord.

But the sharpest clue is in the way that is shown by the baby Mary bears, who though he was in the form of God did not count equality with God-power, high estate—a thing to be grasped but humbled himself and became obedient unto death, the way of this child who though he was rich yet for our sakes became poor. Therefore God has highly exalted him. I am sure that many years later as she watched the agonizing death of her child, Mary pondered through tears how God had exalted this lowly handmaid of the Lord and what that required of her.

18

"... Who Hast Made
of One Genome ..."

Last summer, amid the fusses and arguments over gas prices, political candidates, Supreme Court decisions, and Labor Party problems, the president of the United States and the prime minister of Great Britain joined with two scientists to announce the decipherment of the human genome, "the set of instructions that defines the human organism," as the *New York Times* put it in the lead sentence of its report, which also described the achievement as "a pinnacle of human self-knowledge" (June 27, 2000). While one of those statements is descriptive and the other evaluative, together they accurately report a stunning and epochal moment, not only in the history of science but also in the continuing effort to answer the question "What is a human being?" (Ps. 8:4; 144:3; Job 7:17; compare Heb. 2:6).

The announcement was a little deceptive in that the process of deciphering the human genome has been going on for a long time and is not yet complete. In some respects the hoopla was primarily a way of getting the two major investigative units, one private and one public, into a more cooperative stance to carry on a process of investigating the structure of human life that will carry us far into the future. The basic research involved in this enterprise has large ramifications for clinical and therapeutic possibilities that will take decades to emerge.

It also has ramifications for theological and ethical work that can hardly be missed. Indeed, the announcement by the president was notable for its culmination in an extended theological and moral reflection in which he spoke of the decipherment as "learning the language in which God created life." President Clinton also identified one of the next horizons before us as "the horizon that represents the ethical, moral, and spiritual dimension of the power we now possess." We probably do not even know yet how much power this gives us in defining the human, but that both knowledge of the human and power for shaping human life and destiny are significant outcomes of this scientific project is not in doubt.

Implications for understanding the nature of the human abound. Not least of these is the way that the genetic decipherment points to and identifies our individuality as human beings, our uniqueness as separate persons, while also making startlingly clear our oneness with the rest of humanity. Very small variations in the genetic code are what make us unique, different from every other person. The knowledge that can be gained out of the genome mapping is clearly both revelatory and full of power. It can tell us individually much about our physiological future, our propensity for certain diseases. It can also help scientists develop sensitive diagnostic tests to uncover that propensity, or lack of it, as well as therapies that can be highly tailored to a person's genetic profile. Health science will surely become even more person-specific than it already is. Medications will be developed not simply for a particular disease but for a particular person, so to speak. At a minimum, physicians and scientists will know more about when and for whom various therapies and procedures are most appropriate and necessary.

Such knowledge, of course, may be too much for us, not in the sense of the psalmist that we cannot attain it (Ps. 139:6), but precisely because we can attain it and so learn more about ourselves than we may want to know. It is not all good news to know that it is possible to find out more about our physiological destiny. Such knowledge can be positive in that it may enable us to modify that destiny for good. But the knowledge of a high propensity for breast cancer or heart disease or Alzheimer's can be as terrifying as it can be helpful. It has the potential for turning us more into fated creatures than creatures of hope. If most of us can dismiss the astrologist's claim that our destiny is written in the stars, it will be more difficult to forget that our destiny truly is written in our genes.

That our individuality cannot be reduced to a matter of genetic code, however, is evident from the exception to the rule, that is, the genetic makeup of identical twins. The shared genetic identity of identical twins does not mean two persons who are simply clones of one another. Personality, mind, spirit, and affects are shaped by many other things as well, and the significance of the genetic makeup must not be allowed to obscure the many other aspects of the human—both as a species and in our particularity—that belong to the work of the Creator and the answer to the psalmist's question. Whether or not he views the matter at all theologically, Craig Ventnor, one of the two project directors in the genome decipherment race, said at the White House announcement that he learned out of his experience as a medic in Vietnam that the human spirit transcended the physiology that is controlled by the genome.

If, however, knowledge of the structure of the human genome heightens the knowledge of our individuality and its sources, it also underscores the commonality of the human race and our commonality with the rest of creation. The former is demonstrated biologically in the degree to which the genomic structure of all human beings is markedly similar. As President Clinton put it, "Human beings, regardless of race, are more than 99.9 percent the same." Furthermore, the genetic similarity of all human beings to one another is closer than the genetic similarity of other species, even the apes. The oneness of humanity has a biological ground. As some scientists have pointed out, the differences among us, at least genetically, are only skin deep. Our biological commonality with all other human beings is a characteristic feature of the human species. It is one of the things that defines the human in distinction from other species.

Yet the commonality of the human species is no more strikingly demonstrated in the decipherment of the human genome than is our commonality with the rest of creation. We have long since assumed a relationship between human beings and primates. Even antievolutionists cannot help noticing how much apes act like human beings in many ways. But our commonality with other living creatures has a dramatic demonstration in the process of uncovering the human genome. It is somewhat disarming to discover that the fruit fly provides major clues to the human genomic structure, that of the 289 genes that are known to cause human diseases in mutated form, 177 of them have counterparts in the fruit fly. Even more appropriately humbling for human beings is to discover the commonality "of mice and men." If the image of the mouse has provided a rhetorical and literary point of sharp distinction from human beings, the actual makeup of the mouse turns out to be markedly similar to our own. In its summary of information provided by the Department of Energy's Human Genome Project, the *Times* said this: "Almost every human gene has a counterpart in the mouse, with similar DNA sequences and basic functions. If the 23 pairs of human chromosomes were broken into smaller blocks, those pieces could be reassembled to produce a serviceable model of the mouse genome."

What is evident from all of this is that genomic investigation is serving to confirm one of the basic principles of evolution, that is, that living beings share a common ancestor. Such awareness, however, has not deterred scientists as well as others from being awed by the mystery of God's creative activity. According to Nicholas Wade of the *Times*, Frances Collins, the other project director who stood with the president at the formal announcement, has said that the genome project has filled him with awe as it revealed something only God knew before. In his remarks at the White House, Collins said, "We have caught the first glimpses of our instruction book, previously known only to God."

When the Bible speaks of the knowledge of good and evil as a way of speaking about the maturity of an individual, it recognizes implicitly that knowledge usually brings with it some kind of power, and power has its dark side. The excitement over the implications and possibilities of the decipherment of the human genome has not blocked out awareness of the serious possible misuses of this knowledge and the need for the human community to engage in serious discussion about what are proper and improper uses of this new knowledge. While it is clearer than ever that human beings have most things in common, the ability to be more precise about the differences may lead to genetic racial differentiation that can feed the fires of bigotry and racism. One hates to think how detailed knowledge of the genetic code would have been used by the scientists of Nazism, to cite an extreme example.

But other problems of a more complex sort are before us. Will sophisticated knowledge of the genetic makeup of individuals and what that offers by way of identifying health dangers expand the sharp gap between delivery of health services in the West and the rest of the world or between the better off and the lesser off in the rich nations? Will huge amounts of money be funneled into developing more precise therapies for persons in North America and Europe than on the prevention and cure of AIDS in Africa?

It is safe to assume that such things will happen unless the church and other religious communities resist, even if it is often against our own interests. That will not be easy to do. One of the clearest indicators of the way self-interest controls our lives is the way in which health problems in an individual take over body and soul and inhibit the capacity to see beyond one's self to focus upon the needs of others. When I am hurting, it is hard to worry about your hurting. Christian faith has taught us that it really is possible to think in a quite different way, but I doubt if we can bring that off unless the imitation of Christ truly guides us and unless we do it as a community. I do not have the power on my own truly to set the good of the other first. With the support of others, that may happen. Like so many other social issues before us in contemporary society (for example, the control of guns), the new genetic knowledge will press upon us the search for a common good.

The ethical issues of cloning are also before us in a sharper way. If anything, the whole matter of altering genetic codes and shaping biological life is more complicated as a moral issue than ever before. There will be ways to inhibit diseases and alter the makeup of future persons for good. Biological destiny will no longer be as blind as it has been in the past. We will be inclined to resist fate by taking things into our own hands. But tampering with the genetic code is morally explosive. There is no way we can know now what will be the outcome of modifying the genetic code, that is, reprogramming the human genome, even if the effort is well-intentioned. Attempting to improve on the genetic code, whether in individual cases or in general, is something that science needs to resist until we are clearer about its consequences. Once science is able to do something, it is hard to hold back, but conservatism is appropriate when the issue is defining and modifying human nature. The line between therapeutic developments in light of the new knowledge and modification of the genetic code to inhibit negative developments and guarantee positive ones will be very fuzzy. "Creatureliness" does not define our relation to other human beings but to the God who made us. The knowledge, power, and freedom God has given to humankind have always been a potential for good and for evil. The two possibilities are still with us in these new developments. Like the splitting of the atom, marvelous scientific discovery once again opens doors of disaster as well as doors of hope.

There is a further moral issue that may not be as evident but is at least disturbing. It is the degree of commodification of the human that is apparent in the rush to patent the genes that are being deciphered. Private enterprise often contributes significantly to scientific advancement, and patenting of scientific results is as common as dirt. One should pause, however, at the prospect of patenting the discovery of how we are made. It looks as if there is a sense in which as human beings we are, biologically, for sale. At least there is a serious effort to control the knowledge of our biological makeup through the patenting process.

Once again, therefore, scientific discovery and technological capacity raise very large moral and theological issues. The church needs to be at the center of the discussion of those issues, which is why we are planning an issue of *Theology Today* in the next year or so to be devoted to technology and its implications for faith and life.

The various comments about this discovery by scientists, politicians, and journalists have confirmed something I have long suspected. It is the degree to which the most ultimate matters cannot be talked about finally only in scientific terms but must invoke the language of poetry. With regard to the decipherment of the human genome, Harold Varmus, president of Memorial Sloan-Kettering Cancer Center, has said, "There's a metaphor contest going on." So in the early articles on the announcement of the decipherment, the human genome was compared to a pigsty, a pearl, an atlas, and a hodgepodge. One of the most common images is that of a blueprint, but frequently one hears the genome characterized as the "book of life." As one commentator said, "Scientists are falling over each other for the prize for the most apt analogy." Varmus indicated that his favorite metaphor was that of a kid with a clock, taking it apart, laying out the pieces to try to understand what makes it tick, and then putting it back together again.

It is doubtful that the scientific community will reach a consensus about the best metaphor or analogy for the structure of the human genome. There are no final metaphors. What is salutary is that the scientific community finds itself pressed to search for an adequate language to speak about its discovery and cannot do so simply within its own territory. The reach for a more poetic form of speech to talk about the human genome is an implicit acknowledgment that even in this highly technical enterprise there is an openness, an ambiguity about the reality encountered so that it cannot be contained simply in rational and scientific description. The poetic proposals are a way of saying we do not have this matter fully in our control. The makeup of the human cannot be reduced to the language of scientific analysis. Even those for whom that speech is primary find themselves grasping for a way of speaking that is larger than that, communicating the fullness of what is before us in the beauty, complexity, and awesomeness of human nature. I venture to suggest, as would some scientists, that in such efforts we may encounter a suggestion of transcendence, a recognition that our scientific speech is penultimate and our scientific analysis not the last word. Dare one say further that this scientific pursuit of the metaphorical may create a bridge to the language of Scripture, where poetry and figurative speech are often the preferred mode for thinking about the things of God?

19

What Sense Do We Make of the Ending?

From 1997 to 2000, a group of theologians and scientists working together under the auspices of the Center of Theological Inquiry—and longer on theological input than scientific input—engaged the question of what science and theology, separately and in conversation, have to say about the last things, about the end of everything and the consummation of everything, or, to use the title of the collection of essays that came forth as a result of these conversations, about the end of the world and the ends of God.[1] The movement from the *end* of everything, a fact whose reality is evident but whose significance is not—or is, at least, ambiguous—to the *consummation* of everything, a hope whose significance is evident but whose reality is beyond or short of demonstration, is not an easy move to make. The problematic is evident in the difficulty of securing scientists willing to engage in a conversation about anything but the factual, that is, the *end*. On that they are very good, as witness the clearheaded and in ways frightening report of William Stoeger on "Scientific Accounts of Ultimate Catastrophes in Our Life-Bearing Universe," in the aforementioned volume.

It is much easier to talk about and create a conversation between science and theology about the beginning of the universe or about creation than it is about the end of the universe or about the eschaton. In the former case, neither science nor theology presses to try to comprehend what is before the beginning. The origin of nothingness may evoke a certain amount of curiosity, but it does not touch us. It is beyond as before and so does not worry us. But the disappearance or end of what has been is another matter. The whither of ourselves, our world, our memory, our history is the beyond that continues and gives meaning or does not continue and signals absurdity. It evokes either

83

hope (so the apostle Paul) or stoic cynicism (so Steven Weinberg: "The more the universe seems comprehensible, the more it also seems pointless"). It does not leave us untouched.

It is at this point that the Bible comes in, either as a kind of lifeboat to rescue the situation or an embarrassment from another age, to put the matter in rather extreme terms. For it is only out of the revelatory claims of Scripture that eschatology arises as a theological topic and as an assumption about reality that requires faith to engage with science to get some sense of the ending. The ending itself is less a problem than what the ending signals. Both science and theology assume what the Bible says with poetic power, that the world will come to an end, comprehended in one scientific scenario as the final explosive outcome of natural forces at work over billions of years, in another as a cold and unending death in an infinitely expanding universe. At that point, science stops its projections. There is nothingness or an ending. The silence of science at that point is an anticipation of the silence of the universe.

The Bible gives reason for hope and speaks about the future with hope and about a future that is God's, the only ground for hope. Scripture does not do this simply. Indeed, it is not always easy to identify what is eschatological speech or text in Scripture, particularly in the Old Testament but also in the New. At least there is always the question of whether the text, especially if it is a prophetic text, speaks about an end that is on the near horizon or the end that is the farthest horizon. So it is that some texts may have behind them the experience of exile as opening up a larger dimension of hope within a cosmic framework of chaos and new creation and a personal framework of trouble and new life. In other instances, for example, the Isaiah Apocalypse (Isa. 24–27), whose historical context is highly debated, the text seems to move back and forth between death and an end experienced or anticipated within the history known to the writers and an end that is cosmic and the undoing of creation. That end, however, seems also to envision the work of the Lord in (1) newness of personal being (resurrection), (2) newness of social existence (here as elsewhere in Scripture represented particularly in the image of the new Jerusalem rather than homecoming from exile—but are those really different since home is always Jerusalem, whether new or old?), and (3) new cosmic creation inferred from the character of the final judgment as the undoing of the old creation. The biblical texts thus invite us to think about—and to engage science in thinking about—the way in which the end of the world is experienced on both near and far horizons and the way in which death and newness are realities to be understood at several levels: the personal, the sociocommunal, and the cosmic.

There is a realism to the biblical anticipation of the end, not only in its symbols and images but particularly in its realism about death, a point Donald Juel underscores in his essay in *The End of the World and the Ends of God*: "The reality and finality of death cannot be dispelled by arguments. Only God can raise the dead." In full recognition of this, a theology of the end is as much a theology of the cross as it is a theology of glory. The sure reality is death. The hope against hope is that God will redeem through the risen Christ—an act, Juel reminds us, that is available to us now only as promise.

The Scriptures seem always to pose the matter of the end in relation to the expectation of *newness*, or they speak about a newness that is cosmic in scope and is indeed a new creation, a transformation of the *old* and a transformation of the *whole* ("Behold I make all things new" [Rev. 21:5]. So eschatology from the perspective of Scripture is not simply about the end or about death, which is surely a part of all ends whether personal or cosmic, but about the newness that explodes from the end. The texts raise the question of newness in the work of God and lead us to ask about newness in the created order that is visible to us through the lenses of science as well as through the pages of Scripture. As Hans Weder says in his contribution to *The End of the World and the Ends of God*, "It makes a decisive difference for the concrete shaping of hope if the universe is gifted with the unpredictable new or not." John Polkinghorne has pressed the fact that one cannot expect simply the same old thing, that newness is simply recapitulation of the former reality, a point that Michael Welker pushes with equal vigor in rejecting notions of resuscitation as the clue to resurrection. There *is* continuity. It is God's creation that is made new; it is our selves that are resurrected; it is Jerusalem where the community gathers in the new creation. But the matter of the universe as we know it will end or suffer the death of infinity, and the carryover of the pattern in the resurrection will surely take place in a divinely mutated matter, to use Polkinghorne's way of speaking. Hans Weder sees an anticipation of this interplay of continuity and discontinuity in the personal dimension in Paul's distinction between *psychic* body and *pneumatic* body, where the "body," one's whole person, is the dimension of continuity, and the natural and the spiritual are the elements that mark discontinuity. As Paul puts it in 1 Cor. 15:44: "It is sown a physical body, it is raised a spiritual body. If there is a physical body, there is also a spiritual body."

Furthermore, the Jerusalem that is the center of sociocommunal existence in the end is the "heavenly" Jerusalem, not simply Zion redivivus but the Jerusalem come down from heaven (Rev. 21:2, 10)—an image that implies radical transformation—into a world where there is no more weeping and crying, itself an astonishing instance of discontinuity. The "pivot point of hope," to use Walter Brueggemann's phrase, found in the words of assurance, the divine promise, "Do not be afraid, for I am with you," means that the transformation from sorrow and suffering into joy that is experienced now only in part becomes the fullness of the new creation. So the Scriptures appropriate images and experiences of the community gathered at a feast and the choirs of heaven and earth singing for joy together at the end as at the beginning.

Finally, the Scriptures indirectly raise the issue of our language and mode of discourse. What language is appropriate for our speaking about eschatology and new creation? It may be that here our best mode of speech may be the language of poetry. That is, the indirect, non-literal, and figurative language of poetry may provide the proper medium for speaking about that which finally outruns all our scientific description and theological explanation and can only be imagined. At least, the Bible finishes the story that way.

20

Terror All Around

We look for peace, but find no good;
for a time of healing, but there is terror instead.
Jer. 8:15 and 14:19

In the fall of 2001, as these words are being written, there is no longer any thinking that starts from scratch. The events of September and later have unsettled things for all of us, and we can hardly think about anything without the intrusion of this unsettlement into our minds. We know there is a larger picture, but September 11 marks some kind of beginning or ending, even if we are very unsure which it is and what it means. This unsettled existence has a corollary: It is very difficult to speak about anything and assume that several months later what one has to say will be remotely pertinent, much less wise. Contingency is the order of the day, and it may be permanent.

Editorials do not customarily begin with a text, not even in *Theology Today*. But since nothing is quite the same right now and customary rules and assumptions have become unglued, I have an editorial text in the words quoted above from the prophet Jeremiah. The question, then and now, is where and how to find the good when there is "terror all around" (Jer. 20:3, 10). Elusive as the answer to that question may be, there are some things that, at least right now, seem to belong to its pursuit.

Surely, in this time of terror, there is a new understanding that if the good is the aim of all things (so Aristotle), it really is the good we have *in common*. The United States political order in the year 2001 was on a dogged move to claim that the national interest is to be found in separating ourselves from others, in a resistance to common national efforts to protect against weapons, guard the environment, and keep the peace. All that came to a screeching halt on September 11. We assumed we could work out a national good on our own, that in fact *our* good is best pursued apart from the larger global good or without cooperative efforts. Furthermore, many of us have assumed also that within the polis the individual good can only be pursued when everyone is left alone and the political body—the catchword, of course, is "federal government"—is the enemy of the good, a necessary evil to be kept tightly under control and out of our lives.

The massive reversal of American national and foreign policy in the face of terror all around and the revival of some congeniality and bipartisanship in politics as well as dependence upon the federal government to provide security and economic support—indeed, to protect, promote, and enhance the common good—has changed all that. In so doing we have been reminded anew that our life and death are truly with our neighbor. There is good news and bad news in that claim, but its reality cannot be avoided. There is no life that is not lived in community, as T. S. Eliot reminded us long ago. Communities have many definitions and varied contexts and complexities. All of us belong to many, but only as those communities of our lives represent and seek shared understanding of what it is that effects the good of the *whole* and how that may be sought, even if imperfectly, can the good of *each and all* come to fruition.

John XXIII in *Pacem in Terris*, and many others, have told us that the common good cannot be defined or limited by the nation-state. That seems so obvious it hardly needs to be mentioned, except for the fact that we belong to a nation-state that often, and especially recently, has acted on exactly the opposite assumption. The terror all around us probably has not produced a serious change of philosophy in those who govern the nation, but it has at least produced pragmatic efforts to find a way to act in concert to achieve the human good. In our heady economic comfort, we have lived alone and let our neighbor die. Now in the face of death, we have rediscovered our neighbor, only to find both that we need him and that he frightens us. Yet it is not altogether clear that the good we seek in common really does transcend national interests. Will we fall back behind our national borders if and when the terror that is all around us abates?

There is a tension here, experienced corporately and individually. The precariousness of our common existence within a threatened nation and our consequent fears and concerns draw us closer into community, a closeness reflected in visible symbols, from the prominent and unabashed display of our national emblem, to hand-holding, to people keeping in touch, to crowds at Yankee Stadium and Central Park ostensibly to cheer a baseball team or hear celebrities talk and sing but more probably to be together with others. The terror all around brings us together in varied communities—family, corporate and institutional, religious, and many ad hoc new groups of shared experience—all of which are pieces of the larger national community to which we know ourselves so clearly to belong. At the same time, we are highly conscious that we cannot pursue a common good for ourselves that does not take account of the whole human community, of disparate nation-states and their particular needs, of large religious communities with different understandings of the good and not even shared understandings of it. Even as we look inward to find the good, we are forced outward by circumstances that will not allow us to close in on ourselves, even when every instinct is to do so.

The presence of *threat*—a more concrete way of speaking of contingency—raises the issue of the common good afresh even as it exacerbates the tensions just described. No longer can the good we have and seek be confined to academic, political, and ecclesial debate; it is a matter of survival. Philosophical positions will be brought to bear, as always, but they cannot be for the sake of winning. They will have to be for the sake of living. Maybe it has always been that way. Now we know that we cannot afford ideological correctness at the cost of the common good, however such correctness be defined. The choices before us have always been the same: life and good, death and evil (Deut. 30:15). Never has it been more clear, however, that we must find the way to choose life and good (Deut. 30:20), that the two are inextricably combined.

Terror all around means further that the question of the common good has a great deal to do with the presence and uses of violence in our society. Violence is the evil that has confronted us; violence is the means by which we attack it; violence is the everyday staple of our cultural life, from abusive personal relationships to public use of violence in executions and everything in between. Stokely Carmichael's comment is as pertinent as ever: Violence is as American as apple pie. The good we have in common cannot be confined to material goods, to the possibility of prosperity for large numbers. The common good is a matter that has pervasive political, social, and cultural dimensions. It has to do with the reality of war but also with what we see and watch in our entertainment. The issue is not simply a matter of what makes us feel "good," but whether our cultural norms participate in a denigration of the virtues and more specifically whether they elevate violence to an acceptable dimension of the community's life.

In the context of this journal, it is appropriate to recognize that the good is to be thought out and worked out in both public and ecclesial ways. Choosing between *res publica* and *ecclesia* as contexts for achieving the common good seems less and less an option, though it may be very important to think about the one in distinction from the other and to recognize varying modes of pursuit. The church exemplifies the human community. It *is* the human community in its life, in its sinfulness, and in its hope. Furthermore, the threat experienced as members of the larger national community, which we really are, and the contingency such threat effects may so undercut the search for the common good, or at least its realization, that the church, of which we also really are members, remains the only avenue, or at least an avenue, wherein the common good is experienced—in symbolic ways and in actuality, around sacred tables and family tables, in prayer for others and the feeding of the poor, in visible local gatherings and in the *oikumené*.

The church's concern for the good, however, is always in behalf of the larger community, in behalf of the world, and never more so than when terror is all around. It may live out that concern in countercultural ways, but its *hope* is not ecclesial, not a hope of the church but a hope of the world. The church has this larger hope as something in which it has participated from the beginning. The Old Testament is not reticent about the common good, about what God intends for "all the families of the earth," or how it is to be achieved (Gen. 12:3). It tells a story of the life of a particular community called into being to mediate the good—the biblical term in this instance is *blessing*—for the whole. The church has its beginning in the complex Genesis story of how the seed of Abraham effected blessing among and for other peoples, through peaceful mediation (Isaac and the Philistines), through economic support (Jacob and the Arameans), through wise leadership (Joseph and the Egyptians), through prayer and intercession for the unrighteous and the wicked (Abraham for Sodom and Gomorrah). In that story, the church hears a claim made upon its present and continuing existence.

There will always be some blurring between the church's understanding of its task or mission as bearer of God's redemptive word, as agent of God's blessing in and for the world, as those who pray for the world, and the church's sense of a public responsibility to uphold the democratic goals of life, liberty, and the pursuit of happiness. (Deuteronomy offers a substantial polity in behalf of just such goals, lest we tend to consign them to modern enlightenment.) These are not contrary to each other, but they are not automatically the same. So one of the tasks of the church is to enhance those goals in constructive and critical fashion. It needs to be unafraid to stand in support of the public definitions of the common good when those resonate with its understanding of the purposes of God in the world. It needs to be quick to challenge those definitions when they are by intention or actuality counter to the way of righteousness and justice in the world (Gen. 18:19), when they do not offer peace and healing in the face of terror and no good.

In these days, I find myself returning to one of the more prophetic voices of our time, Paul Lehmann, because he offers a frame of reference that may help us seek and find the good when terror is all around. It is there in his well-known understanding of the goal of divine activity and the task of Christian ethics as doing what is necessary to make and to keep human life human. This frame of reference offers two handles for enabling the community of faith to get at the common good we seek. One is the insistence that our commonality at bottom is our humanness, that with all our necessary talk about various forms and experiences of community, the good that finally matters is our humanity. That the veiled and wan Afghani woman I just saw pictured in the newspaper is my sister has nothing to do with global or religious or political communities. It is because she is human. The incarnation can never tell us less than that.

The other "handle" Lehmann's frame of reference provides is the realization that whatever is going on to conjoin these two aspects of humanness— our commonality and our good—is first of all the work of God and that, even when terror is all around, indeed *especially* when terror is all around if our theology is truly incarnational, the question about what is going on is first of all not about terror but about discerning the work of God. That, of course, can be a scary enterprise. The quotation from Jeremiah that I have offered as an editorial "text" occurs in a prayer of the Judean people in the face of and with regard to what they were experiencing as God's judgment. We have to be very careful about reading God's judgment into any human event—as Jerry Falwell and Pat Robertson were so vividly reminded in the days after September 11— much less in connection with terrible and evil deeds that dehumanize and destroy in the worst way. If, however, we assume a priori that God's judgment cannot be a dimension of our corporate and historical existence, then either we have forgotten our Bible or we have, ironically, allowed the cross to take the sting out of history. The church lives theologically and experientially with the question of whether God's anger is always washed with tears, as it was in Jeremiah's time, and whether judgment is no less disturbing to God than it is to those who experience it. Lehmann's conviction about discerning what God is doing in the world reminds us that while we cannot easily read God into the events of our time, we have to be careful about reading God out of them.

Finally, I would suggest that we remember the sabbath. That is an ancient injunction worthy of fresh appropriation in these days. It is a gift no time can stop, a freedom no tyrant can take away, a rest no toil can hold off, a hope no terror can destroy. The sabbath regularly tells us who we are. It is a recurring remembrance of our redemption. It is an order in an unsettled world of contingency and fear. In the sabbath, we find a foretaste and an apperception of the common good in the rest we receive for ourselves and the rest we ensure for others. In our daily life, with terror all around us, the sabbath is a sign of the world to come, a reminder that our ultimate good is God and our final rest is there.

21

Work and Faith

Profession is a word whose multiple meanings point both to the public declaration of one's faith and to the understanding of one's work as a calling. Thus, it is appropriate for a journal of theology to devote an issue to the subject of profession and the professions. The latter of these two meanings of the term is the focus of this issue of *Theology Today*, but the relation of the former activity, professing the faith, to the professional life is not an unimportant issue.

Much of the intellectual discussion around the professions, whether from a Christian perspective or otherwise, has focused upon the place of ethics in professional life. That is no less the case here. Reduced to the simplest terms possible, a profession is intended to be a combination of *technē* and *ethos*—technical knowledge and practice combined with responsible behavior in such practice—or, more simply, the joining of knowledge and character. The former is as crucial to the definition and enactment of a profession as the latter. All professions have an epistemic dimension. They involve the need for knowledge and ways of knowing. This is most obvious in the process of professional education and training, which generally involves not only years of preliminary preparation but also requires formal continuing education so that one's knowledge of the field remains up-to-date. Indeed, this specialized knowledge is what most clearly distinguishes and separates the professions from one another. The ethical dimensions of different professions often overlap significantly, but the professional expertise of each serves increasingly to distinguish it from any other practice as it makes the profession a valuable work upon which others will call. The patient wants the doctor who is treating her to have the most esoteric, extensive, and specialized medical knowledge possible. The client wants the lawyer to be as familiar as possible not only with the intricacies of the law but also with the myriad of cases that might be relevant to the matter at hand. Esoteric knowledge is the name of the game for the practice of a profession. But the fact that such knowledge is in the context of *technē*, the practice of a profession, means that it is not the pursuit of knowledge in itself that is the aim of the professional. *Using* that knowledge to achieve a professionally successful outcome is the ultimate aim (though this does not mean that every piece of learning in professional study has some practical function). A profession is a calling to *praxis*, not to *gnōsis*.

A further dimension of professional knowledge is the particular knowledge that is gained in the relationships developed with persons and groups in the practice of the profession: the knowledge a lawyer receives in working with a client, a doctor with a patient, a teacher with a student, a pastor with a church member. Here is where ethical dimensions come quickly into play, so that what one knows from a client and how one deals with it are explicitly concerns of professional standards of conduct, as, for example, in the legal profession. In various ways, the practice of a profession involves learning about another person or group in intimate ways that are not part of public knowledge. Such knowing is intrinsic to professions, yet full of dangers. Or, to state it in another way, knowing becomes a *moral* issue as matters of trust and confidence, judgment and vulnerability, join with the larger matter of how the knowledge that comes from expertise is to meet and deal with the knowledge that comes from the one being served in the professional activity. Professional success—and I assume various ways of defining success, but in this case it has to do primarily with meeting the need or completing the task that arises in the professional activity—depends significantly upon the manner in which these two kinds of knowing are brought together, so that the *technē* is not undone by the unethical and moral integrity is not made meaningless by incompetence.

Among the issues perennially facing the various professions, none seems more pertinent or obvious in our own time than the degree to which the practice of a profession assumes a large degree of *trust*—and the presence of trust depends upon *telling the truth*. Trust in a profession to do its work honestly, fairly, and competently is a necessary cultural presupposition, if the profession is to function properly and people are to be served effectively. When individual members of the profession violate that trust, lives are harmed. When the violation of trust is widespread in a profession, the common good is harmed and the culture exposed to danger as well as the malaise and despair that come from a widespread sense that things are not working. Thus, the violation of trust by professionals—by priests, in interactions with parishioners (whether in cases of sexual abuse or in cover-ups); by accountants and business executives, in failing to report the facts honestly; by investment analysts, in neglecting to report their institutional affiliations; by prosecutors and police, in hiding evidence; by journalists, in not reporting what is happening; or by lawyers, in not faithfully representing their clients' interests—can have wide cultural repercussions. In his book *Economics as Religion*, Robert Nelson remarks that "the individual pursuit of opportunistic actions such as corruption and dishonest behavior—creating a climate in which 'trust' does not exist in society—have the potential to undermine the efficient workings of markets."[1] At the time I am writing these remarks in the summer of 2002, American society, indeed global society, is watching that potential for harm become actualized in earthshaking ways. The combination of mendacity and the erosion of trust is devastating the national and global economies.

Professional misbehavior, therefore, is often not confined to "individual cases." It may become widespread to such a degree that the common good is undone. The other side of that coin is the need to recognize from the beginning of one's professional training and preparation that the pursuit of a profession is not simply an *individual* calling, whether this is understood in the quite specific sense of a divine calling or in the more general sense of carrying out one's work as a committed Christian. A profession is also a way of serving the *common good*. Proper interest in one's own advancement in the profession and in adequate compensation for one's successful practice of the required skills—goals that are transparent and always present—needs to be placed alongside a sense of responsibility that is wider than any particular case, any particular moment of practice, any particular client, student, parishioner, or the like. Each profession has its own mode of promoting the common good, to which each professional makes his or her contribution. Whatever that mode, authentic professional practice does not lose sight of the larger common good in the midst of its everyday pursuit of the many particulars of that practice.

Professionals also can let their professionalism be obscured in more subtle ways. Central to professional life is some guiding code of ethics and conduct. This may be reflected in simple formulations, such as the Hippocratic Oath or the Pulitzer masthead, or in more comprehensive and detailed rules of professional conduct. The importance of these formal articulations cannot be gainsaid. Some of the authors in this issue, however, remind us that a written code of ethics is not, in itself, a sufficient basis for professional excellence. Furthermore, regulatory codes can actually impede deeper, more comprehensive ethical reflection and moral argument, as Thomas Shaffer notes in his analysis of the split that has taken place between regulation and conscience in contemporary legal codes of professional responsibility. The danger to which he points is that an exclusive focus on formal professional regulation has led to the consequent elimination of any attention to individual conscience as a factor significant in forming an individual lawyer's professional conduct. Thus, strict adherence to "the rules" can set the lawyer's conscience loose relative to anything outside the explicit regulations.

Such an understanding of ethical regulation has been used, for example, in interpreting the Decalogue. It has been argued that here are some basic rules that leave lots of latitude and freedom. But to do what? How then is one to act within this larger latitude? Furthermore, such an approach, whether in regard to the Commandments or to rules of professional conduct, ignores the way that regulations point beyond themselves and give directions for the conscience. Such guiding codes are thus at one and the same time absolutely necessary as a first level in establishing the ethics of the profession, and also a serious if unrecognized danger when they serve to reduce moral inquiry and wrestling to a merely literal conformity "devoid of moral argument" (Shaffer).

The issue of the place of wealth and power in the life of the professional is unavoidable. The expertise that comes with the practice of a profession creates an inherent power—over the health of a patient, the grade of a student, the judicial fate of a client, the outcome of a lawsuit, or the well-being of a subject under journalistic scrutiny. It also can mean increased personal wealth as a reward for efficiently carrying out one's professional duties. The larger concern, however, is whether one's professional practice is tied to sources of wealth and power in a way that inhibits proper moral conduct on behalf of truth, justice, and the common good. Pamela Schaeffer points to the ways in which an institution like the newspaper can tie its reporting and publishing so tightly toward generating increased income that responsibility for reporting the truth about things that really matter and have to do with the common good becomes secondary. Thomas Shaffer's statistics on the availability of lawyers for the poor are astonishing, but they are hardly less so than those on the availability of ministers for small churches, teachers for inner-city schools, and medicine for the poor. The issues here are complicated. Many conditions can work to focus one's efforts on income-producing activity: pressure for billable hours, increases in malpractice insurance, and the need to support one's family, among others. Given these challenges, it is perhaps not surprising that professional activity on behalf of the weak and the poor in no way reaches a level in which any profession can take pride. At the same time, it is important to recognize the positive examples set by legal aid lawyers and those who make a place for pro bono work, by those teachers who commit their lives to educate the most difficult and most deprived of students, by medical practitioners (doctors and others) in public health and private practice who make room for patients who cannot enhance the professionals' personal wealth but are nevertheless proper recipients of the expertise these professionals were trained to give.

Thomas Shaffer raises the question of the moral value of honor, noting that the honor professionals most often seek—and this is not peculiar to lawyers—is the esteem and favor of others in the same profession. As such, honor may be a value, but it is one of dubious moral significance. If, however, that esteem and honor were cut away from power and wealth and directed toward the practitioners who set justice, compassion, and neighbor love as the primary criteria for how they practice their professions, then honor might properly be a significant indicator of moral integrity and the triumph of conscience over regulation. Anyone familiar with Harper Lee's *To Kill a Mockingbird* will remember the climax of the story, when Atticus Finch fails to gain an acquittal for the black man Tom Robinson, who has been falsely accused of raping a white woman. As Atticus leaves the courtroom, the Negroes at the trial, who have been segregated in the balcony, all rise, and one of them says to the young narrator of the book, "Miss Jean Louise, stand up. Your father's passin'." Justice has failed, but its pursuit has brought professional honor.

This illustration uncovers a dimension of professional life that is too often forgotten. Indeed, it may be required only on occasion and often unexpectedly. It is somewhat surprising to hear the theologian in this issue, Douglas Hall, lift up the need for *courage* in one's profession, but he is not alone in knowing the place of that virtue in professional life. A sense of what it may take to engage the demands of one's profession is implicit in all the essays. Telling the truth in journalism and from the pulpit is risky business. Balancing the conflicting pressures of commodification and medicalization in the medical profession takes courageous doctors. Resistance to the powers that be in the search for justice is often a lonely task. Thomas Shaffer asks if it is possible to be the sort of revolutionary who seems to be called for in both Jewish and Christian traditions and still be a professional. Maybe, but not without a good bit more courage than most of us professionals are wont to muster.

In reading the essays that follow, readers may want to take note of the way in which issues lifted up as significant for one profession (for example, commodification and medicalization in medicine and the separation of regulation and conscience in the law) have analogies in other professions as well. Medicalization seems peculiar to medicine: social ills as medicine. But commodification is a more general problem: teachers and theologians who take on assignments primarily in terms of how lucrative they are; lawyers whose primary criterion is the billable hour. So readers should listen for commonalities and observe how the discussion of issues in one profession carries over to others. Beware, however, of becoming reductionistic. If things were all the same, we would need only one essay for all the professions!

Underlying all of what is said here is a sense, once again, of the overlap of "profession" and the professions. The relation of a profession or of the professions to the profession of faith, to theology and the Christian life, runs through every piece in this issue. And that is where the primary commonality undergirding professional life as a whole comes to life. When Mark Schwehn suggests that teaching is first of all a *human* activity and only secondarily a profession, one begins to see that this is true also of healing and justice and truth telling in public. We would do well to ask first of all how our own profession reflects a basic human calling that is now lifted up so as to become a focus in our life for the common good, or, as several of these essays remind us, for the love of neighbor. In shared understandings of calling, covenant, justice, making whole, telling the truth, and the care of the needy, the professions are a place where the Christian life is lived out and where faith informs daily life in consequential ways. So, in our professional life as in all other aspects of our obedience to the calling that is ours in gratitude to a gracious God, prayer and righteous action, as Bonhoeffer put it, are both the context and the modes of our work as of our life.

January's Child

The holly and the mistletoe must be taken down and burnt
And the children got ready for school.
W. H. Auden, "For the Time Being" (1944)

Christmas is out of the way. So we can get back to business. Whatever the business is. The business of doing research, fighting wars, making money, governing polities, executing criminals, healing diseases, feeding the poor. You name it. The Christmas break is over. The baby is born in the manger. Let Mary and Joseph take over now. We must go on with things as if nothing new has happened. Or at least we *do* go on as if nothing has happened.

I am grateful for the Gospel accounts of the birth of the Christ child. I especially like the Lucan account. When I was a boy in elementary school, I used to go around to various classes and recite it at the request of some of the teachers. After all, that is what preachers' kids were supposed to do! I was not sophisticated enough to call it "the Lucan account," of course. It was the story of the birth of Jesus, and Luke 2 was the narrative we all knew, to which we returned year by year. It is indeed the richest report, the first two chapters of Luke comprising some 130 verses telling of the appearances of the angel to Zechariah and Mary and their resultant songs of praise, the birth of Jesus and the announcement to the angels, the responses of Simeon and Anna, and even the tale of Jesus in the temple. Luke's report dominates the Christmas scene. It is a marvelous story of good news to all the world.

Matthew is another matter. The betrothal of Mary and Joseph, the announcement to Joseph, and the birth of Jesus—it all takes place in eight verses. Then we are on to the next chapter, which is where the trouble starts.

I grew up with Luke; why am I constantly drawn to Matthew 2 now? The story of the wise men was, of course, also a part of my childhood. But familiarity and pleasant associations do not draw me to this story. I expect the shifting focus is the difference between being a child and being an adult.

It may also be the difference between Christmas and Epiphany, between the Christmas break and getting back to business in January. January is where we live, and that is when the trouble begins—immediately after Jesus' birth. Matthew reports a visit of some "wise men" to Jerusalem, asking: "Where is he who has been born king of the Jews?" Luke tells us how the news of the birth of this child brings wonderful words of praise and thanks from Simeon and Anna. Matthew tells us that the first response to the news of this child was anything but joy: "When Herod the king heard this, he was troubled, and all Jerusalem with him." Some translations say Herod was frightened. Either translation is on target. The political ruler of the land and the populace in general were troubled, frightened, scared, greatly disturbed.

Two groups of folks respond to the news of the Christ child's birth in Matthew's story. The magi, learned wise men, whom later tradition thought to be kings, came from far away, without any previous connection with this child, his family, or his people. They knew nothing of any prophecies of one who would come from the tribe of Judah to be God's redeeming and ruling presence in the world. Their reason for being there is simply, "We have seen his star in the East and have come to worship him." It is quite an anomaly, this picture of kings and wise men with priceless gifts, bowing in true worship before a baby born in an out-of-the-way place, of which they have never before known. Perhaps we should take the NRSV's cue and say "pay homage" rather than "worship." But I doubt it. It is not, finally, only the family or poor shepherds who come in awe and wonder. The birth of this child is for the sake of the world, and the homage of the wise men is a foretaste of the bowing of every knee in heaven and on earth and under the earth before the glory of God in Jesus Christ. There are no presidents and kings whose sphere of rule transcends or outruns the just and righteous and peaceful dominion that this baby stamped upon our world so loved by God and so gone awry. There are no intellectuals, no professors, no theologians or divines, whose wisdom frees them from the need of this child's loving and redeeming rule. Here in Matthew's story we see the academy in a strange and unexpected place: gathered around the cradle of a baby. The wisdom of the earth bows down before a little child because in this one the wisdom of God is truly manifest.

But the announcement of this child's birth evokes another response. It is that of King Herod, who claims to want to join the parade of adoring kings but seeks instead to destroy the child and in so doing murders all the innocent babies of the region of Bethlehem. We may and do condemn him, and we are disturbed by the ambiguities of life that this child thrusts upon us. Was Jesus worth one dead baby in Bethlehem? The answer is surely no. But such a question assumes that the providence and purpose of God is a mechanical one that simply has to be plugged in and everything works out smoothly, or, if there is danger, one simply reprograms the plan to make it all work out right—to get rid of snipers and terrorists and murdering rulers. But that is not incarnation. That is not the world God made. That does not embody the freedom we have been given to be God's creatures, responding to God's will, or restricting it, or ignoring it. All human lives are ambiguous and subject to the contingencies of history. If that is so, then surely in this one who demonstrates for us what it is to be human, the ambiguities and contingencies are very present.

Lest we think that is not the case, we learn from this story that before this child of God, this child who is God, can speak or think or love, or do nearly anything else, he has disturbed the universe and led to the slaughter of the many for the sake of the one. That is the disturbing dark side of Christmas. Or is it that January uncovers the immediate conflict between the rule of this child and the rulers of this earth, the abrasive and unending friction between every human rule and the claim of God in Jesus Christ against all other claims to rule. The birth of this child was not all sweetness and light. There is no redemptive word in Herod's slaughter of the innocents and the inconsolable weeping of all the mothers of Bethlehem. It would not even help very much if we could demonstrate conclusively that no such massacre happened. We have been told, the Bible tells us, that the presence of this beautiful babe, this sweet Jesus, can evoke the brutal murder of many as sweet as he. We cannot walk around that. All we can do is live with it and think it through as far as we can go.

To that end, here are some further thoughts. Herod was indeed perceptive in seeing the threat in that innocent birth. He sensed and feared the divine upheaval of the human systems of power that was set loose in that seemingly peaceful and ordinary event in Bethlehem. He discerned the threat to every human throne and every seat of government that this child brought into the world. How Herod perceived that so well we are not told, but his prescience is to be acknowledged. Maybe he remembered that exultant song of thanksgiving Hannah sang after the birth of Samuel, giving praise to God as one who brings low and also exalts, who raises up the poor from the dust, lifts the needy from the ash heap, to make them sit with princes and inherit a seat of honor. In any event, somehow Herod got wind of the fact that something was happening here that made all the powers of this world less powerful than they had been, or at least that they and everyone else thought they were. If that is the case, then nobody's throne, not even Herod's, was very secure anymore.

From his birth, Jesus troubles the political scene. His rule threatens the political leaders and the people who do not want the status quo of political stability challenged. That is, of course, confirmed at his trial and execution, but it is already signaled at his birth. We have a tendency to read Jesus non-politically and take our scriptural clues about politics from the Old Testament. But from the beginning to the end of Jesus' story, his coming into this world is seen as a threat to the powers that be. His advent evoked a holocaust, the murder of innocent Jews. His death was a political kangaroo trial and execution. And the troubling did not stop there. Later in Acts, we hear the word that those who follow this Christ have troubled the authorities and the people again by their preaching: "These men who have turned the world upside down have come here also . . . and they are all acting against the decrees of Caesar, saying there is another king, Jesus. And the people and the city authorities were troubled when they heard this" (Acts 17:6–8).

One set of kings bows down in worship; the other king tries to kill the Christ child. Those are the options in hearing the news of this "king." The text, of course, leaves out another option: Just ignore him. Have we so separated faith and politics that the kings and presidents of this world, the Jerusalems and Thessalonicas, the Washingtons and Moscows and Berlins do not have to worry any longer about this king and his way? Is it likely now that anyone will say of those who follow the way of this king: "They have turned the world upside down"? Or are we forever locked in the January mode of business as usual and the murder of the innocents—which often hides under the guise of just war? As Auden continues in "For the Time Being":

> The Christmas feast is already a fading memory,
> And already the mind begins to be vaguely aware
> Of an unpleasant whiff of apprehension at the thought
> Of Lent and Good Friday which cannot, after all, now
> Be very far off.

The story of Epiphany, of God's manifestation in the birth of a child who evokes murder as well as worship, lets us know early on that God's redemptive work in Jesus Christ is not simple or easy. Behind the glory and joy and wonder of Christmas is a terrible reality in the human psyche that erupts in murder, greed, brutality, and the many other deeds of inhumanity that bespatter our common existence. This story lets us know why though we come to the manger infrequently, we come to the table often. The table and the manger are not far apart theologically—or in our lives. The threat to the seats of government that Herod saw so keenly and fought so outrageously finally did in this innocent babe. There are only two times that Jesus is called king of the Jews: when wise men come to worship him at his birth and when the people and the authorities execute him.

There are babies dying still and mothers who weep for eternity. What we remember at the table is that the one whose birth set forth a rage of murder against many others is also the one who for the sake of many others took the murderous rage that seems to lie in all of us. We have no answer to the terrible question why babies are killed and the powerful destroy the weak and the innocent. The darkness cannot overcome this light that has come into our world. But it will surely try. What we do know is that all this suffering is known to the mother and father of us all, and the only crown that can ever claim our full allegiance is made of thorns.

23

Is There a Place for the Ten Commandments?

Before you answer that question, remind yourself of the recent action of the Alabama Supreme Court to remove the Ten Commandments from their place in the rotunda of the Alabama Supreme Court building and of the many foiled efforts on the part of others besides Alabama Chief Justice Roy Moore to get the Commandments displayed in public places. This failure to gain legal approval for public display of the Commandments comes despite polls indicating that perhaps as many as three-fourths of the American population would support their display in our nation's schools. The Commandments have become a powerful symbol, a part of our culture wars. As is often the case, wars produce extreme options. In this instance, the Commandments are to be either everywhere or nowhere. Put them in every classroom or do not allow them in any public place at all—these are the choices that seem to be before us.

The controversy over the Commandments is, in many ways, rather astonishing. They are constantly in the news, frequently the subject of discussion and controversy, provoking vehement comments and arguments. Jesus' teachings are surely as important to Christians as the Commandments, but they certainly seem less controversial, if contemporary culture and media comment are any indication. It seems as if the war is not so much about the Commandments per se, however, as it is about their proper *place*. Where do the Commandments belong? That question, and the way it impacts our culture, reminds us of the significance of public space and what we do with it. There is not a huge debate going on about the value of the Commandments in themselves and whether they apply or should apply to our lives, but there certainly is a vigorous struggle about what we can and should do with them and, more specifically, where we should put them and what their spatial location implies.

The arguments about public display of the Commandments seem to move between appeal to the separation of church and state and the tradition of nonestablishment of religion in the United States, on one hand, and insistence on public affirmation of our nation's religious roots and moral values, on the other. I do not intend to resolve the issue of where one may and should place the Commandments, but I suggest that the question of their place takes us into some important matters worthy of our reflection.

It may be helpful to recognize that there are some unresolvable tensions inherent in the presence and appropriation of the Commandments in human society. The tension between the *universality* and the *particularity* of the Commandments is one example. There is a long history in the Christian tradition of viewing the Commandments as universal natural law. Even if one rejects that view—and it is one with deep roots, not confined to one branch of the Christian community—it is hard to avoid recognizing that the kinds of directions provided in the Commandments are widely present in a variety of societies and cultural traditions throughout space and time. They are not restricted to Christianity and Judaism alone. The biblical narrative itself recognizes the wider validity and wisdom of these laws and of obeying them beyond the confines of Israel (Deut. 4:4–8). Over against this view of the Commandments as a universal moral framework is the fact that they come from a particular story, are rooted in the worship of the God who acts in that story, and are given to the people of Israel at Sinai to order their life under the God who freed them from slavery. The Commandments depend from the start on a particular story and communal memory of that story as the ground for obedience. They address the totality of life with the Lord of Israel, not just getting along with one's neighbor. So the issue before us is this: Can both the universality and the particularity of the Commandments be maintained so that each has its proper bite on our appropriation and display of them? In other words, can the Commandments have their place in our culture without our assuming either too much about their proper realm of authority or too little?

A second unresolvable tension in the way the Commandments are presented and function in the community that lives under their claim is the tension between *simplicity* and *complexity*. The Commandments come to us in relatively simple form. That simplicity is evident immediately in the way our culture has adopted the term "ten commandments" as shorthand for all sorts of simple rules in every sphere of life. A quick perusal of the nearest bookstore or a browse of the Internet will come up with "The Ten Commandments of the Internet," "The Ten Commandments of Origami," "Ten Commandments for Making Money," "Ten Commandments of Financial Happiness," and so on. The number ten—often regarded as representing the number of fingers on our hands and so keeping things to a manageable limit—combined with the brevity of most of the commandments underscores this simplicity. One may assume that the simple character of the Commandments is, in part, to make them easy to hold on to as well as to hold to. That simplicity is crucial for our appropriation of them. At the same time, however, from the beginning of the story as we have it in Scripture, it is clear that these "simple" rules have to be worked out in the complexity of our lives. Thus, statutes and stories, proverbs and prophecies inform us how these simple commandments are to have their play and give us direction. The presentation of the Commandments in Exodus 20 and Deuteronomy 5 is followed in both cases by more detailed statutes and ordinances. These further "laws" open up what the commandments are about in various ways and situations and over changing times and circumstances. The question before us then is this: Can we learn to live with the Ten Commandments as a charter for a rich, *complex* theological and moral worldview and also as a *simple*, often abbreviated guide for basic human living? Can we appropriate them in their simplicity, without falling into trivialization and reductionism, and in their complexity, without falling into casuistry?

A further unresolvable tension is found in the fact that the Commandments belong to both the *church and synagogue* and to the *culture*. They are a sacred text from the Scriptures of Judaism and Christianity. In the nurture of children, they are taught in both religious traditions. They are undeniably a religious text belonging to religious traditions. At the same time, however, they have come to have influence beyond the more limited scope of religious life, precisely because they are meant, in some sense, to encompass all of life. From the start, elaboration of the Commandments in Torah dealt with how they affect those who do not necessarily belong to the religious tradition—the resident alien and the foreigner—because these others are also neighbors. The good neighborhood that is good in part because it is governed by these directives is also a culture. Apart from invoking a theocracy, the polities that include these Commandments are cultures that are not to be equated with the religious communities who share the story and the text as a part of their tradition. So the question here is this: Can we learn to live with the Ten Commandments as a revelatory center of Jewish and Christian faith that embodies the heart of divine instruction for our lives as much as any text we know, while also acknowledging their role as a broader cultural icon with very wide appeal—and can we do this in such a way that the history, context, and actual meaning of the Commandments do not become lost, distorted, or misappropriated precisely because they are so widely held?

A second aspect to consider in thinking about the place of the Commandments in our culture is the recognition that there are, within the culture, impulses toward their display but also reasons to resist their display. How we regard these contradictory forces will vary from individual to individual and group to group, but we can think better about the proper place of the Commandments by becoming more aware of them.

The impulse to display the Commandments publicly and broadly arises out of several concerns. One is the widespread sense of moral decline in our society. Whether formal studies exist to substantiate that perception, there is surely enough general apprehension of moral decay within the culture that one cannot simply dismiss it for lack of available historical or statistical evidence. Out of that fear of moral decline, but also out of wider concerns within the family, the neighborhood, and the community of faith comes a desire to instruct the next generation in the moral life and a feeling that whatever may help us do that is worth trying. Surely few people believe that simply posting the Commandments in public will bring about increased moral rectitude, but many believe that constant reminders—like the reminders of parents to their children—may have some impact, however modest, for the common good. Underneath this lies a general consensus that all of us share at least some basic guidelines for the moral life and that a number of these are found in the Ten Commandments. They function, to some degree, as what David Tracy has called a "classic." Their publication, therefore, has a cultural appropriateness apart from any specific religious commitment.

Over against this impulse to display the Commandments are some serious considerations that arouse appropriate resistance to doing so. The constitutional and general public understanding of the separation of church and state, which might not be an inhibiting factor in another culture, looms large in ours. Other effects of public display, however, should be considered quite apart from legal and constitutional questions, to which the matter largely has been relegated. The Commandments on general display become an icon but, in this case, a potentially meaningless and impotent one that appears simply anachronistic—a relic from a forgotten past (particularly when it is decorated, written in King James English, and so on). Public display can work against its intended moral purpose. This countereffect is accentuated by the meaningless and trivial ways in which our culture often uses "the ten commandments," whether as a description for any simple set of rules, the subject of cartoons and jokes, or as support for a particular ideology or governmental direction. (Go to Victory Store on the web and you will find, in the middle of bumper stickers, ties, and tee shirts bearing such slogans as "First Iraq, Then Chirac" and "Liberate Iraq," the same merchandise for sale with "Support the Ten Commandments.") These cultural uses will happen whether the Commandments are displayed or not, but their public display tends to feed such trivialization and ideological misappropriation. Further, public display assumes the self-evident character of the Commandments. As I have noted, however, this assumption stands in tension with the fact that the Commandments always need to be interpreted, elaborated, and spelled out. Their simplicity can be distorted into a reductionistic ethic when the need for interpretive specification is ignored. A significant part of the reductionism found in the culture's iconic use of the Commandments lies in its focus on the second table, the so-called ethical table, to the neglect of the first table of the Commandments. While many may support public display of the Commandments as a reminder of our belief in God (the First Commandment), this support generally neglects the Prologue, which is the sole ground for obedience to the First Commandment. Nor is there any serious cultural interest in the question of images or the sanctity of the name of God (the Second Commandment), except in certain oath-taking contexts. Finally, public display of the Commandments obviously flies in the face of our country's religious pluralism, which includes the religious minorities who do not claim any religious connection to the Commandments per se.

There are some things we can do within the community of faith about the Commandments, things that do not resolve all the tensions described but that nonetheless may enhance their "place" in our life. For instance, we can:

(1) Flesh out our concern about the misuse of the Commandments by instructing and directing ourselves as much about the first table of the Commandments as about the second. The Commandments are fundamentally theological—from God and about God.

(2) Think about and obey the Commandments in awareness that they are simple rooms with a great deal of moral space for living under their direction. Both their simplicity and their spaciousness are features that should affect how people live by them.

(3) Affirm the symbolic power of the Commandments and learn how to "post" them afresh. We may, in fact, *need* to post the Commandments and erect stone monuments with the Commandments inscribed on them in order to have them visible and continuously before us. The best place for doing that, however, is where Christians and Jews receive and learn these directives in the broader context of a life of faith: in the sacred spaces of our churches and synagogues, where we and our children learn how to serve the Lord our God and how the Commandments can help us with critical moral and theological issues. The display of the Commandments in the sanctuary is a very old tradition. While the early Puritan churches of this country were more austere, the Anglican churches of the colonial period customarily had—according to the canons of 1604—"the Ten Commandments . . . set up on the East end of every Church and Chapel, where the people may best see and read the same." The

degree of controversy over the Commandments' public presence in our culture today may be in direct, if inverse, proportion to their absence from the religious context that is their proper home.

(4) Explicate the Commandments as the heart of catechetical instruction, as was the Christian tradition from early on. We should ask ourselves if we are giving more energy to guarding the Commandments than to teaching them, to worrying about whether they are "out there" than making sure they are "in here."

24

The Accidental Profession

While professions are usually entered intentionally, that is not always the case. This writer, whose profession is teaching, has discovered—in retrospect—that long ago he fell into another profession quite by accident. I am talking about editing. As I conclude twenty years editing this journal, I am highly aware of how editing has become a large part of my professional life. The work of teaching, research, and writing has taken a turn that many others have experienced as well: engagement in teaching and theology through recruitment and direction of the work of other persons in the process of editing books and journals. This particular moment prompts some self-reflection on what I have been about.

There are certain implicit but important assumptions underlying the enterprise of editing. In this case, they belong to the larger work of teaching, scholarship, and interpretation, but they have their particular nuance from the perspective of editing. Those assumptions include:

- *Reading and thinking matter for culture and society broadly and for faith and life more specifically.* The particular play on this assumption in regard to editing is the possibility of exercising a wider influence on what is read and what matters as one is able to bring more voices and topics to the table.

- *There are things to be communicated to a large and diverse audience.* Particularly in editing a journal, one can develop different angles of approach that reach out and engage varied readers over space and time, who may then become subscribers, thus making possible an extended influence upon their thinking.

- *There is a thoughtful and intelligent audience wanting and needing food for thought.* The task of editing is to find both the audience and the food and to present the latter to the former in such a way that partaking is pleasurable, stimulating, and rewarding.

- *All good writing aims to influence thought and action, but it is possible to accomplish that goal in an indirect way through editing.* The impact is more nebulous and subtle; it may also be more extensive and enduring. All scholarship is ephemeral in a very basic way. Editing a theological journal heightens one's awareness of that, as each issue is identified by date—and so is immediately dated. The converse of that is the opportunity with each issue to be immediate, contemporary, in tune with what is going on and needs to be said. Figuring that out sufficiently ahead of time so that the readers perceptions are in line with editorial intent is one of the daunting tasks of editing.
- *Respect for writers joins with the desire to help authors find an audience and present what they have to say as clearly, effectively, and winsomely as possible.*
- *Rhetoric is the tool and persuasion the goal of an editor's work.*

There are two large facets to all editorial work. One is the process of *shaping direction.* The large responsibility—and opportunity—of editing is to take up an idea or ideas and plan the ways in which those ideas will come to expression, locating and enlisting authors who can think and write in fresh, significant, and interesting ways about the matter under discussion. It involves giving character and identity, whether the edited work is a journal, a collection of essays, or a series of books. The knowledge required is less a specialized or technical knowledge relative to editing. It is knowledge of the field of study in which the planning and shaping take place. Often that is quite specific, but it may be quite broad, particularly with a theological journal. That is why editors have editorial boards and advisors. The large requirement for this facet of editing has to do with articulating an idea, direction, theme, or broader vision in a way that communicates to and draws in authors and is then conveyed to the reader through what those writers have to say.

The character and identity of the edited work are achieved, therefore, in different ways. That happens largely by the editor's choice of materials to be published. The choice, of course, may depend upon and be influenced by what is submitted, particularly in the case of journals. Even here, however, what may seem a fairly passive form of editing can be much more creative and active. An editor can develop contacts and lines of communication that open up the possibility of submissions by the best writers, on topics of recognized interest to the journal, or may discover unpublished jewels through contacts, conversation, and correspondence. There is the further distinction between a refereed journal and one whose content is solely determined by the editors, whether or not the essays are solicited. In the case of nonrefereed journals, the risk is greater, but so are the editing opportunities. The editor's voice may be silent, but it is deeply present in the outcome.

The same is even more the case when editing involves invitation and assignment of essays or books. The choice of writers, the formulation of the subjects or topics, the articulation of the aim and intention of the collection or the issue—these are all large and often time-consuming tasks, but they are how the editor leads and guides the discussion. In this way, there is a significant *authorial* dimension to the editing process. Here the editor's voice may be more vocal in a variety of ways, such as editorials, prefaces, and introductions, where the editor seeks to say what is going on in the particular book or issue before the reader, a process that involves both describing what is there and giving it a particular framework or bent that leads the reader into looking at what follows for certain things or with a certain frame of mind.

This last point already takes us into the other large facet of editing: *presenting the material.* Some of this work is quite mundane but no less important, specifically the actual editing and copyediting of essays and books written by someone else. Writing intended for a public, whatever that public is, should be *good* writing. The canons for that are debatable, but they exist in one form or another, whether in *The Chicago Manual of Style* or in those practices that have proven effective over time in producing clear and articulate communication, in conjoining clarity of expression with persuasive rhetoric, drawing in the reader and leading to the hoped-for goal: the reader's genuine appropriation of the author's interpretation and claims.

The presentation of the material, however, involves other dimensions that may not be noticed particularly by the reader but are designed in some fashion to "trap" him or her, that is, to lead and direct the reader's attention in certain ways. So it is that the table of contents of any journal or any collection of essays is a way of saying immediately what lies ahead and how one should go about getting into the material. There may be times when an author suggests the reader go about getting into the book from some other angle than its beginning or opening chapter, but that is rare enough to seem strange when one encounters it. The presumption is that the beginning is where the reader should begin, that the arrangement of the material makes a certain kind of sense and serves to guide the reader in helpful ways to get at the subject matter of the whole. So the ordering of the contents suggests, sometimes overtly and obviously and at other times more implicitly, that there is a way of understanding what you, the reader, are about to take up. The more the communication that comes from the order and arrangement of the material is implicit, the more the editor may need to rely upon some form of careful introduction to lift up major emphases, interrelationships, and the possibility of a coherence that is not self-evident. Indeed, such introductory efforts may well show the authors of the journal or collection of essays an interpretation of what they have written in a larger context that was not self-evident in their isolated creation of the single essay. Even when the product is the result of a highly planned and collaborative engagement among the authors, the editor's ability to say what has finally come forth often may lead to an "Oh, I see" on the part of authors who now comprehend where they fit in the whole. The reader is given a pathway through the material that makes sense and guides him or her along what would be obscure or difficult without the editor's help.

All professions by definition involve ethical dimensions. Some—medicine, law, and journalism, for example—even have formal codes of ethics. Does the work of editing involve any ethical issues, any matters that have to do with doing good, maintaining trust, and being responsible, moral issues intrinsic to the editorial undertaking? I think it does. These issues have to do both with the writers whose work one edits and the audience for whom one edits it. In the former case, an obvious ethical issue is preserving an author's voice. I well remember one author of a book for which I had overall editorial responsibility lamenting to me that the editorial work on his book had stolen his voice. The complaint was a legitimate one, despite the fact that the editor had done a fine job of improving the manuscript stylistically and otherwise. Letting the writer say what she wants to say and how she wants to say it while also helping her say it as well as possible is one of those editorial responsibilities that may create tension and involve compromise. One of the reasons editors should be writers is to know what it is like from the other side, to experience for oneself the effects of the editing process and how it feels to be rejected, accepted, or heavily edited.

With regard to the editor's ethical responsibility to readers, building and keeping trust is to the fore. Especially for the editors of a journal, the moral issue is upfront, in that they take money in trust from readers who do not yet know what they will receive for their cash. The editor's distance from readers may serve to hide the sense of accountability, but it does not diminish it.

Editing is a highly *mediatorial* activity, bringing author and reader together, acting in such a way that the author's integrity and voice are preserved and heard and that the reader is able to receive, grasp, learn from, and respond to what is written. The balance is not always easy to maintain. One may modulate the author's voice so much in behalf of the reader that it is no longer clearly the words and communication of the writer. Or one may preserve the voice carefully but with the result that it is unattractive and unappealing to the reader. A fundamental responsibility of all editing is to find the proper balance between clarity and rhetoric and between simplicity and nuance. The latter is especially fraught with pitfalls as authors seek to express their thoughts in rich, complex ways, heaping up clauses and creating modes of subordination, while editors work to simplify and shorten, cutting up sentences so that readers are not overwhelmed and perplexed, struggling to understand what authors are saying. Every time I find myself dividing overly long sentences in another person's writing and rephrasing them I am reminded how often I have found my own ideas lose their shaded meaning or nuance by an editor's abbreviation, simplification, and shortening of my sentences. Still, I do not relinquish the editor's pen, for I know that whatever I write can be said better than I do it. Chances are that is the case with most of those authors whose work I have the pleasure and privilege of editing.

Perhaps it is this last pleasant reflection that evokes the realization that the work of editing has become for me a vocation. If I have inadvertently fallen into a profession for which I—and I expect this is true of most others—was not trained, in the course of practicing it I have discovered a part of my vocation, a quite particular aspect of teaching and writing that is a marvelous opportunity to bring about a community of teaching and learning through the medium of books and journals. The occasional note or comment from a writer or reader lets an editor know that sometimes it all comes together and the theological task is carried forward. That is one of the two great joys of editing. The other is the growing number of persons whom I have met as writers and now count as friends, an indispensable requirement for good scholarship. But that's the subject of another editorial!

25

In Praise and Thanksgiving

One of the most familiar and important of all the theological questions is the one that comes first in the Westminster Shorter Catechism. And Presbyterians are not the only ones who know how to answer it by heart. What is our chief end, our fundamental purpose as human beings? the first question asks. To glorify and to enjoy God forever, comes the answer. Our life is fundamentally lived in praise of God and in thanksgiving. Doxology is our reason for being—and joy is the final outcome of God's way with us.

Praise and doxology do not arise *de novo*. The countless hymns of praise, from the song of Miriam and Moses at the exodus to the hallelujah chorus at the end of the book of Revelation, arise out of the structure of faith in the dialogue with God. The story of the deliverance of Hebrew slaves and the word of the cross both tell us that cries of human suffering, pain, and need are heard and responded to by a gracious God. But the dialogue does not end there. The anticipation of God's help and deliverance, or the actual experience of it, brings forth a human response as well. Wherever the hand of God is discerned in the accomplishment of some palpable grace—whether a recovery from sickness, the birth of a child, the restoration of a broken relationship, or the realization of peace in the midst of hostility—human beings respond. They respond in a mode of speech: the hymn of praise and thanksgiving. And they respond in a mood of spirit: joy.

I

The form of the hymn praise is as simple as its logic. It begins in a call to praise, or a declaration of praise. This is then grounded in a reason for praise, an indi-

114

cation of what God has done that evokes such a response. The call and reasons may move back and forth, be long or short, but the form and logic remain the same: Something has happened, and the only way to deal with that is in praise and thanksgiving.

> I will extol you, my God and King,
>   and bless your name for ever and ever.
> ....
> The LORD is gracious and merciful,
>   slow to anger and abounding in steadfast love.
> The LORD is good to all.
> ....
> All your works shall give thanks to you, O LORD.
> ....
> The LORD upholds all who are falling,
>   and raises up all who are bowed down.
> The eyes of all look to you,
>   and you give them their food in due season.
>   —Ps. 145:1, 8, 9a, 10a, 14–15

> O sing to the LORD a new song,
>   for he has done marvelous things.
>   —Ps. 98:1

The logic of faith is a matter of the heart as much as of the mind, of one's demeanor as well as of one's thought. Too often, faith seems dour. But where that is the case, good news has not made its way through. "Do not be afraid. I am with you. I will help you." Such words pervade the Bible, which is full of stories of people who have heard and trusted such news, and thereby have turned from fear and sadness and anxiety to joy and exultation.

Hannah utters her lament for her barrenness and weeps bitterly—until she hears the words of Eli: "Go in peace; the God of Israel grant the petition you have made to him." "Then," the narrator reports, "the woman went to her quarters, ate and drank with her husband, and her countenance was sad no longer" (1 Sam. 1:17, 18b). There is no child as yet; she is not even pregnant. But her whole being is changed, and the transformation issues forth in a song of praise:

> My heart exults in the LORD;
>   my strength is exalted in my God.
>   —1 Sam. 2:1

In Luke 2, the shepherds, the poor of the earth, turn from fear to praise and glorify God because of the good news of a savior—even as they walk back to their hard life in the cold fields outside of Bethlehem.

The whole structure of Exodus 1–15, chapters of Scripture that tell of the salvation event par excellence in the Old Testament, is a movement from *lament* through *salvation* to *praise*. The cry of afflicted Israel goes up to the Lord, who comes to deliver Israel from Egyptian slavery. Then, it is reported, when the victory is won and Israel has seen the great work which the Lord has done, they *trusted* the Lord. And they sang this song:

> I will sing to the LORD, for he has triumphed gloriously;
>   horse and rider he has thrown into the sea.
> The LORD is my strength and my might,
>   and he has become my salvation.
> —Exod. 15:1

Miriam and all the women sing and dance and play timbrels as she sings a similar hymn of praise (Exod. 15:21). In the words of the psalmist:

> You have turned my mourning into dancing;
>   you have taken off my sackcloth
>   and clothed me with joy.
> —Ps. 30:11

Isaiah 40–55 is filled with calls to praise addressed to exiles whose laments by the waters of Babylon were turned into exultant hymns of joy—even while they still sat by those same waters.

II

Psalm 126 is a particularly good example of this genre and pattern. Here we see a response of faith that remembers the delivering help of God in the past and hears God's word of assurance afresh in the midst of a world that, personally and communally, has fallen apart.

> When the Lord restores the fortunes of Zion—
>   we are like dreamers—
> Then will our mouth be full of laughter,
>   and our tongue with joy;
> Then they will say among the nations:
>   "The Lord has done great things with these people!"
> The Lord *has* done great things with us;
>   we are those who rejoice.
> Restore, O Lord, our fortunes
>   like the wadis of the Negeb.
> Those who sow in tears
>   shall reap with shouts of joy.

The one who goes forth in weeping,
    bearing the seed,
Shall return with shouts of joy,
    carrying the sheaves. (Author's translation)

The historical setting out of which this psalm was composed is uncertain. It may well have been the experience of the exile. If it was not that, it nonetheless clearly speaks out of and to a similar situation in which the people are in distress and affliction and Jerusalem has been done in. The psalm has two parts. The first three verses anticipate the restoration of Zion as if one were dreaming. The final three verses pray for that restoration.

The key to understanding the psalm is the recognition that dreams were often regarded as a God-given means of revealing the future and God's plans for that future. What the Lord is doing is thereby known in anticipation. Zion will be restored. We anticipate, they say, the Lord's restoring Zion, knowing now already that then our mouths shall be full of laughter. The present situation appears through that anticipation in a completely different light. It is like the oracle of salvation. The word of assurance has been heard.

The theme and spirit of the song are carried by a double repetition in the song: the action of God (restoring the fortunes of Zion and doing great things) and the community's reaction (laughter and joy). The hope of the psalm, expressed in confident anticipation and equally confident prayer, is that the Lord will restore God's people and God's place. Both sections of the psalm start in hope and prayer for God's transformation of their misfortune, for God's rejuvenation and restoration to life of God's people, whose fate is hard and sad. This is a song sung by a defeated people, a people who have experienced national exile and have sunk into profound depression. But the song that arises out of the vision of the action of God has an utterly different tone to it. We can see it in the repetition of the words of laughter and joy. This song of a defeated, downcast community of faith, whose present experience is the sowing of tears, is literally filled with laughter and joy. A song of joy is what I would entitle the psalm, for the note of laughter and jubilation runs from beginning to end. It is a testimony to faith and to the transforming power of the vision of God's redemptive future. The redeeming act of God calls forth a joy in anticipation, and even greater rejoicing in its actualization.

It calls forth another response as well, one that is an important dimension of the act of doxology. It calls forth confession. The nations, who are often the source of Israel's affliction, are here heard praising the Lord and confessing the greatness of the God of Israel. This psalm makes explicit a feature that is common in the psalms of praise, and it is a marvelous indication of the transforming power of God's saving word and deed. Surprisingly, Israel's experience with God can evoke the wonder, praise, and confession *of others*. Such a notion shatters our limited vision, our tendency to conceive the possibilities of God's way with us too narrowly. Well and good, we may say, for us to praise God for those ways we have experienced God's grace. But is it not somewhat arrogant to suggest that communities beyond our own may find a witness to God's goodness in *our* being led and cared for? For Israel, however, this is not arrogance. Israel knows what a narrow vision forgets: that good news always creates a ripple of joy beyond the immediate circle of those to whom it is directed. Thus, one must ponder the larger marvel that Israel's confession is an echo of the *prior* confession of the nations about the great things God has done for Israel.

I have suggested elsewhere that this is why the praise of God is the most prominent and extended formulation of the *universal* and *conversionary* dimension of the theology of the Old Testament. What blossoms and flourishes in the New Testament proclamation of the gospel is anticipated in the Old Testament's proclamation of the goodness and steadfast love of God. Similarly, the New Testament impulse to transcend ethnic and national boundaries in calling all persons to discipleship to Jesus is anticipated in the Old Testament call to a worship that is appropriate even on the part of those who themselves may not have known the powerful control of their lives by the God of Israel but who hear intimations of it in Israel's praises.[1]

III

A similar pattern of doxological response appears in the twenty-second psalm. The psalmist, who has cried out in great distress, receives the Lord's answer in the midst of the suffering and affliction, and then breaks forth into one of the most extravagant songs of praise and thanksgiving in Scripture (Ps. 22:22–31).

As the cry of the mothers and fathers of old was heard, so God has heard and answered the cry of the present sufferer. God has not abandoned the psalmist in silence. The affirmation of the psalmist that God is present and involved is just as strong as the cries of despair. One cannot take the former any more seriously than the latter. Here is one who genuinely experiences God's transforming and delivering power. It is as real as the sense of hopelessness and death.

This creates an unending litany of testimony, an ever widening circle of praise. At the center of that circle is the one who prayed in agony and now testifies and praises in trust and joy. That testimony and praise takes place before the whole congregation, who are also called to praise because of what God has done for this suffering one. But such doxology is not confined to the immediate congregation. It reaches out to the ends of the earth. The proclamation and praise of the God who delivers in this fashion encompasses even the dead and draws in generations yet unborn. Thus, a wave of praise rolls out from God's deliverance of this one person. The doxology of the lamenting petitioner is public praise, which can and should elicit an astonishingly wide echo of praise. The utterly desolate and isolated individual, a worm, nothing, mocked by everybody, has moved to the center of a universal circle of the praise and worship of God.

Such language—the deliverance of one individual evoking the praise of all the earth—seems surely to belong to the hyperbole of poetic imagery. Let me suggest, however, that once this psalm has become the interpretive clue to the meaning of the death and resurrection of Jesus, as it seems to me the New Testament so declares, there is then a profound consonance between the words of this psalm and the outcome of God's answer to the one who cries to God from the cross in utter despair. On at least one occasion, the response of God to human pain evoked an unending wave of praise that still sounds forth.

So Paul, in what one may hear as a commentary on this psalm, writes:

> "And being found in human form,
>   he humbled himself
>   and became obedient to the point of death—
>   even death on a cross.
> Therefore God also highly exalted him
>   and gave him the name
>   that is above every name, so that at the name of Jesus
>   every knee should bend,
>   in heaven and on earth and under the earth,
>   and every tongue should confess
>   that Jesus Christ is Lord,
>   to the glory of God the Father.
>   —Phil. 2:8–11

Such words come from a letter, written while the apostle himself was in prison, that is one of the primary expressions of the praise and joy in the New Testament. If it is possible for a letter written to friends to be thoroughly doxological, perfecting the praise of God and overflowing in the joy, it is Paul's letter to the Philippians. It is written by a man who, in the midst of whatever trouble comes his way, knows the assuring word of God: "You do not have to be afraid. I am with you. I will deliver you." The result is a document that "shows the transformation of an existence taken up into the praise of God."[2]

IV

At this point, some generalizations can be made about the place and signifi-cance of doxology. These draw upon the material discussed thus far but also go beyond it.

1. *Praise is fundamentally a social or communal experience and as such is an antic-ipation of the universal praise of God.* I do not mean by this that it is impossible to render praise to God as an individual or private act. The point is rather that in its fundamental character, and certainly as it is described, uttered, and acted in the Bible, doxology is rendered in community. There are two dimensions to this.

First, thanksgiving and praise by their very nature reach out, draw in, en-compass, and involve others. Thanksgiving is not private. It arises out of rela-tionship and further enhances and strengthens it. I would dare to say that there are few human acts that serve more to deepen relationships than the expres-sion of thanks. Expressing thanks declares one's gratitude and joy for what someone else has done. But it is not just self-expression. It has an effect on the receiver too, who finds his or her own original act completed, enhanced, and carried further in hearing and receiving thanks—whether by word or by some responding gesture or activity that signals thanks. Whatever else may have gone on in the relationship between these persons, they are now drawn together in a positive bond of kindness and gratitude. What we see happening in the human activity of beneficent act and grateful response identifies, if only indirectly and partially, what takes place in the relationship between God and human beings in the dialogical structure that begins in the cry for help and moves from God's gracious response to the praise and thanksgiving it evokes.

It is also clear from our human experience that joy is a response that ulti-mately does not stay contained. It too is an emotion to be shared. Whether its character in any particular instance is gratitude, wonder, or happiness, when joy arises within us, it inevitably breaks out. And the joy and happiness of oth-ers draws us in. Christian community is thus created, enhanced, and strength-ened in the joy of praise and thanksgiving.

The second dimension of the communal character of doxology is that it opens up that chain of praise that leads to the whole universe praising God. Psalms 22 and 126, and many others, speak of the capacity of God's help received and acknowledged in any single case as being capable of drawing forth an unending stream of praise. Thus, whenever the congregation gathers to praise the Lord, it participates in a developing chorus that shall, in the end, encompass all of heaven and earth, everything that has breath and everything that is, in the glorifying of God. When Psalm 150 closes the Psalter with a call to everything to praise the Lord, that is not simply a literal ending; it is an anticipation, a prefiguration of the praise of God by the whole cosmos, the end toward which everything is moving.

2. *Doxology celebrates human impossibilities that become God's possibilities.* The praises of Israel bore witness to transformations too wonderful for any human capability to bring off. They are what Walter Brueggemann has called "songs of impossibility," setting forth "a distinctive and radical claim in Israel . . . that conventional definitions of reality do not contain or define what God will yet do in Israel."[3] One of the most frequent themes of the psalms of praise is the celebration of God's reversal of the way things are: lifting up the lowly and putting down the mighty, feeding the hungry and giving sight to the blind, making the barren woman the joyous mother of children (Ps. 113:9). All human definitions of the way things have to be in this world are challenged and overturned. The freedom and power of God says that what is laughable from a human perspective (recall Sarah's response to the announcement that she would have a child) is the way things are going to be when God is at work.

In a world that assumes the status is quo, that things have to be the way they are and that we must not assume too much about improving them, the doxologies of God's people are fundamental indicators that wonders have not ceased, that possibilities not yet dreamt of will happen, and that hope is an authentic stance. All this is ridiculous, of course, unless one has seen the wonders of God in the past: the overthrow of the mighty and the setting free of an oppressed people, the gift of life in the face of death, fertility where there was barrenness.

Resurrection defies all human categories. So Christians gather every Sunday to give praise to God for the impossible wonder that raised Christ from the dead. In its act of doxology, the church says to the world that all our presumptions about what can happen are overruled by the wonderful impossibilities that God's power and freedom have wrought.

3. *Praise is useless, and that is one of the reasons we do it.* There are many ways that the documents of the Westminster Assembly are a theological albatross around the neck of Presbyterians, but I consider the first question of the Shorter Catechism a surprising gift and in some ways a rather astonishing answer to the question about what is the chief purpose of human life in this world. It sets aside all utilitarian goals, all efforts to identify moral purpose or worthwhile functions, and claims instead that our primary purpose in life is doxology and joy.

Here is another side of the reality of grace: There is nothing you have to do but to live in the joy of the Lord. In the face of an insistent pattern in secular and church life that leads us always to live and work to accomplish things, to achieve goals, to live useful lives, and to carry on an unceasing array of programs to justify our existence, the sound of doxology frees us to do nothing but give glory to God. The thing that matters most is utterly useless in a world that measures all activity by its usefulness and human worth by capabilities and accomplishments.

It is no accident that the Sabbath is the chief occasion when Jews and Christians give praise to God, for the Sabbath is God's gift of rest and uselessness. It is our reminder that we do not justify ourselves by our work. The Sabbath is useless time and doxology is useless act—and both are to the glory of God, our reason for being.

And here is where music finds its place. (Not its use—its place.) The sound of praise is music. Doxology and thanksgiving do not gain their full expression apart from music. The stories and psalms of the Old Testament reverberate with the sounds of instruments and singing. As the Psalter reaches its end, it becomes nothing but doxology, and every instrument is called to play, every voice to sing the praise of God.

It is strange how much the church worries about justifying the place of music in worship and church. Do we spend too much on it in the budget? Is it right to pay money to professional singers? Is the music too elaborate? I suppose all such questions have their place. But I am confident too that they reflect some reluctance to place at the center something that has no other purpose than to glorify God. "Sing to the Lord a new song" is one of the most repeated lines in the Psalter. The Shorter Catechism suggests that is our reason for being. So let the music of Bach and Mozart, Heinrich Schütz and John Rutter, John and Charles Wesley, Handel and American folk songs, Haydn and Black spirituals, Ralph Vaughn Williams and Isaac Watts ring in our churches. It will accomplish nothing. All it can do is express joy and give glory to God.

4. *Doxology is profoundly subversive*, undercutting all human structures and every human being as pretenders for ultimacy or absolute devotion. That happens first of all with regard to the possible pretensions that we make for our own selves. Praise places us totally outside ourselves. Thanksgiving, whether to other persons or God, is an inherent reminder that we are not autonomous and self-sufficient, and by its very character it directs our positive feelings toward others rather than toward ourselves. Praise to God does that in a fundamental way as it directs our love away from self and *all* human sufficiency. Such praise does not imply that we are unworthy—at least I do not think that is reason for praise of God. Rather, the wonder of God's power and love and grace evokes our admiration and adoration. As we see the beauty of a flower or hear the beauty of a symphony, we may be so caught by it that all attention is directed toward the source of that wonder. In a lovely contemporary hymn, Fred Pratt Green expresses the subversive character of praise:

When in our music God is glorified
and adoration leaves no room for pride,
it is as though the whole creation cried
Alleluia.[4]

Doxology also serves, however, to subvert the claims of any *other* person or structure to have ultimate place in our lives. It is the most visible regular expression of our obedience to the First Commandment. The clearest indication of the idolatrous character of political people or structures is their insistence that citizens or subjects praise them. Praise of God helps us to beware of political leaders whose visage is on posters and walls everywhere and of any party that allows only good things to be said of it. Any community that sings with conviction, "All people that on earth do dwell, sing to the Lord with cheerful voice: Him serve with fear, his praise forth tell," cannot give its ultimate allegiance to a Hitler or a Kennedy or a Reagan or a political party of any stripe.

5. *Prayer and praise are the most explicit and clearest testimonies to the reality of God in a God-denying or God-indifferent world.* Most of our other acts are quite ambiguous and capable of authentic duplication by others for whom the reality of God is a matter of indifference, irrelevance, or nonsense. But doxology and prayer make no sense in a world where God is not present or trusted. The act of doxology is a continuing testimony to another order than the one that assumes we have found all the answers in ourselves and have no other way to go than the path our human minds and wills can identify. One of the reasons we gather for worship on regular occasions is to remind ourselves in prayer and praise that the secular ability to live in a world without taking account of God is neither the last word nor the right one.

6. *The praise of God is the last word of faith.* It is our "end" in life, the end or goal toward which all our life is set—so say the Scriptures, and the Westminster Catechism, and Bach, and Handel's *Messiah*. All the songs and prayers of Israel contained in the Psalter reach their final climax in praise. In praise, therefore, God gives *us* the last word. In the structure of faith, God hears the praise of all that is created. The sound of praise is the glorification and enjoyment of God, the true measure of piety, and the proper purpose of every creature. So, first and last, Hallelujah, the Lord God omnipotent reigns!

26

Rethinking the First Article
of the Creed

Among the most significant and influential works in Old Testament studies
during the last hundred years, surely Gerhard von Rad's *Das formgeschichtliche
Problem des Hexateuchs* belongs near the top.[1] While von Rad's enterprise in
that monograph was a proposal about the formation of the whole Hexateuch
(the Pentateuch and the book of Joshua), his starting point remains one of the
presumptions of our contemporary understanding of the origin of Scripture
and of its central claims. The impact of von Rad's uncovering and elevation of
the ancient Israelite credo is signaled by the fact that one of the most extensive collections of Christian creeds in the English language begins its creedal
history of the church by quoting Deuteronomy 26:5–9, one of the forms of the
Israelite creed von Rad identifies.[2] That starting point for the church's creedal
history, however, creates an immediate tension as one begins to read through
the early forms of the church's creed or *regula fidei* (the term used by Irenaeus
and Tertullian), specifically the Roman Symbol or Apostles' Creed and the
Nicene-Constantinopolitan Creed, the most common and oft-repeated creeds
of the contemporary Christian church. For the Israelite credo disappears from
view in these two primary Christian creeds, and this disappearance has greatly
affected the church's theology and believers' faith. I propose, therefore, restoring the missing clause of the creed. By "missing," I refer not to a clause literally removed from the creeds but rather to the fact that, in their initial
formation, an essential element of Christian faith was overlooked in formulating the first article of the Apostles' and Nicene Creeds—an omission that
has resulted in widespread distortion of Christian theology and relegation of
the Old Testament to a secondary position in the church's faith and life.

THE "MISSING" CLAUSE

I propose that what is missing from the first article of the creed is something like this: "who delivered Israel from Egyptian bondage." The complete first article would then read: "I believe in God the Father Almighty, Creator of heaven and earth, who delivered Israel from Egyptian bondage."

The Christian creed has many functions. One of its most important is to guide Christian interpretation (a hermeneutical function). As John Leith puts it: "The creed is simply the Church's understanding of the meaning of Scripture. The creed says, Here is how the Church reads and receives Scripture."[3] Or, as another scholar has said, the creed is an epitome and summary that guides and directs a proper reading of Scripture. It "provides a guide for the correct understanding of the heart of Scripture and its overall intent."[4] It is clear, of course, from the start that the creed is not a full representation of the scriptural witness. No one can expect everything to be there. But that is not the point. The creed intends to get to the heart of the matter. If, however, the creed is a guide for Christian understanding of Scripture and, in some way, an epitome of what matters most for Christians in the scriptural witness, then what is missing—this neglect of the Old Testament canon and, even more, the failure to speak sufficiently (not exhaustively) about the triune God attested by those Scriptures and confessed by every member of the Christian church—risks creating a large distortion, a misunderstanding of Christian faith.

Why, then, is it important to include this clause as part of the church's creedal articulation? There are substantive theological reasons as well as practical-liturgical and pedagogical reasons.

A THEOLOGICAL RATIONALE FOR INCLUSION

There are important *implicit* associations of the first article with the God of Israel. The expression "one God" in the Nicene-Constantinopolitan Creed—not the Apostles' Creed, which has been the Western church's primary teaching instrument—can be associated with the God attested in Israel's Shema and is certainly consistent with the First Commandment. The image of God as "Father" belongs to the Old Testament as much as to the New.[5] It occurs in reference to God's creative activity (Deut. 32:6; Isa. 64:8; Mal. 2:10) and God's redemption of Israel (Isa. 63:16; Hos. 11:1), as well as to God's compassion (Ps. 68:5). In the church's liturgy and teaching, however, Christians hear and interpret the phrase "God the Father" primarily in relation to the second article of the creed—that is, as the Father of the Son and thus our Father.[6]

In a number of instances, the Septuagint uses the Greek term *pantokrator* that underlies the English "Almighty" to translate the Old Testament term "Sabaoth" in the epithet "Lord of Hosts" and, occasionally, as a noun translating "El Shaddai." The term "Almighty" echoes the Old Testament more than the New. Without reference to the Greek translation of the Old Testament, however, this connection is far from transparent and does not point necessarily and inescapably to the work of the God of Israel.

While some explications of the creed certainly acknowledge implicit connections to the Old Testament in the first article (beyond merely its focus on God as Creator and Almighty),[7] such interpretations are not customary, either in churches teaching the creed or among individual believers incorporating its claims into their faith through regular liturgical recitation of the creed. The interpretive handbooks of Gustav Wingren and Karl Barth serve as examples. For Wingren, the first article of the creed has to do with creation and law.[8] While Barth in no way neglects the Old Testament and its testimony to God's work in creation and redemption in his comprehensive doctrinal work *Church Dogmatics*, his early book specifically addressing the creed, which he says "furnishes, as it were, a ground-plan of Dogmatics," notably fails to develop the first article of the creed in relation to God's election and deliverance of Israel.[9] The theologian Kendall Soulen has stated that "the God of Israel is the firm foundation and inescapable predicament of Christian theology."[10] If the God of Israel is, indeed, the firm foundation of Christian theology, the creed that Christians confess must not be silent on this point.

While God's deliverance of Israel from Egyptian bondage is not the whole of God's redemptive and liberating work, as the credos to which von Rad pointed us make clear, it is, in those credos and elsewhere, paradigmatic and revelatory. The Lord's leading Israel out of Egypt was the central event shaping and determining Israel's story with its God. God's work in Israel—to borrow the title of one of von Rad's essay collections—was determinative for the reality of God and God's way in this world. It was the ground from which Israel learned the character of its God and how to live as God's people. Deliverance from Egypt was not the beginning of Israel's covenant relationship with God. Indeed, the covenant between the Lord and Abraham was the underlying ground for God's redemptive intervention in Israel's situation (Exod. 2:24). Yet Israel's liberation from Egyptian slavery created a people to live in covenant with the one who set them free. The powerful connection between grace and law is opened up and given to the community of faith definitively by the God of Israel in the Exodus. Furthermore, the full revelation of the name and character of God the Father unfolds in the exodus event (Exod. 3). Israel learns the identity and way of its God—as does the church—in the exodus and in all that surrounds it. Whatever is finally decided about von Rad's controversial argument about the historical priority of the exodus story over the creation story in Israel's traditions, there is a theological truth to that ordering that means God's deliverance of Israel from Egyptian slavery cannot be omitted from any sufficient effort to state what Christians believe about God the Father. As the Christian story goes on, insistence on the oneness of God as Trinity depends very much upon the claim arising from the exodus event that Jesus is who God always was.

While the precise meaning of the name of Israel's God as revealed in the exodus story is difficult to determine, the two chief clues to its meaning derive from the narrative setting and are not obscure. One clue is the use of the verb *'ehyeh* ("I am" or "I will be") in the sentence *'ehyeh 'immak* (Exod. 3:12), God's assurance to Moses that when he goes to Pharaoh "I will be with you." The other clue to the meaning of the divine name and the character of the one who bears that name is the unfolding of the exodus story out of God's decision upon hearing the cries of suffering and oppressed Israel "to deliver them" (Exod. 3:7–8). It is no accident, therefore, that the Son of the Father, of the God of Israel, bears the names Immanuel, "God is with us," and Jeshua, "He will save his people" (Matt. 1:20–23). The names of the Father and the Son are the same. The identity of the Son is consonant with the identity of God the Father as the God of Israel.

The American theologian Robert W. Jenson has made the deliverance from Egypt a fundamental dimension of his very Trinitarian theology. While he deals with this matter in a number of places, the opening sentence in the section of his *Systematic Theology* entitled "The Way of God's Identity" begins, "God is whoever raised Jesus from the dead, having before raised Israel from Egypt."[11] Elsewhere, he says:

> To the question "Who is God?" the New Testament has one new descriptively identifying answer: "Whoever raised Jesus from the dead." Identification by the Resurrection neither replaces nor is simply added to identification by the Exodus; the new identifying description *verifies* its paradigmatic predecessor. For at the outcome of the Old Testament it is seen that Israel's hope in her God cannot be sustained if it is not verified by victory also over death. . . . Thus "the one who rescued Israel from Egypt" is confirmed as an identification of *God* in that it is continued "as he thereupon rescued the Israelite Jesus from the dead."[12]

It is only thus that the church knows what this God is like and how the power of the *pantokrator*, the Almighty, is manifest in the world. The link between the first clause of the creed and the second is not only a link between the Father and the Son but also between the identity of God and the identity of Jesus.[13] This continuity is most clearly recognized in confessing the Father

Almighty as the one "who delivered Israel from Egyptian bondage." All parts of this hypothetically missing clause are crucial for the Christian creed. It is in the story of Israel with its defining moment in God setting Israel free from oppression and bondage that one sees that the Maker of heaven and earth is bent toward the weak and the oppressed, toward those who are in bondage and dying.[14] In the biblical story, the first time the Maker of heaven and earth ever appears on the scene in response to any human address is upon hearing the blood of murdered Abel crying out from the ground (Gen. 4:10). It is no surprise, then, when the cries of the oppressed Hebrews in Egypt elicit a divine response. That is who the Father is.

The human bondage is real and can be located. It is in Egypt. The salvation wrought by the Lord of Israel is not a spiritualized deliverance. It is concrete, as real as the body of Christ and the ground for the church's confidence in the power of God to raise Jesus, as God previously raised Israel. God the Father is redemptively at work in the whole of the human story, to set free all who are bound. The historic liberation of Israel from Egyptian slavery is definitive backward and forward as it identifies this God as the one who hears the cries of people and moves responsively in their behalf. Identification of the first person of the Trinity as the one "who delivered Israel from Egyptian bondage" thus incorporates much of what the Old Testament says about God the Father—for example, in the many psalms and stories that speak about the one who gives strength, helps the downtrodden, raises up the weak, and puts down the strong (1 Sam. 2:1–10; Pss. 107, 113, 145, 146).

Elsewhere I have suggested that Psalms 103 and 104 provide a kind of compressed but comprehensive theology, a poetic expression of the identity and reality of God in relation to the human creature and the whole creation.[15] These two psalms exhibit features that compel us to see them not only individually but as a whole to be read together.[16] Psalm 103 is about the *hesed* of God, the compassion and mercy God manifests to "those who fear him." This God is the one who heals and forgives, who redeems and crowns our life, "who works vindication and justice for all who are oppressed," and whose compassion is like that of a father for his children. Psalm 104 is an extended hymn about the Maker of heaven and earth, the Creator and provider of all. But Psalm 104 is inadequate to identify and characterize God without Psalm 103, and vice versa. As further support for this point, these connected psalms are preceded in Psalm 102 by a lament, one that is made paradigmatic and universal by its superscription: "a prayer of one afflicted, when faint and pleading before the Lord" (without reference to David or any other specific biblical figure). The prayer in Psalm 102 also anticipates both Psalms 103 and 104 as a response to it by its reference to the one who hears the groans of prisoners and sets free those who are doomed to die (v. 20) but who also long ago laid the foundations of the earth and made the heavens (v. 25). The poetic theology in miniature that answers Psalm 102's lament in Psalms 103 and 104 is then elaborated further in the next two psalms, 105 and 106, with specific reference to God's hesed manifested in Israel's experience, centering in the deliverance from Egypt.[17] Finally, this block of psalms concludes with Psalm 107, which now makes the cry of the oppressed Israelites in Egypt a paradigm for *all* situations of oppression, whether individual or communal. The psalm repeats the theme "then they cried to the LORD in their trouble, and he delivered them from their distress" (vv. 6, 13, 19, 28), joined with an equally repeated wish: "Let them thank the LORD for his steadfast love" (vv. 8, 15, 21, 31; compare v. 43).

This story of God's work in Israel is at one and the same time particular but also indicative of God's work in the world, a work reaching its climax in what the second article of the creed celebrates; the revelation of God in the life, suffering, death, and resurrection of Jesus Christ. The hypothetical clause I propose to add to the first article of the creed leads into and connects with the second article in a number of ways. For instance, Jesus himself links his own ministry programmatically with God's deliverance of Israel from Egypt in his reading from the prophet Isaiah in the synagogue at Nazareth: "The Spirit of the Lord is upon me, because he has anointed me to bring good news to the poor. He has sent me to proclaim release to the captives and recovery of sight to the blind, to let the oppressed go free, to proclaim the year of the Lord's favor" (Luke 4:18–19).

The verses quoted from Isaiah 56 and 61 are held together by their definition of this one as carrying out a ministry of *release* and *setting free*, a joining of the two texts and a definition of the ministry of Christ through the word *aphesis*, which, in its Old Testament context, means release and setting free from slavery, prison, bonded indebtedness, and the like, but becomes, in the New Testament, also the common word for forgiveness. The Son thus continues the saving and freeing work of the Father revealed paradigmatically in the exodus. The ongoing work of God to release humankind from those chains that bind and destroy life is a central feature of the Christian claim. That divine work includes release from the bondage of sin but also, at least eschatologically, from *all* forms of destruction and bondage, including suffering and death. The one who delivered Israel from death also delivered Jesus from death, and therein lies our hope.[18]

The proposed creedal clause also leads into the work of God in Jesus Christ through its identification of this God as the one who hears the cry of the suffering one on the cross and delivers him from that suffering and death. That is the gospel's central claim. It is uncovered, however, as the way of the one God long before the appearance of the Son in human flesh. Christoph Schwöbel has warned that Christology is in danger when it no longer sees Jesus in connection with his people, the people of the exodus and the promise of the Sinai covenant.[19] The church has succumbed to this danger all too often and finds continuing potential for doing so in the short first article of the creed.

LITURGICAL AND PEDAGOGICAL REASONS

There are not only theological but also liturgical and pedagogical reasons for arguing that the proposed clause belongs in the creed. First of all, the creed is *analogous to Scripture* in a very significant way. It is an ancient document whose authority, force, and claims, however, are fully contemporary. When the individual believer affirms the creed in the church's liturgy, he or she may well know that the creed goes back centuries. In the act of affirmation, however, the creed is not ancient but what "I" or "we" believe or seek to believe in this moment, in this time and place. Its formulation, therefore, is not simply a matter of tradition. It is an assertion of the moment. We can restate the faith and, indeed, many new creeds and confessions have been written over the centuries, not least in our own time. But the Apostles' Creed and the Nicene Creed are, finally, more than mere historical documents. They are living statements of faith—the most contemporary expressions of the church's faith that Christians have. The creed is recited each Sunday in many, if not most, churches. The liturgy, in a proper sense, dehistoricizes the creed, because it does not take it up as a statement from the past to be interpreted, argued, criticized, and contextualized. It is an immediate, contemporary, and quite personal claim about what we believe here and now. Further, the creed is both communal and universal, transcending its temporal origins and the way its original formulators may have understood the faith. What is missing from the creed is not, then, simply an issue in the history of doctrine to be analyzed contextually, interpreted, and criticized. It is missing *now* from the believer's confession, from the Christian's understanding of the God in whom she trusts. A critical part of what Michael Welker has acutely described as "canonic memory" is thus forgotten in the creed. To put it another way, the absence of such a clause controls what part of the canonical story is remembered.[20] A contemporary manifestation of the kind of theological error (in the form of modalism) that can result from our abbreviated first article is liturgical "reform" that avoids male or patriarchal God-language by speaking about the persons of the Trinity in purely functional terms, such as Creator, Redeemer, and Sustainer.[21]

Pedagogical concerns arise as corollaries to the liturgical problems with the first article. The church's catechetical instruction takes many forms, but the most succinct statement of Christian belief, often the primary basis for catechesis, is the Nicene-Constantinopolitan Creed. Thus, confirmation classes, preachers, and Sunday school teachers often take up the creed as a basic formula for instruction about Christian faith, a way of learning and taking to heart what we believe most fundamentally about God. While such instruction can, of course, expand on our simple confession of God as Father in the first article in order to connect that to God's fatherhood of Israel, this extension is by no means automatic or even common, as even a quick perusal of the many catechisms and creedal teaching aids shows.

Finally, elaborating the first article to include God's redemptive work in and through Israel might facilitate dialogue or interfaith relations with our Jewish sisters and brothers. If so, well and good. I do not know, however, whether that would prove to be the case. My argument here does not have to do with that important relationship. It has to do with the desire to see the primary confession of the church be authentic to Christian faith and its understanding of the God who is revealed in the Scriptures, in Jesus Christ, and in the preaching of the Word.

Original Publications

"The W/Right Space" (50/1; April 1993, pp. 1–3)

"Whatever Happened to the Soul?" (50/4; January 1994, pp. 507–10)

"Poetry and Theology" (52/3; October 1995, pp. 309–12)

"Whither the Church?" (52/4; January 1996, pp. 445–48)

"Hallelujah! The Lord God Omnipotent Reigns" (53/1; April 1996, pp. 1–4)

"Teaching the Faith" (53/2; July 1996, pp. 143–47)

"Remembering Our Theological Past" (53/3, October 1996, pp. 285–88)

"Popularizing the Bible" (53/4; January 1997, pp. 435–48)

"Revisiting the God Who Acts" (54/1; April 1997, pp. 1–5)

"Life, Death, and the Hale-Bopp Comet" (54/2; July 1997, pp. 147–49)

"A Strange Kind of Monotheism" (54/3; October 1997, pp. 293–96)

"'A' Is for Augustine, Aquinas . . ." (55/1; April 1998, pp. 1–4)

"Good-bye Seinfeld" (55/2; July 1998, pp. 147–51)

"Theology and Science in Conversation" (55/3; October 1998, pp. 301–4)

"The Millennium Bug" (55/4; January 1999, pp. 491–95)

"The State of the World" (56/2; July 1999, pp. 148–51)

"The Church's First Theologian" (56/3; October 1999, pp. 293–96)

". . . Who Hast Made of One Genome . . ." (57/3; October 2000, pp. 291–96)

"What Sense Do We Make of the Ending?" (58/2; July 2001, pp. 141–44)

"Terror All Around" (58/4; January 2002, pp. 497–501)

"Work and Faith" (59/3; October 2002, pp. 349–54)

"January's Child" (59/4; January 2003, pp. 525–28)

"Is There a Place for the Ten Commandments?" (60/4; January 2004, pp. 473–77)

"The Accidental Profession" (61/4; January 2005, pp. 433–37)

"In Praise and Thanksgiving" (45/2; July 1988, pp. 180–88)

"Rethinking the First Article of the Creed" (61/4; January 2005, pp. 499–508)

Notes

Foreword

1. Leif Enger, *Peace Like a River* (New York: Grove/Atlantic, 2001).
2. Ibid., 3.
3. Ibid.
4. Ibid.

1. The W/Right Space

1. Grant Hildebrand, *The Wright Space: Pattern and Meaning in Frank Lloyd Wright's Houses* (Seattle: University of Washington Press, 1991).

2. Whatever Happened to the Soul?

1. Angela Tilby, *Soul: God, Self, and the New Cosmology* (New York: Doubleday, 1995).
2. Sting, *Soul Cages* (A&M, 1991).
3. Karl Barth, *Church Dogmatics*, III/4, *The Doctrine of Creation* (Edinburgh: T. & T. Clark, 1961), 491, 519.
4. John H. Leith, *Basic Christian Doctrine* (Louisville, KY: Westminster/John Knox Press, 1993), 12.
5. James Barr, *The Garden of Eden and the Hope of Immortality* (Minneapolis: Fortress, 1993).

4. Whither the Church?

1. Peter L. Berger, *The Noise of Solemn Assemblies* (New York: Doubleday, 1961); James M. Gustafson, *Treasure in Earthen Vessels: The Church as a Human Community* (New York: Harper, 1961).

5. Hallelujah! The Lord God Omnipotent Reigns

1. Harold S. Kushner, *When Bad Things Happen to Good People* (New York: Schocken, 1981).
2. Marjorie Procter-Smith, *Praying with Our Eyes Open: Engendering Feminist Liturgical Prayer* (Nashville: Abingdon, 1995).

6. Teaching the Faith

1. Richard Osmer, *Confirmation: Presbyterian Practices in Ecumenical Perspective* (Louisville, KY: Geneva, 1996), 72.

11. A Strange Kind of Monotheism

1. William Stacy Johnson, "The Doctrine of the Triune God Today," *Insights* 111, no. 1 (1995): 10.

12. "'A' Is for Augustine, Aquinas . . ."

1. Andrew Delbanco, *The Death of Satan: How Americans Have Lost the Sense of Evil* (New York: Noonday Press, 1996).

14. Theology and Science in Conversation

1. John Noble Wilford, "New Data Suggest Universe Will Expand Forever, *New York Times*, January 9, 1998, late edition-final.

15. The Millennium Bug

1. Edward Tenner, "Chronologically Incorrect," *Wilson Quarterly*, Autumn 1998.
2. Steven Levy and Katie Hafner, "The Day the World Shuts Down," *Newsweek*, June 2, 1997.
3. Peter de Jager, "Doomsday 2000," *Computerword*, September 6, 1993.
4. Jason Kelly, Y2K: It's Already Too Late (Los Angeles: JK Press, 1998).
5. Michael Hyatt, *The Millennium Bug: How to Survive the Coming Chaos* (Washington, D. C.: Regnery Press, 1998).
6. Tenner, "Chronologically Incorrect."

19. What Sense Do We Make of the Ending?

1. John Polkinghorne and Michael Welker, eds. *The End of the World and the Ends of God: Science and Theology on Eschatology* (Harrisburg, PA: Trinity Press International, 2000).

21. Work and Faith

1. Robert H. Nelson, *Economics as a Religion: From Samuelson to Chicago and Beyond* (College Station, PA: Pennsylvania State University Press, 2001), 331.

25. In Praise and Thanksgiving

1. Patrick D. Miller, *Interpreting the Psalms* (Philadelphia: Fortress, 1986), 68.
2. Daniel W. Hardy and David F. Ford, *Jubilate: Theology in Praise* (London: Darton, Longman & Todd, 1984), 25.
3. Walter Brueggemann, " 'Impossibility' and Epistemology in the Faith Tradition of Abraham and Sarah (Gen 18:1–15)," *Zeitschrift für die alttestamentliche Wissenschaft* 94 (1982): 624–25.
4. Fred Pratt Green, "When in Our Music God Is Glorified," in *Rejoice in the Lord*, ed. Eric Routley (Grand Rapids: Eerdmans, 1985), no. 508.

26. Rethinking the First Article of the Creed

1. ET: Gerhard von Rad, "The Form-Critical Problem of the Hexateuch," in *The Problem of the Hexateuch and Other Essays* (New York: McGraw-Hill, 1966), 1–78.
2. John H. Leith, ed., *Creeds of the Churches: A Reader in Christian Doctrine from the Bible to the Present* (Louisville, KY: John Knox Press, 1982), 13–14.

3. Ibid., 8.

4. Luke Timothy Johnson, *The Creed: What Christians Believe and Why It Matters* (New York: Doubleday, 2003), 59.

5. It is worth recognizing in this context that one of the most powerful expressions of the parental image in the Old Testament is formulated specifically in relation to the exodus: "When Israel was a child, I loved him, / and out of Egypt I called my son" (Hos. 11:1).

6. A representative interpretive example may be found in Calvin's instruction on the Apostles' Creed in his Geneva Catechism (1541). To the question, "Why do you call Him Father?" the catechetical response is, "It is with reference to Christ who is His eternal Word, begotten of Him before all time, and being sent into this world was demonstrated and declared to be His Son. But since God is the Father of Jesus Christ, it follows that He is our Father also." So also in the Heidelberg Catechism the question of what we believe when we say the first article of the creed is answered entirely in terms of "the eternal Father of our Lord Jesus Christ" who "is for the sake of Christ his Son my God and my Father." Origen comments on the fact that "while the title 'Father' as applied to God was of frequent occurrence in the Old Testament, it was the Christians who were first privileged to call God Father in the fullest sense of the word." Quoted in J. N. D. Kelly, *Early Christian Creeds*, 2ᵈ ed. (New York: Mackay, 1960), 135. Kelly argues, with reference to a number of the second-century church fathers (Clement of Rome, Justin, Irenaeus, Theophilus of Antioch, Tatian, and Novatian) that to Christians of the second century, the primary reference in the title Father with respect to the first person of the Trinity was to "God in His capacity as Father and creator of the universe." So also the term *pantokrator* was, in the early period of Christian history, understood primarily in relation to God as all-ruling and all-sovereign (particularly in relation to the created order), though the term quickly became understood as meaning all-powerful. Ibid., 136–37.

7. See, for example, Wolfhart Pannenberg, *The Apostles' Creed: In the Light of Today's Questions* (Philadelphia: Westminster, 1972), 30, and Luke Timothy Johnson, *The Creed: What Christians Believe and Why It Matters* (New York: Doubleday, 2002), chap. 3.

8. See Gustav Wingren, *Credo: The Christian View of Faith and Life* (Minneapolis: Augsburg, 1981). The scriptural index to this interpretation of the creed alludes to just nine Old Testament books, only four of which have more than two references. There is no allusion to the book of Exodus. The Old Testament is virtually absent from the interpretation except primarily for the creation account in Genesis.

9. See Karl Barth, *Credo: A Presentation of the Chief Problems of Dogmatics with Reference to the Apostles' Creed* (London: Hodder & Stoughton, 1936). The same is true of Barth's later interpretation of the creed in *Dogmatics in Outline* (New York: Philosophical Library, 1949), as well as of his commentary on the Apostles' Creed according to Calvin's Catechism in *The Faith of the Church*, ed. Jean-Louis Leuba (New York: Meridian, 1958).

10. Kendall Soulen, *The God of Israel and Christian Theology* (Minneapolis: Fortress, 1996), 1.

11. Robert W. Jenson, *Systematic Theology*, vol. 1, *The Triune God* (Oxford: Oxford University Press, 1997), 63.

12. Ibid., 44.

13. Note Jenson's comment that Israel "confessed communally in paradigmatic parallel to the second article of a three article Christian creed: 'A wandering Aramean was my father; and he went down into Egypt. . . . And the Egyptians treated us harshly and afflicted us. . . . Then we cried to JHWH . . . and JHWH brought us out of Egypt with a mighty hand . . . and he brought us into this place and gave us this land.'" Ibid., 43.

14. "[I]n her own self-understanding, Israel had been created by the deliverer of bond workers from Egypt and by events of their consequent migration through Sinai into Canaan. . . . God is doubly identified by this confession: he is *uniquely* described by the narrative of the Exodus-event, and the one so described has a personal proper name, JHWH." Ibid. (emphasis added).

15. Patrick D. Miller, "The Psalter as a Book of Theology," in *Biblical Texts in Community: The Psalms in Jewish and Christian Traditions*, ed. Harold W. Attridge and Margot E. Fassler (Leiden: Brill; Atlanta: Society of Bibilcal Literature 2003), 87–98 Reprinted in Miller, *The Way of the Lord: Essays in Old Testament Theology* (Tübingen: Mohr Siebeck, 2004), 214–25.

16. The most obvious editorial means of joining the two psalms are the absence of a superscription at the beginning of Psalm 104 to mark it off from Psalm 103 and the use of the sentence "Bless the Lord, O my soul" at the beginning and end of both psalms, a sentence that does not appear elsewhere in the Psalter.

17. There are clearly aspects of Psalms 104 and 105 that lead one to read from the former on into the latter as a kind of continuation of the praise of God's mighty works. For example, Psalm 104 concludes with the wish, "May my meditation (*śîḥ*) be pleasing to him" (v. 34), while Psalm 105 begins with the exhortation to "meditate (*śîḥ*) on all his wonderful works" (v. 2). The "meditation" (spoken out loud?) of Psalm 104 is probably the poem itself, that is, the praise of God that is sung in the poem. So also the meditation of Psalm 105 is the praise of God's wonderful works (*niplĕ'ôtāyw*). The term "wonderful works" looks both backward and forward; backward to God's wonderful works in creation, the praise of the Maker of heaven and earth, and forward into Psalm 105 and its praise of the wonderful works of the Lord in Israel, specifically and centrally its deliverance from Egypt. Note that at the end of Psalm 104 we have the sequence *šîr, zāmar, śîḥ,* and *śāma* as a declaration of praise. That same group of verbs then follows in that sequence in Ps. 105:2–3 with *hithallēl* inserted before the last one. Thus: *šîr, zāmar, śîḥ, hithallēl,* and *śāma.* This is the only time in the Psalter or anywhere else in the Old Testament that this combination appears. It is worth noting further in this instance that Psalms 106 and 107, while extending across the presumed end of book IV of the Psalter in the doxology in Psalm 106:48, continue the pattern begun in Psalm 104 of omitting any superscription. Thus, one reads Psalms 103 through 107 as a unit in response to Psalm 102. The superscriptions and a new group of psalms then resume with Psalm 108, which is a composite psalm made up of parts of other psalms.

18. On this interpretation, see further Patrick D. Miller, "Luke 4:16–21," *Interpretation* 29 (1975): 417–21.

19. Christoph Schwöbel, "Das Christusbekenntnis im Kontext des jüdisch-christlichen Dialogs," in *Gott in Beziehung: Studien zur Dogmatik* (Tübingen: Mohr Siebeck, 2002), 308.

20. On the character and significance of canonic memory or remembrance, particularly with reference to the resurrected Christ and the place of the

Eucharist, see the work of Michael Welker, especially "Resurrection and Eternal Life: The Canonic Memory of the Resurrected Christ, His Reality, and His Glory," in *The End of the World and the Ends of God: Science and Theology on Eschatology*, ed. John Polkinghorne and Michael Welker (Harrisburg, PA: Trinity Press International, 2000), 279–90; Michael Welker, *What Happens in Holy Communion?* (Grand Rapids: Eerdmans, 2000), chap. 8; and John Polkinghorne and Michael Welker, *Faith in the Living God* (Minneapolis: Fortress, 2001), 63–65.

21. The implicit critique of this move is not meant to imply that there is no value in developing a theological understanding of the Trinity that avoids male delineations. On the contrary, that is an important task. It should be done, however, in a way that does not lead to modalism.